Brutally honest and devoid of hyperbole, this is Roelf van Heerden's Executive Outcomes.

Unapologetic, unassuming and forthright, the combat exploits of Executive Outcomes (EO) in Angola and Sierra Leone are recounted for the first time by a battlefield commander who was physically on the ground during all their major combat operations. From fighting UNITA for the critical oil installations and diamond fields of Angola to the offensive against the RUF in Sierra Leone to capture the Kono diamond fields and the palace coup which ousted Captain Valentine Strasser, van Heerden was at the forefront. He tells of the tragedy of child soldiers, illegal diamond mining and the curse of government soldiers who turn on their own people; he tells of RUF atrocities, the harrowing attempt to rescue a downed EO pilot and the poignant efforts to recover the remains of EO soldiers killed in action. Coupled with van Heerden's gripping exposé, hitherto unpublished photographs, order of battle charts and battle maps offer unprecedented access to the major actions as they took place on the ground during the heydays of EO.

Roelf van Heerden decided at a young age that the vastness and unpredictability of the wild African outdoors were far superior to the confines of an office. With his sights set firmly on the next high ground, the next mountain range and the next mirage, he set off on his life's adventure as a soldier. A unique opportunity to break new military ground presented itself at the end of a most satisfying military career as an officer in the South African Defence Force, with Roelf's African odyssey continuing as an Executive Outcomes founder member and commander on the battlefields of Angola and Sierra Leone during the 1990s. It was on these savannahs and in these primeval forests that the interdependency among exceptional soldiers, fundamental to the achievement of great military deeds, surmounted the challenging odds that Roelf recollects in his unassuming style.

Andrew Hudson, a former SADF officer and longtime friend of Roelf van Heerden, holds three post-graduate degrees, works internationally and enjoys travelling. Still a soldier at heart and a firm believer in the axiom 'once a soldier, always a soldier', he divides his time between earning an income, indulging his passion for collecting books on conflict in Africa and road running in weird and wonderful locations. A chance meeting between the two former colleagues a few years ago convinced them both that a book project was essential to a comprehensive understanding of Executive Outcomes. This endeavour has given rise to Andrew's latest interest—recounting the untold stories of true soldiers on the African continent.

FOUR BALL ONE TRACER

FOUR BALL ONE TRACER

Commanding

EXECUTIVE
OUTCOMES

in Angola and Sierra Leone

Roelf van Heerden
as told to Andrew Hudson

30° South Publishers (Pty) Ltd

Helion & Company Ltd

Co-published in 2012 by

Helion & Company Limited
26 Willow Road
Solihull
West Midlands
B91 1UE
England
Tel. 0121 705 3393
Fax 0121 711 4075
email: info@helion.co.uk
website: www.helion.co.uk
Twitter @helionbooks
Blog http://blog.helion.co.uk/

&

30° South Publishers (Pty) Ltd.
16 Ivy Road
Pinetown 3610
South Africa
email: info@30degreessouth.co.za
website: www.30degreessouth.co.za

Designed & typeset by Kerrin Cocks
Cover design by Justin & Kim Zimmerman
Printed by Lightning Source Ltd, Milton Keynes, Buckinghamshire
This paperback reprint for Europe and North America published by Helion & Company Limited 2015

Text, maps & diagrams © Andrew Hudson, 2012
Photographs © Roelf van Heerden, Hendri Engelbrecht & Attie Strydom
Maps & diagrams by Kim Zimmerman
Front cover images courtesy of Roelf van Heerden & Andrew Hudson

ISBN 978-1-910294-71-0

British Library Cataloguing-in-Publication Data
A catalogue record for this book is available from the British Library

For Dee, Vicki, Chantelle, Lindsay and Sharon.
And for soldiers within whose souls the warrior spirit is kindled.
Andrew Hudson

★★★★★

For my beloved Gerda, who was tragically murdered during one of my absences.
For Rudolph Mauritz and Emile, my sons, whose fortitude and sacrifices enabled me
to undertake such adventures; and for Amoret, who was born during the advance on
Cafunfu, Angola, and who had to learn what a father was every time I returned home.
Also for Loraine, for understanding and giving me the space to ponder the past.
To all my mates who, whilst pursuing the same path as I did, often paid the
highest price. I salute you. May our shared exploits remain as close and
as dear to us all as our comradeship.
What an adventure! Long live EO!
Roelf van Heerden

Contents

Illustrations

Relaxing at Barra do Quanza after a day's training at Cabo Ledo, the former Cuban base south of Luanda. Renier van der Merwe and Kolle are on my right.

Training former Koevoet members in the finer points of BMP-2 mechanized drills at Cabo Ledo.

Taking a break between sand models and orders at Cabo Ledo.

Testing the wading capability of a BMP-2.

Photo section 3

Roelf van Heerden, Saurimo, Angola, 1994.

Stand-to in our trenches, awaiting an expected UNITA attack on the EO mechanized force deployed in a forward position west of Saurimo.

United Nations leased Ilyushin IL-76 aircraft framed by a FAPA MiG-23 on the Saurimo apron during the logistic build-up to the advance on Cafunfu.

Posing alongside Pine's MiG-23 whilst it was under repair at Saurimo. The EO MiG pilots provided excellent support during the offensives against Cafunfu and Cacolo.

Battle map depicting the UNITA attack on Saurimo.

Not a good day. The destroyed Mi-17 on the morning after the UNITA attack on Saurimo.

Aftermath of the UNITA attack on Saurimo. One destroyed Mi-17 in the background and one Mi-17 full of chalk-ringed bullet holes.

Leisure time utilization at Saurimo with an Mi-17 helicopter under maintenance in the background.

Senior commanders gathered together a few days before the offensive against Cafunfu commenced. From left: Duncan Rykaart, General Sukissa, garrison commander at Saurimo, Brigadier Pepe, myself.

The provincial commander of the Lunda Sul Province, General Marx, with dark glasses and green uniform, chats to 16 Brigade men during the advance on Cafunfu. Brigadier Pepe de Castro is the tall man with spectacles opposite him.

A BM-21 artillery strike on UNITA positions during the advance on Cafunfu.

Lifting a TMM mobile bridge not far from Cafunfu. The bridges certainly contributed to our mobility.

EO troops stretching their legs during the advance on Cafunfu.

The combined EO/FAA force was required to construct many improvised bridges on the way to Cafunfu. Alfonso, an EO interpreter and a former 32 Battalion soldier, is in the foreground.

An EO Mi-17 helicopter resupplying us during the advance.

Photo section 4

During the advance on Cafunfu I handed over to Hennie and took a few days leave to attend my daughter's birth.

Armoured warfare on the plains of Angola. Jos Grobler is standing on the BMP-2.

EO men advising on the maintenance of momentum during the advance.

FAA special forces troops on their Chevrolet pickup with a mounted 12.7mm heavy machine gun.

UNITA soldiers killed in a contact during the advance.

Vehicles towing SU-23 anti-aircraft weapons into Cafunfu.

EO vehicles move on the streets of Cafunfu after the attack. Are those liquid sandwiches on the BMP-2?

My bunker, protected by an AGS-17, located in 16 Armoured Brigade Headquarters at Cafunfu.

Digging in a BM-21 in the 16 Brigade-defended locality after taking Cafunfu.

The remains of the EO Mi-17 helicopter ditched during the Camaxilo incident. UNITA chopped the helicopter up and transported it to Cafunfu to display to the local population.

The last resting place of the 'Camaxilo four'. UNITA brought their remains to Cafunfu and eventually dumped them at the end of the runway, burnt the bodies and then buried them.

Freddie, my interpreter, digging for the remains of the Camaxilo four. We also found three UNITA troops buried on the far side of the wooden structure.

A skull and a strip of camouflage uniform—remains of the Camaxilo four buried at the eastern end of the Cafunfu airstrip.

Freddie with the possible remains of one of the EO reconnaissance team we lost to the east of Cafunfu before the advance. We found the graves close to the hospital in Cafunfu.

Photo section 5
The EO and FAA order of battle for the advance on Cacolo.

Battle map of the EO and FAA advance on Cacolo.

Battle map of the attack on Cacolo and the occupation of the town thereafter.

Chatting with the EO men during the advance on Cacolo.

A study of EO operators during the advance on Cacolo. Rusty, in the foreground, shares a joke with his gunner as they consume ratpack milkshakes.

Henry van Dyk enjoys the simple pleasure of a bush bath during the advance on Cacolo.

Collecting drums of fuel dropped by parachute from Ilyushin IL-76 aircraft during the advance on Cacolo.

Final orders before the attack on Cacolo.

The EO gunners at Cacolo laying the RM-70 122mm multiple rocket launcher (MRL) mounted on a Tatra. Neels Britz is on the far left, with Ben Burger in the white shorts.

Resupply in Cacolo. An EO Mi-17 helicopter delivers rations and supplies to us in Cacolo.

Contrary to what UNITA expected of us, we occupied the town of Cacolo itself and set about fortifying our defensive positions.

A victory lap through Cacolo after the successful attack.

EO crew members cleaning BMP-2 weapons at Cacolo.

Photo section 6
Orientation map of Sierra Leone.

The EO organization in Sierra Leone.

Graphic representation of the EO plan for Sierra Leone.

The order of battle for Operation Waterloo.

Vanguard of any EO advance in Sierra Leone—the two trusty Land Rovers.

A motley collection of vehicles made up the elements of the advance on Koidu.

The 120mm mortar in action. This weapon and its crew played a vital role during the advance on Koidu.

Mi-24 helicopter and crew taking a break at the airstrip at Yengema, west of Koidu.

An RUF commander and his second-in-command who didn't make it past the RSLMF troops at Koidu.

The macabre traffic circle we were confronted with on our arrival in Koidu. Koidu 'dared' to illustrate its support for the National Provisional Ruling Council led by Captain Valentine Strasser, by erecting this signboard depicting Captain (later Brigadier) Maada Bio, one of the group of five coup members. The RUF obviously didn't take kindly to this.

One of the first things we did after retaking Koidu was to encourage the local inhabitants to return to the town. I arrived at the location from where we addressed the large number of returnees who had come to see who EO was.

Lieutenant-Colonel Tom Nyuma, with sunglasses, one of the five coup members, listens attentively whilst I address the crowd.

Photo section 7

Order group at the EO headquarters at Koidu. Lieutenant Tom Nyuma is sitting in the centre, with Carl Dietz on the right. Ukrainian helicopter pilots are sitting with their backs to the camera.

The thick vegetation on the way to Baiama didn't allow much room to manoeuvre.

PP discussing an upcoming operation with EO troops at Koidu.

A meeting of the Kono Consultative Committee (KCC), an organization established by EO to administer the Kono district. To my left is Nick du Toit and Chief Abu Kongoba II, the Paramount Chief of the Lhei Chiefdom, and Chairman of the Council of Chiefs.

EO men preparing the two Land Rovers before a patrol from Koidu. Jos Grobler is standing at the driver's door of one of the vehicles.

One of the Mi-17 helicopters, on a rat-run mission, landing at the EO base in Koidu. One of the two BMP-2 infantry combat vehicles is in the foreground.

On my best behavior at Koidu, complete with the RSLMF rank insignia of a full colonel.

A Soviet-designed, single-engine light multi-task utility aircraft, the Antonov-2 seen here on the airfield at Yengema, close to Koidu, was often chartered to provide us with rations and other logistic support.

Graphic representation of the operation to remove the RUF from Gandorhun.

Celebrating the successful attack on Gandorhun with 'Fearless' Fred Marafono and members of the RSLMF company. Note the sign in the top left-hand corner of the photograph.

Discussing a problem with the local RSLMF commander and the chief of the Sierra Leone police at Koidu.

Graphic representation of the operational plan for Operation Zenith.

Visit by EO members from Freetown. From left: Myself, a Ukrainian helicopter technician, Andy Brown, Duncan Rykaart, Jos Grobler and P. P. Hugo.

I take leave of Major Kamara (shaking hands), the RSLMF commander at Koidu, and welcome the new commander. Inspector Sesay, the Koidu police commander behind me, looks on. Major Kamara later joined the Armed Forces Revolutionary Council (AFRC) which, after taking over the country in a coup d'état, allied itself with the RUF. When the elected government was restored, Major Kamara was apprehended, charged, and with other officers, shot on the beach at Freetown by ECOMOG officers.

Author's note

A wise man once told me that there are usually three sides to every story—my side, your side and the truth. This book represents Roelf van Heerden's recollections of his time as a member of Executive Outcomes and, whilst time and age do affect one's faculties, a substantial effort has been made in ensuring that the events he describes are 'the truth'. Those inaccuracies that may indeed have crept into the text are, therefore, not intended and should rather be ascribed to receding memories and the mists of time. Any factual improvements to the book are of course welcome and, in the interests of a more comprehensive picture of these times, would certainly enjoy serious consideration for inclusion in any future editions.

A word or two about technical matters is perhaps in order here. I have used a convention in the narrative where the full description of a weapon, vehicle or unit is used the first time it is cited, followed directly by its abbreviation in parenthesis. Thereafter the abbreviation alone is used. A glossary of terms and abbreviations is also included and the full description and abbreviations of these and other applicable concepts are included here as well.

The correct spelling of the names of towns, villages and geographic features in Angola and Sierra Leone can be a source of concern. Ever mindful of the fact that the correct spelling of a town or village in Africa is inevitably influenced by a host of factors, I have elected to apply a spelling format that is simple and appears to be commonly used rather than agonize over whether it is the 'correct' spelling or not.

The photographs used in this publication are of differing quality and, rather than include only those images that would be fit for purpose in a glossy production, I have also included those images which Roelf and I believe are required for the sake of the record. The historic record has weighed heavier than visual appeal as a consequence and the reader is asked to bear with these 'inferior quality photographs' as we believe that they are necessary to assist in illustrating Roelf's narrative.

The battle maps represent free-hand graphic images of the various battles as Roelf remembers them and they have been included to assist the reader in visualizing the passage of events as they unfolded in Angola and Sierra Leone. An illustration style which excludes military symbols has specifically been selected as this opens the visual understanding to a wider readership than would have been the case should military symbols alone have been used.

Finally, a word about soldiers and mercenaries. After almost four decades of participation, study, reflection and contemplation of the military I am convinced that in every nation there exists a small group of individuals within whom a unique energy smoulders. This energy, which is both physical and intellectual by nature, manifests itself in times of national adversity and conflict in what can be referred to as the warrior spirit. I also believe that, once fanned, the desire to release this energy repeatedly becomes unquenchable and it transforms each warrior soul forever. And, life thereafter becomes a constant quest for the fulfilment that manifests itself when the flames of the warrior spirit are fanned once more. If this desire is satisfied within the ranks of an acknowledged national military organization, then that individual will find a home there amongst similar souls for as long as the flames can be fanned. Once this is no longer possible within the confines of a national military organization, then that individual moves on, unfettered by physical or mental limitations, and searches for new opportunities to rekindle the embers. Some people call them mercenaries; others refer to them as private military contractors. I believe that such labels ignore the essence of those unique individuals who are imbibed with the smouldering embers of the warrior spirit. This narrative bears testimony to the warrior spirit and it has been a privilege to be part of it.

Unapologetic, unassuming, yet forthright and brutally honest, this is Roelf van Heerden's Executive Outcomes as he lived it.

Andrew Hudson

Preface

I am sick and tired of the stories and inaccuracies about Executive Outcomes (EO). Nobody wants to tell the story as it actually happened. Everyone has an angle. So, I have gathered the notes, diaries, photographs and video tapes I kept during my time as a member of EO and called on my good friend and fellow soldier, Andrew Hudson, to lend an ear and assist me in putting together a narrative describing the events that unfolded in Angola and Sierra Leone as I experienced them during those eventful years in the 1990s. This recollection then is a record of my time as a mercenary—or private military contractor or whatever else the armchair critics and sages choose to label me—in command of EO forces.

The Angolan part of this recollection covers the very first days of EO as I experienced them, followed by the madness at Soyo, where a new era in African military doctrine was birthed. The focus then moves to my experience as a member of the joint EO—*Forças Armadas Angolanas* (Angolan Armed Forces or FAA) advance from Cabo Ledo, via Saurimo, to Cafunfu, as well as the re-occupation of Cacolo, my last action in Angola.

My recollection of Sierra Leone starts with the tension and expectations surrounding the new contract; the development of the Sierra Leone plan and its successful implementation from the outskirts of Freetown to the diamond rich Koidu area; the stabilization and military administration of this strategic area thereafter by EO, followed by the disappointment of having to leave the country just when the rebels had been brought to their knees.

I was proud to be a soldier; I was equally proud to serve as a member of EO and I assume that my colleagues who served with me share this feeling. As a consequence I haven't made any effort to change names (except in two instances) as I believe that this practice detracts from the authenticity of the narrative and clouds the real story with undeserved secrecy. If my approach does lead to the embarrassment of any of my former colleagues then I wish to state that this outcome is neither desired nor intended.

Was I a mercenary killer, dog of war, or, was I fortunate enough to be part of the evolution of a new type of soldier whose subsequent utility in the early years of the 21st century has vindicated the approach followed by us in the African bush? I leave you, the reader to judge for yourself.

Roelf van Heerden

Glossary

2 SAI Bn Gp	2 South African Infantry Battalion Group, based in Walvis Bay, South West Africa.
3 SAI Bn	3 South African Infantry Battalion, based at Potchefstroom.
32 Battalion	SADF unit formed in 1975, consisting mostly of former FNLA soldiers from Angola.
4 Reconnaissance Regiment	SADF special forces unit specializing in seaborne operations.
5 Reconnaissance Regiment	SADF special forces unit specializing in pseudo operations.
82 Mechanized Brigade	South African Army mechanized brigade which, together with other formations, formed 8 Armoured Division (8 Div).
101 Battalion	One of the nine indigenous infantry battalions raised in South West Africa during the SWA conflict. The headquarters was located in Ondangwa, Owamboland.
102 Battalion	One of the nine indigenous infantry battalions raised in South West Africa during the SWA conflict. The headquarters was located at Opuwa in northwest SWA.
A52 radio	South African-designed VHF/FM short-range man-pack tactical radio with a line-of-sight range of approximately 5km.
AFRC	Armed Forces Revolutionary Council. *See also* JPK.
AGS-17	Soviet-designed tripod or vehicle-mounted automatic grenade launcher. With an effective range of 1,700m, the weapon fires 30mm linked grenades carried in a 30-round ammunition box.
AK-47	Selective-fire 7.62 x 39mm assault rifle, first developed in the Soviet Union by Mikhail Kalashnikov.
Alpha Jet	French/German-developed light-attack aircraft. Armaments include a 27mm cannon in a centre-point pod and five external hard points which can carry a total of 5,600 kilograms of bombs, or two rocket pods, or missiles, or a combination thereof.
Antonov-12 (AN-12)	Soviet four-engine turboprop military transport aircraft, similar in size and capability to the Hercules C-130
Antonov-2 (AN-2)	Soviet single-engine light, multi-task utility aircraft. This aircraft was often chartered to provide EO with rations.
APC	All People's Congress, a political party in Sierra Leone.
area of influence	a geographic area in which a military force is capable of directly influencing operations through the use of manoeuvre forces or fire support.
area of interest	a geographic area in and from which enemy forces could jeopardize the accomplishment of a military operation.
avança	Portuguese for 'advance'. One of Brigadier Pepe de Castro's favourite words of encouragement.
AWOL	Absent without leave, a common violation of most military codes of discipline.

B-10 recoilless rifle	Soviet 82mm smooth-bore recoilless rifle with a maximum (indirect) range of 4,500 metres.
B-11 recoilless rifle	Soviet 107mm smooth-bore recoilless rifle with a maximum (indirect) range of 6,650 metres.
BMP-2	Amphibious Soviet-designed infantry combat vehicle with a crew of three. The main armament consists of a 30mm auto-cannon and the vehicle can carry up to seven infantry troops.
BM-21	Soviet-designed truck with a mounted 122mm multiple rocket launcher. With a launcher pack of 40 barrels, the weapon has a rate of fire of two rounds per second and a maximum range of 20,000 metres.
BTC	Benguema Training College, an RSLMF military training facility near Freetown, Sierra Leone.
Beechcraft B-200 King Air	Twin turboprop transport and utility aircraft .
biltong	South Africa term for dried, salted meat, similar to American jerky.
Boeing 727	Three-engine commercial jet airliner. Two such aircraft supported Executive Outcomes in Angola and Sierra Leone.
boere	Afrikaans for 'farmers', a colloquial reference to South Africans.
braai	South African term for 'barbeque'.
Buffel	Afrikaans for 'Buffalo', a South African mine-protected, armoured troop carrier with a capacity to carry ten troops. Used extensively during the South West African conflict.
bully beef	canned corned beef.
bundu bashing	South African term used to describe vehicles travelling through rough, remote or cross-country terrain.
CCB	Civil Cooperation Bureau, a covert military organization in the SA Defence Force.
CDS	Chief of Defence Staff, the head of the armed forces in Sierra Leone.
casevac	casualty evacuation.
Campo Oito	Portuguese for 'Camp Eight', one of the military targets during the EO assault on Soyo.
Casspir	Wheeled, mine-protected troop carrier vehicle that was used extensively by South African and South West African forces during the conflict in South West Africa.
Cessna 210	US-designed, six-seater, single-engine light general-purpose aircraft.
Cessna 337	US-designed twin-engine, 'push-pull', light utility aircraft.
civvies	military slang for civilian clothing or civilian persons.
Combat Group Course	course qualifying SA Army officers to command an integrated, all-arms combat force at unit level.
CPO	Chief Police Officer, a rank in the Sierra Leone Police Force.

D-1	the day before a military operation commences.
D-30	Soviet 122mm towed howitzer with a maximum effective range of 15,300 metres.
DAF	British 4x4 military cargo vehicle which can carry a maximum load of 4.2 tons or 20 troops.
DCC	Directorate of Covert Collection, a directorate tasked with the covert collection of military intelligence, under the Military Intelligence Division of the South African Defence Force.
D-Day	the day on which a military operation commences.
DF task	Defensive Fire task, an artillery/mortar term for a defensive fire mission.
Dragunov	Soviet semi-automatic sniper rifle, chambered in 7.62 x 54mm.
DShK	Soviet-designed belt-fed 12.7mm, heavy machine gun with an effective range of 2,000 metres.
ECOMOG	Economic Community of West African States Monitoring Group, established by Nigeria, Ghana, Guinea, Sierra Leone and the Gambia in 1990.
ECOWAS	Economic Community of West African States.
EO	a private military company headed by Eeben Barlow, a former member of the South African Defence Force. The majority of the employees who participated in EO operations in Angola/Sierra Leone were recruited from southern Africa.
EO Tac HQ	Executive Outcomes tactical headquarters at Saurimo, Angola.
FAA	*Forças Armadas Angolanas* (Angolan Armed Forces).
FAPA	*Força Aérea Popular de Angola* (Angolan Air Force).
FLOT	Forward Line of Own Troops. Identifies the location of own troops closest to the enemy, for mainly own aircraft in close air support and other air support missions. FLOT can be marked by coloured smoke, helicopter panels or dayglo materials.
força	Portuguese slang for 'keep going'.
forming-up place	or FUP, an area where military forces form up in battle formation prior to the start of an attack.
Fina	a lubricant brand owned by Total.
fireforce	a fireforce usually consisted of a light heliborne force that could be transported to the location of a contact with enemy insurgents to assist with the contact, take over the contact or conduct immediate follow-up operations. The force was usually composed of men from the paratrooper units.
G5	South African 155mm towed gun howitzer with an effective range of approximately 38,000 metres.
gatvol	Afrikaans expression for 'fed up'.
Goldstone Commission	chaired by Justice Goldstone, the commission was appointed

	by the South African government to investigate political violence and intimidation that occurred between July 1991 and 1994. Members of the commission raided the offices of the DCC.
GPS	Global Positioning System.
GRAD-PA	single-round, man-portable rocket launcher that fires 122mm high-explosive shells.
GSG	Gurkha Security Guards Limited, a company employed by the Sierra Leone government prior to the engagement of EO
Gurkha	a soldier from Nepal and North India who serves either in the Indian Army or the British Army. Renowned for the efficient use of a knife known as a kukri.
H-Hour	the hour at which a military operation commences. Similarly, H-60 minutes refers to the time at a point 60 minutes before an operation commences.
Himba	a tribe in Namibia (previously South West Africa) whose traditional home is located in the northwest of the country.
HQ	headquarters.
Ibis Air	charter airline which supported Executive Outcomes in Angola and Sierra Leone.
IDM	illegal diamond mining.
IL-76 Ilyushin	Soviet-designed four-engine multi-purpose military transport aircraft with a range of up to 5,000km and a payload of 40 tons. Used in Angola to transport EO personnel, cargo, vehicles and to conduct air supply.
in loco	in the proper or natural place.
JOC	Joint Operations Committee.
JPK	nickname for Major Johnny Paul Koroma, head of state in Sierra Leone from May 1997 to February 1998, after he wrested control from the elected government in a coup d'état.
junter	South African slang to describe a joy ride or an aimless trip.
Kamaz	Soviet-designed military cargo vehicle with a cross-country capability.
KCC	Kono Consultative Committee.
Koevoet	Afrikaans for 'crowbar', a South African Police unit based at Oshakati, South West Africa that utilized motorized skirmishing tactics with great success against SWAPO insurgents.
Kondecom	Kono Defence Committee, a committee established by EO, consisting of the heads of the uniform services in the Kono district.

Leone	the currency of Sierra Leone.
LZ	LZ.
Makarov	Soviet-designed semi-automatic pistol with a normal magazine capacity of eight rounds.
manne	form of addressing soldiers in Afrikaans, literally translated as 'men'.
modus operandi	method of operating.
M1942	Soviet-designed 76mm gun with an effective range of 13,000 metres.
M-46	Soviet-designed 130mm gun with an effective range of over 27,000 metres.
Mi-17	Soviet-designed medium twin-turbine transport helicopter that can also act as a gunship and can carry 30 troops.
Mi-24	Soviet-designed helicopter gunship capable of carrying eight troops. The Mi-24 has a nose-mounted, four-barrelled 12.7mm Gatling gun and can carry up to 4,200 kilograms of ordnance on six wing pylons.
MiG-23	Soviet fighter aircraft with variable sweep wings, a twin-barrelled 23mm cannon and six external hard points for munitions.
Namibia	independent African country, formerly South West Africa.
NCO	non-commissioned officer.
NDMC	National Diamond Mining Corporation, the state diamond company in Sierra Leone.
NPRC	National Provisional Ruling Council, the body that ruled Sierra Leone after Captain Valentine Strasser took over the country.
Operation Hooper	Codename of a South African Defence Force military operation, in support of UNITA and against the FAA forces in southeast Angola during the 1980s.
Operation Modular	*see* Operation Hooper.
Operation Packer	*see* Operation Hooper.
ops room	operations room, which contains the radios, equipment and staff required to control military operations.
OPSO	operations order, an order that describes a military operation and tasks constituent military forces.
Parabat	South African paratrooper, der. Parachute Battalion.
pega pak	a white spirit or gin brewed in Sierra Leone and available in a convenient plastic pouch.
PAIIC	a clandestine company within the DCC.
PC-7	Swiss-designed and -manufactured light turbo-prop aircraft

	with a ceiling of 33,000ft and a maximum range of 2,630km. Used as a light reconnaissance aircraft, the wings also have six hard points that can carry bombs or rockets.
PKM	Soviet-designed, 7.62mm, belt-fed, light general-purpose machine gun.
PLAN	People's Liberation Army of Namibia, SWAPO's military wing.
PLO	Principle Liaison Officer. The collective name for the three remaining officers who had been part of the group of five officers who carried out the coup d'état which saw Captain Valentine Strasser appointed as the head of state of Sierra Leone and Captain (later Brigadier) Maada Bio as his second-in-command.
RDF	Rapid Deployment Force. The EO force consisted mainly of light infantry teams deployed by helicopter, to conduct reconnaissance tasks, mortar bombardments and follow-up operations.
RPG-7	Soviet-designed portable, shoulder-fired anti-tank rocket-propelled grenade launcher, with an effective range of up to 300 metres.
RSLMF	Republic of Sierra Leone Military Forces, the armed forces of Sierra Leone.
RUF	Revolutionary United Front.
RV	rendezvous, or meeting place.
rat-run	military slang for ration run.
Recce	A colloquial name for a special forces operator, a member of one of the Reconnaissance Regiments of the SADF.
rubber duck	inflatable rubber dinghy often used by seaborne special forces
SAAF	South African Air Force.
SA Army	South African Army.
SA Army Command and Staff Course	Senior course in the SA Army. Presented at the SA Army College in Pretoria, the course prepared senior officers for senior command and staff roles in the SA Army.
SA-2 / SAM-2	Soviet-designed high-altitude, command-guided, surface-to-air missile (SAM) system. The missile has a 195kg fragmentation warhead, a range of approximately 45,000 metres and a maximum altitude of approximately 65,000ft.
SA-7 / SAM-7	Soviet-designed man-portable, shoulder fired, infrared-seeking anti-aircraft system.
SADF	South African Defence Force (pre-1994 designation).
SADFI	South African Defence Force Institute, the military's shopping outlet, similiar to the British NAAFI or the US PX Stores.
SANDF	South African National Defence Force (post 1994 designation).

SDO	Senior District Officer, a senior appointment in the Sierra Leone civil service.
Single tube GRAD-P	Soviet-designed single-round, man-portable rocket launcher that propels a 122mm high-explosive fragmentation rocket with an 11,000-metre range.
sitrep	situation report.
SLCU	Sierra Leone Commando Unit, the RSLM unit trained by the Gurkha Security Guards, under Lieutenant-Colonel Bob McKenzie.
SLP	Sierra Leone Police.
SLPP	Sierra Leone People's Party.
SLST	Sierra Leone Selection Trust. *See also* NDMC.
Sonangol	Angolan state enterprise charged with managing the country's hydrocarbon resources.
SWA	South West Africa, an African country situated in the southwest of the continent. Originally a German colony, it was mandated to South Africa after the First World War. The country became independent as Namibia on 21 March 1990.
SWAPO	South West African People's Organization, the political organization whose military wing, PLAN (People's Liberation Army of Namibia), fought an insurgency conflict in South West Africa.
SWATF	South West Africa Territorial Force; comprised nine indigenous infantry battalions, headquartered in Windhoek.
Sul Africanos	Portuguese for 'South Africans'.
T-62	Soviet-designed, main battle tank with a combat weight of 45.7 tons, a crew of four and a 155mm main weapon with a 7.62mm PKT co-axial light machine gun and a 12.7mm DShK anti-aircraft machine gun
Tatra	military truck manufactured by Tatra, an established vehicle manufacturing company in the Czech Republic and the third oldest car manufacturer in the world.
Telstar	term used by SADF members to refer to an airborne aircraft through which radio messages are relayed.
Texaco	a US oil company.
tiffy	SADF slang for a member of the Technical Services Corps in the SA Army; a military vehicle mechanic, der. artificer.
UNITA	*União Nacional para a Independência Total de Angola*, The National Union for the Total Independence of Angola.
URAL	Soviet-designed, general-purpose 6x6 off-road diesel-powered vehicle. Used for transporting cargo, troops and railers on all types of roads and terrain; it also serves as the launching platform for the BM-21 multiple rocket launcher.

VHF	very high frequency.
VIP	very important person.
vlamgat	Literally translated from Afrikaans as 'flame hole' or 'flame arse', the slang for a Mirage, from the jet's afterburner.
vlamgatte	Afrikaans slang for SAAF Mirage pilots.
whitee	slang for white person.
ZU-23-2	Soviet towed twin-barrelled 23mm anti-aircraft cannon. Manually aimed and fired, the weapon was designed to engage low-flying aircraft at a range of approximately 2,500 metres as well as a selection of ground targets and vehicles.

Roots

I come from a stock-standard military background. After completing my national military service at 2 South African Infantry Battalion Group (2 SAI Bn Gp) in Walvis Bay, South West Africa in 1973 I studied mining engineering but after six years decided that my talents lay with the military. After rejoining the South African Army in a permanent capacity in 1978 I was immediately transferred to South West Africa (Namibia) where I served as a young staff officer in the headquarters of the South West Africa Territorial Force (SWATF HQ) in Windhoek. After a whilst I was transferred to 102 Battalion (102 Bn) at Opuwa in Kaokoland, an area in the north-west of South West Africa where I spent four very enjoyable and rewarding years working with members of the local tribes who had been recruited into the South West African Territorial Force (SWATF). This experience was to prove handy later in my career.

In December 1981 I married Gerda and was subsequently transferred to 3 South African Infantry Battalion (3 SAI Bn) in Potchefstroom, South Africa. My prolonged stay at Opuwa had caused me to fall somewhat behind in completing my SA Army promotion courses and I had to catch up. I made it back up to standard, in my view, in a very short time, although Borries Borman and Jan Bierman at the Infantry School in Oudtshoorn were never satisfied unless there were a large number of red circles around the answers in my examination books.

I attended many courses during this catch-up period and I trained many soldiers thereafter, all good preparation for the intensification of the insurgency conflict in South West Africa. In 1985, after completing my Combat Group course, I was transferred to 82 Mechanized Brigade (82 Mech Bde) in Potchefstroom where I gained valuable experience in conventional warfare. I enjoyed my time here and my conventional stint peaked when I attended the SA Army Command and Staff Course in Pretoria and was transferred thereafter to 2 SAI Bn Gp in Walvis Bay.

It was during my staff course at the SA Army College in Pretoria that I was recruited into the Civil Cooperation Bureau (CCB), a military organization the details of which I will not describe here, for understandable reasons. With the pay grade of a colonel in the military and the seniority of a manager in the CCB, I initiated and ran a number of very sensitive projects. When the CCB was disbanded and its members were thrown to the wolves by the politicians, I was transferred to the DCC within the Military Intelligence Division of the South African Defence Force (SADF). I can, today, still recall the shit taste of political betrayal. My time at the Directorate of Covert Collection (DCC) ended in January 1991, once again due to the fact that the security pillar of the South African order was on the retreat and had given way to pressure. I was simply asked to resign.

The recollections of soldiers about some or other high adventure during their career are often preceded by a wry smile and a reference to being at the right place at the right time. This was true in my case as far as my post-SADF career was concerned. EO, a little-known private organization headed by Eeben Barlow, a former colleague of mine in the CCB, was on the lookout for soldiers for a military operation in the northwestern corner of Angola and a number of former CCB and DCC soldiers, myself included, exited the foxholes in which we were sheltering from the political storm and grasped this job opportunity, realizing that this was probably the closest we would get to the life we really loved, to the vocation we were very good at and which we still desired to practice.

Despite the fact that EO was representative of a new era in soldiering in Africa, so different from the infamous African mercenaries of the 1960s and 1970s, the organization's activities immediately fuelled the imagination and creativity of the media who couldn't grasp the fundamental difference between us and our predecessors. Hence, in an era pervaded by so-called political correctness in South Africa, we were tarred with the same brush. The same untruths, generalizations and tripe that appeared in the media was also repeated verbatim in the officers' and non-commissioned officers' messes in the SA Army, SA Air Force, SA Navy and SA Medical Service, sensationalizing everything. It was no small wonder then that journalists began to accuse EO of romanticizing mercenaries.

The perceptions of Executive Outcome had really got out of hand.

Roelf van Heerden

PART 1
ANGOLA: HELPING A FORMER ENEMY AGAINST A FORMER ALLY

SOYO AND THE BIRTH OF A NEW TYPE OF AFRICAN SOLDIER, MARCH 1993

Background

The town of Soyo is located in the northwestern corner of Angola, on the Congo River and this is where Colonel Pepe de Castro, the local *Forças Armadas Angolanas* (FAA) commander and his opposite number from the *União Nacional para a Independência Total de Angola* (UNITA), the government's mortal enemy in the ongoing twenty-year civil conflict, had manned the Joint Monitoring Headquarters during the disastrous peace initiatives of the early 1990s. Soyo had been overrun and occupied by UNITA during a surprise attack which ended the short-lived era of peace between the two forces. Colonel Pepe, as he was known, and the FAA forces had retreated from the area and UNITA had gone on to occupy large areas of Cabinda, the oil rich enclave just north of the town, as well. This was tactically sound from their perspective as Cabinda borders on Zaire (now the Democratic Republic of the Congo or DRC), a country which was positively disposed towards UNITA. After the withdrawal of the FAA forces from the area their commander, Colonel Pepe knew full well that within the ranks of the FAA it was expected of an operational commander who had lost a position such as Soyo to be told by General João Baptiste de Matos, the head of the Angolan Armed Forces, to retake that position.

The occupation of Soyo by UNITA had effectively halted the oil exploration and production activities of Heritage Oil as a number of drilling sites on land as well as other expensive equipment in Soyo had fallen into UNITA hands. Tony Buckingham, the head of Heritage Oil and a former British special forces soldier, together with a second former special forces soldier of British descent who went by the name of Simon Mann, set about negotiating with Sonangol, the Angolan state oil company, to persuade them to retake and occupy the oil-rich Soyo province with Angolan government troops so that the production of the sought after Soyo sweet oil could resume. Their arguments found favour, particularly when the two businessmen suggested that the government troops could perhaps be augmented by a force of battle hardened South Africans. It was of course in Angola's interests to restart the flow of oil revenue to finance the costly conflict with UNITA and General de Matos eventually gave the green light for a contract with a security company, known as EO, to retake this province in cooperation with FAA government troops.

Eeben Barlow, a colleague from my SADF and CCB days who had established EO, started the wheels rolling to fulfil this contract and began recruiting people to establish the desired force level. He had also decided to recruit people through his circle of friends and in this fashion he obtained the services of Buks Buys, a former captain in the South African Special Forces, who he appointed as the commander of the operational unit, whilst Harry Ferreira, Phil Smith and Lafras Luitingh were appointed as the three platoon commanders. It was evident that Eeben had complete trust in these men as he had operated with each of them at some point in his military career. Each platoon commander was tasked to recruit around fifteen persons for their platoon. The operation was highly classified for two obvious reasons. The town of Soyo had been taken by UNITA using the advantage gained by surprise and the whole of the Soyo province was now under UNITA's control. The closest UNITA troops to Soyo, however, were deployed in the coastal town of Ambriz, approximately 120 kilometres north of Luanda; this effectively isolated the Soyo area, making it vulnerable to a surprise attack. The other reason for the high security of information was that a security breach in South Africa itself could scupper the operation even before the force had left for Angola. It was also naive to think that covert military ties, including the exchange of information, no longer existed between South Africa and UNITA.

Part of the solution was to create and circulate a credible cover story amongst the recruited members and strictly apply the 'need-to-know' principle during all phases of the operation itself. It was decided that the cover story was to run along the lines of a mountaineering expedition somewhere in Central Africa. Each recruited member was required to buy mountaineering equipment, including two shirts and two pairs of pants, a gold coloured pair of Hi-Tec hiking boots and all the necessary accessories such as socks and the like from none other than Trappers Trading, an outlet that specialized in selling outdoor clothes and equipment. From later discussions it became clear that many of the wives hadn't really believed the cover story from the start, but the men folk persevered with it for the benefit of the children and any other inquisitive persons who happened to witness the preparations for the operation. We all knew that a successful cover story has to be well thought out and carefully coordinated but I believe that most perceptive people would probably have found the cover story difficult to swallow. From where had the sudden desire to undertake a mountaineering expedition in Africa sprung? Questions about departure dates and the identity of the expedition leader were asked. Was Buks Buys qualified to lead a mountaineering expedition? Why were we taking compasses with us on a mountaineering expedition? I kept my side of the bargain and persisted with the cover story as I believed in the importance of security as a critical success factor for this operation. The gods smiled kindly on us and the cover story held for the four days that it took for us to leave South Africa in small groups and regroup in Namibia. In any event we succeeded in leaving without the cover story being blown, all set for a six- to eight-week military operation that would take us, via Namibia, to Angola before our return to South Africa.

We also decided that the mountaineering expedition cover story did not have to be believed by everyone and during the first meeting of the group at the Fountains Valley Resort in Pretoria some part of the truth was leaked. We learnt that we were on our way to protect oil rigs and that the enemy in this operation was UNITA. This was of some concern to me as it was somewhat difficult to imagine myself aiming a weapon at members of a force alongside whom I had fought during Operations Modular, Hooper and Packer, the South African Defence Force's military operations in support of UNITA, aimed at halting the FAA advance into southeast Angola during the 1980s. Not only had I fought alongside them, I had participated in joint planning cycles with them in Rundu, Namibia as far back as 1986. This was going to be awkward to say the least.

There were of course, a number of serious concerns and unknowns about the operation. Would the political storm burst in South Africa before we returned and what about all the possible enquiries that could emanate from the South African National Intelligence Service, the Security Police and Military Intelligence? We were in actual fact skating on very thin ice, in that we could have been perceived as being a threat to South Africa, especially during this period of delicate negotiations with the African National Congress (ANC). If one looks at some of the EO members involved in the Soyo operation—people who had an intimate knowledge of the inside workings of each headquarters of each security organization and structure in South Africa—and add the fact that the Angolan government and their armed forces supported the ANC's goals, and the ANC's Quattro base was close to Luanda, our operation could have been perceived by the South African government as a very real threat to the country's security.

By now I had become accustomed to having to cut all ties and lie low until further notice. I had already experienced the feeling of sitting in the CCB headquarters, only to learn all of a sudden that some or other police element has climbed over the outer walls in an effort to seize documentation. I had actually been located at the alternative headquarters when this event took place. Dolf, a colleague of mine, and I immediately relayed instructions but the ladies at the office had luckily already stuffed the files under the fridges, but they couldn't do anything with the steel trunk packed full of money.

Notwithstanding these agonising concerns I really believed that things would work out in the end and my analytic capability would ensure that healthy decisions were made and sound judgement was exercised.

Recruitment

I believe that Eeben Barlow didn't agonize much about his decision that the people he was going to use were to be former 32 Battalion members or Special Forces members. With the exception of a few members who hailed from the more conventional forces in the SA Army, the majority of the EO contingent in actual fact consisted of his colleagues and friends, some more obscure than others. The Soyo force was organized into a small headquarters element under Buks Buys, with three under-strength platoons, each fifteen strong, and a total strength of 54 souls when we first arrived in Angola. This initial contingent had only two black soldiers, both former members of the Special Forces. This ratio was destined to change radically as EO evolved.

When the recruiting for EO started I was a senior member serving in the DCC within the SA Defence Force's Military Intelligence Division. The previous week I had received my second 'discharge' from the SADF and I was at my wits end as I didn't really know what was to become of me.

The Goldstone Commission had recommended that the whole group of ex-CCB members currently serving in the DCC, including myself, should leave the DCC and the South African Defence Force. Included amongst these 'outcasts' was a close acquaintance, Harry Ferreira, who had worked in my DCC region, could speak Portuguese, was an ex 32 Battalion member, and was also one of Eeben Barlow's friends. After being appointed as a platoon commander in EO, Harry approached me and asked me what I was going to do next. At the same time he gave me an indication that he had something for me to do. I received a very general briefing and was asked if I could recruit a few of my old CCB colleagues. I duly contacted a few former members and they indicated that they were interested. The issue was not what, but where and how many of us were going to undertake this job. A number of questions came to mind and I failed to reach answers, which I believed would probably be provided at a co-ordinating session. I had committed to providing feedback to Harry by the following Monday, 1 March 1993, and it was during this session that he informed me that I was to be appointed as his second-in-command, or platoon sergeant, for the operation. I was rather taken aback by this as I had already achieved a number of relatively significant military milestones to date, including having passed the SA Army's Command and Staff Course, served as the second-in-command of 82 Mechanized Brigade, and having been a regional manager during my time in the CCB and in the DCC. I was informed that this was the way things were in EO and it was a case of first come, first served. This saying evolved over time into what later became the unofficial EO motto: Fit in or fuck off! In true soldierly fashion I realized that I would have to be patient and act with fortitude as I was convinced that there would be many occasions where my military qualities would be sorely required. I didn't even know who the other platoon commanders were, nor did I know Buks Buys.

By Tuesday, 2 March 1993, a sense of urgency was evident as much still had to be done. Recruitment had to be completed, procurement of equipment had to be completed, administration had to be finalized and a clean break had to be made from South Africa as soon as possible in order to keep the operational security intact.

On Wednesday evening we gathered at the Fountains Valley Resort in Pretoria to coordinate our progress. This was the first time that we had all gathered together and I was led to understand that the first flight had already left with an advance team consisting of a number of administrative personnel. Eeben Barlow told us in general terms what the job was about and the latest cover story that we were going to guard and ensure the safety of oil rigs. When the time for questions arrived a number of those present wanted to know who had been appointed as the force commander. Eeben didn't identify the person by name and merely stated that he had already been appointed and that he had left with the advance team. A few members asked why I had not been appointed as the commander. After all I was staff qualified and, as a full colonel, the person with the highest military rank. Eeben maintained his position that the force commander had already been appointed and that he had already left for our destination together with the three platoon commanders. It was obvious that this decision was not open to debate.

The next surprise we received was when Eeben informed us that we were scheduled to fly out to a transit destination over the next two days. So, things had to move along at a brisk pace. The next day we ambled off to Trappers Trading and duly acquired the civilian clothing for the climbing expedition. The cover story was accepted at face value by the shop assistants and it gained further credibility in the process.

I had been allocated to No. 3 Platoon where things were generally progressing well. I knew most of the members of the platoon and was therefore in a position to register my own private reservations about the capabilities of a few of the men, based on my experience with them at DCC. I did not, however, doubt their friendship and good intentions—something which is crucial when a small group of people are involved in an external task of this nature.

Gerda, my wife, had not been very enthusiastic about this undertaking from the outset. But, having classified me as a stubborn person on a number of previous occasions—not the least of which was related to a visit to the South African Defence Force Institute, the SADF shopping outlet, to buy baby milk powder only to see me return three hours later with a new video cassette recorder under my arm and no baby milk formula—she understood when I informed her that we were due to fly out on the Friday evening.

On the Friday morning, 5 March 1993, I visited the DCC at Military Intelligence headquarters in Pretoria to receive my last military documentation and with that another chapter in my life came to an end. I said my goodbyes to those people who wanted to greet me in a friendly manner. Not everybody was all that attached to me, especially the commander, Brigadier Tolletjies Botha, who had previously not taken kindly to my warning that Judge Goldstone, who was investigating a possible 'third force' within the South African security forces, would still locate us, expose us and compromise a number of operators. On the day that this event actually did take place Brigadier Botha had left the building to play bowls, true to the SADF tradition of sport parade on a Wednesday afternoon. Wednesday sport parade was the last thing on the minds of the members of PAIIC whose offices were raided in his absence that afternoon, and I was left with the task of informing Judge Goldstone and all his policemen that the commander was not in the building and that I actually did not work at DCC either—I was merely delivering documents. Our professional relationship had not been enhanced at all by this incident.

There were others, including Jan 'Bal' van Rensburg and another hanger-on, Borries Bornman, who were not very enamoured of me either. I will never forget the presentations made to Brigadier Tolletjies Botha on the short term survival strategy of the DCC, with a view to the negotiation politics between the government and the ANC. The two elected syndicates who made presentations in actual fact consisted of a DCC syndicate, led by Borries Bornman and a former CCB syndicate, led by myself. The main thrust of my presentation was a recommendation that DCC should become truly covert, to the extent that it should almost 'go underground'. The recommendation was summarily shot down as it had a financial implication which would increase the budget from its current levels. On the other hand, Borries Bornman provided a cheaper option which provided for an intelligence product based more on computerised resources.

I did manage, however, to accede to my immediate boss, Koos Louw's request that I explain to him how the CCB had actually worked. Tolletjies Botha also wanted to know how the CCB worked and operated, but what they actually found very difficult to accept and understand was that the *modus operandi* of the CCB exposed their own incompetence and unprofessional approach.

I left that day with a promise that I would be in contact once my discharge documents had been processed. Little did I know that within a short period of time this same DCC would be tasked by the military to find out more about the activities of a certain group of mercenaries of which I was a member. In addition, little did I know that during the operation in Soyo my wife would be contacted by members of DCC with a request to get hold of me and convince me that I should return to South Africa immediately, as the task we were undertaking was not the right thing to do. Perhaps I knew too much about South Africa's military presence in countries such as Zaire (now the Democratic Republic of Congo) and the Comoros and many other projects outside South Africa.

Mercenary or what?

Friends remain friends, especially when the friendship is based on a set of truths, and preferably nothing to do with politics.

One of the highlights of my military career in the SADF had been the opportunity to make contact with and operate with UNITA. During the time I served as a company commander at 102 Battalion in Kaokoland my troops were deployed into Angola alongside UNITA troops. During my years of service at 3 SAI Bn I had also been deployed on operational tasks into Angola and I liaised directly with UNITA from my Angolan base located at Chiede. I regarded the UNITA forces as my friends and allies and it had been a pleasure to work with them. They were trustworthy and eager to learn from us. On my part I learnt from them about how to get on with a campaign without the benefit of a substantial support and logistic effort, how to maintain a sense of determination in the face of adversity, and how to adapt the tactics and techniques that we had taught them to prevailing conditions. I also came into contact with UNITA during Operations Modular, Hooper and Packer, in the vicinity of Cuito Cuanavale, in southeastern Angola. As the primary member of the operations staff (SO1 Operations) of 82 Mech Bde I regularly worked with Colonel Sivukuvuku, my UNITA counterpart. He always appeared neat and clean, due in all probability to the fact that UNITA officers each had a few batmen. The UNITA troops really performed well during operations. Wherever we came across them, whether it was in Mavinga, the Lomba River, or at Tumpo, just east of Cuito Cuanavale, they impressed me. They also had their limitations. In general though they applied what they had learnt from us—after all a right flanking attack remains a right flanking attack despite the fact that there may be an obstacle between the attacking force and their objective. In essence, leadership on the lower levels up to and including company level is very important, especially when one is engaged in the more flexible type of operations. Once I entered Angola as a member of EO I realized that I knew what they knew, whilst UNITA had not as yet fought against South Africans.

Eeben Barlow, probably with tongue in cheek, had mentioned in passing that we were to be deployed in an area which was under threat by UNITA. At the time I didn't give this information too much credence or prominence, as I had learnt that throughout the many battle appreciations that I had carried out during military courses, I would merely have to be wary of UNITA. In short, we would have to be able to defend against UNITA offensive operations.

I realized with finality at that point that I was now actually a mercenary. The country that pays me received my services, irrespective of where in the world the services were to be carried out. This was the mechanism by which I could justify the fact that in 1987 and 1988 I had fought as a member of the SADF alongside UNITA and in January 1993 I had operated alongside the FAA against them. The actual detail related to the way I would carry out this task would probably differ as it would be determined by the output of my battle appreciations and the contents of the subsequent operations orders (OPSOs). I also knew that an operation order would undoubtedly be forthcoming once the EO force had arrived in Angola.

There was too little time left to reflect in any depth on the Angolan Government's feelings about me as a South African soldier. The *boere* (colloquialism for South Africans) had fought on UNITA's side, had supported them for so many years logistically, and on the battlefield with close air support and indirect fire support, as well as on a tactical level with deception actions deep into their rear areas. Here we were again. Only this time round we were members of EO, effectively a bunch of mercenaries, moving deep into Angola to support FAA troops. I didn't ponder much about whether the Angolans trusted us or not. I avoided conversations with officers (including my good friend Colonel Pepe de Castro) where jokes were made or serious discussions held about the measure of trust with which the South African members of EO were regarded. I also refrained from sharing any jokes, whether told over a Black Label whisky or not, about how a particular person reacted under heavy fire or how another person fled during a certain contact with UNITA forces. Colonel Pepe de Castro did once tell me, however, with some relish, that as a young and much slimmer FAA captain he had once been forced to escape and evade South African troops as they chased him, with the support of helicopters. When he felt that he couldn't run any further he literally dived into an ant-bear hole to escape the attentions of the South African helicopter gunship.

By the end of the day on Friday, 5 March 1993, all the members of my platoon had left Jan Smuts Airport (now O. R. Tambo International Airport) in Johannesburg and had arrived at Eros Airport in Windhoek. We overnighted as unobtrusively as possible in a motel in the southern suburbs of the capital city. We had received instructions to lie low and to leave Windhoek at 0400 the next morning from Eros Airport, close to the motel, via two Cessna 210 aircraft. We were en route to Cabo Ledo, a military base situated on the Atlantic coast about one hundred kilometres south of Luanda, the Angolan capital. The flight was uneventful and we landed safely that afternoon on a well maintained runway where the members of the EO advance party met us. It was obvious that the long runway had been designed to handle much larger aircraft, including the Soviet-built IL-76 Ilyushin cargo aircraft.

Later that evening we learnt that Cabo Ledo had been a Cuban base during the 1980s and that the government was in the process of renovating the facility. I realized that there was very little movement on the base and that very few FAA troops could be seen. We only made contact with Antonio Lucas, a FAA major who issued us with FAA equipment, weapons and ammunition. I couldn't help making a few wry remarks in the store as we received the easily identifiable FAA uniform and belt. I smiled, however, when I realized that we were being issued with brand new AK-47 assault rifles and magazines. I was entering a new era, and this was the first of many changes I was to experience over time. The change in basic weaponry was of no real consequence to the former Special Forces and 32 Battalion guys who had pseudo-operations experience, as they had been used to carrying these weapons.

I was now inside a former Cuban base in the very heartland of what used to be one of South Africa's priority enemy forces. Talk about fundamental change. In my days as a SADF soldier I would have given a lot to have been able to penetrate Angola as far as this location, gather intelligence and carry out a few operations on small scale, and to exfiltrate thereafter. These were daydreams; the reality was that I was on the other side now, and it had not really been all that difficult to switch mentally from fighting for UNITA to fighting for the FAA. It would not be all that difficult to pull the trigger when UNITA soldiers appeared in my rifle sights either.

My previous mentors, including Lieutenant General Witkop Badenhorst, had always said that a soldier should know his enemy 'inside out' and now here I was with high levels of knowledge of both sides of the equation, something that was of great assistance to me during our cooperation with FAA and our operations against UNITA. We were indeed highly valuable assets. Would I ever forget how, during the intelligence appreciation on military courses we were required to dissect the enemy in great detail, to know the enemy thoroughly in order to formulate detailed, 'fat' deductions and conclusions about their probable courses of action that sounded like short stories? Practical experience of course spawns a different reality, which in turn develops its own theory. The reality was that the well known expression circulated by General Jannie Geldenhuys, a former Chief of the South African Defence Force, which stated that one should "Do what you can with what you have" was very apt, especially in Africa. Well, with how little can one actually cope? I had already realized that in this role the support that we had been used to as South African Defence Force soldiers did not exist. I actually didn't really want to dwell too much on military theory at this point as I was convinced that perseverance would be a more highly valued commodity in the operations we were about to undertake.

Preparation and training

Whilst we were in the process of drawing our small arms, chest webbing and other kit, one member of our group stumbled past me to the door of the store. It was evident from his demeanour that this young man was really looking forward to the action. He unfortunately didn't have enough arms and hands to carry the large number of weapons, piles of ammunition and the kit that he had drawn from the store, so he was forced to make use of his pockets as well. What a sight. There were other light hearted moments as well. This time it was a man in

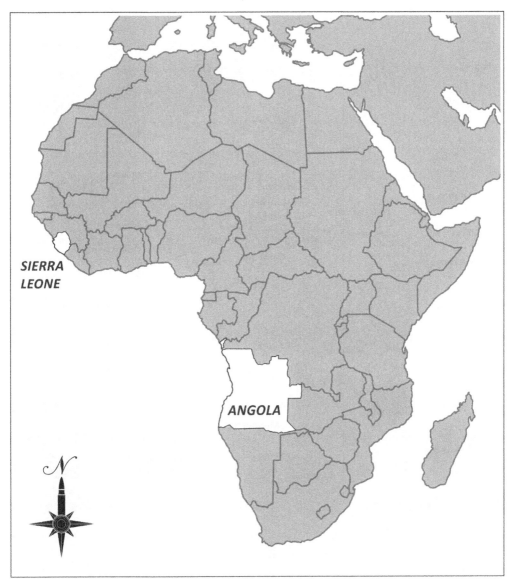

SIERRA
LEONE

ANGOLA

Map of Africa depicting Angola and Sierra Leone.

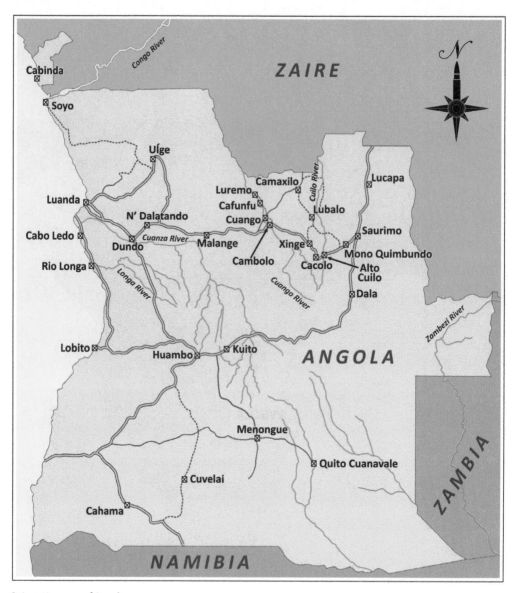

Orientation map of Angola.

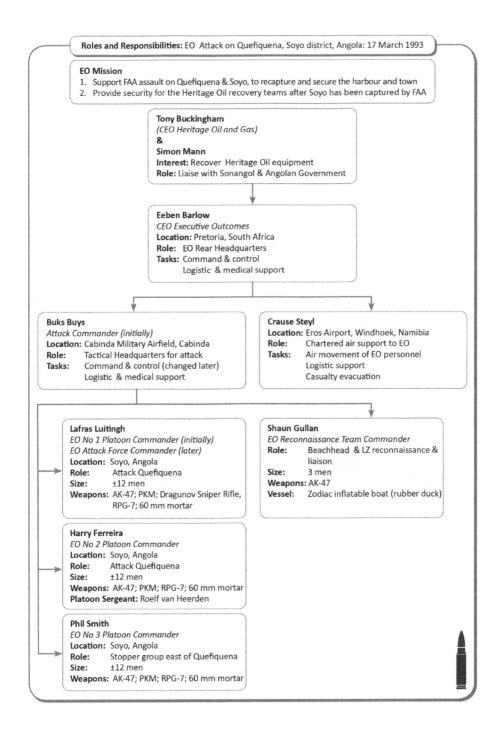

Roles and Responsibilities: EO Attack on Quefiquena, Soyo district, Angola: 17 March 1993

EO Mission
1. Support FAA assault on Quefiquena & Soyo, to recapture and secure the harbour and town
2. Provide security for the Heritage Oil recovery teams after Soyo has been captured by FAA

Tony Buckingham
(CEO Heritage Oil and Gas)
&
Simon Mann
Interest: Recover Heritage Oil equipment
Role: Liaise with Sonangol & Angolan Government

Eeben Barlow
CEO Executive Outcomes
Location: Pretoria, South Africa
Role: EO Rear Headquarters
Tasks: Command & control
Logistic & medical support

Buks Buys
Attack Commander (initially)
Location: Cabinda Military Airfield, Cabinda
Role: Tactical Headquarters for attack
Tasks: Command & control (changed later)
Logistic & medical support

Crause Steyl
Location: Eros Airport, Windhoek, Namibia
Role: Chartered air support to EO
Tasks: Air movement of EO personnel
Logistic support
Casualty evacuation

Lafras Luitingh
EO No 1 Platoon Commander (initially)
EO Attack Force Commander (later)
Location: Soyo, Angola
Role: Attack Quefiquena
Size: ±12 men
Weapons: AK-47; PKM; Dragunov Sniper Rifle, RPG-7; 60 mm mortar

Shaun Gullan
EO Reconnaissance Team Commander
Role: Beachhead & LZ reconnaissance & liaison
Size: 3 men
Weapons: AK-47
Vessel: Zodiac inflatable boat (rubber duck)

Harry Ferreira
EO No 2 Platoon Commander
Location: Soyo, Angola
Role: Attack Quefiquena
Size: ±12 men
Weapons: AK-47; PKM; RPG-7; 60 mm mortar
Platoon Sergeant: Roelf van Heerden

Phil Smith
EO No 3 Platoon Commander
Location: Soyo, Angola
Role: Stopper group east of Quefiquena
Size: ±12 men
Weapons: AK-47; PKM; RPG-7; 60 mm mortar

Executive Outcomes order of battle for the assault on Soyo.

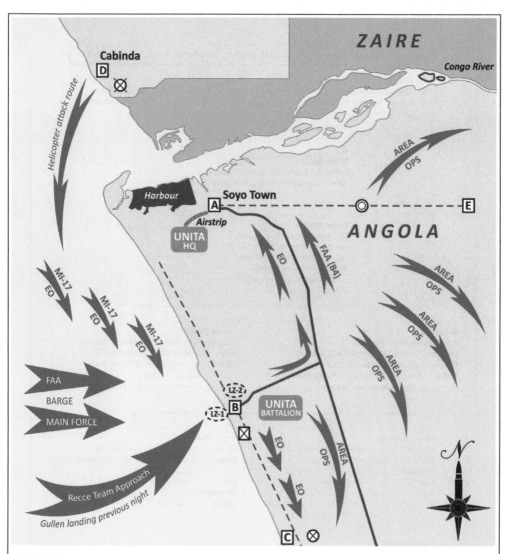

NOTES:

- A Soyo Town and Airstrip - UNITA HQ before attack. Taken over by FAA & EO.
- B Quefiquena Oil Installation - UNITA Battalion
- C Camp - Oito (Camp 8)
- D Cabinda
- E Sumba
- ⊗ Missile site from where Phil's PC-7 was shot at
- ⊗ Emergency landing site for PC-7 on Cabinda soil
- ○ Phil shot here
- ⊠ Buks Erasmus shot here
- -- · Secondary Road
- ▬ Main Road

Map depicting the Soyo operational plan.

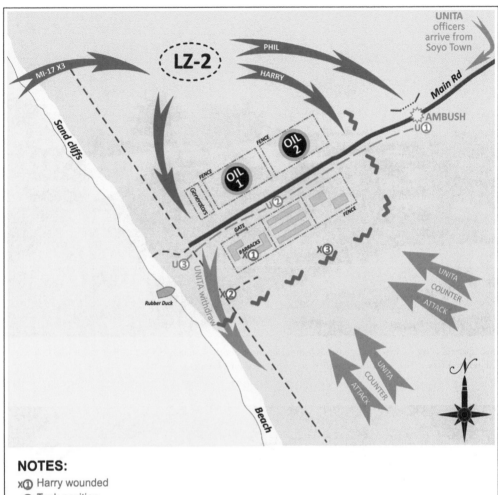

NOTES:

x① Harry wounded
x② Tank position
x③ EO defensive positions on night after attack
u① UNITA officers react from Soyo Town. Taken out by Phil's platoon
u② UNITA officers in Mitsubishi double cab killed by Harry/Louis
u③ Final position of Mitsubishi double cab

The attack on Quefiquena, near Soyo.

Soyo operation staging area—J.C. Erasmus leaning against a poorly maintained SA-2 surface-to-air missile at the Cabinda military airfield after the operation was postponed for 24 hours.

Quefiquena —The inflatable dinghy used by the Executive Outcomes reconnaissance team to reconnoitre the Quefiquena target before the attack. The sand cliffs adjacent to the beach are also visible.

Quefiquena—UNITA officers killed by Phil's No. 3 Platoon as they approached Quefiquena from Soyo. The irrigation ditch and long grass around the objective area are also evident.

Quefiquena—The seaborne landing. The barge carrying FAA troops and equipment was turned parallel to the shore by the current and the tide, and the DAF vehicle in the foreground was squashed as one of the T-62 tanks moved onto the beach.

Quefiquena—The beach after the landing. Once under fire the FAA troops and their kit parted company.

Quefiquena beachhead on the second day after the attack. The T-62 tank was stranded on the beach due to a burnt-out clutch. Thereafter, it was used to deliver inaccurate indirect fire; its rusted hull is still visible on the beach today.

the same platoon as I, who had a police background, who told me that he was a sniper. It was indeed difficult to suppress my amusement when, a little whilst later, he asked me on which side of his body he should carry his revolver as he was already struggling to sling both his AK-47 and his Dragunov sniper rifle over his shoulders. I heard later that he had left the revolver. We were well kitted out and the choice was left to us to draw the number of uniforms we wanted. We were even issued with good quality shorts. The packing of this large amount of equipment into one's rucksack was the only problem. As an infantryman I had been taught to keep kit light and to a minimum. "Light, as for darts," we used to say, as we would always have to carry it on our backs into the back of beyond.

The messing facility spoiled us in that it was neat and clean, the rations were of good quality, there was no shortage of beer and the bar also served wine, brandy and whisky. In the evenings we had to prepare to fend off mosquitoes and if there was one person who detested every single mosquito under his mosquito net it was Kolle Olivier. He would hunt these erring mosquitoes down with a torch inside his net until he found and disposed of each and every last one of them.

On the second day after our arrival at Cabo Ledo, Buks Buys, our commander, addressed us with these words, "Come *manne*, let's do it". A stocky man with an ever present serious expression on his face, he was doing his bit to convince us of the viability of the operation. He was, however, somewhat out of his depth and had to rely on the battle hardened platoon commanders to get things done.

The training phase was chiefly directed towards refreshing our existing knowledge and experience of battle drills on platoon level, weapon handling and our familiarization with the other weapons and equipment with which we had been issued. Communication between the platoon members had to be established as soon as possible and the buddy-buddy system was instituted in all seriousness. I must say that there was precious little that the platoon members needed to learn. After all, we were all hardened veterans. All that was really required was the allocation of correct positions to each person and an orientation as to who was situated on each man's front, rear, and flanks, and the rest fell into place almost naturally. The platoon was indeed ready for battle.

Buks sent for me at some juncture during our time at Cabo Ledo and, as I walked to his accommodation, I wondered what was afoot as I had been appointed as a lowly platoon sergeant in this organization. Buks invited me to sit next to him on his bed and we watched the television monitor on his cupboard and listened to the heavy breathing as the lead character in the movie 'serviced' his girlfriend. I also observed a satellite phone with its antenna deployed outside the area allocated for our office space. We had really organized ourselves pretty well.

"Rudolph, I understand that you are staff qualified," Buks stated. After the subsequent discussion I left Buks, having agreed to complete the tactical appreciation for the operation and then hand it over to Buks who would then present it. On my return to the rest of the men in the platoon I heard one of my section leaders say that a number of the former Special Forces members, especially those who had operated with him before and knew his *modus operandi*, were opposed to him being the commander of the operation. They remarked that their previous experience with him, linked to his limitations, was being repeated here and this was why he was able to give me, a platoon sergeant, the 'order' to complete the tactical appreciation so that he could take the credit.

The next day I duly got behind a map and started the appreciation. There was very little accurate and reliable information or intelligence available. On the contrary, Buks told me that they had 'estimated' the strength of the UNITA forces in the area in which we were to operate at 25 soldiers. I just had to smile. I had to make a massive mental effort to consciously engage my brain to start thinking, analyzing and planning a number of levels lower than what I was used to as a staff officer on division and brigade level. Having said this, it didn't take too long before the enemy paragraph of the appreciation was completed. The only available detail on the terrain was derived from a 1:250,000 map. Buks also handed me a brief pamphlet on the oil storage tanks at Quefiquena (also known as QQ). The pamphlet had one small photo of the oil tanks taken from an aircraft at an oblique angle, and a sketch plan of the tank farm, which was a great help. That was the sum total of the detail we had on the terrain at Soyo.

It wasn't too difficult a task to develop a simple, yet practical plan to take and hold our primary objective—the oil storage facility at Quefiquena. It was also a relatively straight forward exercise to plan the subsequent operations leading up to the re-occupation of the remainder of the province by the FAA forces. Simple plans are vital as so much can go wrong if a complicated plan is carried out with so little available information. It was more irritating to hear, via a signal message that we received a little whilst later, that the 25 UNITA troops deployed in the vicinity had in fact decreased to 15 men. I had not been informed of the strength or location of the enemy in our area of influence around the objective, nor did I have any accurate information on UNITA dispositions and activities in the area of interest, located further afield. I needed the information on the dispositions urgently in order to plan what would be required of us after we had taken the objective area, from where we could expect a counterattack, what mutual support was available to UNITA and what movements of UNITA reserve forces and firepower could be expected. My concerns about the vagueness of the basic information, coupled to the rather wide assumptions that I had been forced to make as a result, were not assuaged by hearing that only time would bring the answer to this question.

Tony Buckingham and Simon Mann visited us during the planning phase and asked if we would prefer to use helicopters during the operation. This made the plan so much easier to carry out and we all responded immediately with a strong affirmative. Tony obviously had a great interest in the success of the operation and he listened very carefully to our plan. We were not allocated any additional manpower other than the FAA battalion that would approach from the sea and 'drive the UNITA force' from the target area. The allocation of helicopters did make a great difference though.

The planning for the operation indicated that a strengthened FAA infantry battalion would be attached to the effort. What was, however, unclear was whether the EO force was attached to the battalion for the operation or whether they were attached to us. We did know that the unit consisted of approximately 800 troops who had just completed their basic training. In other words the troops would be able to fire and maintain their weapons and demonstrate some knowledge of basic musketry and field craft. We should have had sufficient time to jointly practice battle craft on platoon and company level but this did not actually take place. The battalion had arrived at Cabo Ledo too late and no formal marrying up drills, joint training or rehearsals took place at all. Not a very auspicious start to say the least.

My limited experience and knowledge of the FAA command structure at that point had already indicated to me that the leadership of their middle level management and officer corps were not strong at all, and this situation made it necessary for colonels and brigadiers to become physically involved and micromanage matters on the very lowest levels of command. It had become necessary for General de Matos, the head of the FAA, for example, to liaise personally with us regarding the plan for the offensive. It was not encouraging at all, although we appreciated his attention for other reasons, namely the emphasis on a high level of surprise and secrecy.

Our greatest concern was still the composition and state of readiness of the FAA battalion who were going into battle with us. The fact that we were not able to liaise with the battalion or train with them before leaving on the operation had made the plan a whole lot more difficult and complex to carry out successfully. It was also abundantly clear that the EO group would have to carry out the first phase of the operation on its own. We hoped that the main FAA force would then link up and support us thereafter for the subsequent phases of the operation. The use of helicopters piloted by inexperienced aviators was another issue. We were aware that they had never undertaken helicopter assault operations before and we realized that this was a potential disaster just waiting to happen. By this time our own training and preparations had virtually been completed and all that was left was to grab hold of a few last things and make a few arrangements before we left for the operations area.

The initial design for battle called for both the EO element and the FAA battalion to move via air and various seaborne transport means to the vicinity of the target area at Quefiquena. Thereafter the EO force would establish and secure the beachhead for the FAA battalion to land, and this would be followed by the assault on the objective by the main force consisting of the FAA battalion. The additional difficulties and lack of liaison had, however, forced us to amend the plan for the attack on Quefiquena as follows:

Stage 1

Phase 1: Air reconnaissance of the objective area by EO and training by EO and the FAA battalion at separate training locations.

Phase 2: The movement of the main equipment, including T-62 tanks, to Cabo Ledo for seaborne transit to the deployment area.

Stage 2

Phase 1: EO moves by air to the Cabinda enclave and marries up with the air element for the attack.

Phase 2: EO reconnaissance team moves by sea to the target area on D-1, reconnoitres possible helicopter LZs (LZs) at Quefiquena under cover of darkness and acts as a radio relay station between EO and the main FAA force.

Phase 3: The FAA battalion at Cabo Ledo loads the main equipment onto two barges, embarks and moves northward by sea to undertake the beach landing at Quefiquena on D-Day.

Stage 3

Phase 1: At H-60 minutes the EO force leaves Cabinda in three Mi-17 helicopters, carries out an airborne assault operation on Quefiquena, via the LZs indicated by the reconnaissance element, and secures the beachhead.

Phase 2: The FAA infantry battalion arrives in the vicinity of the objective by sea and carries out a beach landing once EO has secured the bridgehead.

Stage 4: The FAA battalion force occupies the target area, prepares to cut off the town of Soyo and neutralises UNITA thereafter.

Stage 5: The combined EO and FAA battalion secure and occupy Soyo province so that oil production can resume.

With D–Day having been set for 16 March 1993 and the whole operation due to last approximately four weeks, we presented the plan to General de Matos, who expressed concern that there were only 34 men in the EO assault group. When asked if he had any further guidelines for us, he merely shook his head and said: "Just do it."

I believe that his concern was related to the proximity of the identified LZ to the objective. He was also worried about the fact that the helicopters, with Angolan FAPA pilots, would have to take off at 0500 in the morning when it is still dark. The FAPA pilots had not been trained to undertake night flying missions. In addition they would not take kindly to being required to land so close to an enemy position. Even before the presentation started, General de Matos let slip that in accordance with intelligence source reports there were now only approximately six UNITA members in and around the target area. I maintained that we should not change the plan even if there were 100 UNITA soldiers on the objective.

It was clear by now that the protection of oil rigs was not an apt description of our task. We were preparing to fight a deadly battle against an enemy in well prepared defensive positions, before even contemplating the protection of the oil installations at Soyo.

Well, we had come so far we could just as well go for it. The plan was relatively straight forward, and its main advantage lay in the tactical surprise that would be achieved in the execution thereof. This was, of course, dependent on the fact that the reconnaissance force would not be located by UNITA before the airborne assault took place.

Heliborne assault on Quefiquena

On D-1 (15 March 1993) we all waited patiently alongside the FAPA Antonov-12 (AN-12) transport aircraft for our pilots to get the show on the road and fly us from Cabo Ledo to Cabinda, the staging area from where we would undertake the first light helicopter assault on the target at Quefiquena.

The reconnaissance team, consisting of three former members of 4 Reconnaissance Regiment had already left for Luanda and beyond. They would eventually reach the target area by means of a commercial vessel and approach the beach thereafter by means of an inflatable rubber dinghy during the night of D-1/D-Day. This action was vital to the success of the operation as they were required to locate the enemy deployments on the target, identify and then talk the air assault helicopters into the LZs at H-Hour.

We landed at the military airfield in Cabinda and were immediately taken to an isolated military base at one end of the runway, as our presence was supposed to have been kept a secret. In the far distance I was able to see large oil storage tanks and this made me think of the exploits of Captain Wynand du Toit, a SADF officer from 4 Reconnaissance Regiment who, during an infiltration operation in the 1980s, had hit a lemon here, was wounded and whilst the remainder of the force exfiltrated successfully was located by the FAA forces, captured the next day, and spent two years in Angola as a prisoner of war before being released as part of a prisoner swop. My head spun as I could also see a SA-2 anti-aircraft missile battery deployed around the airfield. The atmosphere on the landing strip itself was charged with energy, but on closer inspection I realized that none of the missiles could be employed effectively, as they had been poorly maintained. This made me think back to some of the trans-border operations I had undertaken into Angola with the SADF between 1978 and 1989. The majority of the Angolan equipment that we had came across or expropriated looked in a similar condition.

We checked and rechecked our kit and prepared for the start of the operation the next morning. Then we received word that D-Day had been postponed by 24 hours. I wasn't at all sure if this was altogether a wise thing to do. Nevertheless, on reflection I realized that the decision could have been precipitated in order to allow sufficient time for the FAA battalion on the two barges to move into position offshore, or it could be that the reconnaissance element had run into a problem. We never got to know what the reason for the delay actually was as our means of communication were very poor. I saw Buks wandering around the temporary tactical headquarters with a frown on his face, only to learn from the other men that this was a permanent feature of his appearance during operations. He told us to be patient. My problem was that the element of surprise dissipates over time and our ability to astound the enemy with the helicopter assault would be significantly diluted as a result of any delay. The wait until the next morning felt much longer than it actually was.

By 0400 on the morning of D-Day, 17 March 1993, we were all up and had deposited our surplus kit at the FAPA headquarters for safekeeping until such time as it was expedient for them to fly it out to us. By 0500 we had been allocated to the three FAPA Mi-17 helicopters nd the pilots had started to wind up the engines for takeoff. It was still pitch black outside.

We had no communication with the reconnaissance group on the ground at the LZ and Buks, Lafras and I agreed that in the event that we did not make any contact with them, we would land the helicopters at LZ No. 2, an area to the north of the objective located approximately 100 metres from the buildings that we knew served as the accommodation of the UNITA forces at the objective. With this in mind the three Mi-17 helicopters flew in a southerly direction over the sea whilst keeping some distance between themselves and the town of Soyo itself in order not to give away our presence and intentions. As we flew along the coast we also realized that the landward side of the beach was elevated approximately twenty to thirty metres above the level of the sea and in addition to the darkness, this enhanced our cover from sight.

At 0615 the helicopters flared and we began the final approach to the objective, which was located approximately 500 metres inland from the beach. Suddenly hard reality hit me and I saw that with the long grass on the LZ the pilots were refusing to land and we were forced to jump the two metres to the ground from the hovering aircraft. I was carrying my personal kit and weapon, as well as an A-52 radio and a 60mm mortar tube, and the momentum created as I dropped the two metres from the helicopter caused the A-52 radio I was carrying on my back to slam into the back of my head. We had not rehearsed this at Cabo Ledo as the helicopters weren't initially part of the plan, but they turned out to be an absolute bonus in approaching the enemy, even if the jump had left me as dizzy as hell. The choppers lifted and flew off in a northerly direction whilst we moved at best speed to the allocated forming up places under the bulky weight of our kit. There was no time to waste. Phil's No. 3 Platoon had been tasked to act as a stopper group on the left flank to the east of the objective on the main road from Soyo. Harry's No. 2 Platoon, of which I was the platoon sergeant, together with Lafras's No. 1 Platoon were required to advance to contact from the forming up place north of the objective and clear any UNITA resistance as we proceeded in a southerly direction through the objective. Phil's platoon would remain in position whilst the other two platoons consolidated in a southerly direction after the attack. Phil's task held the most danger as it was from his direction that the UNITA reinforcements located in the town of Soyo would most probably react in support of the element at the Quefiquena oil depot.

We skirmished forward through the long wet grass, which was approximately three metres high in certain spots, until we came to a deep drainage ditch, about one and a half metres wide and three metres deep, that we had to cross. This type of activity becomes somewhat more difficult when one is weighed down by the extra weapons and equipment. All of a sudden we heard the first shots and deduced that they had been fired by Lafras's platoon. I remember thinking that the six UNITA soldiers that the so-called intelligence briefings had detailed must be wide awake by now as the battle was becoming more ferocious by the second.

My group was in its allocated position and had yet to encounter any resistance on our flank or from the front. We did hear a brief exchange of fire in the vicinity of Phil's position to the east of us but this abated after a whilst. I remember thinking that Phil was a good operator and he would control his fire. A moment later, however, a new firefight broke out in his vicinity. Things were quiet on our immediate front but over the radio we heard that three vehicles, a double-cab pickup truck and two sedan vehicles, had reacted from Soyo town towards the objective area and had burst through Phil's position on their way to assist their troops in the area of the objective. Phil had succeeded in stopping two vehicles but the pickup had broken through and was making a getaway on the tarred road towards the main gate of the oil depot. Fortunately, Lafras's group was in a position to cut off the pickup and engage it. The vehicle sped through his position, received a number of good bursts of fire and hurtled through a T-junction, then over a drainage ditch and finally it disappeared into the long grass. No sounds came from the vehicle at all. The two sedan vehicles had been rendered out of action by Phil's fire but we did recover one—a Toyota Corolla—which we used as a means of transport thereafter.

It was clear by now that the sporadic firefights were only happening on Lafras's front. Harry and I decided that we would join him and provide support where required. We divided the platoon into one group of seven people under Harry, who would join Lafras, and a second group of six people under my command that would carry out a cut off action to the south of the objective.

Lafras updated us on the current situation from his perspective. It emerged that whilst we were disembarking from the helicopters we had disturbed about six platoons, consisting of a total of approximately 200 UNITA soldiers, whilst they had been engaged in a period of physical training. Some UNITA soldiers were carrying weapons, others not. They had been running in platoon formations on the tarred road around the objective when they realized that the three FAPA helicopters were dropping FAA troops in the distance. They had obviously hastened back to their base at best speed to pick up their weapons, ammunition, uniforms and other equipment in order to commence the defensive battle for the area. I was shown where a bunch of these soldiers had not made it in time before the gate to the fence around the objective had been closed. They obviously had realized that to climb over the high fence was too risky and had attempted to climb under it despite the tightly spanned wire. Scraps of torn uniform had been caught on the bottom of the wire and an AK-47 had even been left in haste. Time had obviously been of the essence for these UNITA troops but it must have been hilarious to have observed this scene unfolding.

We took up our agreed position and from the silence on the front it appeared that UNITA was in the process of reorganising themselves, as we knew they always did, and that this process will take place in quick order. In the meanwhile they were probing our positions with fire and lobbing a few speculative mortars in our general direction.

We decided that in view of the number of UNITA troops on the objective, coupled to the fact that we had already made contact with them, we would have to occupy and hold our present position until the linking force had joined up with us. I could see the sea from my position and there was not the slightest indication of any ships or barges bearing FAA forces. The immediate implication of this state of affairs was that we would have to work very economically with our ammunition and water until such time as it could be replenished. It was also pretty clear that we were effectively cut off from any support until the linking force had disembarked. During the afternoon a deathly silence descended over the area and after a further period of consolidation we vacated our prone positions and stood up not too much the worse for wear, with only two members of the platoon slightly wounded. Harry had been shot in the wrist and a second member, Jeff Landsberg, had been shot in the foot. I took over the command of the platoon from Harry. During this quiet time our medical orderly, Verny Lange, attended to the two wounded persons and we also managed to revive an old URAL cargo vehicle for possible future duties of a transport and logistic nature. It also became clear to Lafras that we would experience problems evacuating the wounded as we only had limited medical support with us. We also determined, based on our brief encounter and experience with them that morning, that a request to scramble the Mi-17 helicopters for this purpose would most probably result in a no show on the part of the FAPA pilots. The battle was still too young and matters were still too uncertain for them to fly to and from the objective. Verny did, however, keep a good, trained eye on our casualties.

Seaborne landing

At about 1500 that afternoon I heard a very loud explosion in the direction of the sea. This was followed by another shot and I observed a vessel sailing on a course for our position. The UNITA forces had obviously also seen the vessel and the explosions were emanating from a position where they were launching 122mm rockets at it from a single tube GRAD-P rocket launcher. I informed Lafras of the situation and we agreed that I would oversee the beach landing and make contact with the on-board FAA commander. I would brief him as to the situation on the ground so that he could deploy his troops on those fronts where we knew the enemy may try to break out that evening.

It also dawned on me at this point that Buks was nowhere to be seen. I had not heard from him on the radio either. I guessed that his style was one where he drove everything from a position in the rear and that he would join us later. I only learnt later that Buks had been relieved of the command of the operation and that Lafras had been appointed as the commander on the ground. I was, therefore, liaising with a commander on my flank who happened to be the actual commander on the ground. This is what I had expected all along as we had grown up in the military believing that a commander's place was with his troops.

The approaching vessel was indeed one of the barges loaded with FAA soldiers and equipment. Once it had reached a distance of about 800 metres from the shoreline I took three of my men with me and moved down to the beach to wait for the landing to take place. I thought back to the beach landing operations I had helped plan during my military days in the SADF and compared them to the scene unfolding before me. Here was the hard reality and I had to swallow it, bitter as it was. I noticed a large figure on the vessel waving to try and attract my attention. I waved back and this is how we established communication. I indicated to him that the area was safe for his forces to land. The GRAD-P rocket launcher had stopped firing by now and the landing operation could proceed with somewhat greater safety.

I was unaware of the problems that had beset the FAA forces during their preparations at Cabo Ledo. Instead of two barges with approximately 600 troops and main equipment on board, only one barge had arrived. It later transpired that after the two barges had got underway from Cabo Ledo as planned, one had developed engine trouble and both had been required to return to port. All the equipment on the unseaworthy barge was cross-loaded to the seaworthy vessel, which now carried four T-62 battle tanks and four DAF cargo vehicles as well as 600 troops. Needless to say, the vehicles had been incorrectly loaded. The tanks had been loaded first and the soft skinned DAF cargo vehicles were parked in front of the exit ramp. This oversight was to be the source of a major problem during the disembarking operation.

It is hard to describe the utter chaos that unfolded in front of my very eyes over the next two to three hours. Once the barge had hit a sandbank close to the beach, as was planned, it became somewhat stranded and the depth of the water in the vicinity of the exit ramp was still two metres deep, far too deep to unload troops or vehicles. The imminent high tide conditions would add a further element of complexity to the existing situation. Despite this the landing went ahead.

The large ramp of the barge had hardly crashed into the water before the first wave of FAA troops burst down the ramp into the water. It was easy to see that these troops had become really *gatvol* with the boat trip and they were equally determined to leave the barge come what may. Just when they believed that they were about to find themselves safe and sound on dry land they were actually sinking to the bottom of the sea in at least two metres of water. A sea of problems indeed! My colleagues and I threw down our weapons and rendered whatever assistance we could.

I looked up to see if the commander on board the barge was going to provide any guidelines or leadership, or even abort the landing and try again from a shallower or safer location. This was not to be.

"*Força, Força,*" was all I could hear from the commander, as he shouted at the troops from his position on the bridge of the barge. I began to realize that the lives my colleagues and I had saved would be in the minority as this fiasco continued to unfold. We then decided to stand aside as wave after wave of troops continued to stream from the barge's ramp into the sea, spurred on by the voice of the commander screaming and ranting at them without respite.

We also realized that the incoming high tide was turning the barge's stern northward, and swinging its ramp entrance parallel to the beach, making the unloading of the tanks and vehicles that much more difficult. The next moment one of the cargo vehicles closest to the ramp was started and it began to reverse off the front of the barge. The vehicle actually fell from the barge and started making its way towards the beach, with the driver's head just visible above the water. The vehicle actually managed to build up a little momentum and moved about thirty metres, bringing it in line with the edge of the water, before it came to a grinding halt. It was not going to be moving from that position for a very long time. The second DAF followed and it too reversed towards the rear of the barge. By now the barge had turned almost parallel to the beach and the vehicle fell straight into the sea. The driver didn't even attempt to drive it out of this position and the vehicle stayed put in that position, minus its driver. By this time the FAA commander located on the bridge was particularly short tempered as it was obvious that things were not developing according to his plan.

UNITA had obviously seen what was about to happen and they began to carry out probing attacks from the south of the objective area. Our EO platoons had their work cut out for them to hold our current positions. Lafras briefed us as the situation developed and I informed the FAA commander on the barge that chaos would erupt if he didn't hurry up and complete the landing.

I personally met and briefed the FAA commander, Colonel Pepe de Castro, as soon as he set foot on the beach. He was an enormous, blunt man, built like a heavyweight boxer, with a habit of following up his commands with physical action to drive his point home and remove any doubt as to his intent. He sent his company commanders, together with their troops, to take over from EO with the sole purpose of repulsing any UNITA counterattacks so that by last light the position could be secure. In the interim he had given the command that two of the four T-62 tanks should be offloaded. The first tank started up, left the ramp, dropped into the two-meter deep water and the brave driver persevered, narrowly missing the stranded cargo vehicle that lay in his way. He surprised us all and, like a real life James Bond, drove the tank out onto the beach. Now for the next tank, which managed to drive over and crush the stranded cargo vehicle in the water as it made its way to the beach. Reasonably successful, if one ignores the fact that in the process the second tank's clutch had burnt out. Colonel Pepe de Castro then decided to keep the remaining cargo vehicles and T-62 tanks on the barge until later. It was time to make contact with the immediate enemy.

Together we moved on foot to the road where we had parked the URAL cargo vehicle that we had commandeered and repaired earlier that day. The vehicle was loaded up with ammunition from the barge and it became all the more urgent to distribute it to the troops as the fire was becoming more intense towards the south. Colonel Pepe, as he was known, used this position on the road as his temporary headquarters whilst his intelligence officers fanned out to obtain as much information as possible about the situation on the ground. My limited knowledge of Portuguese, together with Colonel Pepe's equally limited capacity in English, made communication a real challenge, especially now that Harry Ferreira, our official interpreter, who had an excellent grasp of Angolan Portuguese, had been wounded. It was getting late and Colonel Pepe wanted us to secure the next high ground, located in a southeasterly direction along the coastline and closer to our second objective at Campo Oito, before last light. This was a bit over ambitious as the FAA troops did not have the experience or the know-how to keep the UNITA troops under pressure, partly due to the poor standard of their mid-level officers.

At last light the UNITA force broke through the FAA forward troops and penetrated along the road to where we had been located earlier that same morning. The situation seemed hopeless. The position where Colonel Pepe and I were located next to the vehicle came under intense fire and I expected a projectile from a RPG-7 rocket launcher to hit the vehicle at any moment. I quickly gave the command that the area should be evacuated under cover of intense fire. Fortunately nobody was injured in the ensuing process.

The UNITA counter-attacking force was eventually halted at the same position where EO had pinned them down that same morning. We then dug in for the night after the UNITA force had been repulsed. As platoon leader and platoon sergeant I had to look after the replenishment of ammunition in my platoon. I undertook this task personally as everybody else was busy digging in and it was already last light. I took two men and got into the Toyota Corolla that Phil's group had stopped earlier on during the day. The vehicle's doors and boot lid had been removed by now and I drove it down to the beach, loaded a few cases of 7.62mm ammunition for the AK-47s, 60mm mortar bombs and a few cases of RPG-7 ammunition into the car, returned to the EO position, distributed the ammunition and then began digging in. UNITA was certainly keeping us under pressure in the hope that we would abandon our defensive position before last light. With the FAA forces in disarray it was left to the EO men in the hastily dug positions to hold the defensive line. Harry, my wounded platoon commander lay beside me, silent and in deep shock, with his arm thickly bandaged. All I could do was encourage him to be strong. Our positions were not deployed in depth as we had insufficient people to achieve this and I dug in close behind the rest of the platoon, just deep enough to protect myself from direct rifle fire.

Once guard duties had been sorted out I returned to my position and fell asleep. It had been a long day, but I was somewhat satisfied with progress, especially after seeing the only T-62 tank deployed on the road, adjacent to us as part of the defensive position. This was tactically incorrect but I learnt quickly that the FAA had adapted their bush war culture and the Soviet conventional warfare doctrine to the requirements of the Angolan conflict. One is never too old to learn. I realized how quickly one simplifies the life of a poorly equipped African soldier with limited training by deploying tanks, even as few as one per company. Firepower plays a large role, especially against UNITA who had no tanks in this area.

During the night our rest was broken by a long burst of small arms fire followed by 82mm mortar explosions. The UNITA forces were so close to our position that we could hear them screaming the fire orders. We responded with effective 60mm mortar counterfire and the UNITA probing attack fizzled out. It was evident that they were intent on keeping pressure on us. In the early morning hours they tried once again, only this time they advanced along the road and tried to neutralize the T-62 tank by firing a number of RPGs at it. The tank crew were waiting for the UNITA force and they fired one round of the main gun at a position thirty to forty metres ahead of them in the road and the UNITA attack came to a speedy conclusion once again.

Consolidating our gains

The next morning, 18 March 1993, heralded the first of a number of anxious days. It transpired that the T-62 driver had been killed by UNITA small arms fire during the night and his body lay draped over the tank. This was the first of a large number of losses over the next few weeks and all we could do was bury them where they had fallen, without any type of ceremony at all.

Our mission was clear—we were to advance towards the next high ground to the south of our position, take it and to dig in there and hold the position. The distance to the high ground from our current location was approximately 800 metres.

Colonel Pepe was a real driver, pacing up and down behind the troops with an AK-47 in his huge hands. If the troops even dared to leave their positions on the front, even to replenish ammunition and water, he would fire at them without any show of emotion at all. I saw him wound one of his own troops in the hand. Needless to say the soldier returned to his post without any medical aid. But, by the end of the first day between fifty and sixty wounded FAA soldiers had gathered in the headquarters area and nine FAA soldiers had been killed. And the end was not in sight yet.

The EO contingent got together and we numbered 32 of the original 54 members who had started out from South Africa such a short time ago. At this point we came to the conclusion that we were missing one person. I remembered seeing him last during the vehicle rumpus whilst we attacked the position during the first part of the previous day. We eventually located him, broken hip and all, in one of the three meter deep drainage ditches around the objective. Our casualties were starting to mount. Some of the EO members obviously didn't visualise that this was a possibility when they had been recruited. I didn't actually blame them all that much, but the immediate aim was to persevere, to stand together and support the government forces in order to achieve what we had set out to do. Most of the EO members found little difficulty in understanding this. Their faces were a dead giveaway and it was relatively easy to distinguish between the 'talkers' and the 'doers'. I was disappointed and surprised at the behaviour of a number of the men. Some of them could have performed better whilst others performed well. Once again some of the members asked where Buks was, implying that if he was not here with the troops in battle he should be fired.

Over the next days we progressed in phases and bounds in a southeasterly direction towards Campo Oito. Sometimes we remained in the same trench for up to three days, followed by a large bound forward to the next tactical terrain. UNITA resistance was starting to crumble as a result of the sustained pressure we had brought to bear on them, but it was being achieved at a high cost as measured by the FAA casualty rate. On the seventh day after the airborne landing we carried out an early morning attack on the UNITA defensive positions. Some of us took part in the attack. EO as an entity had not been tasked to partake in the attack, but we duly divided ourselves evenly amongst the FAA troops to support them where the need was the greatest. In addition to the members who had joined the attacking force I assisted the 82mm mortar group and Mauritz le Roux assisted the mine sweeping teams, whilst another large EO team was involved in obtaining ammunition, transporting it to the front and distributing it, as this was where the greatest needs were. Most of the EO men assisted in line with their particular speciality or qualifications. It was in this fashion that Buks Erasmus, who was a member of one of the assault force platoons, lost his life when a UNITA rifle grenade hit him and exploded, shredding him to pieces. This was very difficult for us to accept and even more so for Ivan van der Merwe, his best friend alongside him, who had been with him from their days together at 32 Battalion. His body was evacuated to the logistics area in the rear where

Lafras requested his immediate evacuation to Cabinda. Eventually the helicopters arrived to evacuate the dead and wounded after we had sent umpteen dire threats. All our losses, casualties and dead, were evacuated that day. The EO element had been reduced even further by a number of the men who had decided that enough was enough and that they were far better off back home in South Africa than at Soyo. Buks Buys visited us briefly and told us that he was worth much more to us in Cabinda than on the ground at the front. We accepted this with a pinch of salt. We were, however, happy with Lafras on the front.

We were progressing well in taking the target area around Quefiquena and the time arrived for us to take the last piece of terrain in order to guarantee a safe LZ for the helicopters. We took the terrain and achieved the objective by digging in well and repulsing a surprise UNITA first light attack thereafter. EO had only one fatality that first morning—a delayed RPG back blast as a result of a moist booster charge. I escaped a certain death when a UNITA mortar landed in my individual trench and exploded whilst I was alongside, assisting the 60mm mortar team. Once the last piece of terrain had been taken we could catch our breath somewhat. It was clear that UNITA had realized that the key to the battle was EO and they concentrated their fire and thrust on our position. They knew that once we had been removed as a force, they would win the battle

From Cabinda we were ordered to consolidate before commencing Stage 4 of the operation, which involved the occupation of the target area by FAA and preparations to cut off the town of Soya and neutralize UNITA. Lafras tasked Phil and myself to return to Cabinda and take turns in flying a set of reconnaissance missions in a PC-7 light reconnaissance aircraft to locate and confirm the UNITA positions south of our position, as they had made a clean break and withdrawn to their rear areas. As a force we were thinly dispersed on the ground to the extent that we found it difficult to extend the defended locality. To achieve this we would first have to take the town of Soyo itself, where the airfield was located and then fly in FAA reinforcements.

After flying out to Cabinda by helicopter Phil undertook the first reconnaissance mission in the PC-7. He flew low over our defensive positions and the aircraft then gained altitude as it overflew the suspected UNITA positions. We could see the aircraft circling above Campo Oito in the distance where we believed UNITA had regrouped. The next moment Phil informed us by radio that the aircraft had drawn heavy fire from the ground and that he believed that it had been hit. He had in fact seen someone firing at the aircraft with a RPG-7 and the pilot had informed him that the aircraft had a few 'problems'. The best alternative was to make for the Cabinda enclave, some thirty kilometres to the north and try to land at the airfield twenty kilometres further. Phil signed off over the air and the aircraft gained altitude in order to be able to glide if this was required. The engine did in fact stall and they glided as far as they could until they were able to make a successful emergency landing on the beach, where after they were located and picked up by a FAPA Mi-17 helicopter and flown to Cabinda none the worse for wear. The reconnaissance was halted for the time being. We were finally tasked to occupy Campo Oito, a task that the combined force undertook successfully whilst UNITA withdrew at great speed.

The occupation of Soyo

Our focus now shifted to the implementation of Stage 4 of the plan and EO was tasked by Colonel Pepe to withdraw to the rear areas of the FAA battalion deployment to act as a reaction force. By now the number of EO members had decreased to 18 men on the front. We acted as a type of a reserve and where a crisis developed we concentrated our presence and our skills to make life easier for Colonel Pepe. Lafras liaised with Colonel Pepe on a daily basis now and he invited me to accompany him. The three of us became a productive team together and a good working relationship developed between us to the extent that the last two stages of the plan progressed relatively quickly.

After about two weeks we formed an assault force to cut UNITA off from the area between our location and the Zaire River to the north. The UNITA force, however, withdrew during the last moments of the action with all the available vehicles, rations, large amounts of diesel fuel and everything else that was of any value to them. They also blew up the giant power station at the harbour town as a last resort. We could not succeed in cutting off UNITA's withdrawal but two days later we had advanced into the town of Soyo itself. Colonel Pepe gave us the responsibility to look after the town and its surrounding vicinity whilst he, together with his troops, would defend the eastern and southern areas that had already been taken.

We halted our advance and made ourselves at home amongst the destroyed facilities belonging to Fina, Texaco and Sonangol. We had specifically been tasked to control all land movement to and from the town, to control all air traffic and the movement by air of all troops, as well as all logistic provisioning. With the available brainpower and technical skills we were also able to revive a large cargo vehicle that we used to replenish the various FAA tactical headquarters. The FAA forces could also rely on an EO tactical team to support them during all their offensive operations. I was allocated to the logistic support element whilst the tactical support team got hold of a DAF cargo vehicle and transformed it into a combat support vehicle. Harry Carlse, Luis du Preez and the rest of their team professionally mounted a 23mm ZU-23-2 anti-aircraft gun, a 60mm mortar and an AGS-17 grenade launcher on the rear of the vehicle, readying it for action.

One day whilst travelling together with Lafras we made a detour to the beach, where the seaborne landing had taken place, to reclaim our rubber inflatable dinghy used by the reconnaissance team on the night before the assault. The barge was still there with its two tanks and vehicles on board. Later the barge's crew, who had disappeared during the battle, returned and sailed the barge to Luanda under more favourable conditions. The T-62 tank with the burnt out clutch was still on the beach and, whilst one of the DAF cargo vehicles was totally buried under the sea sand, the other was successfully recovered and used by us.

At the end of the contract period, which had been extended from four to six weeks, we anxiously awaited any scrap of news about our immediate futures, but to no avail. Despite the lack of any positive news and the comfort that would accompany a renewed contract we continued with our assigned tasks and persevered, delivering time and again what was required of us, and more.

With the occupation of the town of Soyo, control of air traffic at the airfield had been assigned to EO and EO deployed a Cessna 210, at the airfield from time to time for casevac purposes. A medical doctor also joined us. This was a fortuitous move indeed as both Carl Dietz, the intelligence officer and I contracted malaria and were evacuated by air to Windhoek Medi-City Hospital in Namibia.

During this time our tactical team joined the FAA force in an offensive against UNITA in the Sumba area, east of Soyo and alongside the Zaire River. This operation claimed the lives of two of our men and what made things worse was that their bodies could not be recovered. The deceased included Phil Smith, the one platoon commander during the initial attack, and Tallies Taljaard who had joined us from South Africa three days prior to his death. They had walked into a massive UNITA ambush together with the FAA forces and were forced by the volume of UNITA fire to vacate the area, in an unorganised fashion, under huge pressure. I will always remember Phil as someone who asked where he could be of assistance but who could at times be very reckless. He had no fear and was regarded as a person who had more than earned his spurs as a member of the team. Tallies had just arrived and had been looking forward to engaging with UNITA.

The FAA defensive line had certain weak points as the area it covered was too large for the available troop strength and the troops were deployed too thinly as a result. To penetrate the defensive line was, therefore, not too difficult a task. We regularly reminded Colonel Pepe to obtain reinforcements, but we were led to understand that new recruits could not be trained quickly enough and sent to the front. The inevitable happened thereafter as UNITA broke through the defensive line and penetrated deep into the FAA rear areas. They were, however, repulsed at a later stage.

This action led EO to wonder what could be done to prevent a recurrence but, short of receiving reinforcements, there was little that could have been done to achieve the FAA objective of securing the area. By this time we had also devised an emergency escape plan—a smallish vessel that could convey about fifteen men was kept ready in the event that it was needed. Our fear was, however, that during an escape we would not make it to the north bank of the Zaire River and we would have to consider another alternative inside the territorial borders of Angola. It is much more difficult for South Africans with white faces to melt away into the bush than it is for Angolan soldiers.

Whilst passing through the airport in Windhoek, Namibia, on our way to hospital both our passports were confiscated by Namibian immigration officials at the airport and it was very obvious to us, even in our fevered state of minds, that we were regarded as unsavoury characters by the Namibian Government. In addition to the fact that we did not have visas for Angola, the recent actions of EO in the Soyo area had hit the front pages of the newspapers in South Africa. We weren't entirely sure what this all meant for us at the time.

Whilst we were recovering at Medi-City Hospital it became obvious to us that the hospital manager had realized that she had two mercenaries in her care and she thankfully isolated us from unwanted media visits. Our presence in the hospital had in all probability rung a bell, as Linchy, one of the two black operators with EO, had paved the way for us here and this had obviously left a bad taste in everyone's mouth. After a week we begged the hospital manager to discharge us and with our returned passports in our pockets we flew to South Africa.

Reflections

After our return to South Africa I applied for leave. Eeben Barlow at first asked me if I would take over from Lafras—we had agreed to this previously—at Soyo. I asked for a short period of recuperation first and stated that I would be available in seven to ten day's time. With this in mind I left on vacation with my family. I also learnt about the great fuss in the media and heard that my previous employer—the SADF—had been looking for me. I also learnt about Buks Erasmus's funeral and the media hunt for a group of mercenaries.

On returning to duty after the short period of leave I heard that the EO element at Soyo had been withdrawn to Luanda after the over-extended FAA defence had crumbled under the sustained UNITA pressure. I also read in the newspapers later that Colonel Pepe had been wounded in an ambush and that, true to their style of operations, UNITA had threatened the area again and disrupted the FAA troops. UNITA then retook the Soyo area and controlled the Soyo province once again, only to be driven out later when another EO force returned together with a FAA element.

So, what had come from the mountaineering expedition? I had found the Soyo operation a very valuable experience, in addition to the good salary that we had received. I had been forced through circumstances to wait 39 years of my life before I was given the dubious opportunity to man and defend an entrenched defensive position as a soldier, similar to so many other fellow South Africans during the Second World War. For most of the men it was indeed a strange experience. As former members of the special forces the manning of static entrenched defensive positions was an uncanny experience and they felt claustrophobic. They baulked at the static, exposed nature of the positions and admitted openly that they preferred the space and cover which is derived from open plains, the air or the sea.

Looking back with a view to isolating the main lessons of the experience is somewhat difficult as too many things appear to have taken place at the same time and to attempt to recall them is difficult. Things that do come to mind now include the first helicopter flight to the Soyo target area. This flight would not have taken place had Tony Buckingham not exerted pressure on the pilots. A shortage of ammunition and water was not a good enough reason for him. The other side of the coin was the question as to what can you expect from pilots who land on a LZ which is under mortar fire? I remember an occasion when three Mi-17 helicopters landed on D+3 days under such conditions. The last helicopter to land 'pressed' its tail rotor into the ground and the pilot and his crew didn't even wait to turn off the helicopter's engine, so eager were they to escape on the first helicopter that had landed. The main rotors of the crippled helicopter were still turning and they were already safely buckled into the escape helicopter for their ride out of the LZ.

Another thought that comes to mind is the extent of the FAA casualties and the circumstances that they faced. The wounded were only assisted if a helicopter was on its way to the area. On the other hand the logistic requirements were so great that the helicopters could not keep up with the replenishments needed.

The captain of the barge that was used for the beach landing had never been involved in a contact with an enemy or an opponent before. He calmly brought the barge in to land, totally overloaded, whilst UNITA were firing GRAD-P rockets at it. Thereafter he beached the barge, managed to get it grounded and stuck where it should not beach, and the troops nearly drowned whilst disembarking. To crown everything, the currents during high tide turned the barge and it came to rest alongside the beach, and the remainder of the equipment could not be offloaded. It is no wonder that I found the barge crew racing as fast as they could towards the first helicopter to get out of there.

To cut a long story of the woes that begat the FAA short, the idea that Tony Buckingham and Eeben Barlow had formulated regarding the use of private military professionals held some real merit as a solution for Africa. There is a need for effective action to get things done quickly as this provides the element of surprise which made the critical difference during the attack on Soyo. The nail had been hit on the head. Admittedly, this did exact a price, but the attack achieved its objective. I also think that General de Matos, the supreme commander of the FAA, had realized that this concept could be successful.

The initial contract lasting one month was also extended by two weeks and thereafter by an additional month. This was supposed to have led to a new contract but there was a break in between. At a later stage an agreement was reached with Eeben to the extent that once the contract had been signed the wheels would start rolling once again.

It was also very clear that those EO members who had been part of the initial contract would not consider such a contract lightly in the future. There were a number of hardliners, who would last the pace and the distance, but they were few and far between—a mere handful.

I once read a magazine article on the EO Soyo operation and it was clear from the narrative that the interviewee was one of those EO members who had packed his rucksack and returned home very early on during the operation. I wonder where he got his facts from to colour in the remainder of the operation. This anonymous writer stated that one should not trust one's employers. My question to him is why on earth did he get involved in this adventure in the first place if he thought that it was going to be similar to a Sunday school outing? Why didn't he make his decision when he looked around him and saw the type of people who were going to accompany him into battle? I am convinced that he is one of those who told everyone within hearing range in the nearest bar of his heroic exploits.

THE 1994 OFFENSIVE TO OUST
UNITA FROM CAFUNFU

Preparation and training

When I landed at the military base at Cabo Ledo on 3 January 1994 with a new EO contract, the force in Angola was already in the process of undertaking certain preparations to give effect to the conventional phase of the MPLA government's plan against UNITA. It was also clear that this contract was much larger than the Soyo operation and a quick look around established that the numerical strength of EO had increased steadily, with members from such former SADF units as 4 and 5 Reconnaissance Regiments, 32 Battalion, the Koevoet unit, 101 Battalion and 102 Battalion, amongst others. Collectively the force could be described as a firm base of experienced, battle hardened soldiers from southern Africa.

No sooner had I debussed from the aircraft than I was met by Chris Grové, the 'Main Peanut' at Cabo Ledo, and Nic van den Bergh. Both men were former paratroopers or parabats, as they were known in the SADF. I had also served my time as a student and qualified as a paratrooper at 1 Parachute Battalion in Bloemfontein when I was a captain in the SADF. Let me make myself clear, however, that my operational experience with the 'singing and jumping' parabats had led me to less than flattering conclusions about them. It was in this environment that their true colours were revealed to me when they were deployed as part of the fireforce in Sector 10, Owamboland. They would arrive at the location of a contact with SWAPO insurgents, ask where the insurgent tracks were and, if on inspection, they appeared not to be fresh enough they weren't interested in following up at all. But, to be fair, there were also a number of good parabats.

After welcoming me, Chris Grové volunteered such information that left me in no doubt as to the fact that he wanted me to believe that he had been a colonel in the SADF and that he knew what he was doing. He was a strange character indeed and we didn't have too much in common during the remainder of the contract in Angola or in Sierra Leone thereafter. Later that day Nic van den Bergh informed me that he had allocated me to the conventional warfare wing of the EO force at Cabo Ledo. This transfer placed me under the command of a former SADF major, whilst I had been a SADF colonel. I wondered how they had reached this decision. The major left EO shortly after I joined the wing and the situation resolved itself as I took over the command of the conventional warfare wing.

I found out a little more about Executive Outcome's purpose during this contract and came across an organization chart that to me was too fancy and elaborate for the existing circumstances. My experience at Soyo had shown me that it was vital to 'get the job done' and leave the sideshows out of it. It was also clear that there was a rash of 'rank inflation' in the organization chart. People were appointed in command over people who were better qualified than they were. It was also evident that some of the men had already indicated that they would not work with certain other men. Highly experienced and specialized people had been bunched together with others who hadn't the same experience or specialization. How was it to be expected of the men to adapt without any thought for the development of *esprit de corps*? I also saw and experienced that, aside from Nic, the EO commander, who was now addressed as 'Brigadier', there were decision-making problems between Chris Grové, the chief of staff, and Duncan Rykaart, the second-in-command.

My first assignment was to visit the FAA training area at Funda, east of Luanda. On the way there I had the first opportunity to experience firsthand how the country had deteriorated. In addition to building projects and sites that had been terminated and abandoned years previously, the place was filthy, sewage spilled down the middle of the roads, no refuse was being removed and the infrastructure of the town was not being maintained. The people were, however, peaceful and life continued despite the fact that the majority of the youths under the age of twenty had been born during the Angolan civil war.

When I arrived at Funda the EO element there was in the process of training an infantry company of FAA soldiers. Their standard of preparedness looked to be good. Frans Flakjacket, a former SADF armoured car commander, was training the troops in the employment of the 30mm main armament of the BMP-2. Two qualified infantrymen, Freddie and Johan, were assisting him by providing training in battle drills once the troops had debussed from the vehicles. It was, however, decided that to simplify matters EO should continue this training at Cabo Ledo and I was tasked to reconnoitre a suitable training area. I used a helicopter to carry this task out and Juba, a very experienced former South African Air Force helicopter pilot in whose helicopter I would spend many an hour in the days and months ahead, flew me around in search of a suitable training area. The area north of Cabo Ledo was recommended as it was ideally suited to the training of mechanized infantry but it was too open for advanced training.

I had a training staff of ten men at that point, all of whom were qualified armoured soldiers or infantrymen with a rank of corporal or lieutenant. Everyone, with the exception of a former policeman by the name of Taz, had been operationally employed at some or other time during their careers. I learnt later that Taz had appeared 'out of the mist' to join the Soyo operation. I also learnt to accept that Taz hung, packed, wore and draped everything he could lay his hand on onto his body, as if he was modelling equipment for *Soldier of Fortune* magazine. His kit wasn't complete without the latest fashion in dark glasses and camouflage shorts, with boots that were never fastened. The FAA troops hero-worshipped him because he paraded himself as the Swedish actor, Dolf Lundgren's double. A powerfully built character, he loved entertaining me with all his dental problems for some or other unknown reason.

The 'Main Peanut's' top structure identified the need for a force similar to the highly mobile Koevoet light counterinsurgency forces that had operated so effectively during the insurgency conflict in South West Africa. There were few real takers who actually saw this concept taking off as the current military situation was vastly different and it required a different response as a consequence. There were indeed a number of very experienced and battle hardened people on hand and they had to be gainfully employed. The question now was where? My own experience, as a UNITA ally, at the Lomba River south of Cuito Cuanavale during the FAA offensive against UNITA in 1988, had indicated to me that the Koevoet forces employed there had sought unsuccessfully for an identity and a role in these semi-conventional operations. At our current location there were, however, more former Special Forces, 32 Battalion and other former SADF members than there were ex-Koevoet members.

It went without saying that the Koevoet members employed by EO for this contract were 'seriously after wheels', as their whole operational concept had been based on high mobility offensive operations in mine proof vehicles on company level, with relatively high volumes of direct firepower. The Casspir mine-proof vehicle that Koevoet had used in South West Africa had been developed together with members of the unit and it was well suited to the light skirmish role required of the Koevoet forces under those circumstances. The suitability of Koevoet-type forces in a more conventional role was limited and they could mostly be utilized as advance guards and flank guards, with a possibility of a light reconnaissance role as well.

Over time I succeeded in earning the trust and camaraderie of these former Koevoet men, though it still required an effort on my part to convince them that efficiency and order could be established out of disorder. I had always believed that the majority of Koevoet's successes in South West Africa had emanated from the organized disorder of their high mobility. I was also very aware of the fact that I could learn much from their camaraderie and their culture. When it was offered to me I accepted it and we became a united team thereafter.

Take, for example, the time a heavily overloaded vehicle pulled to a dusty halt in front of me with a new bunch of men to train at the conventional warfare wing. Half the members were *boere* from Namibia, with a few South Africans, whilst the rest were all from the traditional Owambo and Himba tribes of Namibia. I had to train and convert them from a highly mobile, independent, skirmish force into conventional soldiers, something they eventually recognized and accepted after many verbal skirmishes, differences of opinion, potential punch-ups and a large number of brandies. There were a few fundamental differences though. We had been issued with the BMP-2, a tracked, amphibious infantry combat vehicle as opposed to the lightly armoured mine resistant Casspir used by Koevoet forces. In addition, there was a requirement for integrated call signs, group procedures, orders, other disciplines and a higher headquarters to which they were to report. I was fortunate to have the time to convert them at a rapid pace from the flexible Koevoet style of skirmish operations to conventional warfare. My ten members of staff quickly mastered the weapon conversions, as well as the vehicle to armoured vehicle conversion and I modified the group procedures in the interim. The conversion to an acceptable conventional warfare standard was complete within two weeks.

By this time the FAA members of 16 Armoured Brigade had arrived for their training, which was to last for six weeks. Numerically 16 Armoured Brigade would eventually be approximately equal in troop strength and weapons to a SADF mechanized combat group. I was very fortunate in that the brigade commander, under whose command we had been placed, was none other than the newly promoted Brigadier Pepe de Castro, my good friend from the Soyo operation. It did, however, take some time before we could sort out exactly how the EO force would participate in the overall plan for the new offensive

With UNITA driven from Quefiquena the men take a day off in the close proximity of the oil storage tanks. Buks Erasmus, our first casualty only three days later, stands with his back to the camera as he chats with other Executive Outcomes men. Phil Smith, the EO No. 3 platoon commander, is in the middle in the background.

Victory flypast. A FAPA Mi-24 helicopter flies over Quefiquena after the objective had been taken. It did not participate in the attack itself.

The M-46 gun used against us by UNITA during the attack. Originally an FAA gun, we captured it and pressed it into service against UNITA. I was (second from left) part of the Executive Outcomes gun crew at Quefiquena.

Digging in at Quefiquena. On D+14 days we withdrew a tactical bound and dug in to repel a UNITA attack. I am about to start swinging my shovel.

After taking the town of Soyo itself during Stage 3 of the offensive we moved into much-improved accommodation.

Angolan navy visit. The silhouette of an Angolan naval vessel that visited us after the town of Soyo had been secured.

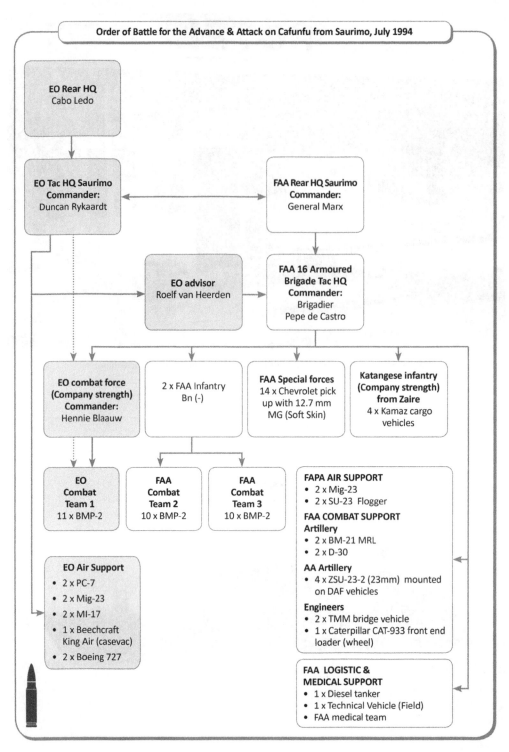

Order of Battle for the Advance & Attack on Cafunfu from Saurimo, July 1994

EO Rear HQ
Cabo Ledo

EO Tac HQ Saurimo
Commander:
Duncan Rykaardt

FAA Rear HQ Saurimo
Commander:
General Marx

EO advisor
Roelf van Heerden

FAA 16 Armoured
Brigade Tac HQ
Commander:
Brigadier
Pepe de Castro

EO combat force
(Company strength)
Commander:
Hennie Blaauw

2 x FAA Infantry
Bn (-)

FAA Special forces
14 x Chevrolet pick
up with 12.7 mm
MG (Soft Skin)

Katangese infantry
(Company strength)
from Zaire
4 x Kamaz cargo
vehicles

EO
Combat
Team 1
11 x BMP-2

FAA
Combat
Team 2
10 x BMP-2

FAA
Combat
Team 3
10 x BMP-2

FAPA AIR SUPPORT
- 2 x Mig-23
- 2 x SU-23 Flogger

FAA COMBAT SUPPORT
Artillery
- 2 x BM-21 MRL
- 2 x D-30

AA Artillery
- 4 x ZSU-23-2 (23mm) mounted
  on DAF vehicles

Engineers
- 2 x TMM bridge vehicle
- 1 x Caterpillar CAT-933 front end
  loader (wheel)

EO Air Support
- 2 x PC-7
- 2 x Mig-23
- 2 x MI-17
- 1 x Beechcraft
  King Air (casevac)
- 2 x Boeing 727

FAA LOGISTIC &
MEDICAL SUPPORT
- 1 x Diesel tanker
- 1 x Technical Vehicle (Field)
- FAA medical team

EO and FAA order of battle for the assault on Cafunfu.

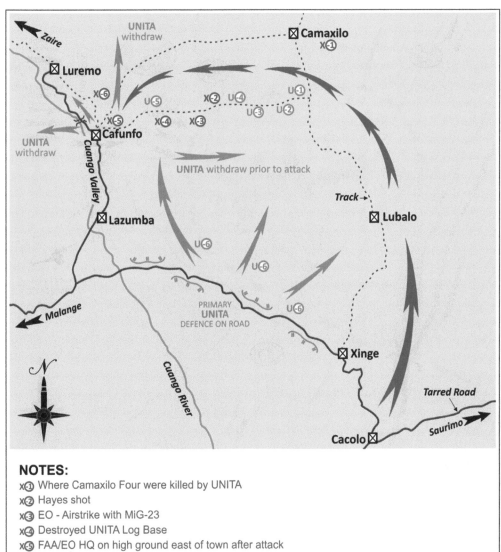

NOTES:

x① Where Camaxilo Four were killed by UNITA
x② Hayes shot
x③ EO - Airstrike with MiG-23
x④ Destroyed UNITA Log Base
x⑤ FAA/EO HQ on high ground east of town after attack
x⑥ L. Bosch PC-7 shot down with 2 fatalities
u① First landmine - 23mm truck taken out
u② First Auxiliary Battalion (UNITA) ambush
u③ Second ambush (Regular UNITA Battalion)
u④ First B-10/B-12 artillery bombardment
u⑤ UNITA Main logistics area (Diesel, Food)
u⑥ Routes taken by UNITA to occupy quick defensive positions as EO/FAA took alternative/unexpected route

Battle map depicting the EO and FAA advance on Cafunfu. We used the alternate, less obvious route to Cafunfu.

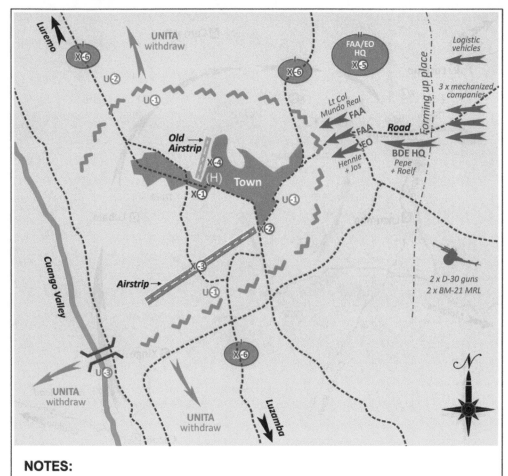

NOTES:

x❶ EO MI-17 pieces found after attack
x❷ Graves of Camaxilio Four
x❸ EO MI-17 (Juba) landing position
x❹ Probable site of EO Recce team graves close to hospital (H)
x❺ FAA/EO HQ dug in after attack (high ground)
x❻ All round defence (FAA/EO) after attack
u❶ UNITA main defence positions
u❷ SAM-7 firing position on Juba MI-17
u❸ Bridge destroyed by UNITA

Battle map depicting the EO and FAA attack on Cafunfu.

Relaxing at Barra do Quanza after a day's training at Cabo Ledo, the former Cuban base south of Luanda. Renier van der Merwe and Kolle are on my right.

Training former Koevoet members in the finer points BMP-2 mechanized drills at Cabo Ledo.

Taking a break between sand models and orders at Cabo Ledo.

Testing the wading capability of a BMP-2.

against UNITA. We all had our own ideas as to how the operation should be conducted. After days of discussions and new guidelines from the higher headquarters we decided that the EO component of the force would be grouped together as a full combat team within 16 Armoured Brigade which was under the command of Brigadier Pepe. I would be the combat team commander and Brigadier Pepe's advisor at the same time. This organizational setup was the source of a number of problems, not the least of which was a communication problem, and I was required to communicate through an interpreter. Command and control passed from me directly upwards to Brigadier Pepe and laterally we had to establish some form of liaison over time. It took time indeed as procedures and drills differed and I was not inclined to cross swords with Brigadier Pepe all the time. The bond of friendship and trust that was established between the other commanders on the ground and myself made life that much easier. I eventually became the buffer between commanders on the ground and Brigadier Pepe.

The relationship between Brigadier Pepe and myself and his officers became progressively better and stronger, to the extent that my own EO colleagues and friends cautioned me against this practice as they were opposed to it. I knew that time would show that this relationship would be beneficial in the long run. I was the only member of the conventional wing of EO who had previous EO experience in Angola. Pine, the oldest, self-proclaimed 'nerd' in EO, who at this point was the operational officer on duty tried to warn me. I decided there and then to ignore him if he dared to display this attitude in the future. If I could chase Taz out of my base because he used finger language to communicate with me, then why should I have to put up with Pine when I know that in a short whilst it will only be the men and I, minus Pine, with Brigadier Pepe against the enemy? Time was too precious and relationships became less complicated as time passed. The use of language between the teams became progressively economic and to the point, to the extent that a few words were sufficient to express a whole concept. I enjoyed this tremendously. Good communication is achieved through confrontation.

Matters were progressing well in the ranks of the conventional force and our programme had developed as planned. We had, for example, achieved a very good artillery capability with the allocation of a battery of D-30 122mm guns and a troop of BM-21 multiple rocket launchers. We resolved the last irritations and issues during an integrated exercise, which included the use of close air support.

During the exercise I was invited to enjoy a ground-pounder's ultimate joy: accompanying the PC-7 pilot as he observed the exercise below. I strapped myself in and calmly let on that I had had exposure to this type of aircraft in my father's Cessna 172 aircraft. We had hardly left the ground when it occurred to the pilot to test this hypothesis somewhat and he indicated to me that when one moves the stick between my legs to the left then this happens and when one moves it to the right then that happens. I experimented under his tutelage and the next moment he let go of his stick and the aircraft was mine. What a beautiful, powerful aircraft. The pilot took me through the paces and before long my lack of exposure and experience in such a situation was evident. I politely asked him to allow me five minutes to recover otherwise my activities would, in all probability, land us up in a situation where his head would be permanently fixed to the back of his seat. He understood immediately. During the ensuing conversation he mentioned that he had taken my colleague, Duncan, for a lesson and had it not been for the fact that Duncan had been dressed in combat clothing, he would have run out of pockets to fill. I realized then that this was the reason why pilots had so many pockets in their flying overalls. My ultimate surprise came when he asked me to help him whilst he flew to the favourite crayfish diving spot located by the EO pilots. I was up for this as he had after all said that my initiation phase had ended. We flew to the area and at a distance of about three kilometres from the sea he indicated a spot where rocks were located close to the surface of the sea. This was evidently where they caught the largest crayfish and he asked me to take over the controls so that he could get a proper GPS fix on the location. With an air of determination I took the controls and flew the aircraft towards the point at an elevation of approximately five metres above sea level.

After having taken the GPS reading he calmly said, "OK, I've got it".

I was under the impression that he was referring to the fact that he had resumed control of the PC-7, and I released my hold on the stick, only to feel after a whilst that we were descending lower and lower towards the surface of the sea. At a point where it appeared to me that we were dangerously close to the surface I heard him shout and pluck the aircraft back into the air. Whilst I was recovering he calmly stated that such things did tend to happen when the cabin control procedure is not followed correctly.

During this phase of conventional training, parallel training was taking place at the EO base at Rio Longa, approximately one hundred kilometres south of Cabo Ledo. A rapid deployment company had been formed and training concentrated on helicopter-borne operations. The main components of the force consisted of ground troops supported by mortars and anti-tank weapons. A strong and experienced reconnaissance team, consisting of former special forces men, was formed as part of this force as well.

I must say here that the same sorry routine took place here as during the Soyo operation as well. Men joined EO, arrived here and either resigned as time went on or fitted in at all cost. This phase of the training at Longa was very frustrating. It is never a wise practice to leave experienced soldiers without much to do but sit around and buy their chocolate and booze on account. Soldiers must be kept busy.

Many amusing incidents took place, particularly when the men's vacation leave periods arrived before the movement to Saurimo. The men were flown to their destinations on a very tight and busy schedule by two medium sized Beechcraft B200 King Air aircraft. Time ran out, some of the men were incorrectly scheduled and too many returned from leave on the same day. The bunch was stranded at Lanseria International Airport outside Johannesburg for two days before the problem was resolved and everybody was back to Angola. Needless to say, the only person who profited from this situation was the barman at Lanseria International Airport, who was forced to replenish supplies three times over this period. Those who required some comfort overnight baulked at the local prices of a mattress, especially when their wives or girlfriends had taken their credit cards into safe custody.

The deployment at Saurimo

At this point of the operation very little was known about the nature and scope of our participation in the coming offensive against UNITA. A very short planning cycle had been conducted in Luanda and Nic van den Bergh had presented his mission to the FAA headquarters planning staff. A number of people were withdrawn to attend the planning session, including Hennie Blaauw and Mike Herbst, two of the more experienced conventional warfare planning staffs. I contributed to the planning cycle effort as a commander, and it was enjoyable since Hennie, Mike and I went way back to the time when 7 Infantry Division, one of the conventional SADF divisions, was responsible for the Western Theatre, which included South West Africa and Angola.

The broad plan was directed by the planning guidelines received from General João De Matos, head of the FAA, and its purpose was to deny UNITA access to the diamond fields at Cafunfu in the Lunda Norte Province of Angola. This was to be achieved by a simultaneous attack along two axes—the Saurimo–Cafunfu axis and the Malanje–Cafunfu axis. EO was required to concentrate almost all its members in Saurimo for the Saurimo–Cafunfu advance, whilst a small EO contingent was allocated to the T-62 tank-heavy Malanje–Cafunfu axis. The BMP-2 infantry combat vehicle was the armoured vehicle allocated to the Saurimo–Cafunfu route, mainly because it was air-transportable and there weren't many bridges left along this axis that could take the 45 metric ton weight of a T-62 tank. The cost of the operation along this axis would have been prohibitive as they would have had to move under their own steam all the way from Saurimo to Cafunfu, whilst on the other axis they could be transported on tank transporters to a location just outside Malanje.

On the face of it we had to accept that UNITA did have prior knowledge of what the government was planning. It was, therefore, a case of keeping the force strength and time-scales as secret as possible in this environment. To date only a few EO members actually knew what the contents of the plan were. The plan would be conveyed to the whole group once the reconnaissance and leave had been completed.

After returning from leave a small group of us left for Saurimo in a FAPA Ilyushin-76 cargo aircraft and on arrival at the base we were made to feel very welcome by the Governor of Lunda Sul Province who treated us to a delicious feast of Portuguese cooking at its best that first evening.

Early the next morning we travelled, secretly, to the airport at Saurimo and conducted a reconnaissance of the airfield, mostly in order to determine where the EO force for the Saurimo–Cafunfu advance should be housed. The buildings were in very poor condition but we eventually got used to this in Angola. After all, this was Africa. Sometime later during the day we managed to get an aerial view of Cafunfu and its surrounding environs. It became all too obvious that we had selected the wrong day to undertake an air reconnaissance mission, as the height at which the aircraft flew and the dry conditions on the ground, coupled to the levels of dust in the air, simply did not enable us to see anything meaningful at all. We were also very concerned that UNITA, through radio intercepts, may have been able to determine that we would be flying over the area and could have deployed forces to lie in wait for us with guided anti-aircraft missiles. As a result the reconnaissance of the terrain did not reveal much, nor did it reveal anything of the enemy forces. From information gained during the planning cycle, however, it was established that there were eight UNITA battalions deployed throughout the area between the Lauchimo River, on the Zaire border to the north and Malanje in the west. We had to assume that they would not be static in their deployment as they had not as yet weighed any options as to how the government forces would be deployed and employed. We returned to Cabo Ledo the next day with very little knowledge of the terrain and even less of the UNITA enemy.

The movement of the EO contingent from Cabo Ledo to Saurimo started in earnest hereafter. The advance team started out first, under the leadership of Duncan Rykaart, the commander of the EO Tac HQ and the last to leave was the mechanized combat team under my command. It was also agreed that the EO rear headquarters in Angola would remain at Cabo Ledo and the training wing would remain in its current location at the Rio Longa base.

As is the case with the deployment of any new headquarters, a settling-in phase was required and we went out of our way to embed ourselves thoroughly. The EO Rapid Deployment Force (RDF) company was accommodated in a row of bungalows closest to the EO Tac HQ and in a large adjacent hanger. The EO Air Wing was accommodated on their own, diagonally opposite the RDF. We all accepted that, as flying types, they preferred to be on their own. The combat team under my command was accommodated in tents close to the EO Tac HQ for a few days until such time as the movement from Cabo Ledo had been completed in total. During this period Ibis Air, an arm of EO, acquired two Boeing-727 aircraft and great was our enjoyment when both aircraft surprised us with a very low-level flypast at Saurimo.

By the beginning of April 1994 the EO Tac HQ started gearing up for smaller operations aimed at gaining control and dominating the area surrounding Saurimo. These operations were also undertaken to prepare and sharpen the EO members for future operations that we all knew were to follow.

The conversion of the EO Air Wing members to the Mi-17 helicopter and PC-7 light aircraft was very successful and we gained a great measure of flexibility as a result. The aircraft roles fitted the requirements of the upcoming operations like a glove, the crews spoke our language—literally and figuratively—flew in such a fashion that we understood the profiles, and were used to them, and knew that they were the solution for the type of bush war we were fighting. EO did, however, struggle initially to marry up and be in a position to coordinate their air activities with the fighter aircraft missions undertaken by FAPA pilots. One will never really know what the reasons for this inability were, but that didn't stop us from hazarding a number of guesses—an expensive machine that could easily be flown away and what not. This lack of trust was, in my opinion, swiftly overcome and the EO Air Wing was used with such success that it became almost indispensible thereafter. The close cooperation between our ground forces and the EO Air Wing became a hallmark of our approach and many successful operations thereafter could be directly ascribed to this phenomenon. Small forces achieved such flexibility from this and left the impression that 'high technology' operations were indeed undertaken by them within an African context. This was due to the skills and approach followed by the veteran pilots of the South African bush war—Arthur Walker, Carl Alberts, Juba and Charlie Tait—and a number of younger men who learnt from them as time passed.

Rapid Deployment Force operations

Whilst we waited for the Angolan forces to complete the logistical preparations for the operation, EO was tasked to continue with actions aimed at fixing UNITA in the Lunda Norte Province to the north of Saurimo. The objective was to conduct harassing actions in order to engage UNITA over a wide front whilst at the same time disrupting UNITA logistic lines through the employment of the EO Air Wing. These actions were to be conducted in such a way that they did not establish a pattern. After all, we knew this was a basic requirement for success in these types of operations.

This phase of the campaign really frustrated me and my men as we had already completed our training and conversion to the BMP-2 and all we could do was sit and wait. By this time my force had left the airfield vicinity and deployed tactically in positions to the west of Saurimo, approximately 15 kilometres outside the town itself. Contrary to the practice followed by our EO colleagues in town and at the airfield we stayed in tents, dug trenches and conducted stand-to drills as part of our daily lives. When we realized that we needed to enhance our personal hygiene we washed out of buckets or visited the nearest river for a convenient place to take a bath. What a joy it was to feel clean after these sessions. I liaised personally with Duncan on a daily basis at the EO Tac HQ in Saurimo by driving in with my driver/assistant and interpreter. The difficulty experienced in communicating with the FAA forces and the local population was such that an interpreter had to accompany one as a matter of course. This was not such a barrier to those men who had previously been members of 32 Battalion.

The first operations duly got underway and Xingi was the first area where the RDF was employed. Costly lessons were learnt during this deployment. I was not involved in the activities of the RDF but the feedback we received from the EO Tac HQ was that the basics of offensive operations and of air-landed operations should never be disregarded. 'No names, no pack drill' as we always used to say.

Pollie, one of the RDF men was shot in the leg and his team had to carry him out of the area. The area in which the team was operating was very mountainous and suitable helicopter LZs were limited as a result. This operation was the ice breaker and its success was very limited. I should mention here that a number of the members of the RDF company leader group had very little previous experience—in fact they were naked as it were. Some of them had only started their military careers in the SADF once the war we had conducted was a thing of the past. Luckily, there were members with years of real combat experience and they were able to manoeuvre the RDF wagon through the drift, as it were. In the interim, the RDF force continued their operations and they wrestled to achieve a viable and reliable operational procedure for the type of operations that were required. As is typical in these types of African operations, the day of reckoning was not far off.

A three-man reconnaissance team consisting of Renier van der Merwe, Steyntjie (Steyn) Marais and Handsome Ndlovu had been deployed deep inside UNITA held territory to the north-east of Cafunfu. Cafunfu was of course our main target and it was situated approximately three hundred kilometres northwest of Saurimo as the crow flies. We were looking for UNITA deployment areas, logistic routes, rear areas, dumping areas and possible areas where they were erecting obstacles on the advance routes of the FAA mechanized force. A second team, led by Meno, had been deployed further north, closer to Quango River valley. They were also required to look for UNITA air routes in order to enable us to threaten their air-supply capability. The two teams were flown into their respective areas under a veil of very strict and elaborate security. Carl, our intelligence officer, and I accompanied Meno's team during their deployment. The area did not look encouraging during the flight that late afternoon; thick mist covered the low lying areas between the hills and the pilot's view was limited. The pilots were not put off by these conditions though. After all they were veterans and true to form, they delivered once more. We felt secure and at ease knowing that they were behind the controls.

Renier's team made contact with the EO Tac HQ shortly after they had been dropped off by the helicopters and reported that their situation was difficult, due to UNITA activities in their vicinity. As time progressed no more reports were received and the members of the EO Tac HQ became anxious and concerned that the team was in for a very difficult time ahead. A PC-7 and the MI-17s were repeatedly sent to establish communication with the team but they returned without any success. By the fourth day after their deployment, however, stress levels in the EO Tac HQ were very high. It turned out that we had lost the entire team, missing presumed dead. The bad news was then reported to the higher headquarters and the parents and wives had to be informed as well. The loss of the team came as a devastating blow to all of us in the field. We all remembered the three men—Steyntjie who, one evening previously, refused to let Renier, Meno and I leave him on his own. He even served us coffee and bully beef and, when we each hinted that we may have a requirement for something stronger to fortify ourselves, 'borrowed' a bottle of brandy from the pilots. After all, the pilots always had that little bit of extra space on the Boeings for their Air Wing colleagues, more at least than for us ground-pounders in any event. That same evening Renier and I analysed and criticized the Soyo operation once again over coffee, bully beef and brandy, as we challenged the different bravados we had experienced there, allocated fictitious medals to deserving recipients, and wrote off Buks as a very poor commander once again.

By now Meno and his team had also realized that there was a strong possibility that they were being followed and they were subsequently recovered in a heroic bid by the helicopters. The team was deployed once again on the inbound flight routes of UNITA logistic aircraft, but they were unable to deploy their SAM-7 missile launcher effectively due to UNITA activity in the deployment areas. They returned from this mission with different ideas. We all realized that to deploy reconnaissance elements with the current backup facilities at our disposal was to court extreme danger. We had to re-direct our thought patterns and use logic and the military appreciation process to determine how UNITA would deploy under normal circumstances to stop the advance of an armoured FAA force, consisting mostly of BMP-2s. We also knew that there was a strong possibility that they had tortured Renier, Steyntjie and Handsome to the end to obtain information about the objectives and order of battle of the FAA and EO force. I realized there and then that both I and my own armoured force would have to prepare ourselves for the worst. This was not going to be easy.

Meanwhile, Duncan was beginning to feel the pressure that was being exerted on him by a number of men under his command. This is one of the greatest disadvantages of this type of security or mercenary organization—call it what you will. The men realized that this operation was not going to be a 'cake walk' at all: there was a possibility that they could disappear, or get wounded or even lose their lives. It was at this point that the 'worm' appeared that had been fabricated by the 'Main Peanut'. Chris Grové arrived from Cabo Ledo, gathered all his parabat colleagues in the operations room in the EO Tac HQ and, without realizing that the room had no ceiling and that people outside could hear him, told his parabat colleagues that they shouldn't be stupid and that they should rather step aside and allow the other EO members who hailed from other former SADF units, such as 32 Battalion, to 'bleed' instead. He told them that the parabats should look carefully after themselves and after each other. It was under these circumstances then that Duncan was forced to make a so-called democratic decision every time it came to the conduct of the RDF operations. A very regrettable and unwelcome chagrin had emerged. Hereafter the RDF platoons were required to conduct their own planning and then to present the results thereof for approval, something which would have been more appropriate to the captain of a popcorn team, not a member of the highly sought after EO. Chris Grové had laid the foundation of this wasteful and selfish practice.

Subsequent to this episode, an operation was planned to harass the UNITA forces at Camaxilo, located to the northwest of Saurimo, by means of a stand-off engagement with mortars. Shaun Gullen, one of the shirkers during the Soyo operation, was the RDF commander and he delegated the planning for this operation to a young inexperienced platoon commander—a certain Taljaard, whose father had been my company commander whilst I was receiving junior leader training at the SA Army Gymnasium in 1972. The plan was presented and even I, as a mere observer during the presentation, was concerned that the same pattern that had been followed during the two previous operations was to be repeated here. This vulnerability was highlighted to Taljaard but he was adamant and, in his ignorance, forced the issue by maintaining that this was his plan, the men were his men and that he believed that the plan would work. The pilots attending the presentation indicated critically that the LZ was, in their opinion, located too close to the town of Camaxilo. Once again, Taljaard egotistically forced his opinion and plan on the decision makers. He also demanded that he should be in a position to enforce the location of the helicopter holding area as he had appreciated where it should be located. We all knew, as did UNITA, that the helicopters were the key element in the attack. UNITA knew that if they could restrict and limit the employment of helicopters then they had succeeded in denying EO the ability to undertake helicopter-borne offensive operations. The helicopters were everything to us at this point.

Once the heliborne attack force had taken off at H-Hour, 'Boss' Taljaard jumped into the PC-7 to act as the Telstar or airborne commander. I knew that Duncan was under a lot of pressure that day due to the fact that the operational planning had drawn so much criticism and there were still many unresolved issues surrounding it.

The mortar fire group, consisting of two crews of 4 men each, manned 82mm mortars with an effective range of approximately 3,000 metres, and with approximately 40 bombs per weapon landed on the designated LZ and within minutes they were in action and on target with their fire mission. The weapon teams were protected by a close protection element consisting of up to 20 men, including observers and Carl Dietz. The purpose of the deployment was to bring about a heavy, accurate bombardment on the enemy target and then withdraw safely by helicopter, before the enemy could react effectively to the bombardment. The fire control commands were coming thick and fast from the PC-7, but they were interrupted by an incoming message from the EO protection element deployed around the mortar fire group. Shots had been heard close to their position, about 100 metres away, coming from the direction of the town. The force deployed on the ground was instructed to continue and complete the fire mission. The fire mission was interrupted once again by sporadic fire coming closer and closer, and the protection element even reported that they were hearing enemy voices through the bush. The order from 'Boss' Taljaard in the PC-7 still remained unchanged—remain at the position and complete the fire mission. No instructions or indications were given to the ground force as to whether they should escape to the emergency rendezvous (RV) or not. At this point the ground force was under a huge amount of pressure but, more importantly, the helicopters were the only extraction option available and they would have to carry this out from an unsafe area.

Suddenly the command was given by Taljaard to cease fire and the helicopters were instructed to lift the force very quickly. At this point I was standing in the ops room at Saurimo with Duncan and I saw that he was exceptionally uncomfortable. All we could hear on the radio was the voice in the PC-7; no voice traffic from the ground force could be heard at all. And then it happened. The shit began to hit the fan. The ground force came under effective enemy fire and we were unable to deduce from the faint radio traffic whether they were on their way out of the area by helicopter or not. We did hear that they had left a number of men behind. This in effect meant that the force had not been extracted in full.

What has actually transpired was that the first of the two helicopters had come in to land at the LZ and successfully extracted the mortar fire group, whilst the second Mi-17 helicopter circled at a safe distance away from the LZ, waiting for the first helicopter to take off and leave the LZ area. Once the first Mi-17 had lifted off, the second helicopter came in to land and whilst the protection team was running towards the helicopter they drew very heavy effective fire from the bush surrounding the LZ. Chaos ensued and the enemy small arms fire succeeded in puncturing the outer skin of the helicopter many times, to the extent that helicopter fuel began escaping from the fuel tanks and Charlie Tait, the pilot, decided that what was left of the helicopter had to be extracted from the LZ there and then. There were indeed still a number of men running towards the helicopter whilst others were still clambering aboard. The enemy fire was so intense and concentrated at this point that some of the men inside the helicopter were hit, one of whom was fatally wounded.

Charlie was doing well as he laboriously enticed the helicopter out of the LZ. Four men had been left behind on the ground. The actual events that took place on the ground thereafter are unclear but from what those who were successfully extracted had seen, it appeared that some of the men left behind on the ground had been wounded and even shot dead whilst approaching the waiting Mi-17. What had actually happened was clouded in uncertainty and the metaphorical fog of battle.

Tait realized that the helicopter was losing fuel at such a rate that the inside of the cabin was covered in spraying fuel and visibility out of the helicopter was severely impaired as a result. He also realized that he would not be able to nurse the helicopter much further and began looking for an emergency LZ where he could put the helicopter down and save the lives of the men on board. After flying a distance of approximately five kilometres from the LZ he put the helicopter down in an open spot in the bush. The Mi-17 carrying the mortar fire group then landed close by and Tait and the rest of his crew, together with all the passengers were transferred and a massive total of 41 men were returned safely to Saurimo in the solitary Mi-17. What a heroic rescue feat it had been to recover from such a chaotic situation.

At this point the EO Tac HQ was under the impression that the only problem was the fact that a few men had not managed to climb aboard the helicopters. Instinctively both Duncan and I said, as one, that the helicopter should turn back and lift the men who had been left behind. We were not actually in a position to make a clear decision as 'Boss' Taljaard had been giving us the incorrect feedback.

It was a bitter, galling, sinking moment when we saw only one helicopter return to Saurimo. Luckily the men had decided that the best thing they could do with the crippled helicopter was to deny its use to UNITA and they had shot it to pieces whilst they withdrew to safety from the emergency LZ in the second helicopter. However, the crippled helicopter just wouldn't catch fire and burn.

Back at Saurimo the doctors had already been warned to prepare to receive a number of wounded men. Once the helicopter had landed it was determined that one man had died and three had been seriously wounded. The two doctors and a number of medics were kept very busy for some time in order to get the situation under control.

The battle at Camaxilo left deep physical and emotional scars amongst the EO men and the bitterness and anger would resurface regularly thereafter. This was the greatest loss of EO men that had been sustained in one contact.

During the debriefing, after the operation, it was concluded that a change of focus should be initiated and that this type of operation should be shelved for a whilst. Despite the fact that EO did manage, in time, to obtain a replacement helicopter from FAPA, this was the last operation undertaken by the RDF Company. The main effort shifted to the training of the FAA forces at Saurimo and the conduct of Special Force type operations. The morale of the EO men was indeed low at that point in time.

In the meantime 'Boss' Taljaard had returned from leave in South Africa with the rumour that he had heard from his colleagues still in the SADF that EO would have to be very careful from then on as UNITA had acquired South African G5 howitzers and we were about to be 'revved' at Saurimo by these guns. We were understandably concerned at this information and uncertain as to whether we were in fact at all safe in our present dispositions and locations. I felt excluded from this fear as my mechanized force had from the outset been deployed defensively and dug in some distance from Saurimo in such a fashion that we were ready for UNITA.

Nic van den Bergh then came to visit us at Saurimo and he gave Duncan orders to prepare and dig defensive positions for the EO force on the base itself. The guard system was to be enhanced and, more importantly, the attitude of the men would have to change for the better.

All the battle indications pointed to the possibility that UNITA was intent on attacking any forces in and around Saurimo. All the units and sub-units, including FAA and FAPA, prepared themselves for a possible attack—all except the RDF. No trenches were dug by the company. Jan Joubert had been instructed to take control of this activity and it became obvious that the order had not reached the men as nothing had happened. Nic van den Bergh shat him out about this dereliction of duty one day in the EO ops room. Jan Joubert merely turned his back on Nic and walked out. Where was Duncan now, when he was required to be present? He was responsible and accountable as the EO Tac HQ commander.

On reflection, this is one of the weak points of the cultural differences between the different forces used by EO. The paratroopers used an informal type of communication to get by and to hell with the rest of the EO force. EO had lost seven men in battle by now and many men had been wounded. Things were not going well. The men had the mutters and command and control structures that had been established under favourable, less stressful conditions were crumbling and fewer and fewer men were willing to take responsibility. After all who wants to write off his men and get them killed? The wheat was being sorted from the chaff. The moaners weren't happy any longer and all they wanted to do was to return to the EO base at Rio Longa where they could fart-arse around as they had done before their tasking to Saurimo.

UNITA attacks Saurimo and EO bleeds again

Speculation and deductions aside, it was obvious that UNITA was preparing to attack the town of Saurimo at any time as they needed to apply pressure on the EO force. All that was unknown was the direction from which they would attack and the size of the force. It was also obvious that EO would be the target, right there in the heart of the objective. We also knew from experience that UNITA tactics dictated that when they attacked a target they penetrated into the target itself. To penetrate an enemy position in a controlled and measured manner without fragmenting one's own force requires that force to be particularly courageous and well-disciplined.

The inevitable happened one night in June 1994. The FAA guard at the main entry gate to Saurimo woke up to the sight of approximately 40 men, whose leaders began to ask him where the South Africans were staying at the base. The next moment he was in full flight, running for his life from this group of threatening individuals, even before he could spit out an answer. Later we determined that this UNITA attacking force could well have been 'high' on some substance.

At 0200 that morning the UNITA force casually entered the Saurimo base area via the main gate, hit and destroyed one of the EO helicopters with an RPG-7 rocket, then moved directly to the electricity generator and severed the electricity cables with an axe. Thereafter the force split into two groups. One group, supported by 60mm mortars, conducted a well-organized house clearing action against a row of bungalows. Their information was not accurate enough though, as the bungalows were empty. The other group moved to the large hanger area where the men of the RDF third platoon were barracked and they initiated a firefight with the latter. They met with stiff resistance. With the helicopter in flames and a lively firefight within the base, the guards deployed on the elevated water tank to the north-west of the EO barracks began to report to the EO Tac HQ what they were seeing.

From the available information Duncan reached the conclusion that the attackers were in all probability drunk FAA troops and he gave the order to hold fire. He had hoped that this would bring the situation back under control. The other guards started reporting that they believed that the attack was being conducted by UNITA troops but Duncan ordered them to hold their fire.

By now the one UNITA group had moved to the front of the bungalows where the first and second platoons of the RDF were accommodated and they shouted at the EO troops to come out as they wanted to talk to them. A firefight broke out and Blackie Swart, one of the RDF men, was fatally wounded in the stomach. He died shortly thereafter.

The other UNITA group moved in the direction of the EO Tac HQ but passed it. Some of the attackers had even looked in through the windows, but they evidently hadn't seen anybody, and moved on.

A new firefight had broken out and the EO Air Wing even got the opportunity to push their empty bottles and glasses to one side and participate in the battle with gusto. The EO Tac HQ vehicle, a green diesel pickup truck, was parked in front of the EO Tac HQ building, outside Carl Dietz's window. Carl, our intrepid intelligence officer, swore that he had no idea why the vehicle picked up so many holes during the attack.

The second of the helicopters had also been punctured by small arms fire by this time. At this stage the UNITA force in all probability realized that they were up against stiff resistance, as the EO force was not about to flee, and was intent on fighting back. They broke contact and withdrew into the darkness and the situation quietened down. The score for the evening amounted to one EO man dead against three dead UNITA members, one burnt-out EO helicopter, one EO helicopter full of bullet holes and one EO pickup vehicle (the quickest vehicle) that looked like a tea strainer. The lion had really been let loose in the sheep kraal.

That night I was asleep in my base outside Saurimo when the sound of a mortar round exploding woke me. I attempted to make radio contact with the EO Tac HQ but there was no answer. I tried a second and a third time unsuccessfully. After a whilst the sound of firing died down and I realized that Saurimo must have been attacked and that people were bleeding. As I lay there I recalled an occasion before the attack, when Carl Alberts (one of the EO pilots) and I had gone into the civilian part of town to have a quiet drink. We had met a man who was identified by a number of the locals as a stranger. The man denied this but on reflection I concluded that he could very well have been a UNITA scout on a reconnaissance mission that night.

The next morning early I mobilized my team and as usual left for Saurimo to liaise with the EO Tac HQ. I drove with a feeling of dread. As I entered the base in my pickup truck I looked towards the helicopter pad and saw that one of the helicopters was evidently missing. I later was shocked to see that it had been reduced to a heap of burnt aluminium scrap, with the tail and rotor sticking out and a smouldering gearbox. I drove on to the EO Tac HQ and found that no one wanted to talk to me. The men I talked to spoke with difficulty and said very little and nobody wanted to look me in the eye. I learnt that Blackie had been killed during the incident. Men were standing around aimlessly, unsure whether the attackers were UNITA or mischief makers and it took some time to assimilate the situation. At last I began to get the picture. This was exactly how UNITA must have felt after we attacked Soyo the previous year—a surprise attack had really shaken them.

UNITA had demonstrated to EO what was to be expected on the road ahead; that they were no pushovers; they could operate effectively by day or during the hours of darkness; they were after us and this attack had been relatively easy to pull off. At first the gate guard had thought that the group that approached him consisted of a number of EO men returning from an operation, as everybody knew that EO acted in this fashion, coming and going at odd times of the day and night; then the gate guard realized that these men didn't look like EO men, and he deduced that they were a UNITA force, especially when they started to ask where the South Africans were.

With the gate guard in full flight a wonderful target of opportunity presented itself in the form of a Mi-17 helicopter and they initiated the battle by destroying the helicopter and the electricity generator. EO members woke up and struggled to determine who was attacking their position. Duncan didn't want to fire at 'own forces' and ceased fire. UNITA maintained the initiative and continued the battle.

It was difficult to obtain any guidelines from Duncan that morning. What I did want to know was whether I should initiate a follow-up action as I had the men, the skills and the means to do it—trackers, BMP-2 vehicles and willing men—men who still had not made contact with the enemy and wanted very badly to close with them. A large number of my men were veterans of Koevoet, the police unit in the South West Africa/Namibia conflict responsible for extraordinarily successful results during follow-up operations against insurgents.

I issued a radio warning order to my force to prepare four BMP-2s for a follow-up operation, then I finalized the operation with General Sukissa, the FAA garrison commander at Saurimo and returned to my base area at breakneck speed. I realized that we didn't have much time and we could expect UNITA to make things very difficult for us. I was sure that they would try to get at least a river between themselves and my force if they could.

I was reminded of all the follow-up work I had done as a young lieutenant in the bush war in South West Africa. Later, as a major in the SADF, it became a real experience every time to outwit the enemy (SWAPO) in a systematic fashion and attempt to achieve control over them. Their technique was to disperse or 'bombshell' and rendezvous later at a previously determined location. My most successful follow-up was during a SWAPO penetration into South West Africa/Namibia in 1981. I took over the follow-up of the SWAPO group from a Koevoet team, whose vehicles were low on fuel, and started the operation after my infantry platoons were lifted by helicopter and dropped on the tracks. The area in which the follow-up took place was located on the flat plateau east of Opuwa in the dry Kaokoveld region of South West Africa. The dry limestone hills caused us to lose the tracks regularly and my Himba troops had to persevere and locate them time and again.

We followed the tracks for two days and were very close to the SWAPO group by dusk each day, but the fading light each evening forced me to stop and break off the follow-up temporarily. After two days my Buffel vehicles joined us on the track and our movement speed increased due to their added mobility. By the middle of the third morning we were very close to the enemy and we made contact with them in the vicinity of a cattle post.

During the contact four SWAPO insurgents were killed. We actually killed them by running them down with our vehicles. After consolidating, we once again followed the remaining tracks. When we had set out on this operation our mission had been clear, and since this group had been identified as the advance component of PLAN's (SWAPO's military arm) so-called Typhoon Group we were instructed to catch one member of the group alive and hold him as a prisoner of war. With this in mind I started following the tracks of a single insurgent who had broken away from the rest of the group. It was already 1400 in the afternoon and it was clear from the tracks that this man was a tough cookie. He succeeded in shaking us off regularly in the limestone hills. At one point we were so close to him that we could hear him running through the thick mopani bush to double back around our team. When he tried this a second time we knew that we were very close to him. The bush was our only obstacle and we had one hour of daylight left in which to capture him. I believed that our chances of capturing him were high and I warned my troops to ensure that he was captured at all costs, rather than killed. I decided to leave the vehicles and continue on foot with six of my men. I was determined to capture him today before last light.

We followed him on foot and it soon became clear that he had gained the impression that the lack of vehicle movement implied that we had given up. The distance between his rest periods became shorter and shorter but he remained vigilant, sitting next to or behind a tree or an ant hill each time. We continued to follow up at a quick pace, in an extended line formation.

My Himba troops indicated to me very clearly what the insurgent's plans were. The man following his tracks indicated to me that the insurgent was looking for a place to rest. The next instant a shot was fired out of the bush in front of us and I shouted to my men not to shoot to kill, but to keep him occupied. I moved out to a flank and saw him, lying behind an ant hill, oblivious to my presence. My troops could see me clearly as I moved out to his rear and literally pounced on him, shouting at him to drop his weapons and lift his arms into the air. He calmly moved his weapon's change level to the safety setting and placed it on the ground in front of him. The subsequent harvest of weapons, equipment and information was rewarding and I still have his Makarov pistol today.

Back to the present. We picked up the tracks at the main gate at Saurimo and started to follow them in an easterly direction. It quickly became evident from the blood on the tracks that the UNITA force was evacuating a number of their own wounded as well. After a whilst the blood spoor disappeared, however, and we came to the conclusion that the force was making for the Lauchimo River and we tried to make up as much time as possible. It wasn't long before we arrived at the river and located their crossing place. They had crossed in great haste and we could see where they had rested on the far bank after crossing before continuing on their way. They were approximately six to eight hours ahead of us and it was clear that we would not catch up with them very easily. We searched for a place where the BMP-2s could ford the river. Hendri Engelbrecht led the movement and we watched as he followed the course of a small stream then suddenly shouted repeatedly to his driver to stop. The BMP-2, a tracked vehicle, was sliding like a car on a wet road, and eventually came to a halt in the middle of the stream. The riverbank had a gradient of approximately 30 degrees and I knew that we were going to have our work cut out to recover the vehicle. We eventually managed to extract it from the mud by linking two other BMP-2s to each other with towing cables and harnessing their combined pulling power. The gradient of the river bank was, however, too steep and the vehicle remained in the river despite our best efforts. I was in the process of calling in help from Saurimo when darkness overcame us. It was a bit difficult trying to visualize what the help would constitute as General Sukissa wanted to send the only T-62 tank from Saurimo.

We slept fitfully that night out in the bush, on the high ground in the vicinity of the crippled BMP-2. The vehicle isolated in the river did concern me as the night wore on. UNITA were familiar with the way in which South African soldiers carry out a follow-up operation and it was for this reason that they chose to cross the river and use the time required by vehicles to cross the river as an obstacle to delay our movement on their tracks and give them an advantage.

The next morning we started out very early to recover the BMP-2. The more we tried to free the vehicle the deeper it sank into the mud. By now the area around the vehicle was a vast expanse of mud. General Sukissa still wanted to send the T-62 tank to our aid, but just then a FAA trooper appeared out of the blue and gave us all a lesson in tank recovery. He showed us two thin steel cables on the BMP-2, each with a 'buttonhole'. With a long, thick tree trunk placed diagonally across the front of the vehicle the two cables were then used to fasten the trunk to the underside of the BMP-2's tracks. The vehicle was engaged in first gear and then 'pulled' itself out of the mud. Each time the tree trunk had moved under the track to the rear of the vehicle it was removed and fastened to the front and in this fashion we made progress until the vehicle was free of the mud and the river. This delay had put us two days behind

UNITA. The follow-up was called off and we retraced our steps to Saurimo with the bitter taste of failure and defeat very evident amongst us.

In the EO base at Saurimo there was a lot of dissatisfaction about the way things were progressing. Accusations were being thrown back and forth between Nic van den Bergh, Duncan, Jan Joubert, the Air Wing under Arthur Walker, and even amongst the men themselves. Contrary to this my men had become a close-knit unit, located in their defensive positions to the west of Saurimo. There were real problems inside the EO base in Saurimo itself. Nic van den Bergh and the 'Main Peanut', Chris Grové, arrived from Cabo Ledo to investigate the matter, particularly the disastrous attack on Saurimo by UNITA. We were to blame and there was no way of getting around it. Why weren't defensive positions prepared within the base, as instructed? Someone within EO was guilty, despite the fact that we as EO were part of the overall base defence. There were no excuses. All the battle indications pointing to a UNITA penetration or some form of attack had been ignored.

With Nic van den Bergh standing in front of the gathered men to listen to any complaints they brought to his attention, Chris Grové sat on his backside against the back wall of the meeting location with a notebook and pen and said to the people in front of him, "Come on boys let's hear it."

He was never a popular person—not that one is required to be popular to be effective and efficient as a leader—but his popularity decreased even further at this point. He had already received a very clear message from someone—a highly polished AK47 round placed on his pillow.

Nic had hardly started talking when Pine Pienaar, one of the Air Wing's jet pilots voiced his dissatisfaction and like a choir the rest took up the chorus and succeeded in totally destroying any semblance of Nic's authority. He had been humiliated by the men and they threatened to return to the Rio Longa base. Nic in turn threatened to fire some of the troops. In all honesty, Blackie's death, the death of the Camaxilo four and the disappearance of Steyn, Renier and Handsome had caused fear and trepidation to spread amongst some of the men. The possibility of picking up a 'leak' or two, courtesy of UNITA, was not being relished by the men at all.

The EO Boeing was ready on the runway and Nic challenged those who felt the need to leave to emplane. Nic asked me, in front of everyone, what my plans were. I replied that if the logistic preparations had been completed we would have already been in Cafunfu. The EO Boeing filled with men and it took off for Cabo Ledo without me aboard.

The EO men were openly on strike and the only persons left to continue operating, in addition to my own men, were a few helicopter pilots, plus Duncan and Carl Dietz. I even had to send a number of my men to Saurimo base to help them stand guard. Once the striking men had reached Cabo Ledo approximately 30 of them were fired. The remainder who had not been fired were paratroopers who had been let of the hook by the 'Main Peanut'. They were tasked to assist with the training at Rio Longa thereafter.

My mechanized force did receive a boost from the affair as Simon Witherspoon and a few of his mates who had been amongst the strikers returned to Saurimo and joined us.

Obviously Simon and his mates from the RDF who had joined the mechanized force had reached a conclusion that the risks and dangers were more manageable within the ranks of the EO mechanized group. This was not necessarily the case, as subsequent actions would prove.

During this phase the men of the mechanized force in the laager area outside Saurimo started to take things even more seriously and with everyone's consent a rank structure was instituted to give a formal structure to our force. The events to date were reviewed in detail and the number of men who had lost their lives in this short space of time was carefully tallied. In addition the men realized that the offensive against UNITA at Cafunfu had not even started yet. A few of my men considered the situation and decided that it would be better for them to return to the Rio Longa base to help with training, or to stay at Cabo Ledo. They had to make their decision quickly as the offensive was not far off and they would then be required to accompany the mechanized force on this offensive.

If you have been a member of the Recces—the South African Special Forces—for your whole military career it is a nightmarish change to adjust to the life of a mechanized soldier. At the same time it is also a new challenge and I was truly grateful to the few men from the RDF who had joined us for the offensive and made a worthwhile contribution to the effort. They paid the price of course.

I often refer to the day at Lafras's house when all the men signed the EO contract. It is such an easy thing to do: just sign the document and you are a member of a private security company. But in actual fact it is considerably more difficult to process the implications once you have signed. Similarly it is just as difficult to process, once you are in mortal danger, to decide whether you are doing what you are doing for the money or because this type of work is in your blood. Members of the mechanized force had adherents from both schools of thought. We had work to do. EO, as a company, was bound to carry out the contents of an agreed contract, and we were loyal to this undertaking. The men were loyal to this, despite their individual feelings—as time would tell.

I also had a discussion with Duncan about rank inflation. The EO top structure had faulted here in my opinion. Nic van den Bergh and 'Main Peanut' Grové had issued ranks to inexperienced men who later failed in battle and were removed. It was just so unnecessary and sad that some men had to die in the process before these errors were rectified.

Final preparations

The offensive against Cafunfu was due to start as the logistical preparations and stacking had virtually been completed, as had the planning.

FAA's 16 Armoured Brigade, with the EO company strength combat team, was assembled in an area outside Saurimo to the west of the Lauchimo River. From radio intercepts we had learnt that UNITA now realized more than ever before that the threat from Saurimo was more aggressive and intensive than they had anticipated. Aggressive action is after all one of the principles of the defence. We deduced that UNITA would have to initiate a battle to fix the FAA forces at Saurimo before they commenced the offensive against Cafunfu. We, on the other hand, realized that area operations would have to be continued and maintained at their present intensity in order to prevent the Saurimo force from becoming a static, and dead, UNITA target.

We received information that UNITA was massing in order to threaten us from the vicinity of Dondo, to the south of Saurimo. As a result General Sukissa had deployed small occupation and screening forces in the smaller towns to the south of Saurimo. Great was our surprise when we heard the sounds of battle one morning not far from the deployment area of the mechanized force outside Saurimo.

There was no reaction from the FAA HQ though as there were no vehicles with which to react and communication was poor, with only one high frequency (HF) radio per company. General Sukissa asked me if I would go out and have a look at what had happened and report back to him. Freddie, my interpreter, and I jumped into my Chevrolet rover vehicle and sped southward towards Dala to assess the situation.

As we sped along I realized that what I was doing was the very opposite of what should be done. EO's approach to operations relied heavily on the combat doctrine of the SADF. I hated indecisiveness, I hated what had become of EO, and I hated the fact that we had failed at Xingi and Camaxilo. I also hated the fiasco and aftermath that had taken place at the EO base at Saurimo. It was time for a change and I knew that it was contingent on the mechanized force to bring this about.

Freddie, my interpreter, an efficient, former 32 Battalion platoon sergeant sped on, avoiding the potholes in the tarred road, swerving drunkenly left and right across the surface area and alongside the surface as well. We encountered more and more groups of locals fleeing northward towards Saurimo. As we neared the area of fighting we came across more and more FAA troops who had evacuated their defensive positions. The troops stopped me and provided feedback. At first light UNITA had surrounded their defensive position and fired on it. All their equipment had been destroyed, including a BM-21 multiple rocket launcher and an M-46 artillery piece that had only been received from Luanda the previous week. This equipment had been earmarked for the Cafunfu offensive and General Sukissa had penny packeted it to the outlying areas of Saurimo contrary to the doctrine which dictated that by last light the equipment should be back at the HQ in Saurimo. His plan had been to attack UNITA the next day, but he had been pre-empted and the defeat was costly.

In the meantime, I sent one of my elements to strengthen the defensive positions around a bridge approximately three kilometres outside Saurimo. It was also probable that UNITA intended to destroy all bridges that led westward from Saurimo, in order to cut off the MPLA force and make it difficult for them to advance on Cafunfu. UNITA's offensive operations around Saurimo started increasing in intensity and the locals reported a large UNITA force to the southwest of the town as well. We followed up with a ground force of two platoons supported by the airborne PC-7 but it soon became clear that the information was more than a day old and the UNITA force had already withdrawn from the area to the main route between Saurimo and Cacolo.

Brigadier Pepe de Castro, the FAA commander of the Cafunfu offensive, was now ordered by General Sukissa to move a force to the town of Mona Quimbundu, west of Saurimo, in order to occupy the no-man's land between Saurimo and Cacolo to the southwest. Brigadier Pepe used one of his combat teams and my HQ to test our marrying up success and aggression. His method of occupying the area can best be described as an all-out dash.

This was my first experience of a very unsure, but aggressive, Brigadier Pepe de Castro, who would first eat a handful of cassava roots and then give his troops verbal orders, punctuated by expansive gestures. The mission was simple—charge at the enemy, penetrate their front, turn around and attack the enemy from the rear.

We took off at best speed with eleven BMP-2s and the driver of the leading BMP-2 was none other than Lieutenant-Colonel Mundo Real, our colleague from the EO attack on Soyo (then a captain) who was fearless and whose only inkling of fear had been totally smothered by marijuana. We penetrated the UNITA defensive line at Mona Quimbundu with little effort. UNITA had obviously seen the attacking force and decided that the terrain did not hold any advantage for them, as it was ideal for the deployment of armour. Brigadier Pepe wiped the perspiration from his brow and Lieutenant-Colonel Mundo Real carried a permanent broad smile, indicating that he wished to exploit further. We returned to Saurimo without leaving any forces behind to occupy the ground we had taken.

I returned to this location two weeks later, however. This time it was without an FAA ground force as I conducted a night movement with my combat team to the deployment area eleven kilometres from the town. We carried out a rocket attack on the town whilst a FAA force stood by as the main attacking force on the town itself. The operation was supported by a PC-7 aircraft armed with 68mm rockets.

Unfortunately, the FAA force provided incorrect co-ordinates for its position and the fighting vehicles on the forward line of own troops (FLOT) were peppered with shrapnel from the close air support provided by the PC-7. This incident escalated into a dispute between those who believed that the co-ordinates given for the vehicles were incorrect and those who believed that the air support was too close. We knew that we would resolve this issue quickly when we gathered at the general's house. It would merely cost us the inconvenience of convincing the general that our pilots were experienced professionals who knew how to navigate in the bush.

I must say though that up to this point Laurens Bosch's PC-7 had been hit twice by enemy fire, without any adverse effects, and a wry smile on the part of Laurens himself. This specific incident happened when he was flying behind Pine Pienaar and returning from Cacolo. At the bridge at Mono Quimbundu a sizeable UNITA force was waiting for them and they conducted their normal anti-aircraft drills. In so doing they succeeded in hitting the exhaust of Laurens's aircraft with small arms fire.

After this reactive action at Mono Quimbundu another reaction operation took place, only this time the EO combat team was included. This provided me with the opportunity to test the battle preparedness of my own troops. The operation involved a night movement, partially by means of a 'bundu-bashing' off-road movement technique, and the occupation of a position south of Mono Quimbundu. Our navigation was spot on and I confirmed the result the next morning with a PC-7 flypast.

With a BM-21 multiple rocket launcher in direct support we provided artillery fire from a southerly direction, in order to avoid the risk involved in the delivery of overhead fire. Brigadier Pepe attacked the objective at Mono Quimbundu itself from the east with a combat team with close air support from an EO PC-7. UNITA obviously did not challenge our force, they vacated their positions at Mona Quimbundu, withdrew along the main road and strengthened the existing positions at Cacolo, approximately eighty kilometres southwest of Mono Quimbundu. So far so good. The cooperation between the EO combat team and the FAA forces had been successful and the ground-air liaison was working well. The logistic preparations and the stacking had achieved a level that allowed us to start the offensive against Cafunfu proper.

Taking Cacolo

There were a few logistical requirements that had not been satisfied as yet, including the provision of spare tyres and wheels and certain types of ammunition. As a mechanized ground force we became irritated at having to sit around waiting for things to happen and I became increasingly vexed as I believed that we were giving UNITA more time to dig in and improve the preparation of their defensive positions. I was also keenly aware of the fact that they were grinding us down and exhausting us with their guerrilla actions whilst each day's successful diamond production in Cafunfu was adding to their advantage over the FAA government.

The intent of the Cafunfu offensive was to deny UNITA access to the Cafunfu area and remove their ability to sustain hostilities through the revenue from diamond mining. To achieve this, a two pronged offensive to occupy Cafunfu had been planned along the Luanda–N'Dalatando–Malanje–Cafunfu and the Saurimo–Cacolo–Cafunfu axes respectively.

16 Armoured Brigade, the combined EO and FAA combat group concentrated at Saurimo, was earmarked to undertake the eastern thrust of the offensive and it consisted of a headquarters plus three mechanized infantry battalions (each with a strength equivalent to a SADF company), one of which was composed of EO forces; a FAA special forces platoon on fourteen Chevrolet pickups with mounted 12.7mm heavy machine guns; artillery in the form of two BM-21 MRLs, two D-30 guns; four ZU-23-2 anti-aircraft artillery pieces mounted on DAF vehicles; two mechanized TMM bridging vehicles and a wheeled Caterpillar CAT-933 front-end loader; as well as a diesel tanker and a technical support vehicle. In addition, the force was supported by a poorly equipped FAA medical team and a signals unit with the bare minimum levels of spares and accessories, as well as four Kamaz cargo trucks set aside for the transportation of the Katangese troops we were due to pick up north of Cacolo.

By this time the higher headquarters in Luanda had decided that UNITA had reached such an advanced stage in the preparation of the controlled demolition of the bridge over the Cuilo River at Alto Cuilo that, with an eye to the future after the offensive, the FAA force should at all costs prevent the bridge from being blown by UNITA. This turn of events and decision exerted a profound influence on the planned offensive. The priority now was to conduct a surprise attack on UNITA at Cacolo, to the west of Alto Cuilo, with a strengthened combat team along a route far south of the planned axis of advance from Saurimo, directly to Cacolo. The new route would follow the road southward to Dala and thereafter veer west through Alto Chicapa, before turning northward to Cacolo, a deviation of approximately 400 kilometres. The eventual attack on Cacolo would be supported by FAPA elements as well.

Brigadier Pepe de Castro called me one afternoon late and said, "Russo, you and Colonel Nevis must take the EO combat team, the platoon of commandos in their Chevrolet pickups, as well as the one under-strength FAA combat team; move along the southern route; occupy the bridge over the Cuilo river east of Alto Cuilo; and then occupy Cacolo. The main aim of this operation is to prevent UNITA from destroying the bridge over the Cuilo River."

I completed my planning and issued orders later that afternoon to Jos Grobler, my new second-in-command, as Johan Maree, the previous incumbent, had no intention of picking up another leak (injury) and had left. It was somewhat difficult to get everyone galvanized into action as we had been deployed in a static position protecting the bridge over a tributary of the Luangue River at Mona Quimbundu for some time now. The *braai* (barbeque) grids and the improvised cold boxes did not fit safely and well inside or on the outside of the BMPs and a number of serious threats were required before the priorities changed and the care of the braai equipment was subordinated to the need to get mobile and start the offensive. From this point on there were no more arguments, however, only cooperation, and it was a pleasure to have such a strong group of men under my command.

In preparation for the 'bundu-bash' or off road movement to Dala we formed the combat team up in its correct order of march east of Saurimo and alongside the main road which stretched southward from Saurimo to Dala. My greatest concern was for the lack of spare wheels, and after a mere two kilometres two vehicles had already picked up one puncture apiece. After a serious moan session on the radio back to the EO Tac HQ in Saurimo I was informed that I should not worry and that everything would work out for the better.

Once we had crossed the start point for the movement the troops' morale soared, especially the 'Special' Commandos who created great enthusiasm amongst the rest of the troops, something that to me looked more like a lack of battle discipline than anything else. I comforted myself in the knowledge that we had experienced the commander's same enthusiasm and convincing behaviour before we had left Saurimo when he demonstrated to us how to prepare the BMP-2 for a river or water obstacle crossing at the local water storage dam. This must have been something he had learnt during his two years in Cuba.

My concern that we would soon come to a grinding halt due to punctured tyres was realized within a short space of time when I saw a DAF ration vehicle with only three wheels. The tyre on the fourth wheel had been so damaged that it had slipped off the rim but the driver was nevertheless lucky to be able to keep up with the rest of the column. I immediately adapted my Western value of mobility as this had been a first for me. That same day more Chevrolet pickups experienced problems with spare tyres. The problem was solved by the

FAA commanders by merely pointing to the front with an index finger and stating that that the problem would be solved somewhere in the future. Notwithstanding the punctured wheels we actually didn't do too badly on the first day.

We were moving at an average speed of between six and ten kilometres per hour, which was not at all bad for a mechanized force, and we planned to cover the 150 kilometres to Dala within three days. The FAA commander, Colonel Nevis, and I found we understood each other quite easily until we experienced problems with a BMP-2 that was overheating. I suggested that the BMP should return to Saurimo as the speed of the advance up ahead would be adversely affected by its slow movement. Colonel Nevis refused, saying that he needed the vehicle's firepower. My opinion was that we could always make a plan if we didn't have sufficient firepower—we could manoeuvre or phase an activity for example, but if one is forced to stop in a BMP-2 due to engine problems then one is stranded. Colonel Nevis actually meant that he would utlize the BMP-2 until it came to a standstill and was unserviceable, then he would abandon it. Another lesson I still had to learn—there was no such concept as the recovery or repair of unserviceable vehicles in Colonel Nevis's mind. I convinced him that we should tow the vehicle as far as possible. He wanted one of my BMP-2s to undertake the towing but I refused, and it was at this point that we clashed.

We were into the third day of our advance and we were entering an area controlled by UNITA. The only reason why we had not been stopped or shot at was that the terrain was ideal for tank and mechanized movement and any action on the part of UNITA would have led to casualties on their side. Our first real obstacle on the advance appeared—a rather insignificant river. The successful crossing of this obstacle kept us busy for rather a long time and we realized that this was to be a recurring event as the advance progressed. The wheeled vehicles didn't have the same degree of mobility as the tracked vehicles and we soon saw the proof thereof—every logistic vehicle and other soft-skinned vehicle had eventually lost its bumper due to rough towing practices. Our speed decreased further as the towed BMP-2 required attention and the towing vehicle was overheating.

We reached the outskirts of Dala, expecting some resistance from UNITA, so we moved into battle formation and prepared to make contact with groups of UNITA forces aiming to resist or delay our progress. To our great surprise we found that Dala had been totally deserted once we had occupied the high ground outside it and we could see the column of dust as the UNITA forces pulled out of the town. We took over and overnighted there, happy to learn that the main FAA force would be ready to leave Saurimo within three days. We planned to advance to within effective artillery range of Cacolo before they commenced their movement from Saurimo. We still had a long way to go.

The FAA troops had a habit of setting the bush alight wherever they went. This practice nearly cost us dearly here as the wind changed direction once they had ignited the fire blazing towards our position. The vehicles all had to be withdrawn from our defensive positions and parked in the middle of the road in order to escape the raging bush fire. As fate would have it we couldn't get the ammunition vehicle started. I had visions of the DAF cargo vehicle exploding and fragments shooting into the air. Chris Frazer's BMP-2 was the closest to it and he drove it through the fire, lined the BMP-2 up with the cargo vehicle's nose and shoved the vehicle out of the danger area of the fire. He hadn't even waited around to see whether there was a driver on board the DAF or not—he shoved and asked questions later. In any event the ammunition had been saved. We left the area as the order of march of our vehicles had been badly disrupted by the fire and it was a mess. We banned the burning of any enemy positions from that day on. We were not certain that this would actually be adhered to by the FAA troops as their morale was high and their discipline was sure to be sorely tested.

Hennie Blaauw joined me along the route. He had been involved for some time with the western FAA pincer movement along the Malanje axis. They had T-62 tanks as their main equipment but had encountered very stiff UNITA resistance on the way. They had eventually abandoned the advance somewhere to the west of Malanje as the swollen rivers had become insurmountable obstacles. At the same time that Hennie was being flown in, Nic van der Bergh and General Marx, the FAA commander of the Lunda Sul province, decided to visit us. The helicopters landed, offloaded the persons they were required to offload and without any warning took off and flew to Saurimo. Nic van der Bergh and General Marx were left behind until 'further notice'. Nic was very angry and decided there and then that he would not undertake another staff visit to the front due to the fact that he had been left behind.

I asked Nic where he wanted to travel—on the inside or outside of a BMP-2, the latter with all the implications of less protection against the enemy and vegetation. The two visitors decided to make use of the inside of a BMP-2 as they didn't feel like bleeding. In addition to the oven-like temperatures inside the BMP-2 they gained first-hand experience of the battle culture exhibited by the FAA forces on the ground, with the killing of pigs and the local dogs as well as members of the local population, the razing and burning of settlements and the wild shooting that took place during this orgy of violence. Nic didn't feel at all happy about this way of doing things and pleaded with General Marx to change this *modus operandi*. The EO Tac HQ at Saurimo rerouted the helicopters to our position and in this way saved Nic from having to sleep in the bush with the rest of us on the ground. Once again Nic stated that he would not undertake another staff visit to the front due to the nature of his reception on his arrival.

The speed of our advance was hampered by the BMP-2 that still had to be towed and we were running out of serviceable towing cables as their quality was so poor that they were continually breaking. We decided to leave two BMP-2s and their teams with the unserviceable BMP-2 and in this way substantially improved our chances of reaching Cacolo within a day. The next visitation of bad luck upon us took place shortly thereafter. One of our BMP-2s detonated an anti-tank mine and the force of the explosion bent its driving axle, immobilizing it and we were forced to leave it behind as well. In addition, we received the less than encouraging news that UNITA had picked up the direction of our movement and had detonated a controlled demolition on an important bridge over the Cuilo River on the main axis of advance. This bridge had been identified by all parties to the conflict over the years as key terrain, and UNITA had now decided to destroy it. Obviously their appreciation had indicated to them that this act would halt our movement and advance on Cafunfu.

On reaching Cacolo, Colonel Nevis and I decided that our force should overnight on the outskirts of the town and the next morning we entered it for the first time without encountering any resistance at all. UNITA had withdrawn from one of their best known locations, which they had occupied for a number of years, without firing a single shot. UNITA had always been very considered and calculating in similar actions that they had taken against FAA attacks and would allow the FAA forces to penetrate the target area only to cut them off thereafter. In this instance they miscalculated as they would have had to come up against the EO force, which was deployed as the fire support base for the FAA combat team. We had calculated that the whole town would have been encircled by UNITA-laid minefields and we kept our vehicles on the town's roads as a result.

The remainder of 16 Armoured Brigade had already started to advance westward from Saurimo towards Cacolo by now and the possibility of encountering UNITA-laid landmines along the route was such that they restricted their movement to the use of the existing roads. The two TMM bridging vehicles were included as part of their advancing column as well.

My wife, Gerda, was expecting our third child at any time and Lafras was present when I requested a few days leave in order to be with her during the birth. Hennie and I formalized the handing and taking over ceremony with a toast of good South African brandy right there on the helicopter LZ before I was flown out to Saurimo. He would take over command for the remainder of the advance. I arrived at Saurimo at last light and enjoyed a quick and welcome shower under blackout conditions. The EO Air Wing's Beechcraft B-200 King Air was ready and waiting on the apron for Lafras, Shaun and myself. We took off and flew southward, eventually landing at Lanseria International Airport north of Johannesburg sometime after midnight. Lafras gave me a lift to Johannesburg International Airport and I flew on to Namibia at 0700 that morning. I slowly but surely began to realize that I must still look a mess—covered in the accumulated dust and grime of fourteen days in a mechanized column on and off dust roads in the Angolan bush with no chance of enjoying a proper bath or shower except for a quick wash at Saurimo in the dark. Only when I inspected myself in the mirror at the airport did I actually realize how covered in dust I still was. I used the waiting time in the early hours to make a serious attempt at improving my state of personal hygiene. When I arrived at Windhoek airport later in the day I was still being stared at by people, including Gerda, who tactfully enquired after my state of personal hygiene. I was overjoyed to be reunited with my wife and family—three months is a long time to be away from home and one's loved ones, especially if there is no break in this time. Amoret, our third child—the daughter we had both hoped for—was born within the week and I was filled with joy as Gerda had so wanted a daughter in addition to Rudolph Mauritz and Emile, our two sons. She was bitterly disappointed during the morning of the birth as my mother-in-law and I could just not make it in time to the theatre to witness the birth event. I waited outside and kicked my heels for a whilst until I was allowed to see her, bristling with anger and disappointed that we could not continue the tradition of experiencing the birth together, as had been the case with our two sons. The joy of our newborn daughter soon outshone this disappointment, however. Amoret was hardly a week old before I had to return to Angola, as the quest to take Cafunfu awaited, and the hard reality of this hit me like a pole axe.

Cafunfu—the advance and attack

I returned to Saurimo in the EO King Air and, once on the ground, was transferred by helicopter to Cacolo that same day, as the main FAA force was ready to move from that location the next day. At Cacolo, Brigadier Pepe de Castro and I greeted each other as long lost friends. I told him that I would be acting as the EO advisor and liaison officer from here on and that Hennie would command the EO combat team. At the same time General Marx, who had accompanied the flight to Cacolo, issued his last guidelines for the remainder of the advance before he too returned to Saurimo.

A deception operation was carried out just before the main force was scheduled to start their advance. Xinge, a town approximately 30 kilometres outside Cacolo, on the main road from Cacolo to Cafunfu, was subjected to a probing attack by an FAA combat team to give UNITA the impression that the main force was about to follow the expected axis of advance along the main road to Cambolo (and ultimately Cafunfu). In fact the main force was actually going to continue the advance along a far right axis roughly parallel and approximately 75 kilometres to the north east of the main Xinge–Cambolo–Cafunfu route, and then swing in a westerly direction to converge on Cafunfu from the east for the advance to contact and the final attack. Once the probing attack had been carried out the combat team would then rejoin the main advance on Cafunfu and take up the rear.

From feedback received, and from UNITA radio traffic intercepts, we concluded that UNITA had fallen for the trick. As a result of this they directed their defensive posture along the main route and prepared, and dug, their defensive positions accordingly. By using the far right route we had gained the initiative and, once UNITA had discovered that they had indeed fallen for the deception, they were forced to cover their rear areas very quickly. Of more concern to UNITA was the fact that we were in a position to threaten their rear areas and endanger their logistic dumps.

We moved for five days without any incidents and reached Camaxilo, the location where the RDF team had received a hiding from UNITA and EO had lost four men. As planned, the axis of advance swung here in a westerly direction en route to Cafunfu. We had hardly swung in this direction when we ran face-to-face into UNITA forces. The resistance they put up was light and it was clear that UNITA had pushed a number of young, inexperienced troops out ahead of their forces. We knew that the experienced UNITA veterans would be deployed in and around Cafunfu.

Brigadier Pepe continuously emphasised that the success of the advance depended on the speed with which the force advanced. We weren't doing too badly at all despite his concern. With Hennie, Jos, Hendri and Chris Frazer as part of the advance guard we were actually doing very well. Lieutenant-Colonel Mundo Real actually gave Hennie some stiff competition during the advance—Hennie's combat team would lead the advance, then Mundo Real's combat team would lead, each using a one-up formation. If the resistance stiffened then a two-up formation was followed with the road as the axis of advance and the boundary between each combat team.

It puzzled us that up to this point in the advance we had not experienced any mine incidents. This ended a few kilometres outside Firiquich south of Okanguala, where we detonated a landmine in closed terrain. The unfortunate vehicle was a DAF cargo vehicle on which a 23mm ZU-23-2 anti-aircraft weapon was mounted. What a loss. We stripped the vehicle quickly and continued the advance.

From this point onward we decided to bundu-bash, avoid the roads at all costs and follow a traditional bush-breaking route. As a consequence the soft-skinned vehicles were exposed to harsh terrain for which they were not designed, and we ran the gambit of punctures and more vehicles that had to be abandoned due to breakdowns and their inability to keep up with the advance. Our greatest loss was that we were forced to leave the diesel tanker vehicle behind as it didn't have sufficient rubber left on its rims to gain purchase in order to move forward. The Caterpillar CAT-933 front-end loader that had accompanied us all the way from Saurimo was a godsend and it contributed time and again to the restoration of our forward momentum. It even towed vehicles. But it could only tow so many. We were comforted that our decision to advance through the bush was correct when we could actually see old vehicle mines that had been planted in the road over the years, washed up to the surface by the rain and weather. The road had probably last been used at least three to four years previously and it was clear that it would not be used in the near future either. This was why UNITA had been caught totally unaware by the approach along an easterly route to Cafunfu.

We came across a number of obstacle-like terrain forms but the CAT-933 saved us time and again. We simply built a bridge or built a road until the whole force had crossed the obstacle. The CAT-933 was also the source of its fair share of sport. The driver of the CAT-933 could only drive the vehicle itself and he had no idea how to utilize the bucket at all. Rusty, one of my BMP-2 commanders was an old South African Army Engineering Corps man and he certainly knew how to handle the machine. We quickly employed Rusty in this role, not without frustrations, however.

Brigadier Pepe kept getting personally involved in the road and bridge building activities. This frustrated Rusty to the extent that at a certain point Brigadier Pepe's hand signals became too much for him and he simply stopped the CAT-933, rid himself of his frustration by letting lose a very racist remark, and jumped off the machine. This flabbergasted Brigadier Pepe, as he believed that he was explaining what to do so very clearly. We were obliged to calm Rusty down and plead with him before he came to our road construction rescue once more. Rusty was one of those people who should be told what to do and then left to complete the task on his own, in his own way. He was an action person, not a talk person. He was also inclined to express his feelings by using his fists and he wasn't afraid to receive counterpunches. He was the ideal person for the job.

We knew and could also see that the terrain was closing in as we approached Cafunfu. We also knew that this spelled trouble for the mechanized force. UNITA made contact with us and tried everything in their power to delay or stop us. They ambushed our advance guard, attacked the rear guard of the advance, and carried out flanking attacks on the middle of the force. The killing groups of their ambushes numbered up to three hundred soldiers at a time and the firefights were intense and heavy, but our success lay in the momentum that was maintained by the main force. It was always heartbreaking to see how we had to abandon vehicles—only two of the Chevrolet pickups used by the commandos were still part of the advance. These vehicles would sustain up to as many as three punctures, and the spinning of the rear wheels as the punctured vehicle's tyres slowly disintegrated, would cause it to overheat. As the number of serviceable pickups decreased, so the number of passengers on the BMP-2s increased.

The BMP-2s began to look like bamboo thickets as more and more troops sat on the outside of the vehicles as opposed to the hot inside where one's view is reduced to the small vision blocks and the AK-47 firing ports. The SADF training we had received came into its own here with the conduct of immediate action drills, first to the right for an attack from the right, then to the left for an attack from the left, as well as for attacks from the front and the rear. I knew what to expect and I don't think that Brigadier Pepe was caught unawares either. He told me that he had learnt his lesson from a series of contacts he had had with the SADF when he was still a captain serving in the south of Angola. Why would he not know how UNITA operated then? Brigadier Pepe and I had known each other for a year now and I knew that when the whites of his eyes were prominently visible he was annoyed with me. Brigadier Pepe was pleasantly surprised by the performance of my troops and this in turn created energy amongst the FAA troops. They became all the more daring, to such an extent that they would fire at the enemy, then flee without any control at all, and then ask, as if surprised, where the South Africans were.

The channelling effect of the terrain at Firiquich brought the advance to a standstill as it consisted of a large number of low hills and these features could be very well utilized by UNITA to delay our movement. UNITA did indeed use them to great effect during their delaying actions.

We eventually called a halt at Firiquich, as the vehicles descended into chaos and piled up to such an extent that we obviously had become an easy target for UNITA. As feared, UNITA opened up on us a moment or two later and GRAD-P 122mm rockets and D-30 artillery rounds exploded around us. Things got so bad that I radioed Hennie and asked him to move his combat team to the far right of the axis of advance in order to create space for the main force to spread out more. We saved the situation in this manner. Brigadier Pepe and I decided after a quick map appreciation that the most probable position from where the UNITA fire was coming was an area of high ground approximately four kilometres away from our position. We tasked the BM-21 MRL to launch a salvo of ten rockets at this area and, as always, Neels Brits our artillery commander was there. The main force was deployed in a fishbone formation alongside the road and the BM-21 tasked with the fire mission was behind my vehicle. I hit the ground quickly as the fire mission commenced. The elevation of the rocket trajectory was so low that I felt a hollow feeling in my lower stomach as I took cover. But I recovered quickly. The fire was accurate and the UNITA actions stopped.

That night we were restless indeed. UNITA was well known for their ability to conduct infiltration night attacks. I was, however, comforted by the thought that it was highly unlikely since they would have to conduct a thorough reconnaissance first and there wasn't sufficient time to do this and attack all in the space of one night.

My bottle of whisky that I had received from Major Sam the FAA Logistics Officer at Cacolo had lasted well up to this point. Both Neels Brits and I fully accepted that this brand of European whisky had been blended specifically for the Angolan market, unlike the single malt whisky we would have preferred. Nevertheless it was adequate for the current circumstances and it made the difference between sleeping with one or both eyes closed.

We knew that UNITA had business to conduct with us the next day as they had to stop our advance. Having the advantage and background of a staff qualification in the SADF, I had a good impression of what a formidable effort it takes to swing the direction and main focus of a well-prepared defensive system in another direction. It requires a massive effort to swing the axis of advance that UNITA had appreciated we would follow—the Cacolo–Cuango route—to the far eastern route we were actually following. UNITA were, therefore, required to swing their defence from a general southerly orientation through ninety degrees to an easterly orientation.

Notwithstanding this, Brigadier Pepe and I realized that we were starting to tackle the UNITA veteran soldiers. I issued orders to my men that, as far as tonight was concerned, defensive preparations should take the form of a proper slit trench for each man. This is where an infantryman feels safe and secure. I was exposing my men, especially my ex-Koevoet men, to trench drills. I knew that the Casspir vehicle that Koevoet had used in South West Africa was the ultimate vehicle for their operations and that they had not been very favourably disposed towards the infantry drill of the SADF. We all eventually have to learn the basics though.

We also realized that the next day would be difficult and we would face stiff resistance. UNITA were not an easy enemy to overcome. We contacted the EO Tac HQ at Saurimo and forecast that things would become all the more difficult as we neared Cafunfu. Duncan informed us that he would be tasking the *vlamgatte* or fighter pilots to assist us. I was comforted as I knew that both Pine and Bosch would be able to deliver the required support with their MiG-23s when called upon to do so. Hennie was tasked to indicate the FLOT to the aircraft, when required.

The advance on Cafunfu continued and I briefed Hennie that we expected serious opposition from UNITA up ahead. UNITA would do everything they could to stop us and we would have to support all movement with indirect fire and close air support.

I remembered my experience at Soyo where FAA air support amounted to the far off sound of something which may have been an air-delivered bomb or a rocket exploding in remote areas of the battlefield, far away from where it was actually needed, inside the actual fighting on the ground. Air support from the former SA Air Force pilots was an absolute dream by comparison—always on time and on target. Nevertheless, there were a few exceptions that only contributed towards proving the rule. During the advance from Firiquich we were surprised by the MiG-23s and this raised everyone's morale. Suddenly UNITA's artillery fire was no longer a real threat, and the advance was progressing apace. At a certain stage whilst the MIGs were overhead the advance guard reported that it had observed many defensive positions and they expected heavy resistance from UNITA from this location. Hennie got his troops to debus and advance on foot over a wide area together with Mundo Real's troops. This action was supported by Pine Pienaar and Bosch in MiG-23s and our jubilation at the great air support was quickly deflated by a FLOT that had been incorrectly marked or a short drop. Hennie and Jos Grobler screamed at me over the radio that the bombs were falling behind them and they advised that we should terminate the air support mission immediately. The error was in all probability due to the limited visibility in the poor light and the thick bush where the FLOT had been marked.

Hennie continued with the advance until the closed terrain once again forced him to debus with his troops. He sent an element of his force forward on foot to clear any resistance and to gather any appropriate battle information.

This combat patrol did indeed come across a UNITA force in well-prepared defensive positions alongside the roadway and a firefight ensued during which Nick Hayes was killed. The route was cleared but we had lost Nick, a good guy who had been a good soldier; a young man who kept to himself, except when there was work to be done, and then he would go into action with notorious bravado. His body was evacuated that same day to Saurimo by an EO Mi-17 helicopter.

This was our first EO fatality along this route, but the memory of the Camaxilo incident was still fresh in our minds and it was difficult to get over this fatality as well. On the contrary, it is always hard to get over losses in battle. In my mind I also knew that once we had signed the contract with EO we had to accept everything, especially the danger and possibility of injury and death. We couldn't afford the luxury of becoming emotional about the loss of our fellow soldier. Our thoughts remained with him for some time, however.

The day had to continue. EO had the sharp end to contend with, but there was such a variety of military professions and skills in this small group of men, and the close relationship between the men, as volunteers, had already been forged to the extent that they were able to get through the negative effects of this tragic loss. This loss was my personal casualty as well. I am not one to dwell on casualties but this was my first casualty as the commander of the EO force in battle, and it made me think all the more about how to continue the offensive with this mechanized force.

UNITA did not disappoint us either, and the next morning our first cup of coffee was interrupted by a fire mission carried out by a single D-30 gun. I didn't know it at the time but we would hear a lot more from this weapon in due course. The column's movement closer to the gun position forced them to cease fire and withdraw as they were obviously not prepared to lose the weapon at this stage. They were also firing at our column with a B-11 recoilless gun during their withdrawal. The mutual support between the D-30 and the B-11 allowed them to maintain effective fire on our column. What made things difficult for them was the fact that the high trees limited their choice of deployment areas and the utilization of the weapons. There wasn't sufficient time to prepare proper gun and recoilless gun firing positions and the crest clearance for the D-30 trajectory remained a critical issue.

Roelf van Heerden, Saurimo, Angola, 1994.

Stand-to in our trenches, awaiting an expected UNITA attack on the EO mechanized force deployed in a forward position west of Saurimo.

United Nations leased Ilyushin IL-76 aircraft framed by a FAPA MiG-23 on the Saurimo apron during the logistic build-up to the advance on Cafunfu.

Posing alongside Pine's MiG-23 while it was under repair at Saurimo. The EO MiG pilots provided excellent support during the offensives against Cafunfu and Cacolo.

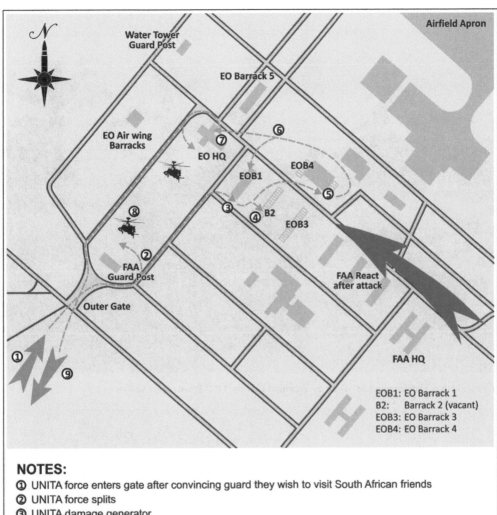

Battle map depicting the UNITA attack on Saurimo.

NOTES:
① UNITA force enters gate after convincing guard they wish to visit South African friends
② UNITA force splits
③ UNITA damage generator
④ UNITA attack vacant Barrack 2 (B2)
⑤ UNITA then attack EO Barrack 4 (EOB4) and meet stiff resistance
⑥ UNITA force spilts to attack EO HQ and EO Barrack 1 (EOB1). Blackie killed at EOB1
⑦ UNITA attack EO HQ from the rear
⑧ EO MI-17 helicopter burns out
⑨ UNITA escape route

Not a good day. The destroyed Mi-17 on the morning after the UNITA attack on Saurimo.

Aftermath of the UNITA attack on Saurimo. One destroyed Mi-17 in the background and one Mo-17 full of chalk-ringed bullet holes.

Leisure time utilization at Saurimo with an Mi-17 helicopter under maintenance in the background.

Senior commanders gathered together a few days before the offensive against Cafunfu commenced. From left: Duncan Rykaart, General Sukissa, garrison commander at Saurimo, Brigadier Pepe, myself.

The provincial commander of the Lunda Sul Province, General Marx, with the dark glasses and green uniform, chats to 16 Brigade men during the advance on Cafunfu. Brigadier Pepe de Castro is the tall man with spectacles opposite him.

A BM-21 artillery strike on UNITA positions during the advance on Cafunfu.

Lifting a TMM mobile bridge not far from Cafunfu. The bridges certainly contributed to our mobility.

EO troops stretching their legs during the advance on Cafunfu.

The combined EO/FAA force was required to construct many improvised bridges on the way to Cafunfu. Alfonso, an EO interpreter and a former 32 Battalion soldier, is in the foreground.

An EO MI-17 helicopter resupplying us during the advance.

They weren't doing all that badly. They succeeded in harassing us to some extent. On the other hand, we weren't all that eager to run blindly into artillery fire.

We received information from our radio intercepts of UNITA radio traffic that UNITA was about to use poisonous gas against us. I knew the capability of UNITA to get hold of such munitions and this information spread amongst the troops like wildfire. A little later we were on the receiving end of UNITA indirect fire once again and requested the support of the MiG-23s. Adding to our indirect fire problem was the fact that the thick bush and high trees made crest clearance problematic for our indirect weapons as well. With the MIGSs we had air superiority, after all. Bosch was overhead quickly and had a reasonable idea of the general bearing along which the enemy artillery position was located. His close air support was spot on and the enemy fire was silenced for good. As he pulled up after delivering his munitions Bosch tracked their delivery, saw them explode on the target and witnessed the flames and smoke erupt at the gun position.

I issued radio orders for the resumption of the advance but the momentum was very slow due to the closed terrain and the troops were forced to debus and advance on foot at regular intervals. All of a sudden the command radio net became very active and it was clear that there was chaos at the front. One of the BMP-2 drivers had fainted and it was deduced that this may have been the result of poison gas. In addition, a number of the troops on the ground reported that they had smelled gas and this caused panic to spread. Everything settled down once the driver had come round, complaining that exhaust fumes had leaked into the driver's station of his vehicle. It was at this moment that Bosch's air target had been located on the ground and it became clear that the artillery ammunition and charges that had been ignited by Bosch's MiG was the root cause of the gaseous smell in the air. Two UNITA vehicles had also been rendered unserviceable during the attack. The delaying actions undertaken by UNITA now had to rely more on ambushes and mortar fire. I began to understand the concern for a gas attack better as the main force passed the remnants of the enemy artillery position. The smell of explosives and burning munitions was pervasive and could easily have led to this confusion.

The movement speed with which Brigadier Pepe was so fixated was not always to our advantage as UNITA knew that they could pin us down at night. One afternoon we advanced until late and established the night laager area just as the sun was setting. All my training dictated that this area should be reconnoitred before the time and that the setting up of the laager should be done tactically. I witnessed all the training I had given my EO men at Cabo Ledo, as well as the training of the FAA leader group, being jettisoned because Brigadier Pepe was in a hurry, and his timing at last light was not well judged. The result was a long list of weaknesses and vulnerabilities that were exposed; the laager areas were too small, fronts weren't properly covered by fire and individual troops were too concentrated together, especially outside the laager area. My concerns increased as the sun set and all the vehicles rushed to move into a deployment area before last light.

I raised my concerns with Brigadier Pepe, knowing full well that I had no control over the FAA troops; on the contrary, all the EO troops in the advance, including myself, were actually under his command. This made the situation untenable and it erupted that very night. I had been taught, and I had also trained the EO troops to carry out stand-to drills at last light and at first light. These drills include a set of tried and tested activities that are virtually universally applied in armed forces throughout the world. However, the further we moved, the more the stand-to drills were watered down, all in the name of speed and momentum.

To add to my concerns, one of my BMP-2 vehicle commanders mentioned that he wasn't at all able to sleep restfully due to the lack of discipline during stand-to drills, and he had been forced to sleep with one eye open when he had previously operated with a FAA combat group on the route between Luanda and Malanje. EO had been employed chiefly in an advisory role in this instance and Hennie Blaauw and Mike Herbst were in command of the EO troops attached to the combat group. As they progressed the combat group paid less and less attention to tactical movement and UNITA caught them in their vehicle laager one night and gave them a severe hiding. Chaos ensued as UNITA infiltrated the laager area and, as of old, started the battle from within the laager. UNITA caused a lot of damage and a number of the FAA tanks were destroyed whilst they were still on the tank transporter vehicles.

I could see that we were about to experience a similar set of circumstances. During the early evening I heard the distinct cough of 60mm mortars as they left their tubes. The bombs landed inside the laager and a number of my EO men were wounded. What happened during the next thirty minutes brought a wry smile to my face. I actually couldn't do anything to change the situation from my position in the middle of the laager but I watched as panicking FAA troops let loose with heavy, undisciplined fire aimed at the outskirts of the laager, to ward off any UNITA attack. Due to the less than optimal tactical disposition and haste to establish the laager we had become vulnerable to fire directed from the outside of the laager into the circle, as well as uncontrolled defensive fire that was being delivered from within the laager. A 14.5mm anti-aircraft weapon suddenly commenced firing from within the laager, recklessly directing its fire into the air, falling branches raining down on the surrounding troops as the outgoing rounds connected with the surrounding trees—no crest clearance and no clear arcs of fire—a basic requirement.

After an initial shocked moment of silence, Brigadier Pepe reduced the chaos and panic to a semblance of control through the use of his thundering voice. Hennie then reported that the EO force had neutralized the UNITA mortar firing position. EO medics then stabilized the wounded men who had picked up mortar shrapnel during the bombardments—one man unfortunately lost a testicle—and the rest of the night passed without incident. A number of FAA troops did, however, report that they had heard UNITA troops digging and preparing positions, possibly 82mm mortar base plate positions, for a first light attack or stand-off bombardment. The terrain was not suited to an attack on foot, such as those conducted by UNITA along the axis of advance or from behind, as was the case during the previous evening.

Even before my full bladder had forced me to leave my sleeping bag and attend to the simple pleasures of nature, the tearing sound of a UNITA 23mm anti-aircraft gun, employed in the ground role, made me sit bolt upright, and immediately thereafter duck for cover.

Although the UNITA fire was inaccurate it definitely had the desired effect on the FAA troops. Brigadier Pepe caused even more self-inflicted havoc by marshalling a platoon of BMP-2s onto the road in order to remove the UNITA resistance. Quick radio orders were given to the effect that the only way we were going to get out of this mess was to continue with the advance. I tried very hard to recall my days in the South African Defence Force's 82 Mechanized Brigade during Operations Modular, Hooper and Packer. I vaguely remembered that the SADF combat groups reported that the enemy (FAA in those days) had used the hasty withdrawal method to evacuate their positions during SADF attacks. I was now witnessing what this actually entailed and I began to form a clear picture of how it happened. There was, therefore, some method in this madness.

I made contact with Hennie who was deployed at the 6 o'clock position in the laager. They would be the last to leave the laager area and they remained under enemy fire to the end. Their departure was delayed further after the last BMP-2 of the previous combat team detonated a vehicle mine as it was leaving the laager. The vehicle was gutted and burnt out on the spot, still with some of the troops caught inside it. The absolute necessity to put some distance between us and this laager area became paramount now. Brigadier Pepe had by now managed to get his own BMP-2 going and inserted the FAA combat team as the advance guard. Some of my troops had lost their tempers at this chaos and spoke to me in animated tones about it. I also had information that one of EO's BMP-2s had serious problems with piston rings that had given in or oil pipes that had burst. Black engine oil was being pushed out of the exhaust which, on the BMP-2, is situated very close to the crew commander and the gunner. I had the opportunity to see these two a number of times later in the advance and they were pitch black from the oil fumes, with wide white eyes and white teeth when they spoke. The language that the two used was colourful, well-embellished with the required adjectives, and rounded off with a number of internationally recognized hand signals. I accepted that in the heat of battle these exchanges would in all probability be the actual means of communication. There was little time for mincing words or standing with one's hands in one's pockets. I put it all down to the speed of the advance that had to be maintained, that the combat group could not stop for one vehicle, that there was a technical team moving at the rear to resolve such problems and that these differences could be easily sorted out over a couple of beers. Brigadier Pepe received the news of the BMP-2 that had burnt out and he indicated that the advance must continue. Big-hearted man that he was; he had no time now for the peripheral details in life.

We were about two days from Cafunfu now and Brigadier Pepe didn't want to waste any time. Only one more night under the BMPs and then we would be able to settle into thoroughly prepared defensive positions. The terrain was less broken here, with fewer hills and more open areas, and each side could derive some advantage from the topography. UNITA had only one more night to carry out penetration attacks before such tactics would become all the more difficult.

The next night passed uneventfully and I was up early, concerned and thinking about the approach route along which we should take Cafunfu. We had very little information and we had no idea of UNITA strengths at Cafunfu, the direction of their defence, minefield locations, outposts or escape routes. These issues had woken me early and I had a feeling that at Cafunfu we could expect large numbers of casualties, something we had managed to avoid during the advance so far. Brigadier Pepe was not talking to me and I didn't believe that he actually had a plan as to how he was going to take Cafunfu. I talked to Hennie and the men and we agreed that we would have to take things as they came and be more accommodating towards the way FAA approached things.

The EO combat team was, once again, deployed as the advance guard at this point. Their location was not far from mine but just a little too far to walk over for a chat. During the advance I had to repeatedly remind all components of the force to keep to time schedules. I knew from my experience at 82 Mech Bde that the movement and integration of forces to achieve the correct order of march was usually a headache for the commander during the start of any operation. If the schedules for the order of march are not followed then the whole operation goes pear shaped from then on. Hennie and I had already discussed this and he reminded me once again that the ex-Koevoet members of the EO combat team did not think and see things in the same way as a soldier with conventional warfare training and experience. They also insisted that they should still think according to the 'Koevoet way'. The group-think approach on their part had to be accommodated and it actually strengthened us as we had to make provision for temperamental differences even in battle.

I could feel the anger at Hennie surfacing at the back of my throat, but I controlled it and it subsided somewhat as the morning quiet was disturbed, as previously, by the sight and sound of incoming red and green tracer fire. A few RPG-7 projectiles flew low overhead as well and I realized that this was in all probability a UNITA first light attack on our position. A quick estimate of the focus of the attack on our laager indicated that it was in the vicinity of the EO forces. I knew that by this time in the morning nobody would still be asleep on the top of their BMP-2s. I also knew that there would be a rush to get out of their sleeping bags and ensure that the main weapon of the BMP-2 was ready for action. I also knew that the fish bone drill—where vehicles stopped alternatively on the left and right of the axis of advance and deployed with their main armament aimed towards the outside and ready to come into action immediately—was always applied by sub-units within a laager. So, if the crew don't relish being exposed to enemy fire then the crew commander and the gunner would slip inside the vehicle through the rear door, carry out a little panel beating of the 'stuff' inside the vehicle until they managed to get into position in the command turret and gunner's station. Some of the men had exceeded my prediction and before I could scream a warning at them a number of 30mm weapons started firing. I felt good because as soon as our counterfire became effective UNITA lifted their fire.

This first light attack really achieved little for UNITA and, with no losses on our side, Brigadier Pepe indicated that I should lead so that the force could advance. I moved to the EO BMP-2s. There Hennie related his frightening experience during the first light attack. His regular morning constitutional had found him a few metres from the BMP-2s on the outside of the laager so that he could conduct his ablutions in peace. The natural world of bushes and trees around him suddenly underwent a metamorphosis and took on the shape of human forms. His mad scramble on all fours back towards the laager was accompanied by the rounds fired from the weapon of a very startled UNITA soldier. Neither of the two men's actions had been planned but they certainly saved EO from conceding a large number of casualties. Hennie was clearly very 'relieved' and couldn't stop talking about it.

We were on the move again shortly thereafter. The movement of the attacking force had changed to a slow, careful pace. It was very evident that UNITA was in the throes of a considered, all-out effort to arrest the movement of the combat group. It also became very clear that their presumption had been confirmed; our movement along this approach was not part of a deception plan, but the axis along which the main FAA attack was proceeding. UNITA could perhaps expect a probing attack along the other possible attack route. We could also observe that UNITA's delaying forces on the advance had become all the more skilled and we deduced that the real veteran fighters were located here now. Ever since we had passed Camaxilo it had become all the more evident that we were no longer dealing with inexperienced or young UNITA forces.

I believe that UNITA had come to the conclusion that FAA were not going to be effectively stopped, since the FAA forces had hauled out all the stops and they had the support of South African mercenaries. This thought pattern on the part of UNITA made EO and FAA very wary around Cafunfu, as we had a very good idea of UNITA's capabilities. In any event the adrenaline began to pump through my system and I experienced, once again, the slightest shiver through the veins and stomach from the excitement.

As is the case with any attack into the rear areas of an enemy we expected a few surprises and we were not disappointed. It didn't take long before we heard surprised exclamations and excited chatter from the leading troops up ahead.

Hennie reported back that the area they were covering looked to him like a logistic area. Many minor roads and grass huts were to be seen throughout. The light resistance was cleared relatively quickly, the area was investigated and it was concluded that it really was a logistic centre. Soon the troops reported that they had found large stocks—estimated at five tons—of tinned meat and tinned fish and we replenished our immediate ration requirements but left the Brazilian bully beef as the expiry date looked suspicious. The men laid into the tinned sardines with gusto and this variation in our rations was most welcome. After all the Portuguese ration packs we had used to date contained only one tin of meat—anathema to any South African.

Just before we left the area Hennie reported over the radio that he had discovered a large fuel dump. On closer inspection I could see the drums, all painted black and packed under branches. We estimated that there were eight hundred drums in the area. I asked Brigadier Pepe what should be done about this find at this specific point, as the momentum of the advance was more important than replenishing our reserves. I was concerned that we would have to destroy the fuel dump only to sit immobilized as a combat group without fuel within a week. I also knew that we were moving into UNITA's heartland and once we were inside Cafunfu, UNITA would try to cut us off and then our logistic needs would have to be replenished by air.

Brigadier Pepe didn't take long to decide that our diesel tanker still had sufficient reserves and that an unnecessary replenishment would only weigh it down and limit its capacity to keep up with the force. He also believed that we had sufficient fuel with which to take Cafunfu. The fuel vehicle had been built to run on proper compacted surfaces and the CAT-933 had been forced to support it all the way to Cafunfu in any event. It was unnecessary to say that I wasn't too surprised to see the column of thick black smoke billowing into the air behind us as we left the area. UNITA had to be denied access to the resource. This amazing sight also had its disadvantage as it allowed UNITA to gauge where we were located in their rear areas.

The effort involved in flying in one hundred and sixty thousand litres of diesel from Kinshasa to Cafunfu must have been substantial, followed then by the movement by normal cargo tipper vehicles into this rear logistic area. UNITA had indeed been dealt a telling blow as it must have taken many months to achieve this level of reserves.

EO was now leading the advance to contact and the front elements had reached the outskirts of Cafunfu. Hennie and I decided that the lack of reliable information on the enemy was such that we would advance systematically, step by step. There was sufficient light left in the day for us to be able to gauge the tactical situation on the outskirts of Cafunfu accurately if we were not able to take the town of Cafunfu itself that particular day. Brigadier Pepe and I had already decided where the combat teams would deploy once we had taken Cafunfu. He had also confided in me the previous evening and explained in great detail why he had been appointed in his current capacity, and that he definitely had a point to prove, particularly after the price FAA had been forced to pay at Soyo.

The opinions he had and his bravado to date became all the more comprehensible as a result. I must emphasize that FAA was in command of the operation and there was a fine distinction to be made between the circumstances when EO were in support and when they would initiate and take the lead.

Brigadier Pepe had been deployed at Cafunfu on a previous occasion together with General Mackenzie—previously a member of UNITA and a great friend of South African forces and now of the EO troops—and General Marx. The chief of the FAA forces, General de Matos had reached an understanding with all his commanders that in the event that a FAA strong point or position was overrun and occupied by UNITA, that FAA commander would regroup and, once the logistics allowed for it, attack UNITA and re-occupy the position. So, this attack was Brigadier Pepe's dream and possibly his ultimatum. Usually the successful re-occupation of a position such as Cafunfu would be linked to a promotion for the FAA commander as well. The pressure was certainly on Brigadier Pepe to deliver.

Brigadier Pepe now left the attack on Cafunfu itself to EO to handle. He instructed Neels Brits, the EO artilleryman at his headquarters, to bring the guns into action in preparation for the attack and we confirmed that the EO Air Wing would react on our command from Saurimo.

We approached the high ground to the east of Cafunfu very carefully and entered hull-down positions to observe over the front. Cafunfu looked deserted and quiet, but we were not deceived by this apparent state of affairs. After all UNITA would all be in their defensive positions, waiting for us. They would rely heavily on the minefields surrounding the town and hope that we ran into at least one of them, after which they would surely bring artillery fire to bear in the hope of pinning us down. We didn't have too many options on our side. The terrain had a number of lateral folds which we could use to our advantage for cover and the tactical movement of the troops on the ground. The appreciated location of the UNITA minefields channelled our mechanized force's final approach to the town and forced the axis of attack to follow only one route. Brigadier Pepe shouted to us over the air that we should get moving and not waste time. Hennie then gave his troops the command to start the attack. We had decided before that we would only use indirect or overhead fire once we had made contact and closed with UNITA forces.

Jos Grobler and his platoon moved in and reported that they couldn't see any enemy movement or active defensive positions. We quickly realized that UNITA was either in the throes of enticing us into a massive ambush or they had decided to implement the alternative, namely to withdraw from the town and consolidate their position. We soon realized that the latter was the course of action that they had selected and carried out—not a bad option on the part of UNITA at all.

Cafunfu was a ghost town as we entered it. There was not a single soul on the streets—not even a stray dog. Our EO combat team swept through the town en route to their exploitation boundary. By this time Mundo Real had joined the attacking force on its right flank to save time and clear the town before dark. The force progressed well and it was soon established that there were no UNITA forces within the bounds of the town.

During last light I heard conversations over the command net reporting the presence of two shipping containers on the outskirts of the town alongside a small retail outlet. Hennie obtained permission to open the containers, by firing at them. I immediately realized that up to this point not a single shot had been fired during the taking of the town, and that it would be totally unnecessary to start firing shots at this point. My instruction fell on deaf ears and I heard the first shots being fired, followed by a deathly silence. I learnt later why.

By last light Hennie and his combat team had taken up positions to the south of the town, alongside the dirt landing strip. Mundo Real was instructed to also take up a position south of the town adjacent to Hennie's position. I, together with the combat group headquarters would take up a position on the northern side of the town with the third combat team, the remainder of the echelon vehicles and the vehicles towing the anti-aircraft element.

Just as darkness fell Mundo Real reported the presence of a lone BMP-2 within the confines of the town itself. It appeared that the vehicle had no occupants or guards in the immediate vicinity. Hearing this Brigadier Pepe called me immediately and asked me why I had allowed this to happen. My immediate reaction was that I didn't believe that my troops would summarily leave a BMP-2 unattended, as had been reported—not my troops. I immediately tried to contact Hennie but received no response over the radio.

At that point Laurens Bosch was overhead in a MiG-23 busy clearing small pockets of resistance on the outskirts of Cafunfu with the aid of the aircraft's 23mm guns. I had made contact with him and asked him if he had any contact with Hennie. After assisting me to re-established contact with Hennie, Laurens left the area for Saurimo and Hennie and I were able to pursue the matter of the deserted BMP-2 further. Hennie informed me that the deserted vehicle was indeed his vehicle and I was forced to humbly report this to an irate Brigadier Pepe, who immediately demanded to know all the relevant details regarding the incident.

My efforts to make contact with Hennie again were unsuccessful and I was forced to drive over to the EO position. By this time it was after dark and I had no alternate choice but to take the risk of moving in the darkness as Brigadier Pepe had demanded an answer. I passed the deserted BMP-2 and followed the tracks of the other BMP-2s in the darkness. I reached the landing strip and came to an area where the tracks of a number of BMP-2s had turned in circles on the landing strip. I called Hennie on the radio but there was no response. I began to realize that my current location on the landing strip was the closest FAA/EO position to UNITA and this concerned me somewhat. The fact that I had no communication with Hennie had made me furious. I also had misgivings about the BMP-2 I was in—over the last seven days it had continuously required a tow or a push to start due to an engine defect. I was, therefore, unable to turn off the engine and listen to see if I could perhaps hear them. During our last communication, whilst I was still in the brigade HQ, Hennie had informed me that he was located on the western end of the runway, and to the north of the runway itself.

Unsuccessful and dejected, I decided to turn and make my way back to the brigade HQ. At this very point the BMP-2 'decided' to cut out and we were marooned. There we were, my interpreter, my driver, an FAA major and me, all in the open on the landing strip. For all I know we could be in the arc of fire of my own men.

We spent the rest of the night on the BMP-2, not daring to debus for fear of the possibility of encountering mines. Our only comfort for the night was a bottle of Johnnie Walker Black Label whisky, still in its container, that we had picked up intact on the landing strip ten minutes previously. We thought at first that it was a booby trap but after careful consideration from the top of our BMP-2 we realized that the item had clearly fallen off a vehicle not too long ago. My interpreter, an energetic ex-32 Battalion sergeant daintily slipped off the BMP-2 and grabbed the find. To be realistic, passing the night in such an exposed position was not at all pleasant, despite the comfort provided to us by Mr Walker. The night dragged on and on and we all stood guard simultaneously.

Early the next morning when it was light enough, my interpreter and I decided to risk a walk along the landing strip. We had appreciated that UNITA would in all probability mine the landing strip but we were incorrect and we reached the shoulders of the landing strip in one piece. Now we could search for Hennie and the rest of the combat group on foot.

All of a sudden I saw some of the Katangese troops—who had joined the FAA offensive close to Xinge—who had been deployed on the laager's flank. I was hailed and beckoned to join them. I perceived that a high-spirited, light-hearted atmosphere prevailed amongst them. On closer inspection I also came across Hennie and I saw that the members of the EO combat team had built themselves defensive sangars by piling cartons of beer on top of each other. All of a sudden the happenings of the last 18 hours quickly fell into place and the sealed container, the deserted BMP-2, the bottle of whisky on the landing strip and the radio silence all began to make sense.

The atmosphere between Hennie and I had to be cleared as a priority now—meaning the lack of communication and the indiscipline resulting from the overuse of alcohol long before any celebrations were warranted. I was offered a beer, congratulated on the successful effort to date and duly informed of the details of the find. The single shot fired the previous evening from a BMP-2's main armament through the container had resulted in a jet of beer pouring out of the bullet hole, much to the amazement and amusement of all. The result was predictable and the looters tried by all means, including radio silence, to keep the secret until further notice. All work and no play makes Jack a dull boy. Hennie and I parted ways there and then, still with a feeling of animosity between us.

The whole incident resulted in Brigadier Pepe claiming the BMP-2 as his personal vehicle, resulting in one vehicle less for the EO combat team. The vehicle's mechanical fault was sorted out quickly, but EO had lost a vehicle. The confiscation of the BMP-2 was indicative of something that would rear its ugly head a number of times and it was at such times that the questions and doubts were raised in my mind as to how far one really should trust one's former enemy. Initially UNITA had been my ally and I had worked regularly with them during my younger days in the SADF. Now the situation was suddenly different, and UNITA was literally in my firing line. I realized this but it was difficult to remain cool-headed when the confiscation incident was still simmering.

Over the next few days we made good progress in occupying the key areas around Cafunfu and the defended locality became well established. Despite this, UNITA had already launched a probing attack on the southern defensive positions around Villa Cafunfu, approximately three kilometres from the town itself.

EO had an internal agreement that, after approximately every three months of service, the members in the field would take a break and enjoy a period of leave. It was time for a break now. The arrangement was that during the leave period half the EO force would be on leave whilst the remainder would remain on duty and assist with the development and completion of the defended locality to the south of Cafunfu, a direction from which it was most likely that any UNITA attack would emanate. I must have had the wrong end of the stick. Duncan discussed the matter with Hennie and, without my knowledge, it was decided that everyone should take a break, excluding myself and eleven other EO members who had recently been on leave. When I heard about this I mentioned to Duncan that Brigadier Pepe would not take very kindly to the arrangement, whereby one third of his force at Cafunfu would suddenly disappear on leave. Notwithstanding this, Duncan asked me to convey this piece of information to Brigadier Pepe. I made it clear to Duncan once again that this would not go down well with him. Brigadier Pepe was indeed very unhappy with this arrangement and immediately contacted General de Matos who contacted EO and all the men were promptly prohibited from leaving the area.

Over the days that we waited at Cafunfu for the leave crisis to resolve itself UNITA did indeed reorganize themselves. It was clear that their immediate objective would be to break the FAA defensive cohesion and cut us off logistically from the other FAA forces. The only route that could be used to support our force was the route that we had utilized during the advance on Cafunfu. We conducted a platoon-size reconnaissance patrol, an activity which brought back information to the extent that Cafunfu had been surrounded by UNITA. In addition, UNITA could and would bring relatively effective D-30 artillery fire to bear on us on a daily basis from gun positions to the west of the Cuango River, which we could not cross with a large force.

We were also fired upon by B-10 and B-11 recoilless rifles from the south. To date these bombardments didn't constitute any real problem as we were properly dug in and entrenched, with overhead protection which we had commandeered from the town itself. The only problem was that all the logistic replenishment had to be undertaken by helicopter and effective artillery fire could terminate this.

Initially we had a helicopter LZ located within the 16 Armoured Brigade headquarters area. Brigadier Pepe very quickly put a stop to this practice as we became an artillery target every time a helicopter came in to land. I had to identify a number of alternate LZs and send their co-ordinates through to the EO Tac HQ at Saurimo. The destination LZ of all subsequent visits by helicopter from Saurimo was provided by us in code, and transmitted at the last possible moment before the helicopter landed.

The time for the EO members to take their leave eventually arrived. That morning Carl Alberts landed in his Mi-17 at the edge of the brigade headquarters position. I went to meet the helicopter and stood chatting with Alberts through his window. All of a sudden D-30 shells began exploding about 30 metres from the helicopter. We decided to say our immediate farewell quickly before the helicopter was hit. There would be time for idle chatter on another occasion.

The tragic loss of Laurens Bosch

With the majority of the EO members on leave, my circle of friends had shrunk and it would be up to the eleven EO troops and I to support FAA at Cafunfu as far as we could. Over the next few days the harassing fire from UNITA increased in tempo and accuracy to the extent that they became a regular nuisance.

We changed our helicopter resupply techniques at Saurimo to the extent that every time a helicopter flew to Cafunfu it was to be preceded by a Pilatus PC-7 which would try and locate the D-30 gun that was harassing us. Fortunately for us we could hear the sound of the gun firing approximately two to three seconds before the shell exploded—enough time to scramble to the closest trench or bomb shelter. In any event we had to get rid of this nuisance to make life a little easier for the helicopters at least. Over the next few days matters progressed very well, the D-30 couldn't fire at us due to the prowling PC-7s, and the pressure on the helicopter pilots whilst they were on the ground was reduced substantially.

We were still subjected to UNITA bombardments, however, and since they were no longer able to fire at the helicopters whilst they were replenishing us, they decided to bombard our ground positions once the helicopters and the PC-7 had left the area.

On one specific helicopter replenishment day the weather was very misty in the Cuango River valley to the west of Cafunfu and visibility was very poor, particularly for Laurens Bosch, the PC-7 pilot and his passenger on this particular flight, an EO administrative member by the name of Daniel Scheurkogel, based at Saurimo. Laurens apologised for not being able to locate the UNITA D-30 at all, and asked for clearance to circle in the vicinity for an additional five minutes, after which he would leave with the Mi-17 helicopter for Saurimo. I thanked him and Laurens continued his task. Once the two Mi-17 helicopters had unloaded their cargo the first empty helicopter took off, bound for Saurimo. With pilots Carl Alberts and Arthur Walker still on the ground in the second helicopter we suddenly received a radio message from Laurens that his PC-7 had been hit. The source of the fire was not known to him. He stated that his cockpit was full of smoke and breathing and visibility was becoming a problem for him and his passenger. Carl and Arthur pleaded with Laurens to remain calm and together they gave him quick directions on how to carry out an emergency landing at Cafunfu. Laurens replied that he would not be able to make it back to Cafunfu and that he would have to land as soon as possible. Carl and Arthur offered to extract Laurens and Scheurkogel wherever Laurens landed and they took off immediately to be as close to him as possible whilst he undertook the emergency landing.

By now Laurens had identified his emergency landing strip, a disused road approximately 12 kilometres north of Cafunfu. Suddenly Laurens's voice could no longer be heard over the radio net. I could still communicate with Carl, who by now was searching for Laurens, and reported to him that the whole area where Laurens had identified his emergency landing strip was teeming with UNITA troops.

According to Carl the PC-7 had made a perfect emergency landing and Carl was on his way to land next to the wreckage. He reported that he could see Laurens and Scheurkogel where they stood next to the road under a tree with their helmets in their hands. By this time Carl and Arthur had seen that a very large number of UNITA troops in the vicinity had realized that the PC-7 had been downed and it was clear from their movements that they wanted to cash in on this windfall.

The situation was critical and, in order to exit as safely and as quickly as possible from the extraction, Carl swung his helicopter through one hundred and eighty degrees and landed. As soon as his wheels touched the ground he shouted for Laurens and Scheurkogel to board the helicopter as he could already see UNITA troops storming towards him in the road, firing as they ran. The fire was so intense that I could hear it in the background as Carl talked to me over the radio. The Mi-17 flight engineer, an Angolan, refused to move to the rear of the helicopter to help Laurens and Scheurkogel aboard. Carl asked him whether the two were on board but there was no sign of them.

By this time the helicopter crew were in danger of losing their lives if they remained on the ground any longer and they took off. During the episode the helicopter's tail rotor had sustained damage to such an extent that a massive vibration could be felt throughout the airframe. Once they were airborne Carl screamed to me over the radio that his helicopter had developed mechanical problems and that Laurens and Scheurkogel were not on board. He recommended that I should enter the area with a ground force to locate and rescue Laurens and Scheurkogel. He stressed once again that the area was teeming with UNITA troops.

Carl also mentioned that his helicopter would not make it to Cafunfu and that he would land it on the dirt road on the outskirts of the town as any further flying would damage the gearbox. An anxious Carl contacted me a little whilst later and confirmed that he had landed the helicopter within the FAA defended area on the main road to Luremo and that he was leaving the aircraft in the care of the FAA troops deployed in the immediate vicinity. Hereafter Carl and Arthur were picked up by the other Mi-17 flown by Juba's team and they returned to Saurimo. Sadness and a sense of helplessness must have overcome them as they left the crash site. Taking into consideration that Arthur Walker had received two Honoris Crux decorations for bravery whilst in the SADF and Carl Alberts was also the recipient of an Honoris Crux decoration, it was highly unlikely that they would ever have left a fellow pilot in distress. I could plainly hear the strain and distress in their voices over the radio as they requested my immediate assistance to help their grounded colleague.

I hastened to Brigadier Pepe and conveyed the bad news to him. I gave quick orders that my BMP-2 team and two other BMP-2s were to react immediately to search for and rescue Laurens and Scheurkogel. We left the brigade headquarters with my three BMP-2s and eleven men, travelled through the town and turned onto the main road that ran in a northerly direction towards Luremo and the Zaire border. I had demanded more troops and BMP-2s from Brigadier Pepe, as I was under strength, and he contacted me to say that I should pick them up as I passed Mundo Real's position. His combat team was deployed to the north of the town and represented the northern component of the defended locality.

Mundo Real took too long to get his troops together for my liking and Phillip Katana, one of my crew commanders and an ex-Koevoet warrant officer, Stefan Crause and I left his area in our BMP-2s at best speed to rescue Laurens and Scheurkogel. Before I left his position Mundo Real's troops warned me that they had seen UNITA troops as close as 400 metres from their forward positions. By this time I was so focussed on getting to Laurens as soon as possible that I gave no consideration to the implications of this latest information. We were about to take on UNITA with three BMP-2s and eleven men.

We had hardly moved 800 metres along the road when we hit the first UNITA ambush. We carried out an anti-ambush immediate action drill to the right and opened fire with all we had, winning the firefight. Once the fire had dissipated I gave orders to move further. I realized what Carl had meant when he reported that the area was teeming with UNITA troops. It appeared to me from the many, many footpaths in the area that UNITA was dominating the area by actively patrolling it on foot.

We hadn't moved much further before we drew heavy fire from UNITA troops again. At this point my vehicle was leading and I was concerned that, if I moved at best speed straight ahead and penetrated the ambush position and the rear BMP-2 picked up a problem then it would be without the support of the other two BMP-2s for a long period of time, and there was a danger that it would then be overrun and seized by UNITA. I decided to clear this resistance first before continuing with the main task. We fought through a total of four UNITA ambushes before we eventually came across the location of the downed PC-7. Laurens had executed a perfect emergency landing, the only problem being that the PC-7 had slipped a little off the road as it had come to a standstill. I stopped my vehicle alongside the PC-7 and climbed off alone and reconnoitred the area. A great silence overwhelmed me, as I had so hoped to find Laurens and his crew member here, but there was no sign of them.

I could also see where Carl's helicopter had landed and where the blast from the rotors had flattened and swept the surrounding area. All of a sudden I saw a blood-stained area. Disappointment started to overwhelm me as I also came across a piece of shoulder muscle that had belonged to a white person. In the same vicinity I then found a piece of material that had obviously belonged to a green flying overall. I instinctively knew then that Laurens had not made it. What puzzled me was where the rest of his body was located, and where was Scheurkogel? What had become of him? I shouted his name but there was no answer. I did manage to pick up a small piece of material that had obviously been part of a pair of blue jeans and I guessed that this could have belonged to Scheurkogel.

Momentarily I reflected on just how excellent a pilot Laurens was. He always found time to go the extra mile and he didn't understand what it was to be afraid. And now he had completed his last good deed for me because he was the one who had offered to check just that one last time for the location of the D-30 for me. My thoughts were brought rudely back to reality by the crack and thump of AK-47 gunfire directed at us. I ran back to my BMP-2 to give quick radio orders to my men. As I pulled the radio harness over my head I heard Brigadier Pepe calling me over the command net with a request for feedback. I needn't have worried about the UNITA fire—Phillip's BMP-2 opened fire with its 30mm cannon and cleared the UNITA fire to our rear. The 30mm cannon rounds burst through the bush lopping off branches as he returned the UNITA fire. Phillip's Koevoet days had stood him in good stead today—deliver maximum fire on the enemy initially in order to keep their heads down then follow this with selective fire.

Brigadier Pepe had by now asked me for the umpteenth time for feedback. I explained that the feedback was negative and that all that remained was a bloody track, with indications that a vehicle had evacuated them in the direction of Luremo. I also explained that I had tried to determine what weapon had actually been used to shoot the PC-7 down and it appeared that it was a 23mm anti-aircraft cannon rather than a missile. Brigadier Pepe ordered me to destroy the PC-7 completely and then to proceed to Luremo, another ten kilometres to the north to carry out a probing attack. This should provide us with some valuable information. I didn't have much choice and I knew that UNITA didn't like surprises at all. After all, we were still riding the wave of success after the advance from Saurimo. Why not ride it a bit further now?

As we left I fired a number of bursts from the 30mm cannon into the PC-7 and then traversed the BMP-2's main armament in the direction of the route to Luremo. All of a sudden I saw UNITA troops taking aim at us with two RPG-7s and I realized that within a split second they would fire these weapons. I tried to slip back down into the turret but my flak jacket got caught. It felt like an eternity before the first rocket propelled grenade left the launcher on its way towards us. Fortunately it hit the ground in front of our vehicles and ricocheted over us. By this time I had managed to extricate myself and I got behind the main armament's control arms. Before I could do anything further, however, the second rocket powered over our heads, missing us altogether. I decided there and then that I had led the movement for long enough and ordered Stefan Crause to lead the formation, followed by my vehicle, with Phillip Katana taking up the rear. The route did not differ much from the previous 15 kilometres—it was teeming with UNITA troops.

A successful rescue effort to lay our hands on the remains of Laurens was not to be. We were forced to a standstill responding to the UNITA fire coming from our left flank. We gave it all we had and with the fire from the 30mm main armaments and the co-axial 7.62mm machine guns we succeeded in thwarting the enemy effort. We didn't get off without any problems though—Crause's BMP-2 had thrown a track and there we were, stranded in the middle of UNITA territory. He recommended that he and his driver would be able to remount the track as long as we delivered covering fire when required. The two men deserved great credit and after 15 minutes they had succeeded. An amazing feat! I knew that he had some mechanical knowledge and that he was not one to shirk at all, but to carry out this task in such a short time, with UNITA observing your every move from the surrounding bushes, took some doing. If nothing else it helped to focus their minds.

With the rear doors shut and his thumbs up sign to me that all was well, clouds of smoke gushed from their location as the BMP-2 engine started. I signalled by hand that Philip was to take the rear and I would lead, only this time we would move back in the direction of Cafunfu. I contacted Brigadier Pepe and stated that it would not be possible for a small force of three BMP-2s to assault Luremo successfully. I also told the accompanying two BMP-2s that there were not enough daylight hours left to clear any light resistance along the route. We would only stop if one of the BMP-2s gave any mechanical trouble. We moved at best speed thereafter and ignored UNITA's attempts to stop us.

During the movement I located a well laid out deployment area where 82mm and 60mm mortars had been set up for a bombardment on the stranded PC-7. It was clear that our speedy movement had disturbed them and they had grabbed the weapons and fled into the surrounding bush, leaving the bombs arranged neatly in rows beside the now empty base plate positions.

After reaching Mundo Real's defence positions I stopped for a whilst to give him feedback on the enemy situation since this was in his area of responsibility. At the same time I noticed Carl Alberts's helicopter where he had abandoned it across the valley. I decided to go and inspect it. When I arrived at the helicopter I walked to the tail rotor vicinity and my worst fears were confirmed. From the blood and the damage to the rotor it became clear that Laurens must have run smack into the tail rotor and I believe he was probably killed instantly. The rotor must have mangled him to a pulp and the impact had caused the aluminium of the blades to crumple, bend and fold, whilst the surface of the helicopter's tail area was covered in his blood and human tissue matter. Not a pretty sight.

Now things started to make sense to me.

Carl, the pilot, had reported over the radio that he could see Laurens and Scheurkogel at his twelve o'clock position. Then, as he had descended for his landing, he had carried out a 180 degree turn. Laurens and Scheurkogel had approached the rear of the helicopter through the dust and inadvertently ran into the tail rotor. Scheurkogel was in all probability less seriously injured and, once he had come to his senses, had tried to gather what parts of the limp and shattered body of his colleague he could. By the time Carl Alberts had lifted, Scheurkogel hadn't reached the rear area of the helicopter yet. What a terrifying moment it must have been for him and Laurens, if he had still been alive. I also knew that UNITA troops were already in the proximity of the helicopter LZ and it would have been a matter of minutes before they would have been captured.

On this very sobering and serious note I returned to my BMP-2 and drove back to the brigade headquarters to give feedback to Brigadier Pepe. After giving him a summarized version of the incident I wrote a sitrep (situation report) and sent it to the EO Tac HQ at Saurimo. It had been an exhausting day for me, a day that I shall never forget. That night I collapsed into a deep, exhausted sleep. I didn't know it then but the next few days would also produce their fair share of equally interesting developments.

Reflections

We spent every day enhancing and developing the defensive positions around Saurimo. Brigadier Pepe couldn't emphasize it enough, and I was very aware from my own experience, that once you hunker down in your trench UNITA is forced to physically come and get you out. I ensured that the EO element at the brigade headquarters, small as it was, was well entrenched and dug in. Our defensive positions were developed to what we in the SADF referred to as Stage 3, which included overhead cover and overhead protection. My only concern was that the entrance to my defensive position faced in the direction of the enemy artillery. I had a permanent concern that the day would come when an enemy artillery shell would arrive at my front door.

We also had the opportunity to lick our wounds now and the technical teams were very busy repairing vehicles—first combat vehicles then the other priorities. I got a view of the condition of our only two D-30 guns. One had capsized and rolled whilst being towed, the other had lost its wheels. This was the inevitable result of having to break through the bush, at speed, instead of using the roads. One of the ZU-23-2 23mm anti-aircraft cannons had also overturned whilst it was being towed and had been rendered beyond repair. In general the vehicles were in a very poor state: headlights and other lights had been smashed, windows had been shattered, a number of wheeled vehicles had no tyres and punctured wheels were the norm everywhere.

I couldn't help reflecting on Brigadier Pepe's train of thought and focus up to this point. In actual fact things are simple in an African war; keep the momentum going, because if you stop for the minor obstacles and vehicle breakdowns the enemy will cause even greater damage to your force. We just had to move from a temporary laager area to the next laager area. Serious resistance was cleared and those vehicles that had to be towed would follow in the rear of the force. It was also clear why Brigadier Pepe would become very impatient with the *Sul Africanos* who would advance in bounds and carefully follow doctrines. As members of the SADF we had been taught to care for our equipment very, very carefully and to nurse it— probably a product of the impact of the sanctions imposed on South Africa. In addition, one of the constants that guided all our planning for the conduct of operations was the limitation referred to as 'minimum own force casualties'—a product of the fact that the SADF used conscripts and the senior SADF commanders and politicians were very sensitive to public opinion on the war in SWA and Angola. The record did, however, show that when EO was leading the advance, or at the leading edge of matters, the force was never surprised by UNITA nor did it ever run blindly into a UNITA ambush or delaying position. In addition, we suffered mostly light personnel casualties, the blood pressure of all involved hardly got out of control, and there were very few surprises.

I enjoyed watching Brigadier Pepe regularly losing his temper as Mundo Real took over the fighting without any communication, consultation or consideration of his position as the brigade commander. In short the FAA way of waging war is something one learns in the bush. It is a combination of the former Warsaw Pact doctrine, adapted to suit African conditions, and determined by the availability of weapons and combat troops. There was always a shortage of both in Angola. I also learnt that it is possible to get by with the minimum, and it also made me think that this is probably why wars in Africa never really 'end'. I should also state that Brigadier Pepe was not all that easy to get on with and he was notorious for his ability to take risks on the war front. Some of his subordinate commanders feared his daring, whilst others praised him. He remains an intimidating character, large at over two metres tall—a massive personality who knows no bounds. Fortunately he had given up drinking. In his younger days he would physically damage his many watering holes, especially if one considers that he was a heavyweight boxer as well. He ruled 16 Armoured Brigade with an iron fist, as opposed to commanding it.

By this time the local inhabitants had begun to return to Cafunfu from their hideaways in the surrounding bush. This in itself brought about a number of problems. The greater the scope of the return the greater the possibility of a successful UNITA infiltration attack on the town or our positions. After all, UNITA had occupied this area for a long time after they had driven the FAA out in February 1994. Brigadier Pepe told me that he had learnt a valuable lesson during this time. He proved me wrong since I had always maintained that UNITA were more at home in the bush than occupying towns, whilst the FAA was tied to the towns. Brigadier Pepe disagreed and stated that in the Cafunfu area he had learnt during the previous FAA occupation that the town should be avoided and that was why he had prepared such thorough defensive positions for the brigade headquarters on the high ground in the proximity of the northeastern border of the town.

This discussion with Brigadier Pepe reminded me of the time I lay in 1 Military Hospital in Pretoria, during December 1987, recuperating from wounds sustained during Operations Modular, Hooper and Packer, the SADF operations in alliance with UNITA against FAA

During the advance on Cafunfu I handed over to Hennie and took a few days leave to attend my daughter's birth.

Armoured warfare on the plains of Angola. Jos Grobler is standing on the BMP-2.

EO men advising on the maintenance of momentum during the advance.

FAA special forces troops on their Chevrolet pickup with a mounted 12.7 mm heavy machine gun.

UNITA soldiers killed in a contact during the advance.

Vehicles towing SU-23 anti-aircraft weapons into Cafunfu.

EO vehicles move on the streets of Cafunfu after the attack. Are those liquid sandwiches on the BMP-2?

My bunker, protected by an AGS-17, located in 16 Armoured Brigade Headquarters at Cafunfu.

Digging in a BM-21 in the 16 Brigade-defended locality after taking Cafunfu.

The remains of the EO Mi-17 helicopter ditched during the Camaxilo incident. UNITA chopped the helicopter up and transported it to Cafunfu to display to the local population.

The last resting place of the 'Camaxilo four.' UNITA brought their remains to Cafunfu and eventually dumped them at the end of the runway, burned the bodies and then buried them.

Freddie, my interpreter, digging for the remains of the Camaxilo four. We also found three UNITA troops buried on the far side of the wooden structure.

A skull and a strip of camouflage uniform—remains of the Camaxilo four buried at the eastern end of the Cafunfu airstrip.

Freddie with the possible remains of one of the EO reconnaissance team we lost to the east of Cafunfu before the advance. We found the graves close to the hospital in Cafunfu.

in the southeast of Angola. This particular campaign centred around the key terrain in and around the town of Cuito Cuanavale. During my recovery period in the hospital my sister, Theresa, who was a lieutenant in the South African Medical Services of the SADF, came to visit me. She had a friend by the name of Manual Ferreira, a Portuguese expatriate and great supporter of UNITA, who she later married. During a particular visit to me at the hospital Manual accompanied her and gave me a copy of the book entitled 'Hostage' by Glen Dixon. The book recounted the experience of the author—an expatriate worker on the diamond mines in Cafunfu—after his capture by UNITA during their successful attack and occupation of Cafunfu in December 1984. I could still clearly remember the sketches in the book, illustrating how UNITA had attacked the town itself. And now here we were— an FAA and EO force—attacking the town in virtually an identical fashion. We actually didn't have much choice, as this axis of attack follows the high ground, thus the correct military option to follow. The important lesson that Brigadier Pepe had learnt was that if it is your intention to defend the town then you should achieve this from positions outside the town, based on the maximum utilization of the available high ground and other terrain. Glen Dixon also mentioned in his book that once the town's electricity supply had been severed, the total population of the town had left in haste and disappeared into the bush with only those possessions that they could carry on their backs. This was the only viable way in which they could survive and look to a better life in the future. It was also a fact that in such areas everyone was related to everyone else—the Angolans had family members who fought for UNITA, whilst others fought for the FAA—a real civil war.

It was also a clear battle indication, once the local inhabitants of Cafunfu returned to the town, that the risk of a confrontation between UNITA and FAA had virtually disappeared. After all they had information from their sources on both sides of the conflict. What was, however, actually somewhat disconcerting was the fact that Brigadier Pepe had allocated two houses in Cafunfu to me for use as accommodation by the EO contingent, and one of these houses had been the house allocated to Glen Dixon before his capture by UNITA. We appreciated, however, that the brigade headquarters on the high ground outside the town itself was much safer and preferred the bunkers to the two luxurious houses.

Locating fallen colleagues in Cafunfu

I used every available day to scour the town with a fine toothcomb, looking for any clues which would assist with the location or fate of the lost EO men and those who we believed had been killed. I agreed with Brigadier Pepe that I would use my few men for protection as we had a suspicion that UNITA had scouts inside the town. We could deduce this from the accuracy of their artillery bombardments. We deduced further that UNITA was not finished with the South African 'traitors'. They had already got their 'knife' into a few South Africans, but UNITA first wanted to gather information, especially after the invasion of Cacolo and Cafunfu. Brigadier Pepe informed me of a number of plans that he was hatching, but stated that he would first have to receive the necessary authority from Luanda before he could go ahead. In the interim I was free to undertake my recovery missions as long as I attended the morning and evening conferences at the brigade headquarters.

I started by looking for locations in the town that looked like UNITA offices and jails. I did locate a number of possible places but was informed by the local population that they only knew of one man who had been admitted to the hospital and he was later observed walking freely around the town without any guards at all. He was a white person but it was not clear whether he was a South African or not. The locals also took me to the now-deserted UNITA headquarters in town and told me that on a particular day 19 UNITA officers had died in the building. It didn't take much to see why this had happened—on that particular day the town had been bombed from the air by EO pilots and a bomb had exploded on the front stairs of the building. Laurens Bosch was no longer around to take credit for this, nor was he around to receive the diamond promised by General Mackenzie to any EO pilot who could accurately bomb the UNITA HQ in Cafunfu. If the bomb had detonated ten metres closer to the centre of the building it would have killed many more UNITA troops. According to the locals it was here, on these very same front stairs, that UNITA had displayed three bodies, of whom two had been white and a third black. I was certain that the locals were referring to Renier, Steyn and Handsome. The story around the three men unfolded slowly though, as there was very little information about their movement and their mysterious disappearance.

I managed to meet a local hospital assistant, by the name of Patrice, who was prepared to tell the story as he perceived it, on condition that I came to see him alone in the hospital. I made this happen and listened as Patrice explained that UNITA had called all the town's inhabitants together as was their custom. On the veranda of the UNITA headquarters lay a number of bodies under military ground sheets. After first ridiculing and poking fun at the 'enemy' at length they removed the ground sheets and there lay three South Africans. According to Patrice, it was evident that the two white men had been dead for some time and that the black man—Handsome Ndlovu—had been executed sometime later. UNITA also informed the crowd in great detail how they had outwitted the three dead men. I deduced from Patrice that Renier van der Merwe, the stick commander had been unable to make a clean break from UNITA and that they had enveloped the group before ambushing them.

Patrice was not able to tell me what UNITA had done with the bodies but said that he thought that they had been buried adjacent to the military barracks located on the eastern side of the tarred landing strip. Armed with this information I located the most likely area and studied it with a fine toothcomb together with my interpreter and after a few days I came across a number of shallow graves, but the bodies had been exhumed and all that was left was one skull, with all the signs that the person had been shot in the head at point blank range in the temple area. I estimated that this could have been part of the remains of Handsome. This area was located on an escarpment right on the outskirts of the town on one of the most probable UNITA infiltration routes and, since the area had been left open in favour of a deployment by Mundo Real further to the north it was a risky endeavour to wander around for too long, and I didn't spend much more time here as a result.

I now turned my attention to the Camaxilo incident where four EO men had disappeared.

An area behind the former UNITA headquarters drew my attention. A collection of military articles and kit lay around and I could see that it included South African military webbing, including a number of HF and VHF radio sets. Then I discovered something of importance: a number of fragments of the EO piloted Mi-17 that had been abandoned at Camaxilo were piled neatly in a heap, as if they had been arranged for people to see. It was obvious that UNITA had instructed their forces at Camaxilo to transport all the remaining components of the helicopter to Cafunfu to show it to the other troops and indicate to them how successful they had been. I then returned to the hospital to find out more about the matter from Patrice. He mentioned to me that he didn't know whether the helicopter components had anything to do with the Camaxilo incident. He did mention that the fragments had come by truck from the eastern military areas where UNITA had experienced recent successes

What he did mention was that on another occasion UNITA had called the whole town's folk together and an 'exhibition' was held of 'certain mercenaries'. He said that he had seen three bodies. He also said that the bodies had been dead for some time and that one man had also been admitted to the local hospital subsequent to the 'exhibition' of the 'Camaxilo Three'. The man had been wounded in the arm and had reportedly been hidden amongst the local population by some of the locals, but they were in no position to attend to his wounds and eventually they had handed him over to UNITA. The people who handed him over were murdered by UNITA because they had hidden him from them. I was taken to the room where he said a white patient had been hospitalized. I tried to get a description of the man but Patrice said that there were so many UNITA members around him and in his vicinity that he had decided to avoid the area. From the conversation I then deduced that it was probable that the dead soldiers were I. Coetzer, J. Loubser and R. Nitzche whilst the wounded man could have been Dolf van Tonder.

I asked Patrice what had happened to this man who had wandered around at the hospital and all he could add to this mystery was that the man had been paraded in front of the local community at the football field to the west of the town and that he had maintained a low profile thereafter. What had happened to him once our force had advanced on, and taken, Cafunfu was unknown. He had most probably moved with the UNITA troops northward towards Luremo as they withdrew from Cafunfu, and that was the last that Patrice had seen or heard of him. I tried to get more information on the location of any other graves but he told me that UNITA never allowed bystanders to obtain any knowledge of the location of graves. He also mentioned that UNITA had shot and killed certain of its own members because they had been 'traitors'.

This information led me once again to return to the landing strip to search for more clues. I came across a wooden frame planted in the ground, like a set of crosses, on the very eastern end of the landing strip. On the eastern side of the framework the surface area had a number of heaps, whilst an area on the other side of the frame had obviously been burnt. Bodies had been burnt here, but they had not been buried thereafter.

I decided to return the next day and dig where the heaps were. We didn't have to dig very deep before I came across old tyres that had been burnt. Under these tyres I came across the gruesome remains of our three lost comrades. The bodies had not burnt away completely, the camouflage was still recognizable and the arm of a white man with blond or red body hair had not decomposed yet. I had no doubt at all that these three bodies belonged to what we referred to as the Camaxilo three, buried whilst still in their uniforms and boots.

I gave thorough feedback to Duncan regarding the findings and he instructed me to send the skeletons to Saurimo for further handling by EO's headquarters. The remains could not be processed from Saurimo onward as requested, however, due to international conventions regarding the conveyance of deceased persons across international borders.

By now I had, in my opinion, obtained enough information about the EO members who had been lost or killed. What was still unknown, however, was the confirmed identity of the man who had recovered in the hospital and had been observed wandering about unattended. What had become of Scheurkogel? I guessed that they had in all probability not lived beyond the outer borders of Luremo. Sadness filled us all as we could not pay our last respects to our fallen comrades who had paid the ultimate price. We wanted to do something to improve this grotesque grave site which didn't even have a stone to mark its position, but we decided to leave it unchanged in order to minimise any possible tampering by the local inhabitants.

Sojourn at Saurimo

It was not all that strange to hear that EO was attracting an unprecedented amount of media attention, especially in South Africa. During the Soyo operation, where we supported FAA, we used silence very effectively. News of our battle casualties was beginning to affect us now though. To date EO had established an impressive record as far as casualties were concerned. In fact, we had done particularly well, given our limited numerical strength during the offensive, and the fact that to a large degree our success in the field could be ascribed to the application of the golden principles of warfare and a good measure of 'guts'. It was a matter of falling back on the well-conceived, tried and tested SADF doctrines that had given us a frame of reference which in turn produced the self-confidence to deliver and persevere. On the other hand I would repeatedly remind my men that our situation was totally different from the operations previously undertaken by the SA Army, the SA Air Force and Koevoet, and that we would have to make do with what we had, where we were, when required. We experienced many frustrations, there were many mistakes made and more embarrassments were to follow.

By now the media was hungry for something out of Angola into which they could sink their teeth. The intelligence community was just as eager to obtain information—from South Africa's national intelligence organization right through to the military intelligence Division. It would merely be a matter of normal procedure for a person such as Eeben Barlow to keep his eyes and ears open for any signs indicating that EO was being infiltrated by an intelligence organization. I also strongly believed that Eeben had planted his own informants within the military intelligence division itself—after all he had been a member of this division himself, just as I had. We knew how they operated. It was just a matter of time before we located two members of the national intelligence organization who had been planted within EO's ranks. Fortunately they left the service of EO before they were formally and publically exposed.

I was also the recipient of information that indicated that members of the EO Air Wing had smuggled examples of the missiles and rockets that they were using in Angola to South Africa—a very embarrassing situation when it was exposed. Fortunately the most serious flames were extinguished before the situation got out of hand and led to a confrontation.

The management of EO was very strict as far as security and breaches of security were concerned, cameras in the field were limited to certain persons, and the media was only handled by the top-level management of the company. I supported this approach for the Saurimo–Cafunfu operations as it allowed the forces in the field to get on with the job without the distraction of the media. EO, however, remained a sinister organization to the general public. The results of its activities, however, spread like wildfire throughout Africa and this enhanced the chances that additional clients would wish to make use of this organization as an extension of their own armed forces.

Sometime after we had settled at Cafunfu we were visited by General Marx. He also preferred to stay overnight in the well prepared brigade tactical headquarters location and travelled to the centre of the town to carry out his various command functions during the day. Brigadier Pepe would not budge out of the tactical headquarters, and I could not recall that he had ever left its location overland at all.

General Marx's visit brought about a number of changes. Firstly, there was a change of focus for the EO force deployed at Cafunfu from operations to a primarily training role. General Marx required 400 trained FAA troops from the local population at Cafunfu and EO was instructed to train them. The Angolan Air Force had also decided that henceforth all logistic replenishment and supply would be delivered by means of parachute-assisted air drops. The Angolan Air Force would use their Ilyushin Il-76 aircraft for this task and the Mi-17 helicopters would be used for the evacuation, transport and return of personnel.

During this time, Duncan decided that Carl Dietz, the intelligence officer at the EO tac HQ at Saurimo should pay a visit in order to update his intelligence framework. By this time UNITA had moved to the very outskirts of Cafunfu and their artillery bombardments were so accurate that the EO helicopter pilots had a serious case of the mutters about safety, ingress profiles, the Cafunfu schedule, and whether it was an EO flight or an Angolan Air Force flight.

During Carl's visit I had the opportunity to initiate my new LZ plan. I would move by road to the selected LZ position and wait for the helicopter, only providing the co-ordinates of the position to the pilot during the last minutes of his approach, just before he was due to land. What surprised me this time was that Arthur Walker had decided to approach from a very high elevation and then to spiral down to the LZ from this height. Arthur and Juba landed their helicopters on the LZ, much to the joy of the EO members deployed at Cafunfu as they had brought post, rations and beer. Equally important was the fact that they were EO people, our people, with whom we could converse in our own language. The aircraft didn't stay long on the ground as UNITA was already targeting the known LZ areas with their artillery and we could be under fire at any moment. We wished them a hasty farewell and I briefly talked to each of them about their return route to Saurimo. Arthur's helicopter was airborne first, followed by Juba who was piloting the second Mi-17. Just about the time that Juba had completed the second circle of his upward spiral above me I heard a very loud crack and an explosion and as I looked up at Juba's Mi-17 I saw it had been hit by a projectile which seemed to penetrate right through the helicopter. My first thoughts and words to the FAA major standing next to me was to ask him why his troops were firing at the helicopter, because the projectile, possibly a SAM-7 or an RPG, had been launched from approximately 1,000 metres from our position. It could have been even closer. At the same time Juba screamed over the radio that his helicopter had been hit and that he was losing height and would have to undertake an emergency landing. He spoke to Arthur and said that his intent was to land on the dirt landing strip if he could. Fortunately he landed safely around the halfway mark of the dirt landing strip. Arthur attempted to land alongside Juba's helicopter but the accuracy of the UNITA artillery fire in the vicinity of Juba's downed helicopter was such that Arthur was forced to land right at the end of the runway, adjacent to the position of the graves of our fallen EO soldiers.

I jumped into my Kamaz cargo vehicle and drove at best speed to Juba's position on the dirt landing strip where he and his team were running in the direction of Arthur's helicopter at the end of the runway. By the time that Percy, the helicopter technician, had moved his large frame into Arthur's helicopter, UNITA had adjusted their artillery fire and the rounds were now exploding in our proximity. I warned Arthur that he should not attempt to egress using a high flight profile and that he should fly as low as possible. If a single SAM-7 was being used, as I suspected the missile to be, then there would be another for the second helicopter. It was clear now that Cafunfu was not a place for sissies. The chances of getting into or out of this place alive had suddenly diminished substantially.

I inspected Juba's helicopter and confirmed that a SAM-7 missile had hit the helicopter from behind, on the turbine exhaust vent. The turbine itself had not been damaged but the helicopter had lost a piece of one of its blades. Juba and his team had been very, very lucky to get away with their lives. The downed helicopter was to remain where it was, guarded by FAA troops, until such time as it could be recovered at a later stage.

With this incident fresh in our minds, Brigadier Pepe decided to send out daily patrols within the defended locality. Eye witnesses had reported that they had seen the SAM-7 backblast as the missile had left the launcher. The weapon itself was actually located at a later stage very close to the LZ and it was deduced that the firing team that had done the damage had abandoned it and then melted back into the local population. UNITA was in the process of getting over the shock of losing Cafunfu and they were gaining confidence by progressively clawing back into a position of strength.

I was also convinced that they were getting a share of the rations that were being delivered by means of the air drops. A number of troops who were involved in recovering the air-dropped pallets, especially those that had landed far from the tactical headquarters, became involved in firefights with UNITA in order to establish authority and ownership over the cargo. Generally speaking, however, the air drops were very accurate; sometimes even too accurate—often the two-ton pallets would descend to within a hair's breadth of the headquarters tent in the tactical headquarters.

With the helicopter flights becoming less frequent the price of cigarettes and sugar rose. Previously a carton of ten packets of cigarettes fetched up to 50 US dollars and a twelve and a half kilogram bag of sugar would cost up to 300 US dollars. This price was so high due to the fact that sugar was the only missing ingredient required at Cafunfu to enable the locals to concoct a potent white alcoholic spirit.

The visits from the EO Tac HQ at Saurimo to Cafunfu began to decrease in frequency and number and my time was mostly occupied in training the 400 troops for Brigadier Pepe. The first group of recruits numbered 140 and they were instructed by Freddie, an ex-SADF second lieutenant, Frans 'Flakjacket', an armoured car commander, and Freek, my interpreter and a former 32 Battalion non-commissioned officer. The training, however, progressed in a stop-start fashion. The recruits had been mustered partly on a volunteer basis, and partly through the use of force and, as a result, we spent an awful lot of time running after them and looking for them. I had no assistance from the FAA forces as they were all engaged in trying to keep UNITA at bay. UNITA was indeed re-organizing to re-take Cafunfu. My training team and I worked at a feverish pace to achieve the first objective, namely the graduation of the first 140 trained FAA soldiers. Once they had been trained all that remained was for them to be issued with equipment. We did not get past this stage and the recruits later became totally demotivated as their equipment failed to arrive, and on top of this they had to stand guard according to a seemingly endless schedule.

What was even worse was the incident that took place one day whilst we were on the soccer field busy with training. All of a sudden we were bombarded by indirect fire from two different positions at the same time. This wasn't regarded as a joke by anyone and the recruits wasted no time in scattering in all directions. To me this development was all the more concerning. Not only did UNITA have a problem with the Mi-17 helicopters, they had a problem with my training programme as well. If only I could locate the bastard who was acting as the UNITA forward observation officer. For all I knew he could even have passed within a few paces of me any number of times, without me being able to recognize him for who or what he was.

Brigadier Pepe instructed me to undertake a military appreciation of each and every possible UNITA approach route to Cafunfu. This included physically following the routes as well. I first completed a map appreciation and concluded that as far as UNITA approaches to Cafunfu for an attack were concerned, any direction was suitable from their point of view, since the terrain was characterized by a number of folds which UNITA could use to good effect whilst they were on foot. UNITA could also make use of a route from the west which crossed the Cuango River and allowed them to carry B-10 and B-12 recoilless rifles across a damaged bridge over the river.

I undertook a few day patrols to the area around the bridge with a platoon of FAA troops. One morning we moved out in two Kamaz cargo vehicles and on reaching the bridge came across a number of Brigadier Pepe's troops mining for diamonds in the riverbed. They assured me that they in fact had the surrounding area totally under control as they had been deployed for this task for some time now, a fact that was obviously untrue. That evening I informed Brigadier Pepe of this matter and he became very annoyed, not because they were mining illegally, but because he did not know about it already. He then asked me to identify the platoon that had undertaken these activities. The next day I moved to the same area with the same vehicles but this time I located the FAA platoon on the high ground approximately one tactical bound from the river. This was an improvement and I spent the rest of the day completing my tactical appreciation of a possible UNITA attack from a westerly direction. Once completed I started the return journey to the combat group tactical headquarters, with one cargo vehicle ahead of my vehicle, as the protection detail in the order of march. We had not travelled very far before I heard an almighty explosion in the road up ahead, followed by silence. When I arrived on the scene I saw that the vehicle had detonated an anti-tank mine and that it had lost a wheel. The co-driver had picked up some shrapnel but the remainder of the troops were unharmed. We determined that the mine had been laid that morning, in all probability after we had passed this point on our way to the river.

On my return Brigadier Pepe did not take kindly to this news at all, and I sensed that he was becoming all the more uneasy about the way in which UNITA was slowly but surely increasing their ability to penetrate into and between the sub-units deployed throughout the defended locality, and the fact that he was losing control of the area.

At the order group the next morning both General Marx and Brigadier Pepe blustered out the orders. The defence of Cafunfu was analyzed under a magnifying glass and it was discovered that subordinate commanders did not have proper control over their troops, there was too much movement taking place and the troops were poorly disciplined. Brigadier Pepe personally berated every operational officer under his command. The tactical headquarters unit commander wasn't spared either. To add insult to injury we took our first fatality in the base itself that night as the headquarters protection unit deployed its nightly patrol. UNITA fired one round from a B-10 recoilless rifle and the shot landed right next to a troop just as the patrol was deploying.

Things were not looking good and General Marx and Brigadier Pepe decided to regain the initiative and take the offensive. The area of operations for the first phase would include 16 Armoured Brigade's immediate area, with phase two including Luremo and its vicinity, in a bid to drive UNITA a safe distance away from Cafunfu. During phase three General Marx would deploy the northern and southern combat teams further from the centre of Cafunfu and enforce proper patrol activity. This allowed us to win a breather from the constant harassing tactics employed by UNITA in and around Cafunfu. A third combat team was established by using the EO equipment that the men had left when they departed on leave. The force was regarded as the depth component of the brigade and it was tasked to act as the reaction force as well.

UNITA was not unsettled for long though and they began to concentrate on night operations; one aspect of warfare in which they really excelled. In response Brigadier Pepe redeployed the combat group second-in-command to the forward troop areas in the hope that this additional brain power would be beneficial. He sustained a telling blow with the death of Colonel Nevis whose DAF cargo vehicle detonated a vehicle mine en route to the combat group headquarters in Cafunfu. Progressively the FAA force was, however, able to reverse the situation to the extent that the tactical conditions that were present just after Cafunfu was taken by FAA had once again been established. Disciplined, continuous monitoring of the enemy situation would be required for this situation to prevail.

During this period we experienced a deathly silence as regards helicopter activity. In the rare cases when a helicopter flew to Cafunfu, the pilot would fly a roundabout route in order to avoid the UNITA early warning systems. At this point one of my men, Neels Brits, came down with malaria. After discussing his condition with General Marx, the latter agreed that Neels should be evacuated. The EO Tac HQ in Saurimo, however, refused to evacuate him. Since this was a pure EO matter, the EO pilots were required to fly and they were not at all inclined to do so. Duncan was not in Saurimo at that time and he had left Jan Joubert, the Saurimo Training Team second-in-command, in command of the EO Tac HQ. I was not impressed with this appointment, as he was a youngster who had been put in a tight spot before. A rather desperate effort was launched to get aircraft into the air to casevac Neels and it became evident that Jan did not have the ability to convince people as the pilots regarded the area around Cafunfu as being totally unsafe for helicopters. We were all stranded. Nobody at the tactical headquarters wanted to take responsibility for this unwillingness to act and Neels was left at the mercy of the FAA medics for a whilst. This support was just not good enough. We had expected a better response from Jan Joubert. Neels did eventually recover but he was never the same joker that he had previously been.

We also learnt that the FAA force that we had left behind at Cacolo to occupy this key location had chosen to vacate the town and disappear from the scene. FAA had deployed an under-strength company of infantry there, supported by artillery. The tragedy was that in their haste to leave they had left the artillery weapons intact for UNITA to take over.

It also became time for all the EO men at Cafunfu to take a spot of leave. What complicated matters was that nobody at Saurimo wanted to fly to Cafunfu, particularly in view of the fact that two weeks previously General Marx had left Cafunfu in a Mi-17 helicopter and the aircraft and its occupants had come to grief in an unknown fashion, very close to Cafunfu. No search and rescue effort was even launched and we later learnt that one of the two Mi-17 helicopters had been shot down, but General Marx had made it home safely to Saurimo.

A few days later we received instructions that EO was to withdraw in total from Cafunfu; something that disappointed me severely. I felt that we couldn't just up and leave General Marx and Brigadier Pepe in the lurch like this. Unfortunately I had no choice. I was also instructed to fly out the equipment that belonged to EO, especially the controlled items of equipment. I packed my Kamaz cargo vehicle with the equipment and kept it ready on standby in case the helicopter arrived unannounced. The unease amongst some of the FAA troops was evident and their desire to fly out to Saurimo was so great that they followed this Kamaz vehicle wherever it went, in the hope that it would lead them to the designated helicopter LZ. True to form, the scuffle around the helicopter turned into a real fist fight as the authorized FAA passengers fought the unauthorized passengers for a seat on the helicopter. Since helicopter security was an EO matter I was regularly forced to act strongly and would always demonstrate a consistent approach.

On this specific day I stopped the vehicle with the equipment in the centre of the town and waited till the last moment before I indicated the LZ to the helicopter. Just before the helicopter commenced its final approach I took off in the vehicle and left all the curious onlookers and unauthorized passengers behind. On this day the LZ was positioned on the gravel landing strip, scene of Juba's previous emergency landing. I watched with great surprise when I saw that instead of the regular two helicopters that arrived, there was only one. The helicopter also approached from a very high altitude and spiralled downwards to land on the LZ.

I indicated to my FAA driver that he should bring the Kamaz vehicle closer so that we could offload and load the helicopter quickly, before the hordes from the town arrived to fight for a seat. As this was taking place the pilot indicated to me via hand signals that he would not take any cargo. I had a sudden crisis on my hands. I had either to leave with the controlled items of EO equipment or I had to stay. I sent my interpreter out to talk to the pilot. He brought back the disappointing news that the helicopter was only running on one turbine and that during the spiral combat landing the second turbine had actually cut out as well. The pilot decided to take a chance and powered down the aircraft in an effort to restart the turbines from scratch.

As he commenced the start-up procedure UNITA fired at the helicopter with a B-10 recoilless rifle and the projectile landed some 200 metres from our position. The pilot decided there and then that he would only load the eleven EO men and their personal equipment. He flew through the start-up procedure and indicated with his thumb that he was about to take off. At once I realized that Freek, my EO interpreter, who had translated my discussions with the pilot, was only now able to fetch his own equipment from the Kamaz vehicle, and that he was not yet aboard. The helicopter was about to take off without him. I jumped up and rushed forward to the cockpit and shouted that the pilot should stop so that Freek could get on board. Only then did I also realize that the pilot was the only crew member on the aircraft and that this had been the case for the whole flight. No co-pilot, no flight engineer, only a pilot in an otherwise empty cockpit. I also saw that he clearly had no time or inclination for side shows and he galvanized the helicopter into the air there and then. He then decided to fly out low over the bush and treetops in a southeasterly direction. These were truly anxious moments. Freek had just made it into the helicopter in time by throwing his bags in and launching himself into the many willing hands of the EO men inside, who helped him get aboard safely. He had very nearly been left behind and it would have been highly unlikely that this pilot would have returned to the LZ to pick him up.

I shuddered to think what had transpired in Saurimo that had led this pilot to fly on his own. It was no wonder that he had been so anxious to depart and had given those desperate hand signals once he realized that we wanted to stuff the helicopter full of men and equipment. I later learnt from the pilots in the EO Air Wing at Saurimo that he was one of the better helicopter 'drivers'. This was fortunate as the flight back to Saurimo was undertaken at treetop level all the way. The EO pilots were good, in fact they were excellent. But I never had the occasion, when flying with them, to remove the leaves and branches from myself whilst in flight and to rather close the window to prevent this happening during the rest of the flight. We were flying so low that it literally felt as if we were flying through the trees. This was one of the most hairy flights I had ever undertaken. We eventually landed safely at Saurimo and I reported our situation to Duncan. The response was a shrug and a comment that the equipment—radios, support weapons and other controlled items—would have to be recovered at a later stage.

We were almost on leave and I began to visualize the two glorious weeks at home. What a wonderful time to look forward to—no UNITA D-30 bombardments, no B-10s and no nagging concern about a possible night attack. We made a mean stand that night at the local EO pub. The place was packed with all my old mechanized combat team members from the advance to Cafunfu, who had returned from leave. I learnt from them that there were fresh opportunities and prospects in the offing for the EO mechanized combat team and I brought myself up to date with these aspects that night in the operations room at the EO Tac HQ.

The command structure had also changed at Saurimo. Duncan was no longer in command. He had been replaced by Hennie and Jos had taken over Hennie's place in the mechanized combat team. I also learnt that a large EO training wing had been established and that a large group of FAA troops was being trained at Saurimo. The majority of the members of the command group of the EO Rapid Deployment Force had moved westward to the other training base located on the Longa River, just south of Cabo Ledo. People had also been transferred to other projects in Luanda, elsewhere in Angola, and South Africa.

The next day we boarded the EO Boeing 727 and en route to South Africa landed at Cabo Ledo. Nic van den Bergh was on the runway and he asked how things had gone at Cafunfu. I responded by regurgitating a number of superficial pleasantries. I respected Nic's appointment, but we definitely differed on a number of fundamental issues. I told him what the good relationship that had been established with FAA actually meant. I stated that I thought that the withdrawal of my men just after we had taken Cafunfu was out of line, as was the lack of support from the EO Air Wing thereafter. I also stated that the antics that followed thereafter with Jan Joubert were the result of the lack of air support and that the EO withdrawal from Cafunfu at this point was inappropriate. The FAA force needed support there now more than ever and I believed that Hennie should be transferred immediately to Cafunfu to provide support and advice to General Marx and Brigadier Pepe. I was even prepared to cancel my leave as I believed that the current situation was not the correct course of action. So much for that; I was not the commander, and I did not necessarily have knowledge of the whole picture in order to comment on this as well.

Later that night I landed at Johannesburg International Airport and the men joyfully took leave of each other. Some retired to the pub and fought the war all over again, until their eyes were bloodshot and the barman had shouted that this was the last round for the umpteenth time. By this time I was an old customer in the airport's corridors as my connecting flight to

Namibia usually only departed the next morning at 0700. I had no desire to be involved with South African family and friends at that time of the morning whilst I waited for the flight and I usually bedded down there and then on the floor. There are very few people in the airport at that time of night and I was tired. To sleep in a facility of this nature can be difficult though; not because of the hard floor; but rather the high white walls, as high as the trees in the bush; and the rows of chairs, arranged in such long rows that my eyes hurt. What a contrast to what I had experienced barely 48 previously.

I lay and thought about the world alongside me in the airport as compared to the world I had experienced over the last three months. Two totally different worlds: one characterized by violent battles and restricted, suffocated movement, whilst the other experienced peace, where one can simply board an aircraft and discover the world. The differences were just so profound.

My 14 days' leave at home was both pleasant and frustrating. The duration was actually only 11 days, if one takes into consideration the day's journey after arrival from Angola, the one day to travel from Namibia to Johannesburg and the one day's travel back to Angola. During this leave I stayed put at home and didn't budge. If the children were at home I didn't move, except to pick them up and drop them at their boarding school and then take the family out or go camping. It was in all probability very difficult for Gerda and the children as the leave vanished so quickly and the children only really saw me on weekends. This pattern would repeat itself every three months, year in, year out, for a number of years. It remained a source of frustration and the day I had to board the aircraft for the journey back to Angola was always a very difficult time—I was difficult because Gerda couldn't seem to get used to this departure day; and Gerda, because she was concerned as to what could happen to me. She also believed that I should carve out a new career for myself, but on the other hand what does one do with an old soldier, who has only known war? Old soldiers, according to the well known saying, never die, they merely fade away.

RETAKING THE STRATEGIC TOWN OF CACOLO

Preparations

On my return to Saurimo in September 1994 I realized that things had indeed changed at the EO Tac HQ. Hennie Blaauw had been appointed as the EO Tac HQ commander, Jos Grobler had been appointed as the mechanized force's commander, the EO Air Wing was under the command of Arthur Walker and the RDF had been closed. The RDF men had been transferred to the EO training teams at Saurimo and Rio Longa.

On the political front UNITA was considering making peace through the Lusaka Accord, an agreement between the two belligerents. There was a singular lack of trust between the two parties and, despite the fact that the Lusaka Accord was virtually a reality, the FAA was trying to carry out a number of moves on the Angolan chessboard before it was actually signed. It was for this reason that we all agreed that it was important that we should retake Cacolo within 14 days.

I was appointed as Hennie's second-in-command at Saurimo, despite the fact that I had actually expected to return to Cafunfu. There was a marked reluctance on the part of Nic van den Bergh to clarify what my role was to be at Saurimo though. It was clear by now that I would not be allocated any EO troops with whom I could return to Cafunfu as there were insufficient troops with a mechanized orientation to support both the retaking of Cacolo and the activities at Cafunfu. It was also obvious that UNITA would rather focus their effort on the siege of Saurimo, as Cafunfu could not remain in FAA hands if UNITA exerted pressure on Saurimo. The FAA had therefore decided to protect Saurimo at all costs and, since General Marx and his men were sitting at Cafunfu, Saurimo was an easier target to take for UNITA.

At Saurimo we remained vigilant as well whilst we waited for the arrival of the additional BMP-2s from Luanda. The lack of BMP-2 vehicles was, of course, due to the fact that we had left our vehicles at Cafunfu after we had successfully taken the town. The new armoured amphibious vehicles arrived on an irregular schedule; those that did arrive were not completely kitted out; there were no spare parts and this meant that a cannibalization programme had to be set up and sustained to keep the fighting vehicles serviceable.

The plan was for EO to establish a reaction force and to undertake probing attacks and threaten UNITA areas and positions even before UNITA could reach the outskirts of Saurimo. The EO Air Wing was also tasked to destabilise UNITA on the fringes of the EO and FAA area of influence. MiG-23s were used to reach the furthest targets and the specialist elements within EO planned to identify strategic locations, destroy them and deny their use to UNITA in order to constrict UNITA vehicle movement.

We did, however, have a headache. Cacumbi was in the hands of UNITA. In addition, Cacolo and the area to its east, including Alto Cuilo and Mono Quimbundu were all controlled by UNITA. This area was situated astride what was regarded as UNITA's most important north-south logistic route inside Angola. UNITA was to a large degree dependent on the aid provided by President Mobutu of Zaire. These logistic supplies from Zaire were transported by road from Kinshasa to Kikwit inside Zaire, then along the roads to the east of the Cuango River and across the Angolan border to the Xinge and Cacolo areas, as well as Alto Chicapa further south. There were vast areas along the route where any aerial view of the many kilometres of the road itself was impossible due to the dense, impenetrable cover of vegetation above it. It was also the reason why UNITA hung on so grimly to the high ground at Mono Quimbundu. In short one does not target UNITA's logistic route lightly as it represented their major survival artery. If this route was denied to UNITA then they would be forced to move logistic supplies via Lubumbashi in eastern Zaire, then southward through Zambia and to the east of the Cazombo bulge to Jamba. To sever the existing UNITA logistic route meant that Cacolo had to be retaken and occupied by FAA and to this end the logistic build-up slowly began to arrive at Saurimo in preparation for the operation. At the same time the men's mechanized battle drills, which had become rusty, were polished up once again.

On two occasions probing attacks and follow-up operations were launched to keep UNITA away from the close proximity of Saurimo and prevent them from exerting undue pressure on the town itself. EO incurred casualties during both these operations. To the south of Saurimo one man was lost when, on attending to the needs of nature one morning, he triggered the tripwire of a jumping-jack mine. His injuries were such that he died before the medical orderly could even attend to him. The second casualty took place during a follow-up operation whilst an EO force was chasing down the tracks of a UNITA force. A BMP-2 hit a rut at speed and the force of the resulting jolt and whiplash was such that it broke the neck of one of our men, instantly rendering him a quadriplegic.

The preparations were, however, continuing apace. Jos commanded the EO element of the attacking force, and he was teamed up with Colonel Palma of the FAA. The total force consisted of the EO mechanized combat team with ten BMP-2s, a FAA company of mechanized infantry, supported by D-30 artillery, 82mm mortars and a RM-70 multiple rocket launcher (a heavier version of the BM-21 mounted on a TATRA truck).

The advance

Morale was high as the force departed Saurimo heading towards Cacolo. The route and the terrain were not entirely unknown to us as some members of the EO force had already passed along this route during the advance on Cafunfu, giving the men some measure of comfort. Things did not, however, progress without mishap. Since Brigadier Pepe and the combat group had last moved along this route to take Cafunfu, UNITA had used this period of time to plant mines on the shoulders of the road, especially in the vicinity of bridges. During the previous advance Brigadier Pepe had maintained the momentum through the deployment of two TMM mobile bridge vehicles and he had kept mainly to the tarred road, only using these vehicles to assist movement over previously destroyed bridges.

UNITA really wanted to make sure that a second FAA advance along this route would not be as easy as before and many mines were discovered. The subsequent clearing operations took up a lot of time before the force could cross the bridges. One FAA officer lost his life and one EO soldier lost his sight during these mine-clearing operations, whilst one of the EO BMP-2s detonated a mine and had to be abandoned.

Jos contracted malaria and was casevaced to Pretoria. Hennie then decided to send me out to take command of the offensive. I was just beginning to enjoy the administrative tasks associated with a second-in-command at the EO Tac HQ at Saurimo, and here I was once again back in the bush. When I arrived at the head of the advance the men were in the throes of crossing yet another river. It was also evident that UNITA forces were in the vicinity. After all, it wasn't that difficult for them to hear the vehicle mines being detonated, and we expected to make contact with UNITA at any time.

My first day with the force did not proceed well and a number of our troops reported that they had observed UNITA movement just as our force was about to establish a temporary vehicle laager area. I decided that this area would then be vulnerable to a possible attack and I planned a quick movement of the laager area to a new location. The move was done at speed as it was already last light and there was very little time left to reconnoitre the new deployment area. I persevered and pushed ahead in the dark.

I didn't sleep a wink that night as I expected UNITA to hit us at any time. I could even hear the UNITA forces carrying out trooping throughout the night. I expected a first light attack on our force but it was not to be. I remained convinced that a UNITA attack was inevitable, however, even after the sun rose without any UNITA actions to accompany it. There were just too many battle indicators to ignore.

That morning, just after I had sent three BMP-2s to patrol ahead of the force on the advance route and clear any minor pockets of UNITA resistance, Hendri Engelbrecht contacted me and reported that they had come across a number of unmanned fox holes and trenches next to the road. I then issued a warning to the whole force to be prepared for UNITA resistance along the route. Colonel Palma, the FAA commander, was however very optimistic and left me to continue the command and control of the force's movement.

I established an order of march in the forming up place which provided for three BMP-2s a tactical bound ahead to lead in an open formation astride the main road, followed by three BMP-2s in the middle and one as the rear guard. As soon as we had started moving the rear guard reported that they had just drawn effective small arms fire. They cleared this resistance quickly with the assistance of the 30mm cannon on their BMP-2s and we could move on in short order.

The bomb actually burst just as the whole force started moving again. A UNITA force attacked us from the front, as well as the centre flank and the rear and we were forced to take UNITA on along the whole length of the combat team. We drew heavy small arms, 60mm and 82mm mortar fire, as well as RPG-7 fire. The team that complained the most was my team who were being transported on the rear of a Kamaz cargo vehicle after their BMP-2 had detonated a tank mine and had to be abandoned. They reported that one of our men, Jan

Kellerman, had been wounded and that he had already lost consciousness. I couldn't actually do much at that point other than get the force out of this position and then request a casevac from Saurimo.

It took us a good half hour to repulse the UNITA attack. We were then only able to attend to our wounded soldiers. Fortunately the EO team had two very good medics and they did their best to stabilize Kellerman. The dilemma was whether we should carry out the casevac immediately with the risk that the helicopters could be in danger, or first move out of the area and then conduct the casevac without the same level of danger to the helicopters. Our man was badly wounded, with a gunshot wound in the head. The bullet hole in the roof of the vehicle indicated that UNITA must have had snipers deployed in trees. This factor made me conclude that we should first move to a new location before undertaking the casevac. My medic, however, convinced me that the wounded man would not make it if we still had to move. I made sure that the area was safe and that the fighting vehicles were formed up in such a way that they could react quickly, but the undertaking remained risky none the less.

I had another problem as well. During the fighting four of the EO men had decided that they had had enough of this and they resigned on the spot, with the aim of leaving the front on the casevac helicopter. It came as a surprise, but this was not the place to exchange blows or argue as we had a seriously wounded man on our hands and an even more serious tactical situation. I accepted their resignations on the spot and arranged for their evacuation together with Kellerman, as any postponement would have made them a logistic problem, and they would also have had a very negative effect on the morale of the remaining fighting men. Coincidentally, these four men were part of the team whose BMP-2 had detonated a landmine and they felt that they didn't have the necessary armoured protection to continue. I gave them the benefit of the doubt and the credit for taking the punch and dodging the bullet thus far.

We didn't waste any more time as the light was failing and I wanted to be out of the area before dark. To attempt a laager in this area would be to invite catastrophe. We got the wheels rolling and ran into another ambush scarcely five kilometres from the previous contact. The UNITA group was in all probability the same group we had encountered that morning who had moved in bounds to a new position.

At last light, with troops debussed and walking in open formation beside the vehicles, we decided to stop and deploy in a laager in the immediate vicinity of the road. Just as we were starting the laager drill UNITA launched a last light attack, but the damage and disruption was minimal and only one FAA soldier was wounded. I directed my medics to attend to him, but they reported to me that the man would not live to see the sunrise and all they could do was make him comfortable. Our medical supplies had not been replenished after the day's casevac and we had to work sparingly as a result. The next morning we were very surprised to find the severely wounded FAA soldier—with a shot having just missed his stomach, a shot through the leg, and two shots through one arm—sitting up in his stretcher smoking a cigarette. He was successfully casevaced to Saurimo sometime later.

We realized that the road ahead would become all the more difficult and up ahead the broken terrain, together with a valley, confirmed this. The troops remained on foot and we

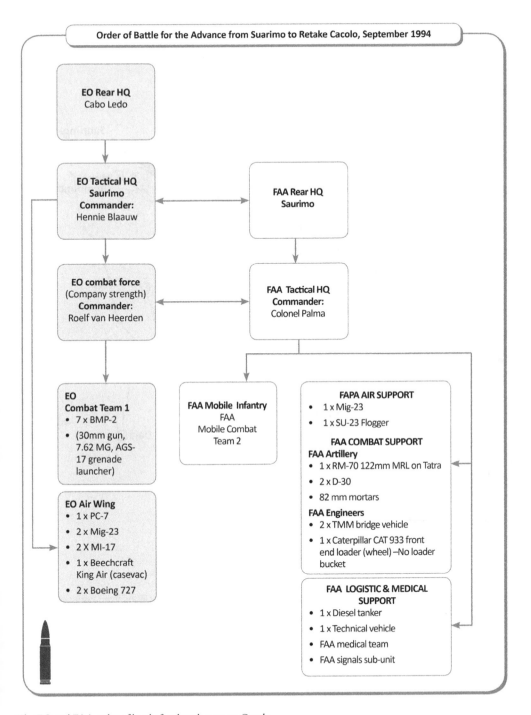

Order of Battle for the Advance from Suarimo to Retake Cacolo, September 1994

EO Rear HQ
Cabo Ledo

EO Tactical HQ
Saurimo
Commander:
Hennie Blaauw

FAA Rear HQ
Saurimo

EO combat force
(Company strength)
Commander:
Roelf van Heerden

FAA Tactical HQ
Commander:
Colonel Palma

EO
Combat Team 1
- 7 x BMP-2
- (30mm gun, 7.62 MG, AGS-17 grenade launcher)

FAA Mobile Infantry
FAA
Mobile Combat
Team 2

FAPA AIR SUPPORT
- 1 x Mig-23
- 1 x SU-23 Flogger

FAA COMBAT SUPPORT
FAA Artillery
- 1 x RM-70 122mm MRL on Tatra
- 2 x D-30
- 82 mm mortars

FAA Engineers
- 2 x TMM bridge vehicle
- 1 x Caterpillar CAT 933 front end loader (wheel) –No loader bucket

EO Air Wing
- 1 x PC-7
- 2 x Mig-23
- 2 X MI-17
- 1 x Beechcraft King Air (casevac)
- 2 x Boeing 727

FAA LOGISTIC & MEDICAL SUPPORT
- 1 x Diesel tanker
- 1 x Technical vehicle
- FAA medical team
- FAA signals sub-unit

The EO and FAA order of battle for the advance on Cacolo.

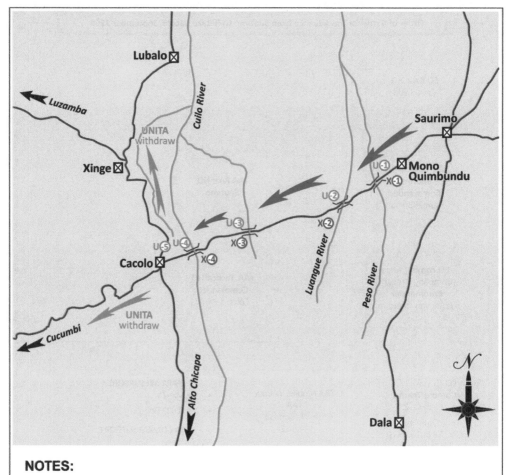

NOTES:

x① Detonated landmine (EO man lost eyes)
x② Keller killed just after river crossing
x③ Stand-off attack
x④ Cuilo River Crossing. FAPA airstrikes
u① UNITA tried to stop EO/FAA with mine fields
u② UNITA defended all river crossings
u③ Major UNITA defence position, supported by artillery. (Failed)
u④ UNITA could not withstand EO/FAA pressure. Only quick defensive positions from here on
u⑤ UNITA did not defend town

Battle map of the EO and FAA advance on Cacolo.

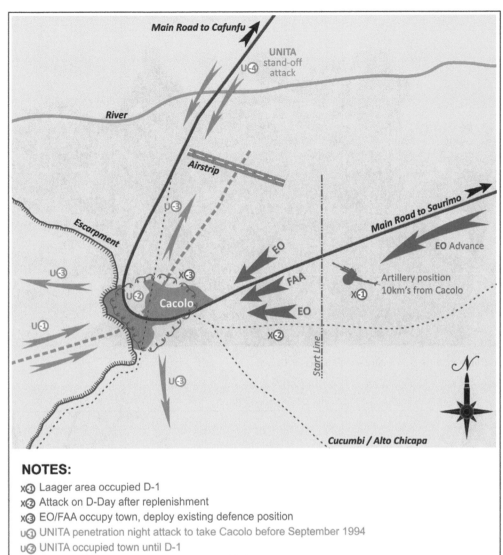

NOTES:

x① Laager area occupied D-1
x② Attack on D-Day after replenishment
x③ EO/FAA occupy town, deploy existing defence position
u① UNITA penetration night attack to take Cacolo before September 1994
u② UNITA occupied town until D-1
u③ UNITA withdraw by D-Day (September 1994)
u④ UNITA stand-off bombardment with 120 mm mortars D+3 weeks

Battle map of the attack on Cacolo and the occupation of the town thereafter.

Chatting with the EO men during the advance on Cacolo.

A study of EO operators during the advance on Cacolo. Rusty, in the foreground, shares a joke with his gunner as they consume ratpack milk shakes.

Henry van Dyk enjoys the simple pleasure of a bush bath during the advance on Cacolo.

Collecting drums of fuel dropped by parachute from Ilyushin IL-76 aircraft during the advance on Cacolo.

Final orders before the attack on Cacolo.

The EO gunners at Cacolo laying the RM-70 122mm multiple rocket launcher (MRL) mounted on a Tatra. Neels Britz is on the far left, with Ben Burger in the white shorts.

Resupply in Cacolo. An EO Mi-17 helicopter delivers rations and supplies to us in Cacolo.

Contrary to what UNITA expected of us, we occupied the town of Cacolo itself and set about fortifying our defensive positions.

A victory lap through Cacolo after the successful attack.

EO crew members cleaning BMP-2 weapons at Cacolo.

stayed on the road, trying not to waste time. Many areas were marshy, with a number of streams and rivers. Whilst it was better to make use of the road to maintain the momentum of the advance, UNITA had no difficulty in finding us. We walked for kilometres at a stretch, but it was safer that way.

The troops on the front reported that the terrain had closed in ahead and that they had observed movement. We employed the 30mm AGS-17 grenade launcher pintle-mounted on a BMP-2 to provide speculative fire into the bush on both sides of the road. The advance continued without interruption knowing that ahead one of the tributaries of the Cuilo River had to be crossed. I called a halt once the reconnaissance troops up ahead had confirmed that they had reached the banks of this river. Colonel Palma and I moved forward and made an appreciation of how we should cross this obstacle. It was very clear that UNITA could utlize this obstacle to great advantage and I issued a warning order to my men that the leading three BMP-2s were to cross the valley under cover of indirect support fire. Hendri would lead once Neels had deployed the RM-70 multiple rocket launcher for support fire in a direct role. This is not the way to do it and I am sure that this drill would have raised the eyebrows of a good number of my former commanders in the SADF.

The valley was approximately three kilometres across with a high ground on the opposite side where the road entered a cutting—a perfect place for a UNITA ambush and killing ground. I gained the impression that UNITA wanted to show us here what they had recently announced over the UNITA radio station. They were going to stop the advance to Cacolo by using everything that we, as the SADF had taught them. We deployed into the bush astride the road and advanced.

Neels reported that his rocket launcher and the 82mm mortars were ready for their fire mission and Hendri moved forward carefully on command. Hendri was tasked to inform me once he had crossed the bridge and passed through the cutting so that I could adjust the indirect fire further forward along the road. Once he had established a firm base on the high ground on the other side of the river I would send the next element forward through the valley.

Neels launched a salvo of 12 rockets from the RM-70 and they exploded on the opposite high ground, covering the area on both sides of the road with effective fire. What a sight to behold. The bombardment worked so beautifully, it gave the onlookers goose bumps. This was followed by fire from the 82mm mortars and Hendri advanced in good time across the valley to link up with the support fire until he reported that they had observed a booby trap. He fired at the booby trap, which was embedded in the banks of the cutting, with his 30mm cannon and shot the charge to pieces. Problem solved.

Once Hendri had secured the high ground on the opposite side of the valley I sent the second element across. When I arrived on the other side I studied the terrain and found the deployment area where UNITA had set up their D-30 guns to fire at us. There were many indications of a hasty retreat by UNITA. The cutting was indeed the killing ground and the exploding booby trap was the signal for the UNITA guns to fire. By sending a platoon of three BMP-2s out ahead and bombarding the high ground with indirect fire we had defeated the aim of UNITA's plan, forcing their infantry to leave their positions.

We didn't waste any time as I wanted to get ahead before last light. With this successful obstacle crossing behind us we took comfort in the fact that the crossing of the Cuilo River just east of Cacolo would not be all that difficult. I informed Hennie in Saurimo that we would in all probability experience heavy resistance and that we would require close air support. We overnighted approximately 15 kilometres from the Cuilo River in order to allow ourselves a full day to undertake the river crossing. Early the next morning Nic van den Bergh and Hennie visited us by helicopter. We received a resupply of rations and this perked us up for the day ahead.

I positioned Hendri and his platoon at the front with the task of securing the eastern riverbank of the Cuilo River before the rest of the force crossed. The terrain didn't allow us to support this movement with observed rocket or mortar fire. The trees were very high and their branches formed a closed canopy above our heads, not allowing us acceptable deployment areas and raising safety concerns due to limited crest clearance. The UNITA forces had located Hendri as he was advancing towards the river bank by observing the black exhaust smoke from his BMP-2 as the driver increased the power output to push over a tree or bush and they bombarded his position with a D-30 gun. I was forced to call in air support and a FAPA pilot, Captain David, came to our assistance with a MiG-23. Without this air support it would have been a very slow task to secure the banks of the Cuilo River. Captain David neutralized the UNITA indirect fire successfully and I must give him credit for his efforts. Generally speaking, I was not really impressed with the accuracy of the Angolan pilots but this man was an exception, achieving success with a combination of bombs and 30mm fire.

As he dived on a point target and bombed it or strafed it, part of his feedback always included the words, "Next target please."

The day came to an end and we still hadn't crossed the river.

The next morning I sent the whole FAA infantry company on foot to the river bank. They secured the area without experiencing any resistance from UNITA and we spent most of the remainder of the day clearing the area of UNITA landmines, anti-personnel mines and booby traps. Once a lane had been opened up through the minefield to the river we moved the TMM mobile bridging vehicles in to lay the bridge. Unfortunately one of the TMM vehicles had detonated an anti-personnel mine and we wasted a lot of time changing the wheel. The spare wheels were far back in the echelon, packed on logistic vehicles and they had to be rolled in by hand up and down the hills. I had to get at least one part of the total force across the river by nightfall to secure the bridgehead otherwise this could become a bloodbath. There was no defendable terrain near the river and UNITA could easily attack us on the river bank from both sides.

Colonel Palme and I motivated and encouraged the troops as they worked to cross the river. The sweat was glistening on my brow as the last troops crossed and the TMM bridges were lifted. The operation had progressed exceptionally well, especially if one takes into account that both bridge spans of the TMM bridges had had to be linked to each other in order to bridge the width of the river. Once we had entered a laager area on the western side of the river I reflected and realized once again, as was the case when we were in Cafunfu, that we were cut off from Saurimo by road and that our only support was by air. A truly sobering though, we would have to be brave. Colonel Palma and I shook hands with all the leader group members and congratulated them on the successful river-crossing operation.

We were about one day's journey from Cacolo by road now and I ordered the FAA troops to debus and advance on foot as I was convinced that the route would have its fair share of ambushes and I didn't want any unnecessary casualties. We led the advance in a two-up formation with two BMP-2s travelling cross-country on each side of the road, and infantry on foot between them. On two occasions UNITA tried to ambush us but the volume of fire delivered by Altus, an EO BMP-2 crew commander and the men on his front was such that UNITA had to withdraw each time. These actions reminded me of the advance to Cafunfu, where our momentum, our motivated troops and the experience of a few masters couldn't stop us. We pressed on that day until we were approximately eight kilometres east of Cacolo but struggled to find a suitable area for our laager as the terrain was open with no cover and very little with which to camouflage ourselves. We were eventually only able to establish a laager after dark that night.

The next morning we were frustrated by the inability of the forces in Saurimo to replenish us and the final advance on Cacolo had to be postponed as a result. Once the replenishment had been completed we advanced to take Cacolo, forming up in battle formation on the southern side of the road and approaching Cacolo with the BMP-2s leading the advance to contact.

From our experience at Cafunfu I knew what UNITA tactics to expect. UNITA would have an all-round defence around the town and when attacked would allow us to penetrate the defence perimeter and enter the town, then they would close ranks, surround us and bombard us with artillery, soften us up and then attempt to disintegrate our cohesion and dislodge us through infiltration night attacks.

We moved to cut a wedge through the defensive perimeter on the southeastern side of the town. During this movement we were rather surprised to find a number of local inhabitants still in the town. They duly informed us that UNITA had actually withdrawn and we entered the town unopposed and swept it carefully for any signs of booby traps. We actually found a number of booby traps, unexploded ammunition and abandoned equipment but no large weapons or supply dumps at all.

The occupation of Cacolo

Contrary to what we had done at Cafunfu, I decided to take up defensive positions inside the town itself and we utilized the existing trench system to full effect. The defence was deployed in such a fashion as to cover attacks from the northeast and the southeast. In the west there was a high escarpment and both Colonel Palma and I agreed that it was highly unlikely that UNITA would attack along an approach from that direction. The most possible direction from which UNITA would attack was from the north. There was also a possible infiltration route from the south along the road that entered the town from Cucumbi.

There was a small neighbourhood within the town area where the local people now lived after UNITA had cleared the rest of the town of inhabitants. Since we didn't want any local inhabitants in the areas of the town where we deployed, we located our positions so that they were outside our defended locality. I placed the BMP-2s on all the strategic approaches to the town and Colonel Palma and I set up our headquarters in the middle of the town next to the church.

The first week after the taking of the town turned out to be restful as no overt enemy activity was experienced. We expanded and improved the defensive positions to cover all the existing defensive gaps and Colonel Palma activated our intelligence gathering capability. Initially no reports were received of any UNITA activity though. During our second week, however, a local man reported to us that he had been captured by UNITA and interrogated about our deployment. He said that he had had no choice other than to answer and tell them what he knew. They had also beaten him up because he had dared to tell them that we had deployed within the town itself. UNITA obviously disputed this piece of information as it did not appear to be 'correct'. To UNITA, the South Africans were always intensely focussed on the correct deployment in the most tactically sound area possible. I felt rather good after hearing this, but admitted that I didn't really have much choice as UNITA had planted so many landmines around the town that we only had one of two choices to make—either sit in the town itself or deploy a good five to eight kilometres outside the built up area. We had decided that the town was the correct place under the circumstances and the escarpment and UNITA minefields provided good protection.

I did spend a lot of time enhancing and improving the defence and the defensive positions. Every bunker had to have overhead protection as we could expect to be on the receiving end of D-30 artillery bombardments. I also found out in detail which route UNITA had used when they had taken the town from FAA earlier in the year. My old friend Mike Herbst had been in command at the time and he had shown me the welts and scars where shrapnel had hit him during the attack. UNITA had used a night infiltration attack technique and had advanced on foot all along the high ground of the escarpment, then alongside a minefield until they were directly in front of the FAA defence positions. UNITA were not very successful during this attack and had been repulsed, but once the EO forces had withdrawn from the position back to Saurimo the FAA force in the town had been left to their own devices. UNITA later succeeded in their attack, taking over the town and capturing all the FAA artillery weapons and ammunition in Cacolo. We were ready and prepared for them however. Colonel Palma and I regularly visited the defensive positions and made sure that all preparations, routines and procedures were in order.

One night just after stand-to we heard a loud noise in the area where the local inhabitants lived, followed by silence. Shortly thereafter I heard incoming rounds as well as the AGS-17 grenade launcher on Altus's BMP-2 open fire. All of a sudden it was quiet again and it remained quiet for the rest of the night. Despite this we remained alert and on investigation the next morning we found that Altus's man behind the AGS-17 had fired the burst from the weapon exactly on target. The grenades had all landed where a UNITA force had tried to penetrate the defence. He must have taken all the mettle and spirit out of the UNITA attacking group as they had withdrawn in a great hurry, leaving a number of patches of blood behind. Luckily for us no local inhabitants had been injured and the incident also served as a lesson to them as the bombardment had taken place in the bush. Hereafter the loud trumpeting voices of the locals were silent by last light each evening.

For the next week or two things were quiet. We learnt that the local UNITA general at Cacumbi, located approximately 25 kilometres to our west, was more interested in feathering his nest for his retirement and his focus was mostly on mining diamonds to keep the diamond jar full. The peace negotiations were underway and he had not been pressurized into any attacking plans, as long as we didn't disturb him in his lair. We kept to the letter and spirit of the Lusaka Accord and were only permitted to defend ourselves. This meant that no offensive actions were to be undertaken at all and we were literally 'sitting ducks'. So far we had only had to fend off the one attack but we slept with one eye open nevertheless. The good news was that Jos had rejoined us after recuperating from his bout of malaria.

One day I was standing in the signals room when I heard artillery shells exploding in the immediate vicinity. We elevated the alert status to stand-to and waited for the beaten zone of the exploding shells to be corrected and approach our positions. Strangely enough, and despite the fact that we knew that the fire was coming from UNITA, the beaten zone moved away from our location. All of a sudden this strange phenomenon started making sense to me. UNITA had tried to find out from the locals where we were entrenched, and they still didn't believe that we had taken up defensive positions inside the town itself. The other possibility, of course, was that they were enticing us to return the fire, hoping that we would utlize our artillery, which in turn would give our position away. I was one step ahead of them and refused to be drawn into responding. This must have really disturbed them. What must have confused them further was that I also located the LZ for the helicopter resupply runs outside the town itself at a different location each time.

UNITA tried once again to precipitate some reaction from us but this time their artillery bombardment was even further off target. Later investigations revealed that UNITA had, once again, captured a member of the local population and really beaten him up badly. It seems that UNITA were of the opinion that the locals did not want to tell them where the *boer* (South African) soldiers were entrenched. I made sure that my EO men were well prepared to withstand a direct bombardment the next time round as I was sure that UNITA was specifically targeting our EO forces.

My own defence position was also fully prepared with overhead protection against artillery fire, and the coming rainy season. One afternoon at about 1700 I was standing on the rear veranda of the house we had occupied as a headquarters, with my one leg on the low veranda wall, staring at the old church in the afternoon sun. One of my men, who had been to the canteen, was returning with his hands full of provisions and chocolate slabs. As he passed me there was a sudden explosion as a bomb detonated in the upper branches of a tree not far from my position. The EO soldier, caught unexpectedly in the open, reacted exactly as he had been trained to do; he threw the load of goodies into the air and instinctively hit the ground in one smooth movement. Within an instant after taking cover he had gathered all his goods together and was on his way back to the canteen at top speed. To his great surprise the second bomb exploded between himself and the canteen, only this time he held on to his goods in the high port position, turned round and came steaming past me at top speed in the opposite direction, once again on his way back to his defence position. With a quick greeting and the white of his eyes prominently displayed as he passed I realized that he had quickly got the message. I also realized that UNITA had eventually located the EO position within Cacolo. With this type of accuracy there was no need to guess what I had to tell my men.

I should also mention that by now Neels, our EO artillery officer, and I had made a thorough map appreciation of the area. We knew that UNITA would use the terrain very well and that they would estimate distances very accurately. From this we deduced that if they were using 120mm mortars they would in all probability use a base plate position at a small river crossing on the Cacolo - Xinge road. We registered this point as the first defensive fire task (DF task) for our own indirect weapons. After the third UNITA bomb had fallen one of the EO deployment areas reported that UNITA were using 120mm mortars and it was very easy to give Neels the fire control order to fire at the river crossing.

In Neels's vicinity a completely different scenario was evolving, as was undoubtedly the case in a number of other positions in Cacolo at that time. Neels was trying very hard to move from his position to the RM-70 multiple rocket launcher position but the accurate mortar fire was keeping him on the run. Just as he was in the process of laying the rocket pack another bomb would fall and he would retire at speed to the closest trench. This repeated process didn't allow Neels to actually finish laying the rocket launcher properly. To add to this comedy Jos was deployed in such a position north of the town that he could hear the bombs as they left the mortar tubes and he provided early warning as a result. The only problem now was that UNITA had decided to fire on the town with a B-10 recoilless rifle, the projectiles of which had a much shorter flight time than the mortar. The reports from Jos were not 'fitting' into the actual explosions on the ground and we only found out later why this had been the case.

By this time Neels had given up hope of getting safely back to his trench in time and decided to lay the rocket pack come what may. He reported that he was ready to fire and we commenced the first bombardment of UNITA since we had arrived in Cacolo. My fire control order made provision for only four rockets to be fired initially in order to gauge the UNITA reaction. A total silence followed once the rockets had hit their target and that was the last artillery bombardment from UNITA. In fact the rockets were so effective that for the rest of my sojourn at Cacolo, until December, there was no single attempt by UNITA even to threaten to take action against Cacolo. We unfortunately didn't know this at the time and at last light I prepared all the defenders to expect a UNITA attack on foot that night. The men slept behind the main armaments of their vehicles and the strength of the guard contingent was doubled. I passed by all the EO men during last light in order to assess the damage brought about by the UNITA bombardment but found that all was in order and nobody had been injured. The UNITA mortars had found their target however. At one position a mortar bomb had hit the house that the EO men had used as their sleeping quarters, penetrated the roof, and exploded in a small room adjacent to the room in which they prepared their meals. Fortunately they were all outside the house in their defensive positions when the bomb exploded. Thinking about the attack, it would have been very difficult to have flown out anyone to Saurimo if the bombs had injured anybody. We had been exceptionally lucky.

During the subsequent weeks we picked up a number of indicators, especially from the locals, as to the extent that UNITA had regrouped, but nothing came of it.

A very frustrating period followed as we looked for something constructive to do. The town was small and we were forbidden from taking the offensive. We thought of 'visiting' Cacumbi or even fetching one of the BMP-2s that we had left behind during the advance on Cafunfu. The vehicle had detonated a mine and we had left it *in situ* on the road. We shelved all these plans once we learnt that one of the town's inhabitants had detonated an anti-personnel mine and had bled to death thereafter. Even I who would regularly find time to go for a run didn't dare undertake such a hazardous pastime here.

By this time the normal habits prevalent amongst the FAA troops whenever they were employed in garrison-type duties had begun to emerge and they looked for something to do in order to generate extra income. These activities ranged from diamond mining to smuggling cigarettes and alcohol, food and medicine. I understood this approach on their part as they generally received their meagre salary on a very irregular basis and usually only once they had returned from a deployment such as the one at Cacolo.

It was not only the FAA troops who were looking for something to do. My own men felt the same about this idleness and their discipline started slipping as a result. I went out of my way to hold a morning parade, to read from the scriptures and to pray, and to keep them updated as to what was happening during the peace negotiations. The men were also rotated out on leave. It was at this stage that some of the men began to stick their necks out a little and ask questions which they would otherwise not have asked. I made myself somewhat unpopular by following the straight and narrow, as it were.

Some of the men were also very creative during this period and went the extra mile just to be able to get their hands on a little alcohol. I remember well the day that 'Ouboet' Braam, one of my gunners, approached me and, with a hand stroking his beard, informed me that he was busy with a specific project and, if I didn't mind adjusting my programme for a whilst, he would conduct me on a tour thereof. When I asked for more details he replied that he had felt that the 14 days we had to wait between each beer resupply was hopelessly too long. I should mention that the EO beer policy in Angola had been clearly laid down by Lafras and one challenged it at one's peril. Every EO man was allowed two beers a day. To the men at Saurimo this wasn't a problem as there were always suppliers who provided spirits even if it was against the policy. But at Cacolo, where we could hear the helicopters from ten kilometres away on resupply day, the 14 days until the next replenishment was just too long for some. Braam had therefore figured out an interim measure and he was about to reveal it to me. The contraption consisted of a distillation drum that he had removed from the clinic and connected to all the necessary pipes and tubes. It looked like an experiment conducted by a 'mad' professor. Notwithstanding this, Braam enlisted the help of his local sources to gather the most delicious pineapples and process them. I asked him to celebrate the first brew with me and I left it at that. What I didn't ask Braam was who his partners in this business enterprise were. To cut a long story short, I missed the opportunity of tasting the first brew, due to the fact that Braam and his accomplices were not in any mood to wait the mandatory four days until the process had been completed. Their expectations got the better of them on this occasion. As time progressed though they improved and the pineapple juice was a viable and acceptable substitute until the next beer replenishment run took place. I must say that the two beers per man per day rule had been adjusted somewhat to the extent that each man was able to take his full 14 day's worth of beers to his trench, store it there and enjoy it as he pleased. Some of the individual stocks were depleted before others and this is where the local brewery came into its own.

This period of inactivity at Cacolo also brought about a measure of tension amongst the men as they were never really certain whether their contracts would be renewed or extended, and no one really knew if the contract between EO and the Angolan Government would be renewed either, especially in view of the Angolan peace agreement that had eventually been signed. A measure of maliciousness surfaced between the men, which could perhaps be ascribed to professional jealousy. There was obviously never a problem for those who had delivered the goods and had always walked the extra mile. There was also the EO policy of last in, first out to contend with. On balance though all these actions should be evaluated in the light of the fact that we were a group of professional warriors. Not a single man would give way or volunteer to step aside in favour of the next person. Everyone had graduated from a hard school, all had a significant amount of combat experience and this type of behaviour was to be expected. The fact that one could take leave every three months and change one's environment did wonders to decrease the level of frustration amongst individuals. The leave rotation schedule also contributed towards the fragmentation of existing groups of individuals and the formation of new groups, both to the advantage and the disadvantage of EO as an organization.

The Angolan contract ends

I began to get the feeling that EO's contract with the Angolan government had run its course, or that a radical change in the utilization of EO as an organization was imminent. To me UNITA as an organization was on the wane as it was no longer really capable of achieving any meaningful gains in our area of operations. I was also aware of the fact that FAA was also conducting a very large offensive in the central and southern areas of Angola, in UNITA's heartland and Dr Savimbi's birthplace. I was of the opinion that, if he was forced through this offensive to relinquish Huambo, he would in all probability have to reassess his position. I also knew that the latest acquisition of weaponry for the FAA had included 100 BMP-2s, as well as additional Mi-17 and MI-25 helicopters. I expected that additional BM-21 rocket launchers, M-46 and D-30 artillery, as well as other items would also have been acquired.

This indicated to me that the current offensives throughout Angola were a last effort to cripple UNITA militarily. I believed this would actually be achieved by FAA and that it was merely a matter of time.

During this period the United Nations (UN) was of course also deployed and I knew from my days in the SADF what the UN had achieved or not achieved. I was never a protagonist of the UN—not so much the organization and its goals, but the inefficient and pompous way they went about achieving them. The UN staff really aggravated me.

The feeling amongst the EO men at Cacolo was that the Angolan government should not agree to the forced withdrawal of EO from the country. If this did take place then the men would of course be without work, but more importantly, it was hopelessly premature. The FAA forces throughout Angola should use this opportunity to carefully move into position and build up their logistics. FAA would also be aware from previous experience that UNITA would have contingency plans in place to cover the UN deployment to Angola. We also knew that UNITA were masters at digging out contingency plans from their back pockets. Notwithstanding all this, EO would have to wait this all out as I, on the middle management level, had not been briefed about what EO was going to do.

It was Christmas time again and the leave schedules had to be implemented. The arrangement was that each man would be at home or with his family either over Christmas or over the New Year period. The 27th and 28th of December 1994 were busy times on Saurimo airport as men were shuttled to and from Angola in accordance with the leave schedule. I flew out to Saurimo to take over from Hennie whilst he was on leave and, true to the principle of always having one foot on the ground Jos took over from me at Cacolo until I returned from my own leave.

During this period I could clearly see that the waiting was not doing anybody any good. All the FAA and EO troops were irritable and short-tempered. Of course, there were a number of incidents which would concern any commander. The first incident took place during the return leg of one of Pine Pienaar's MiG-23 missions. Whilst still some distance from Saurimo, Pine observed that his fuel gauge indicated a defect. He reported that he had a crisis on board and prepared to make an emergency landing at Saurimo. At a distance of approximately two kilometres from the airfield his MiG-23 experienced a flame out. As a result he had insufficient power to lower and lock his landing gear into position and he executed a faultless belly-up landing, with the landing gear folding and collapsing as he landed. The MiG-23 skidded off the strip and came to a halt approximately 100 metres away. The landing gear and certain areas under the fuselage had been damaged and his aircraft remained in this position for two months before anything was done to repair it. EO offered to assist with the recovery of the aircraft but this was refused. I got the distinct feeling that this was a case of finger pointing.

On another occasion two Mi-17 helicopters flew to Cacolo and en route the helicopter, piloted by Carl Alberts, started vibrating and it appeared that the main rotor blades were the source of the problem. This was confirmed by Carl once the helicopters had landed at Cacolo. The age of this set of blades was such that they had progressively picked up small cracks and, because they had not been replaced, pieces of the actual material of the blades had flown off as the blades rotated. The helicopter was declared unserviceable and the chief pilot made the decision that the helicopter was to remain at Cacolo under the protection of the FAA forces, and in particular within the EO defended locality. Carl then returned to Saurimo as a passenger in the second Mi-17 once they had reported the situation to the control tower at Saurimo. All his flying experience had indicated that the blades should be replaced before the helicopter was flown again in order to prevent further damage to the helicopter itself. In the interim the Angolan flight engineer of the unserviceable helicopter, who had remained behind in Cacolo to look after the helicopter, did not approve of this arrangement and said that he would fly the helicopter out to Saurimo on his own. Colonel Palma banned him from doing this since he was not qualified as a pilot; and secondly he had just been charged due to the fact that he had drunk excessive amounts of the local beer. Once Carl was in the air and on his way back to Saurimo the intoxicated flight engineer decided to take a chance and, without Colonel Palma's authority, boarded the helicopter alone, powered it up and flew successfully to Saurimo.

At Saurimo it was easy to identify the tinny sound made by the damaged blades of the approaching helicopter and the loud cheering at this Angolan flight engineer's feat. He landed the helicopter far from the apron—I think he had been instructed to do so—with the tail rotor barely missing the tarred surface. This was not taken at all well by the EO pilots. There had always been a measure of tension between the EO air wing and the FAPA pilots, and this incident only contributed to the increasing irritation between the specialists. From the beginning of the contract we had always struggled to get hold of allocated helicopters, PC-7 aircraft and fighters. Access to fly fighter aircraft involved the greatest infighting between FAPA and EO and some EO fighter pilots completed their contracts with the MiG-23 allocation problem still not having being solved. Eventually the allocation problem was solved and EO utlized two MiG-23s with outstanding success up to the end of the contract.

What was pretty obvious from the outset was the exceptional quality of the EO pilots. In contrast, the Angolan pilots were not known for their flying skills. Night flying was not an option for them and they refused to fly if they were not back at Saurimo by five o'clock in the afternoon. Their navigation skills left much to be desired and they were regarded as a danger to their own ground forces.

The Angolan pilots were not in short supply of bravado though; something which often bordered on stupidity. Their bravado sometimes suited me as was the case, for example, during my exceptional last flight out of Cafunfu. At other times it was counter-productive as was the case one day when I was in the local street market buying beer for the men. All of a sudden we heard the sound of an approaching Mi-17 helicopter and a moment later it made a hasty landing adjacent to the market place. The helicopter's mission was not known but it soon became clear as the tents and corrugated iron sheets of the market stalls began to take to the air as a result of the turbulence generated by the helicopter. It landed amid a horde of running stall owners vainly hanging on to corrugated iron sheets, cloth and their wares. Everywhere children were running around grabbing spilled sweets, cigarettes and anything else they could lay their hands on for free. Screaming and yelling stall owners chased the children as pandemonium broke loose in the market place. One of the helicopter pilots managed to exit the aircraft through a window in the cockpit and he beat a hasty retreat across the market square. His defence was that he did not want to be involved in the drunken orgy that was taking place at the market. The mission of the drunken helicopter crew then became apparent—they had been on their way to buy beer from the local street market. I trust that they received their deserved punishment when they returned to the airfield.

A tantalizing offer

A few days later a person by the name of Queros arrived at Saurimo. He was a personal friend of General de Matos and had been involved in the training of Angolan Special Forces troops near Cabo Ledo. In February 1994 Rieme de Jager and I had visited him at his training base and I must say his years of experience in the SADF's 4 Reconnaissance Regiment had taught him how to deliver top-quality training. I was really impressed.

This time he had not come to Saurimo to provide training though. He remained secretive about the nature of his mission and I saw him every now and again driving in a vehicle which appeared as if it had been specially prepared and kitted out for the bush. After a couple of days he broke the ice and told me that he now worked personally for General de Matos. Once the peace that everyone was talking about was truly on the horizon he would then initiate General de Matos's mining project, which mainly involved the provision of security. Now that it appeared, for the first time, that there was a commitment to peace on the part of FAA, and this peace was imminent, the Chief of the Angolan Armed Forces was about to concentrate his energies on his business interests in the war ravaged province of Lunda Sul. Queros asked me if I was interested in joining him in this undertaking, as General de Matos had specifically asked him to ask Roelf van Heerden if the latter was interested. Queros was offering me a job to manage the security of his business interests, on behalf of General de Matos. This offer precipitated a fundamental review on my part as to what my career as a mercenary actually meant and where it would go from here. To me, the work as a mercenary was my life. I had always dreamed of becoming a mercenary and now I was living it. On the other hand I couldn't let this new opportunity pass without at least considering its merits.

As I pondered this offer over the next few days, my future appeared to be very uncertain and I thought back to the days when I had worked as a miner on the goldfields of the Witwatersrand in South Africa in the early 1970s. There I would sometimes sit underground and dream of how I would move into Africa and become a mercenary in the heart of the continent. It wasn't long before I heard about an organization that recruited mercenaries for the Congo and Angola. I gathered all my courage and fortitude together and approached a number of organizations in order to learn more about this opportunity. I was unsuccessful and the opportunity dried up.

Long after I had joined the SADF as a permanent force officer, I heard from a friend—a truly interesting character—about another mercenary opportunity. He had eventually landed up in the Portuguese Armed Forces, after having wanted to become a doctor. In Mozambique the bush war had escalated to such an extent that he did not want his family to stay there any longer. Tony de Rocha then decided to leave Mozambique and move to Rhodesia to serve a number of years with the Rhodesian Light Infantry. Once more things did not work out for him and the war culminated in the election of Robert Mugabe as the Prime Minister of Zimbabwe. Tony then moved to South Africa. One day he approached me to tell me that he knew of an Arab state that was very interested in recruiting qualified army instructors from South Africa and if I was interested he could help me by providing me with a number of addresses. I learn that the Arab state in question was the Sultanate of Oman. After pondering this opportunity for some time I decided that, as a captain in the SADF, I had all the prospects of a great career ahead of me and I would be wise not to cut this short. I postponed the decision to become a mercenary until later. Now, years later, I was a mercenary—a member of a very experienced and proficient organization, and I was enjoying my work immensely. I didn't want to give this up just yet.

Queros introduced me to an Italian business colleague of his and he encouraged me to take the plunge and join them. I was told by him that General de Matos was very impressed with me and that this was a real opportunity to get involved in the diamond industry. In addition I couldn't do wrong if I was working for General de Matos. He had, after all, approached me via Queros and asked me to work for him. I asked Queros where the diamond mine was to be located and he indicated that General de Matos had obtained a concession at Cacolo. I immediately started thinking about the UNITA activities in and around Cacumbi, not far from Cacolo. My experience and knowledge of the area was such that I was of the opinion that there were a large number of valuable diamonds there but the UNITA general in the area had indicated, for all to know, that he had no intention of leaving the area until after he had retired. I immediately realized that I would have to go to the Cacolo area, for the third time, and in a private capacity, with a different goal, become involved in battles on behalf of General de Matos to take and defend his diamond concession.

These thoughts kept me awake over the next few nights. I was reluctant to accept the offer, but then again what if it worked out well? I decided to put the opportunity on ice for a whilst. My scheduled leave was due to start and I took leave of Queros, stating that if I was scheduled to return to Angola, I would resign from EO and start working for A-5, General de Matos's organization. During my leave at home in Namibia I told Gerda, my wife, about the opportunity and the job offer. To her this seemed like any other job—away from home—and it didn't make much of an impression on her. Gerda's only concern was whether they would pay the same type of salary as EO paid. This remained an open question as I didn't know the answer either. I tried to forget about it and relax. Nobody knew what the future held—there was a possibility that EO would remain in Angola as part of the restructuring of the new FAA or the contract could come to an abrupt end.

Only time would tell.

PART 2
SIERRA LEONE: DEFEATING THE REVOLUTIONARY UNITED FRONT (RUF), 1995–96

WINNING THE CONTRACT

Politics in Sierra Leone

Sierra Leone's post-independence political history can be characterized as an era during which the country's political leaders attempted to remain in power for as long as it suited them to do so. Tension and instability increased over the years as a result of political and ethnic differences, corruption, and the lavish display of wealth by the ruling elite and, somewhat later, the involvement and interference of the military in politics.

Milton Margai, a medical doctor, respected politician and a founder of the Sierra Leone People's Party (SLPP) led Sierra Leone to independence from the United Kingdom on 27 April 1961 and became the country's first Prime Minister. After his death in office in 1964 the country lurched into a downward spiral of failed governments, coups, rule by junta, military revolts and attempted assassinations by the military over the next decades.

Economically the mining industry in Sierra Leone grew substantially after independence and together with the Sierra Leone Selection Trust (SLST) which later became the National Diamond Mining Corporation (NDMC) was the source of the largest contribution to the country's revenue and wealth. The diamond fields in the Kono district in the east of the country attracted worldwide attention with their vast alluvial deposits around the town of Koidu and along the course of the Bafi and Sewa rivers. Security on the diamond mines in the Kono district was inefficient and illicit diamond mining (IDM) became a serious problem. In addition, the local population pressurized the government to allocate areas to be mined by them outside the SLST/NDMC concessions. This resulted in a mass movement of young men from the Freetown area to the Kono district to seek their fortune. Lebanese businessmen, who had been part of the West African business environment for decades, progressively expanded their activities to include the diamond mining industry as well. Diamond smuggling became a normal household activity, eventually leading to the largest diamond theft in history, where a consignment of diamonds in transit to Freetown was hijacked and smuggled out of the country.

In November 1985, Brigadier-General Joseph Momoh succeeded President Siaka Stevens by becoming the only presidential candidate in a one-party election under the banner of the All People's Congress Party (APC). During his tenure, however, he was viewed as being too weak and inattentive to the affairs of state and the country's economy gradually disintegrated.

By the late 1980's, the administration of the country had largely ceased to function, with rampant corruption on all levels, and soldiers and other government officials not receiving their meagre salaries for up to six months at a time. To make up for this, government officials created their own personal businesses and generated extra income during official government time. Despite this sorry state of affairs, the profile of Sierra Leone did not generate much international news interest until the early 1990s when the country was subjected to an especially notorious period of brutal civil conflict.

The coup d'état, the RUF and the civil war

In March 1991, the first inkling of a civil war in Sierra Leone emerged when a small band of men under the leadership Foday Sankoh, a former corporal in the Republic of Sierra Leone Military Force (RSLMF), began to attack villages in eastern Sierra Leone. The group referred to themselves as the Revolutionary United Front (RUF) and they based themselves in the jungle along the border with Liberia, where they established secure logistic lines into the hinterland of Sierra Leone's eastern neighbour.

The RSLMF, the country's armed forces, never a formidable force, was unable to withhold the pressure exerted by the RUF. In a move to counter this pressure and bolster their numbers, the RSLMF began to recruit new soldiers without establishing very high selection criteria. The size of the force increased from approximately 3,000 to 15,000 men but it had become an ill-trained, rag-tag outfit, even less capable than had previously been the case. The increase in the size of the armed forces had brought a host of additional problems due to poor training, a lack of the most basic equipment, and insufficient and poorly trained leaders. These chagrins allowed Foday Sankoh to get his foot into the door, as it were, and President Momoh lost his grip on the security of the country; his internal logistic lines were stretched to the limit, his army's budget was overextended and a widespread sense of unease descended on his senior officers and men.

Foday Sankoh's increased successes, on the other hand, boosted his confidence and this enabled him to take the initiative when and where he chose. It was widely expected that he would take and occupy vast tracts of terrain in the east of the country as his traditional logistic and moral support came from Charles Taylor, the President of Liberia. The relationship between Foday Sankoh and Charles Taylor went as far back as the days when Taylor himself was fighting a war against the then president of Liberia, former Master-Sergeant Samuel Doe, and later against Presidents Johnson and Koroma. Sankoh could also fall back on the training he and a number of his senior men had received in Libya under the watchful eye of Colonel Muammar Gaddafi.

Taylor had relied on Sankoh to provide him with safe bases inside Sierra Leone. These base areas consisted of tracts of land which, over the years, had been traditionally in dispute between Sierra Leone and Liberia. They extended from the Moa River westwards to the Mano River, which forms part of the Liberian border and from Kailahun in the north, all the way south to the Atlantic Ocean. This area of land had been gifted to the Sierra Leone paramount chiefs only because Liberia could not control it as it was far from the capital Monrovia, and it was inaccessible during the rainy season due to the difficulty in crossing the Mano River, a truly formidable obstacle. The Gola Forest and the marshy area west of the Mano River also contributed to the inaccessibility of the area. It was no wonder then that in 1991 Foday Sankoh selected this area as a base from where he could launch his terror campaign against the rest of the country.

The civil war in Sierra Leone extracted a heavy toll on President Momoh, and the Bo and Kenema areas in the southeast of the country were frequently cut off from Freetown, the capital, by RUF ambushes along the Mile 91 and Kenema Highways. Pressure was also mounting in the diamond mining area in the Kono district, to the north of Bo and Kenema. By March 1991, Sankoh had become so bold that he promised the government, and anyone else who wanted to listen, that he would not rest until Freetown was in his hands.

During April 1992, a group of five young RSLMF soldiers—three captains, a lieutenant and a sergeant—decided to move together to State House in Freetown and personally raise their grievances about the conditions under which they were expected to fight the war against the RUF. By the time the group of vehicles in which they were travelling had reached Hastings Airport, on the outskirts of Freetown, a large crowd of people had turned out to support them. As they moved closer and closer to State House the crowd grew and the possibility of actually seeing the president address them made the atmosphere more intense. Once the crowd had reached their destination, the police security arm allocated to State House realized that they would have to do something to maintain control and they fired a number of shots into the air. The crowd, however, overpowered them and chased them back into State House.

The officers in the group of five soldiers—Captain Maada Bio, Captain Valentine Strasser, Captain Komba Mondeh and Second Lieutenant Tom Nyuma—took the initiative and ran up the stairs of State House to President Momoh's office where they were stopped by his personal staff. No one in the group had expected that they would be able to run into the president's office unhindered. They realized there and then that the President had evaded them and they seized the moment to oust him from office without any legal, legislative or ceremonial process. A bloodless coup d'état had taken place, with fewer shots fired than is normally the case after the raucous parties in the capital on a weekend.

President Momoh was deported to Conakry, Guinea that same day and after his departure the surprised members of the successful coup decided amongst themselves to nominate Captain Valentine Strasser as the Head of State, with Captain Maada Bio as his second-in-command. The remainder of the men in the group were appointed as principal liaison officers (PLOs) to run the ministries and together the group of five referred to themselves as the National Provisional Ruling Council (NPRC), promising the people of Sierra Leone a speedy democratic election—a bold step indeed by these young men.

This dramatic sequence of events was not perceived as holding any advantage for Foday Sankoh. The NPRC members were young and energetic, could develop new ways and means to pull the country out of its current position, they had widespread support and they were very popular amongst all levels of the population. On the war front, the RSLMF did manage to recapture a number of key areas from the RUF through the use of pure storm-troop tactics. This technique became the trademark approach used by Captain Komba Mondeh and Second Lieutenant Tom Nyuma in the company-strength counterattacks on the RUF, undertaken by the so-called Special Group, as they called themselves.

Soon after the establishment of the NPRC its members became directly involved in the war against the RUF, whilst additional confident and trustworthy RSLMF officers were appointed to oversee the day to day running of the government. The Army Headquarters was renamed as the Defence Headquarters and Captain Maada Bio was promoted to the rank of brigadier, replacing Brigadier Kelly Conteh as the Chief of Defence Staff (CDS).

Captain Komba Mondeh was promoted to the rank of colonel and appointed as chief of staff operations at defence staff level, whilst Second Lieutenant Tom Nyuma was appointed in a co-ordinating role at Army Headquarters. The new head of state kept his rank and was widely known and addressed as Captain Valentine Strasser. What became of the fifth member of the group of coup plotters is shrouded in secrecy. A ruthless man who always had to prove his point, he was reputed to have had serious differences with the rest of the NPRC and disappeared from the scene permanently shortly thereafter. Unsubstantiated rumours of him being shot and killed at a beach location circulated but were never confirmed.

The country lurched ahead and by December 1994 Foday Sankoh had succeeded in moving into a stronger tactical position in the eastern regions of the country, to the extent that the Economic Community of West African States Monitoring Group (ECOMOG), a multinational West African armed force established in 1990 by the Economic Community of West African States (ECOWAS), was forced to assist the RSLMF in their attempts to ward off the RUF. Even with the assistance of ECOMOG, however, the RUF was gaining the upper hand and succeeded in establishing a set of temporary bases in the central area of the country in the Kangari Hills Forest, the Malal Hills and the Moyamba Hills, from where they could control the main routes from Freetown to the eastern towns of Mile 91, Bo and Kenema, as well as the route to the Kono district via Makeni, Magburaka, Masingbi and Yengema, where Koidu, the main centre of the diamond fields, was situated. Convoys were ambushed on a regular basis, and vehicles were set alight and destroyed. Looting was commonplace, particularly if the convoy was carrying food, ammunition and arms. The RUF only attacked government positions when they had numerical superiority and only after they had managed to carry out a number of successful road ambushes.

By January 1995, the RUF had progressed to a position in the close proximity of Benguema Training Centre (BTC), the RSLMF training base located approximately 30 kilometres southeast of Freetown. It was at this point that Captain Valentine Strasser and the NPRC decided to investigate the use of external assistance as they had reached the conclusion that, even with ECOMOG assistance, they were not in a position to halt the advance of the RUF on Freetown. They also calculated that it was only a matter of time before they would be forced to withdraw all their forces from the interior in order to concentrate them in a final effort to defend the capital. This would have played into the hands of the RUF as the latter would have had a free reign throughout the country outside Freetown to intimidate loot and rape as they wished.

The death of Lieutenant-Colonel Robert MacKenzie

During January 1995 a group of 60 Gurkhas from a British security company known as Gurkha Security Guards Limited (GSG) was engaged by the NPRC to train approximately 160 men as the nucleus of the Sierra Leone Commando Unit (SLCU). Consisting of ex-British Army officers, non-commissioned officers and former Ghurkha Regiment soldiers the GSG was stationed at Mile 91, a military base at the intersection of the two main roads to Bo and Koidu. The group trained the SLCU members with the intent of conducting operations once the training had been completed and the commando group was battle ready. The GSG commander, Lieutenant-Colonel Robert (Bob) MacKenzie, a very well trained and respected former Rhodesian SAS operator, took charge of the combined force and, considering the fact that the average soldier in the RSLMF was very poorly trained to start with, he had a challenging task ahead of him.

By February 1995 the GSG and SLCU force had commenced operations against the RUF in the Kangari Hills Forest and the Malal Hills. The skills levels of the RSLMF soldiers and the short training programme that they had followed were such that any operations undertaken by the force against the RUF involved substantial risks. This was borne out on 24 February 1995 when the new SLCU, together with the GSG, made contact with the RUF and Lieutenant-Colonel Bob MacKenzie (GSG), Lieutenant Myers (GSG) and Major Abu Bakar Tarrawalli (RSLMF and aide-de-camp to Captain Valentine Strasser) were amongst the many killed during the incident. Their bodies were never recovered. This tragic loss placed the GSG force in a very difficult predicament. They never really fully recovered and their relationship with the senior members of the NPRC deteriorated from that day onward.

Lieutenant-Colonel Bob MacKenzie's GSG men were of a high calibre and he had a good military record, but rumours had it that he had misunderstood the contents of the contract with the NPRC. It was rumoured that the terms of the contract provided for the training of the SLCU to a level where they were battle ready. This process was still in progress when they were forced to switch to an operational role; something for which they were neither contracted nor prepared. The reason for Lieutenant-Colonel Bob Mackenzie's presence right at the front when the fatal clash with the RUF took place is unclear and any speculation in this regard is irrelevant. The fact is that he had been killed and, worst of all, his body and the bodies of some of his officers were never recovered.

The disastrous SLCU attack in the Malal Hills and the continued existence of the RUF stronghold there had brought about a rebel victory and this gave them the added confidence to march on Freetown. Battle space had been created and they leapfrogged right up to the outskirts of Waterloo, a suburb on the southeastern outskirts of Freetown. On one occasion Tom Nyuma, who had been promoted to the rank of lieutenant-colonel, took a small fighting force to drive the RUF out of the area but they were unable to penetrate the bush and returned to Freetown without making contact.

By this time there was widespread concern throughout the country and foreigners were leaving Sierra Leone with no hope of ever returning. Freetown had been a very popular winter destination for a large number of European holidaymakers, as could be evidenced by the number of private clubs and resorts on the peninsula south of Freetown itself. These clubs and properties had all been abandoned and left to be looted and destroyed. A truly grim future awaited Sierra Leone in February 1995 and it faced poverty, humiliation, hunger, displacement and hatred more than ever before.

From the perspective of the NPRC, February 1995 was the turning point. They would either come to grips with the war and win it or witness their own demise. To date they had tried a foreign security force and had failed. I later established that Captain Valentine Strasser had personally initiated the contract with Lieutenant-Colonel Bob MacKenzie without discussing the matter with the other members of the NPRC and, as a result, it was not well received. One of the reasons for this hostility was the feeling amongst the NPRC that a force from the same continent, familiar with existing conditions, would have been better prepared for the job at hand.

Whilst discussing the fateful day with a number of senior GSG officers at a later stage, I came to the conclusion that they had followed up certain information which had stated that the RUF had a presence in the Malal Hills, a remote area between the main routes to Bo and Makeni respectively. These hills are visible from the main road and are protected from the Makeni road by the Rokel Creek, which flows westward to the sea at Freetown. These base areas could be controlled by the RUF by blocking off the entrances from the south with early warning systems linked to ambushes. This area was ideal for a number of mutually supporting temporary bases with a network of footpaths leading in all directions to confuse any person who wished to penetrate the area. It was already well known that the ambushes manned by the RUF on the main road to Makeni might be supported from this area as well.

On that fateful day Lieutenant-Colonel Bob MacKenzie's force was carrying out a follow-up operation, based on information that they had received from local informants. The locals later stated that the operation had come as a surprise to the RUF. The operation involved a small mobile force of Ghurkha soldiers, supported by a number of newly trained SLCU members from Mile 91 that penetrated the Malal Hills and moved directly into the centre of the area controlled by the rebels. The initial route they followed was not as had been planned and Lieutenant-Colonel Bob MacKenzie and Major Tarrawalli were deployed at the rear of the column of vehicles at this point. Once they realized that they were on the wrong route, orders were issued to stop the movement and return to where they had initially deviated from the correct route. The force, which had debussed from its vehicles by then, turned around and walked straight into a rebel ambush.

A lengthy exchange of fire took place and when it ceased all that could be heard were the calls for Lieutenant-Colonel Bob MacKenzie and his other missing officers. For those who know the West African jungle, one does not waste any time looking for the injured and the dead after a contact. There was total chaos as visibility was poor, the bush tracks zigzagged all over the area and for all the members of his force knew, Lieutenant-Colonel Bob MacKenzie could have been killed by the return fire from his own men. Once again, I know exactly what it must have been like for the officer who took charge after the disappearance of Lieutenant-Colonel Bob MacKenzie. Undoubtedly he asked himself whether he should leave the area without conducting a thorough search or not. What and how does one answer to one's fellow soldiers back at the base and, even worse, their loved ones back home, when you return without the full force, dead or alive? No word was ever heard of the three officers again. Lieutenant-Colonel Bob MacKenzie was a brave man and a good soldier. Major Tarrawalli was an up-and-coming officer with a great future in the RSLMF, who had recently returned from a military course in the United States of America.

Low-profile preparations

Whilst this tragedy was taking place in Sierra Leone, I was at home, enjoying my 14 days leave from Angola. During this time I received a telephone call from Lafras Luitingh, asking me to join him on a trip lasting about two weeks. He also asked if I had any interest in a new challenge outside Angola. I eagerly packed my bags, kissed my good wife goodbye and flew to South Africa.

I reported to Lanseria International Airport just outside Johannesburg very early on the morning of 18 January 1995 and, in the dark, I recognized Bert Sachse. A former colleague, an ex-commander of 5 Reconnaissance Commando and an ex-Rhodesian SAS soldier, Lafras had invited him to accompany us on the trip. I later learnt that he had been earmarked as the head the new EO project in Sierra Leone. Six of us, including the pilot, left in a Beechcraft B-200 King Air for Cabo Ledo, in Angola under a blanket of secrecy as to the ultimate destination.

Our team consisted of Lafras Luitingh, Bert Sachse, Andy Brown, Ivan van der Merwe (a brother-in-arms from the EO operation in Soyo, Angola) and myself. The secrecy suited us at the time although I am sure each one of us had our own reasons for embracing this approach. We didn't dare ask but we knew that we would not be disembarking at Cabo Ledo to operate there or elsewhere in Angola. Whilst refuelling at Cabo Ledo I started asking questions about the sudden, secretive visit. After all I had been at Saurimo, Cafunfu and Cacolo for months and had no idea what other projects were afoot at EO. I mostly asked Bert Sachse about things as he was still a member of the South African National Defence Force (SANDF) at the time. EO was always exciting and many things were happening and, as always, gossip was an integral part of the way people communicated with each other. We finally left Cabo Ledo at 0400 and headed north for our next refuelling point in Libreville, Gabon. During the short stop Lafras briefed us on the situation and the mission. Our final destination was Lungi International Airport in Sierra Leone, to the north of Freetown and across the Sierra Leone River from the capital.

After landing at Lungi International Airport we picked up a liaison officer from the Sierra Leone Immigration Department and flew directly on to Hastings Airport, located approximately 20 kilometres to the south, without refuelling. I later learnt that the reason for this oversight was that the Hastings Airport runway was very short and our aircraft was severely overloaded for a safe landing. We even had to move forward and crowd behind the pilot in order to shift the aircraft's mass as far forward under the front landing gear as possible.

At Hastings Airport we were met by Baba Tonkara, a local representative of the former Sierra Leone Selection Trust (SLST) and without much red tape on the apron we left for Freetown by private vehicle. We were transported to a large, impressive house that had belonged to the Minister of Finance in the previous government. This dwelling was to become our home for the next few months. The coastal weather was humid and sticky, and I took an immediate liking to the local atmosphere.

Over the next few days a number of serious discussions took place between Lafras, Captain

Valentine Strasser, Brigadier Maada Bio and a businessman, introduced to us as Bogari Kakkai. I learnt later that since Lafras's previous visit to Sierra Leone and his discussions with the NPRC, things had changed somewhat. It became evident that an organization in the same league as EO had slipped into the country ahead of us and had signed a contract with the NPRC. Bogari Kakkai, the local businessman who had facilitated the contact between EO (Lafras), Allan Patterson (the General Manager of the now defunct SLSJ/NDMC), and the head of state later told me that Captain Valentine Strasser had signed a contract with the GSG. This new information put Lafras in a tight spot, but his years as an officer had taught him to be calm and calculated and he relaxed, waited and observed. This is exactly what we did over the next four months.

Lafras left for South Africa on 24 January 1995. Bert Sachse and Ivan van der Merwe left the next day via Brussels and Andy Brown and I remained in Sierra Leone. Andy and I had not crossed paths before during our SADF days and we had to get to know each other and adapt to each other's abilities and limitations. Over the next few months, however, we became great friends but we also irritated the shit out of each other at times. I was usually the good listener and he was the impulsive one, making wild and sweeping claims and statements.

Andy and I were eventually introduced to our neighbour, a local man, by the name of Al Hadji Tolli who tried his best to ferret out what we were up to in Sierra Leone. Whilst we kept as low a profile as possible we were often bored and one day we asked Al Hadji to show us around Freetown. We were treated to a tour of the Fourah Bay College, one of the oldest English-speaking universities in Sub-Saharan Africa. The campus, built in 1827, was situated on the summit of Mount Aureole and had been run all these years by the Church Missionary Society. We were led to believe that John F. Kennedy had once paid a visit to the university and a building on the campus was in fact named after him. We must have selected the wrong day to visit the college as it soon became clear that the RUF were in the middle of a campaign aimed at influencing the electorate and they had targeted the college. Only when we were actually on the campus did we realize that there was a sense of irritation amongst the students. After visiting the campus secretary we were told that a riot was about to take place and it would be better if we left unnoticed as soon as possible. To achieve this we exited the area through a rather small gate at the back of the campus. The riot was initiated through a propaganda pamphlet issued and distributed by the RUF which called for all on the campus to riot, boycott classes and help the RUF overthrow the government. We left without taking any photographs and Al Hadji was extremely disappointed that he wasn't able to conduct us on a tour of this West African showpiece.

We spent the rest of the morning visiting a number of local markets and ended up on the beach watching the locals casting their nets. As we were about to start taking photographs of this scene the fishermen sidled closer and demanded money from us, thinking that we were tourists. Al Hadji tried to explain to them that we were not tourists and implored them to calm down. One hell of a shouting match erupted and ended when the local fishermen stopped the local police and convinced them that we foreigners had taken pictures of the RSLMF Headquarters. This type of exposure was exactly the opposite of what we intended and we were escorted to the local police station where we could plainly see that this incident was turning into an opportunity for the local police to make some money. I left Andy there to argue it out with them whilst I reverted to our colleagues in town to come and rescue us with the aid of a couple of hundred US dollars. The incident drove us to maintain an even lower profile for quite some time thereafter and I spent more time jogging whilst Andy improved on his pipe smoking skills.

Andy and I also tried to establish a means of communication with the NPRC as we had been instructed to sell ourselves, whenever possible, to this body. It was during this period that the GSG started to fall out of favour with the NPRC as a result of the disastrous Malal Hills operation. We met and accompanied Colonel Charles Mbuyo, the Chief of Staff Intelligence and Colonel Komba Mondey, the Chief of Staff Operations to a number of restaurants where open discussions on the military situation in Sierra Leone took place. We came to the conclusion that the relationship between the GSG and the NPRC was in fact deteriorating and this eventually brought about the opportunity that we had been looking for.

The NPRC was also involved in a series of consultations with their allies, mainly the ECOMOG forces, as to how they could maintain a minimum level of security in the country, and this was followed by a period of relative inactivity on the war front in Sierra Leone. I grasped this chance to take a most welcome break and on 8 March 1995 flew via Abidjan to Johannesburg and overnighted at the EO headquarters in Pretoria. After briefing Lafras on the ups and downs of the discussions in Sierra Leone, he advised me to remain calm and wait as he was certain that the right moment for EO would arrive in good time.

I returned to Freetown on 29 March 1995, via the Ivory Coast, and the stay in Le Golf Hotel in Abidjan made me wonder what had gone wrong in Sierra Leone. The Ivory Coast was at this point a well-developed country, with good restaurants, comfortable hotels, well maintained roads and very friendly French-speaking people. I even tried my hand at the hot and cold swimming bath, watched a few people playing a round of golf and, of all things, saw tourists from all over the globe bird watching. Whilst travelling around town I noticed a group of soldiers and identified them as proud members of the French Foreign Legion. I had always admired the men of the Legion—they were my type of people.

Back in Freetown reality hit me hard—Lungi Airport wasn't a patch on Abidjan International Airport. Gone were the neat and tidy offices, disciplined soldiers and airport officials I had seen in the Ivory Coast and I was confronted by a struggling country and a people battling to survive. Despite this I still actually liked the country as there is something about the friendly Sierra Leone people that is attractive. During the lonely three weeks whilst Andy Brown was on a well-deserved break I spent most of the time setting up a brief profile of EO and working on various operational options with different sets of criteria. It was actually very difficult to work with any degree of certainty as the RSLMF only reacted to enemy actions at that time. They had no operational plan and no routine war activities and they merely rushed from one crisis to the next. The integrity and morale of the RSLMF were also at an all time low.

On Andy's return we obtained an audience with Colonel Mondeh at his home. He asked me what the capabilities of EO were and what type of operations we could conduct. From the ensuing discussions it became clear that he did have a serious interest in our services. He did, however, mention that GSG would first have to complete their contract. He stated that he would contact us again to conduct further discussions. That evening I contacted our EO headquarters in Pretoria and briefed them on the first discussions with Colonel Mondeh and the fact that we would be holding discussions again later that month where things would become clearer we hoped.

On another occasion Colonel Mondeh invited Andy Brown and I to his home and gave me the task, very confidentially, of planning an attack on Joru, the RUF headquarters in eastern Sierra Leone, southeast of Kenema. With very little information, let alone intelligence, on the enemy headquarters I managed to provide him with a broad plan of what we could do, what type of EO force levels would be involved and what the schedule for such an operation could be. He was rather impressed with the presentation and promised to stay in touch with us.

In the interim the RUF had succeeded in bringing immense pressure to bear on the main roads in the interior of the country, especially in the diamond areas, through the use of a number of ambushes. The latest information indicated that the RUF was in the process of building up its forces in the Gandorhun area with the aim of attacking the Koidu/Kono diamond fields. The sad thing about the roads in these areas was that there were no alternative routes. The only alternative was to travel by air, a very expensive option to follow and Alex Zagorski of Soruss Air Limited didn't mind as he was the only one who dared to fly into areas where, on a particular day, the RSLMF might be in control, only to be ousted by the RUF the next. I must admit, this situation really worked in our favour as the pressure was on the NPRC to make a very serious and speedy decision.

Tony Buckingham, a man I had met before under quite different circumstances in Angola, visited us in Freetown on 7 April 1995 with Rupert Bowden, a former United Nations liaison officer. I used the opportunity to brief them on the security situation and the progress EO had made to date.

During our stay in Freetown I had also met with Allan Patterson, an important and knowledgeable figure in the diamond mining industry in Sierra Leone. Since the insecurity caused by the war did not allow him to travel inland, he spent most of his time in Freetown and it became evident that there was a mutually beneficial connection between EO, Tony Buckingham and the NDMC. EO would try and get the government contract to secure the country so that Allan and the NDMC could mine the diamonds.

By now I had become a regular visitor to Colonel Mondeh's mansion. A really nice person, he would send his vehicle to our house after dark and, under the protection of his bodyguards, we would be transported to his mansion. I had also achieved a level of knowledge about the 'who's who' in Freetown and deduced that most of the coup plotters had sent their families abroad to the United State and the United Kingdom where they could be raised within a milieu with a better quality of life than in Sierra Leone. It was also clear to me that the group of young men running the NPRC were relishing their tenure at the helm of the country. They were clearly in charge, they were bold, they were flashy and they were soldiers. I had not as yet met Captain Strasser but had met the other NPRC members and I felt some measure of affiliation with them. They moved in a totally different world from Angola, where the General Staff of the FAA were far, far away from their troops and the conditions on the ground.

They appeared a little hesitant about exactly what they wanted to do, but were not afraid of what they were doing; not sure how and with what capacity they could tackle opportunities, but swift in making decisions to respond to enemy activities. It was just sad that so few people had the heart and the courage that these young men were displaying. I met Colonel Charles Mbuyo in his office a few times—a man who had a collection of cars at a secret location which was never divulged to us. He was very open in admitting to mistakes that they were making, who the enemy really was and how bitter this war really was—with brothers and sisters, mothers and fathers on different sides, some fighting for the RUF, others supporting the NPRC.

On 24 April 1995 the news broke early on the streets—a tactical unit had left for the Sierra Rutile Mine and reclaimed it from the RUF. The next day the whole of Freetown celebrated the return of the mine to the government side; traffic came to a standstill and a jubilant atmosphere swept the whole town into a party mood until late into the night. EO would probably have done things a little differently; in a more pre-planned way, with less casualties and a greater chance of success. Nevertheless, they had dared and had achieved success. Having occupied the mine, the whole force picked up sticks and returned to Freetown, leaving a few brave men behind to protect the area, only to have the RUF attack and drive them off shortly thereafter.

The next day I heard that Foday Sankoh had communicated with the NPRC, stating that he was not at all interested in a settlement, emphasizing that he was in control of two thirds of the country and that one defeat such as the loss of the Sierra Rutile Mine would just encourage him to achieve bolder and bigger objectives. On 28 April 1995 it became clear why Corporal Foday Sankoh knew why no talks were necessary between the RUF and the NPRC. The RUF had driven the government's security forces out of Koidu, the capital of the diamond area in Sierra Leone. This meant that the RUF was in control of the entire Kono district. The main route to Kono could easily be cut off at Njaima-Sewafe, where the Sewa River and the main road intersect, and this meant that the district had become isolated from the rest of the country. The two other roads leading to Kono were inaccessible and under RUF control as well.

This tactical move had given the RUF effective control of all the current mining activities in the district. At this time of the year small miners stopped their physical mining activities and concentrated on washing the gravel to locate the diamonds. It was also the start of the rainy season and the harvesting of rice and other food products had almost ended and stores and shops would be fully stocked. This was why the RUF had attacked the Kono district now. The gravel stockpiles would be bountiful and the shops would be stocked to the roof as the miners would start selling diamonds at any moment.

That same day Allan Patterson accompanied Tony Buckingham on a visit to our house. Tony had come to Sierra Leone to make a number of final adjustments to a 25-year mining concession and to make sure that EO would be in a position to gear up the moment that the security contract was awarded to them. The meeting behind closed doors with the members of the NPRC later that evening was successful. The contract had been awarded to EO and Tony had been successful with the 25-year concession for the mining of the Kimberlitic deposit in the Kono district. A number of important calls were made via satellite phone to Eeben Barlow and Lafras Luitingh in South Africa. We had won the contract.

Gearing up

The next meeting with the NPRC took place in a more open and formal manner and our focus turned towards gearing up for the arrival of the EO force. It was, however, sad to see the movement of the officers of the Ghurkha team as they became less and less conspicuous at Cockerill Barracks, the RSLMF headquarters in Freetown. The only items we took over from them were one Land Rover, ex-military, with a mounting for a pintle-fitted machine gun, and a Tatra cargo truck used for logistic purposes. It had also been decided that the EO force would wear the same camouflage uniform and utlize the same rank structure as the RSLMF. Andy and I were made to feel exceptionally welcome at Cockerill Barracks and it almost felt as if we had always been part of the RSLMF.

On 29 April 1995 we held our first formal meeting with Brigadier Maada Bio in his office. We had finally succeeded in getting together around the same table to start work on achieving the same goals as our RSLMF colleagues. A place was earmarked for an EO office in the RSLMF headquarters and money was allocated to finance any changes that we wished to make to the office itself. There were no limits and Brigadier Bio confirmed that he and I would meet every morning before we tackled our daily tasks. He listened attentively to the EO profile I presented and looked suitably impressed. I did not embellish anything during the presentation as this would only have coloured his perception of EO.

We discussed force levels and the quick arrival and deployment of the EO personnel. I had already received a guideline from Lafras that we could expect to receive approximately 200 EO men for the mission in Sierra Leone. I emphasized and received confirmation that all weapons, ammunition, main equipment and uniforms would be provided by the RSLMF.

Andy and I then visited the military medical facilities and were left speechless as there was no real capability to treat wounded soldiers at all. Our own medical staff inspected the facility later as well and it was decided there and then to transfer all cases to Dakar in Senegal until such time as EO could provide its own medical facility in Freetown.

We were also given the opportunity to reconnoitre the terrain and despite the fact that we were forced to undertake this task with limited means it did actually mean a lot to us. We were given passage on the two Soruss Air Limited Mi-17 helicopters and it was whilst we were flying to the Kono district on 30 April 1995 that I realized just how much destruction had been caused by the RUF rebels. As we approached Koidu I could hardly see an area where smoke was not evident. The town was deserted and houses were burning and smouldering, with a few solitary looters here and there still making off with pillaged items. The town's inhabitants had fled to the north, away from the direction of the RUF advance and we could see them concentrated along the footpaths and crossing streams and rivers to safety.

The rebels had first attacked the southern town of Gandorhun, located approximately 30 kilometres from Koidu and government troops had tried to recapture it without success. I could see that the terrain was hilly in some areas and the vegetation, especially the undergrowth, was very dense. My mind was spinning as the terrain presented a formidable challenge.

It was evident that the RUF commanders had some battle skills as they had refrained from attacking Koidu from the outset. They used a bypass tactic and attacked the headquarters of the RSLMF task force at Motema, some four kilometres away from Koidu. The lack of basic logistic support to the government forces prevented them from reacting to the attacks on Koidu town itself and Lieutenant-Colonel S. A. Sinnah, the task force commander, was only able to manage a weak and unsuccessful effort to recapture his headquarters. He was severely criticized later for his lack of effort as a senior officer and I deduced that this was a case of poor leadership, poor training and no logistic support.

The military headquarters at Cockerill Barracks in Freetown had, however, made some effort to improve this situation and the two young 'bull terriers' from the NPRC in Freetown, Lieutenant-Colonel Komba Mondeh and Lieutenant-Colonel Nyuma, together with Lieutenant-Colonel K. E. S. Boyah were called in again to resolve the situation. The disaster at Sierra Rutile Mine was still fresh in their minds and to them this was just another attack. Lieutenant-Colonel Mondeh and Lieutenant-Colonel Nyuma mobilized a force and entered the diamond area from Bumpe, close to Bo. Their attempt to cross the Kambui Hills area into Koidu met with such tough resistance from the rebels that they decided to pull back to Bumpe. I suddenly realized that this was an African thing—government forces are used to sticking to the main roads and rebels to the bush. It is almost as if there is a tacit agreement between the two forces throughout the continent—you stick to the bush and I'll stay on the main roads.

The next thrust by the government troops succeeded in breaking the RUF resistance and they drove into Koidu itself, whilst being surrounded and encircled by the RUF rebels in the surrounding bush. Lieutenant-Colonel Tom Nyuma took control of the town; Major Kahn was placed in command of the ground forces and, with a number of military police, was responsible for putting a halt to the looting. Despite this the government soldiers and the civilians continued looting everything they could lay their hands on. It was at this time that a phrase was coined to identify and describe troublemakers amongst the soldiers. They became known as sobels, a term derived by combining soldiers and rebels.

We were about to land and the helicopter pilot was searching for a safe LZ, unsure whether the groups of armed men on the ground were friend or foe. I looked out and couldn't tell the difference myself. Eventually he flared the aircraft and we landed. From the instant that the port side sliding door of the aircraft opened, looted items were urgently pushed into the hold of the aircraft from outside and the flight engineer had an uphill battle to prevent the helicopter from being overloaded as we still had to fly to Bo as well. We lifted off as chaos reigned, with soldiers still hanging onto the aircraft's door, trying to accompany their looted items, already inside the helicopter.

The town of Bo looked surprisingly calm to me. Like Kenema, it was located in the heartland of the area controlled by the RUF, but the war had not affected it as it had in Koidu. The terrain in and around the town was open grassland, making it that much more difficult to attack from a rebel perspective, unless they did so under cover of darkness. We spent very little time on the ground before returning to Freetown.

The trip to the interior was of great value to us and during our next meeting with Brigadier Maade Bio we were ready to start slowly building towards a plan for the offensive against the RUF. I told him that I would be preparing a command appreciation in order to ensure that we had no misunderstandings as far as the strategy was concerned. My experience was that they were not up to the operational level on which I was talking and I knew that we would have to understand each other and learn about each other over the next few weeks. We needed to learn, and we needed to teach each other. The principles of war are universal—it was the interpretation that differed and that's what made the difference. I also experienced a lack of patience on the part of the RSLMF and a strong urge to jump into vehicles and race to the battlefront to deal with the enemy.

I had many things to do and arrange as Andy Brown and I were the only EO staff on the ground in Sierra Leone and the different staff functions—personnel, intelligence, operations and logistics—had to be fulfilled. Andy was instructed to develop the enemy (RUF) picture from intelligence that had already been gathered, for my command appreciation. He located the intelligence branch of the RSLMF and when he asked for a briefing on the enemy he was shown the archive, where report upon report was packed from the floor to the ceiling. No conclusions had been drawn from the reports, no enemy plan had been derived or deduced, and no enemy organization chart had been developed. Undeterred, he started digging amongst the piles of reports for relevant and applicable material. After four hours of paging through documents and asking difficult questions he came to the conclusion that this was a futile exercise. There just was no processed intelligence on the RUF as the available material was still in the form of unverified information. We would have to rely on what we could gain from Lieutenant-Colonel Komba Mondeh, Colonel Charlie Mbuyo and Lieutenant-Colonel Tom Nuyama and that was that.

We had the full cooperation of everybody on all levels of the military and the planning indicated that all the preparations would be in place for the EO force by the second week of May 1995, when the first aircraft was due to land.

As part of the contract we were required to draw up a list of the equipment we needed and, as was the case during our contract in Angola, all the main equipment was to be provided by the host country's government itself. Our list of equipment included uniforms and small arms as well as 60mm mortars, 82mm mortars, 120mm mortars, AGS-17 grenade launchers, 12.7mm machine guns, pyrotechnics, night vision equipment, as well as two BMP-2 infantry combat vehicles. The list of items was carefully studied and the reply we received was garbled. The uniforms, small arms and ammunition were no problem to supply, but when it came to the mortars they had to go and dig the weapons out from dusty old stores as the RSLMF was not in the habit of using such weapons. The armoured vehicles were even more difficult to even talk about. We explained that the protection of convoys was made possible and viable

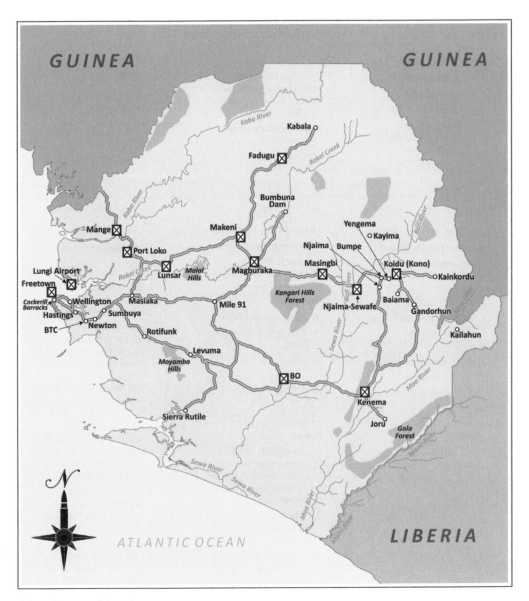

Orientation map of Sierra Leone.

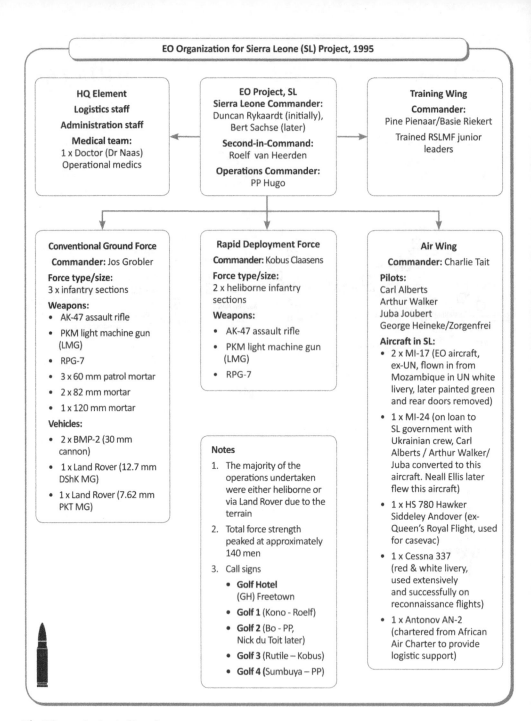

EO Organization for Sierra Leone (SL) Project, 1995

HQ Element
Logistics staff
Administration staff
Medical team:
1 x Doctor (Dr Naas)
Operational medics

EO Project, SL
Sierra Leone Commander:
Duncan Rykaardt (initially),
Bert Sachse (later)
Second-in-Command:
Roelf van Heerden
Operations Commander:
PP Hugo

Training Wing
Commander:
Pine Pienaar/Basie Riekert
Trained RSLMF junior
leaders

Conventional Ground Force
Commander: Jos Grobler
Force type/size:
3 x infantry sections
Weapons:
- AK-47 assault rifle
- PKM light machine gun (LMG)
- RPG-7
- 3 x 60 mm patrol mortar
- 2 x 82 mm mortar
- 1 x 120 mm mortar
Vehicles:
- 2 x BMP-2 (30 mm cannon)
- 1 x Land Rover (12.7 mm DShK MG)
- 1 x Land Rover (7.62 mm PKT MG)

Rapid Deployment Force
Commander: Kobus Claasens
Force type/size:
2 x heliborne infantry sections
Weapons:
- AK-47 assault rifle
- PKM light machine gun (LMG)
- RPG-7

Notes
1. The majority of the operations undertaken were either heliborne or via Land Rover due to the terrain
2. Total force strength peaked at approximately 140 men
3. Call signs
   - **Golf Hotel** (GH) Freetown
   - **Golf 1** (Kono - Roelf)
   - **Golf 2** (Bo - PP, Nick du Toit later)
   - **Golf 3** (Rutile – Kobus)
   - **Golf 4** (Sumbuya – PP)

Air Wing
Commander: Charlie Tait
Pilots:
Carl Alberts
Arthur Walker
Juba Joubert
George Heineke/Zorgenfrei
Aircraft in SL:
- 2 x MI-17 (EO aircraft, ex-UN, flown in from Mozambique in UN white livery, later painted green and rear doors removed)
- 1 x MI-24 (on loan to SL government with Ukrainian crew, Carl Alberts / Arthur Walker/ Juba converted to this aircraft. Neall Ellis later flew this aircraft)
- 1 x HS 780 Hawker Siddeley Andover (ex-Queen's Royal Flight, used for casevac)
- 1 x Cessna 337 (red & white livery, used extensively and successfully on reconnaissance flights)
- 1 x Antonov AN-2 (chartered from African Air Charter to provide logistic support)

The EO organization in Sierra Leone.

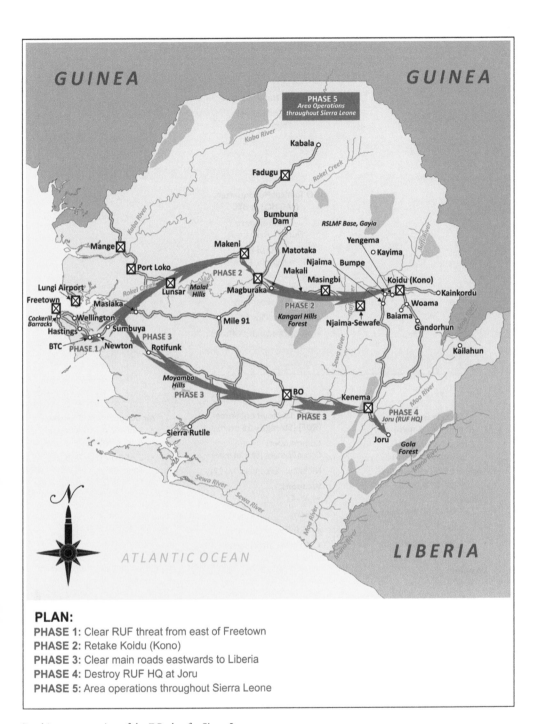

PLAN:

PHASE 1: Clear RUF threat from east of Freetown
PHASE 2: Retake Koidu (Kono)
PHASE 3: Clear main roads eastwards to Liberia
PHASE 4: Destroy RUF HQ at Joru
PHASE 5: Area operations throughout Sierra Leone

Graphic representation of the EO plan for Sierra Leone.

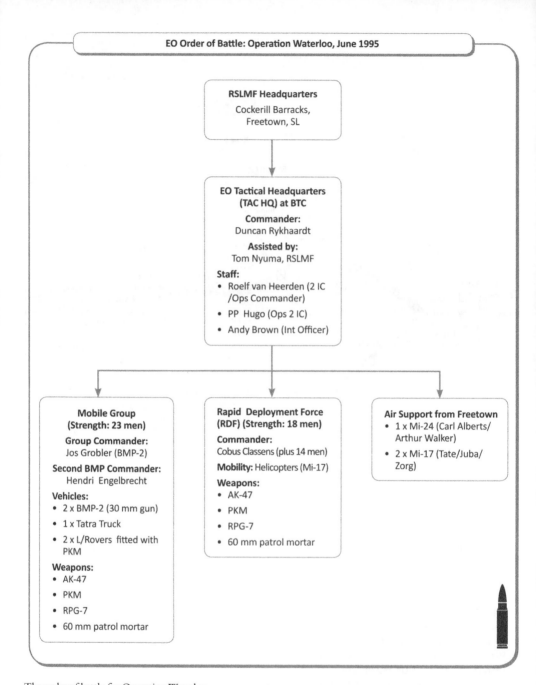

EO Order of Battle: Operation Waterloo, June 1995

RSLMF Headquarters
Cockerill Barracks,
Freetown, SL

**EO Tactical Headquarters
(TAC HQ) at BTC**
Commander:
Duncan Rykhaardt
Assisted by:
Tom Nyuma, RSLMF
Staff:
- Roelf van Heerden (2 IC /Ops Commander)
- PP Hugo (Ops 2 IC)
- Andy Brown (Int Officer)

**Mobile Group
(Strength: 23 men)**
Group Commander:
Jos Grobler (BMP-2)
Second BMP Commander:
Hendri Engelbrecht
Vehicles:
- 2 x BMP-2 (30 mm gun)
- 1 x Tatra Truck
- 2 x L/Rovers fitted with PKM
Weapons:
- AK-47
- PKM
- RPG-7
- 60 mm patrol mortar

**Rapid Deployment Force
(RDF) (Strength: 18 men)**
Commander:
Cobus Classens (plus 14 men)
Mobility: Helicopters (Mi-17)
Weapons:
- AK-47
- PKM
- RPG-7
- 60 mm patrol mortar

Air Support from Freetown
- 1 x Mi-24 (Carl Alberts/ Arthur Walker)
- 2 x Mi-17 (Tate/Juba/ Zorg)

The order of battle for Operation Waterloo.

Vanguard of any EO advance in Sierra Leone—the two trusty Land Rovers.

A motley collection of vehicles made up the elements of the advance on Koidu.

The 120mm mortar in action. This weapon and its crew played a vital role during the advance on Koidu.

Mi-24 helicopter and crew taking a break at the airstrip at Yengema, west of Koidu.

An RUF commander and his second-in-command who didn't make it past the RSLMF troops at Koidu.

The macabre traffic circle we were confronted with on our arrival in Koidu. Koidu 'dared' to illustrate its support for the National Provisional Ruling Council led by Captain Valentine Strasser, by erecting this signboard depicting Captain (later Brigadier) Maada Bio, one of the group of five coup members. The RUF obviously didn't take kindly to this.

One of the first things we did after retaking Koidu was to encourage the local inhabitants to return to the town. I arrived at the location from where we addressed the large number of returnees who had come to see who EO was.

Lieutenant Colonel Tom Nyuma, with sunglasses, one of the five coup members, listens attentively while I address the crowd at Koidu.

through the use of armoured vehicles. The fear of using the country's main roads because of the risk of RUF ambushes was causing the civilian population great suffering and we could really solve this problem with these vehicles. The logistic officer promised to take us to the RSLMF transport park to show us what they had.

As far as air support was concerned, the RSLMF shared their predicament with us. The government already had a contract with a Ukrainian company which had sold them a Mi-24 helicopter gunship with a crew as part of a two-year package and the contract would expire towards the middle of 1995. I informed Brigadier Maada Bio that two EO Mi-17 helicopters were on their way from South Africa and that we would really appreciate the use, by EO aircrew, of the gunship. The reason for this requirement was that our battle procedures required good communications and this would be impossible if the gunship was to be crewed by our Russian-speaking colleagues. We also convinced them that we already had a number of excellent pilots and that they had been flying these toys around under dangerous conditions for many years. The helicopter was allocated to EO on condition that the EO pilots received some training from the Ukrainian-born aircraft commander himself.

Andy and I had some time on our hands now and we decided to visit the transport parks. We were very disappointed to see that, for a start, the parks looked as if a civilian was doing business on a military site. On closer inspection it appeared to be just as we had guessed. The two armoured vehicles were parked at the rear of one of the transport parks, on blocks, with no engines and the transport park personnel confessed that they would not be able to get these vehicles into a serviceable state again. We were a little confused. Were we expected to go into battle against the RUF with only a few Land Rovers taken back from the Ghurkhas? Finally they informed us about the tanks that they could show us. They told us that they didn't think we would be able to use them as they had never been used before. The tanks had been acquired some time before and the RSLMF had never really used them other than as a show of force and for the protection of the head of state.

We asked to see these vehicles and were told that we would have to obtain the permission of State House to visit the premises where they were located. We were granted access and were subsequently shown the position where they were parked. The tanks turned out to be two BMP-2 infantry combat vehicles, a piece of equipment with which we had become very familiar in Angola. At that point the army was using them to defend State House against any enemy approach from an easterly direction. We met the vehicle crews and they showed great enthusiasm, telling us that they had been trained in Nigeria. Our only problem now was to add these two vehicles to our list of requirements and to check their serviceability. The crews reassured us that the vehicles were battle-ready.

Back in Brigadier Maada Bio's office helicopters and armoured vehicles were the main discussion points. We had jumped one step ahead already. Arthur Walker and Carl Alberts, our two gunship pilots, had arrived from Angola and had bonded immediately with the Mi-24 helicopter gunship's Ukrainian pilots. This meant a lot for us and Brigadier Bio agreed that we could train our pilots to fly the Mi-24, and that the EO pilots could fly the aircraft in support of EO operations, with the original flight engineers on board. The two BMP-2 vehicles were released and we were requested to move them to BTC, where minor repairs could be done before we obtained their full use. Much had been accomplished and this indicated the positive response of the RSLMF to our presence and our requirements.

By the end of the first week of May 1995 most of the preparations to receive the first flight of EO men had been completed. The Mile 91 area east of Freetown had also been earmarked for the preparation and training of the EO force once it had arrived.

News of the arrival of the two EO Mi-17 helicopters was greeted with great excitement by one and all. Juba and Jors Zorgenvrei had flown the helicopters in all the way from South Africa and it must have been the trip of a lifetime—all 8,000 kilometres over hostile terrain. Luckily for us the livery of the helicopters was plain white and this made it easier for the whitees flying the lonely route northward. They did have difficulty obtaining landing rights in Nigeria and on one occasion were not permitted to leave the airport building and were required to sleep in the helicopters. We all welcomed the pilots and I began to get a feeling of satisfaction as I saw that the arrangements were slowly but surely coming together. It wasn't only the EO team who was kicking the tyres and admiring the two white Mi-17 helicopters, a large crowd of RSLMF staff stood around and we could see that they were just as happy as we were.

By this time Duncan Rykaart and Naas, our doctor, had arrived with the EO training team. Duncan would command the EO contingent until Bert Sachse arrived. I was appointed as the second-in-command. Quality and courage were added to the team with the appointment of Renier Hugo as the operations commander. We paid a visit to the government hospital where we met Dr Kanu, the director of medicine, who confirmed what support we could provide to each other as the offensive developed. The training team was organized and equipped to help with the training of a cadre of young officers and NCOs from the RSLMF.

We were also introduced to Brigadier Kelly Conteh, the Chief of Defence Staff. He was a fine, very effective senior officer who was pleased at the prospects of the joint mission. He immediately worked hard on the training programme for young officers and NCOs and I felt that we would develop a close and mutually beneficial relationship with him. Lieutenant-Colonel A. C. Kenny met us in his capacity as the Officer Commanding BTC and he offered accommodation for our men as well as providing a liaison officer.

As we approached the arrival date of the first flight of EO operators we finalized the date on which the joint planning cycle between EO and the RSLMF would commence; the date on which the helicopter pilots would complete the conversion to the Mi-24; the accommodation at BTC; and a logistic back-up plan. Our vehicles now included the two BMP-2 infantry combat vehicles, one Land Rover, one Tatra cargo truck and a variety of soft skinned staff cars for local use. The EO office at Cockerill Barracks also moved to a building that had previously been occupied by the RSLMF Air Wing.

We were almost in business.

EO arrives in Sierra Leone

On 11 May 1995 the first contingent of approximately 60 EO operators, with a variety of military specializations and musterings, arrived at Lungi Airport, Freetown. Special arrangements had been made to direct the Ibis Air Boeing 727 to the apron in front of the VIP terminal building where Andy and I received the men before they were airlifted by our own helicopters to the RSLMF Headquarters at Cockerill Barracks.

Meeting up again, after five months, with a large number of the EO operators I had left behind at Cacolo and Saurimo in Angola was an amazing feeling. Wide smiles and exuberant handshakes were the order of the day and I realized how hungry I had become for news from that front. The EO contract in Angola was due to scale down and most of the operators had been transferred to Sierra Leone. The majority were just happy and relieved to move on as some of them had been stuck in places such as Cacolo, where no operations were taking place at all. With the arrival of the first flight of capable, fit young men at Freetown a refreshing, optimistic air of confidence became very evident.

Andy briefed the new arrivals on the intelligence picture and they settled down for their first night in Sierra Leone at the RSLMF headquarters. The beach was close by and the men enjoyed the leisure time there as well as the good company at the Chez Nous Bar, the only bar on the beach at that time. Hassan, the bar owner, had become a good friend to Andy and I and he had allowed us to refrigerate our fresh meat ration there, as refrigerated space was at a premium in Freetown.

The first task was to draw the equipment and prepare the vehicles. Jos and his team worked hard on the two BMP-2 armoured vehicles—track links had to be replaced and the turrets repaired as they had never been properly used. The 30mm main armament on one BMP-2 had been damaged and the gun had to be replaced by a 14.5mm anti-aircraft gun which we mounted outside the protection offered by the turret, exposing the gunner to small arms and indirect fire.

We had become used to this type of improvization and neutralized the danger somewhat by using flak jackets. In short, we had largely to make do with what we had received from the government. The men were doing a good job and they began to take on the characteristics of a force that could overcome the RUF.

Whilst the remainder of the men continued with various training tasks, the leader group participated in the planning cycle for the offensive against the RUF. I fell back on the methodology of the planning cycle I had been taught at the SA Army Staff College in Pretoria by none other than Andrew Hudson. I had been inspired by the example that we had followed all those years ago and was determined to conduct thorough planning just as I had been taught. It is not very often that one has the opportunity, or is in a position to conduct a complete planning cycle, starting with the command appreciation, followed by the intelligence appreciation, the operations appreciation and so on until the operations plan, together with its support plans has been generated, discussed and approved.

The planning cycle started well and the RSLMF officers who attended and participated were attentive and very co-operative. I must admit I could feel that there was a real keenness amongst them to arrive at a well conceived plan and to learn from us about how to conduct real joint planning.

We were all a bit apprehensive about the operation and everyone, from the Chief of Staff right down to the middle ranks wanted to know when we were going to do something. I went out of my way to engage the RSLMF commanders and staff officers at the headquarters to ensure that they were part of the planning process, within the limits of operational security, as I wanted the solution to be a joint solution. If I had not steered the planning in this direction then we would have had a repeat of some of the misfortunes that we had experienced in Angola. Admittedly this approach made the planning cycle at Cockerill Barracks difficult but I tried to lead by example and make it a routine hereafter as well—joint planning whilst fighting the RUF.

Duncan was out of his depth as he had not had the opportunity to attend the SA Army Staff Course and it soon became apparent that this was not his kettle of fish at all either. Duncan nevertheless knew my way of doing things—a joint, combined operations approach with the local commanders even if their operational standard was not equal to ours. I persevered and the approach brought great success in all the operations during the campaign.

The first option that was developed during the planning cycle provided for a speedy end to the war by attacking the RUF headquarters base in the vicinity of Joru, to the southeast of Kenema in the hilltops inside the Gola Forrest. After having neutralized the main headquarters, area operations could then be conducted in the country's southern districts and then move progressively from east to west within each district.

On the other hand, the concept of operations outlined by the second option provided for operations to secure the central areas of the country along the main routes towards the eastern and southeastern districts. This would allow the focus of main effort to move progressively eastward in order to conduct attacks on the priority target areas occupied by the RUF. Once this had been achieved the expansion of operations to other priority conflict areas could take place.

The final option provided for operations aimed at clearing the RUF from the west of the country by neutralizing the threat in the eastern proximity of Freetown, and thereafter penetrating to the east until the RUF were forced into the forest area of the Gola Forrest on the border with Liberia.

Once the presentation of the options had been made by the operations staff I realized that the arrival at a final decision on the preferred option would take prolonged discussions. It was clear that wherever one pointed a finger on the map of Sierra Leone the RUF had a presence. The RSLMF strongholds throughout the country had been totally isolated and there was no single case evident where one could travel from one stronghold to the next without the real risk of being ambushed. I could see by the facial expressions on the headquarters staff that they were earnestly in search of a saviour and a plan for success. In my opinion they were in deep trouble and we had an extensive amount of work ahead of us to achieve any semblance of success.

During the planning session it also became evident that an enemy force in the Waterloo area, southeast of Freetown, had become a real and worrying threat to the capital. Lieutenant-Colonel Tom Nyuma had personally taken a small force on one occasion and tried unsuccessfully to drive them out of the area. It was decided on EO level that we would have to make the decision for the RSLMF, use the principle of starting from a firm base and clear eastward of the capital prior to tackling the remainder of the country.

What was amazing was the fact that the planning group did not appreciate that Freetown, the country's capital, was actually under threat. They had been lulled into a sense of false security by the presence of the ECOMOG forces in Freetown. On my visits to BTC on a number of occasions I had carefully observed the ECOMOG forces and, judging from the relaxed atmosphere and the easy fraternization of their men with the local inhabitants it was evident that they didn't expect any threat either. The makings of a real disaster were very evident.

After lengthy discussions, the third option—clearing the threat from the eastern proximity of Freetown, penetrating to the east and forcing the RUF into the Gola Forrest on the Liberian border—was selected as the preferred option. In short it meant that during the first phase the RUF would be cleared from Waterloo, and this would be followed by operations to clear the highways to the east as far as the Liberian border.

Almost everyone who worked at the Cockerill Barracks was present on the day that the final plan was presented to Brigadier Maada Bio. The office didn't have any air conditioning and we were limited to the use of a number of fans that merely circulated the hot air. Despite the cramped, hot conditions the presentation was a huge success, and everybody in the Cockerill building felt involved in the execution thereof. The next step was to put the plan together on the ground and ensure that the tough part—the logistic support—was in place. The operations themselves would primarily be conducted by EO with their own air support, together with the logistic support provided by the RSLMF.

As far as command and control was concerned, I would command the operation and Duncan Rykaart would stand in for Brigadier Bert Sachse as the latter was still in the process of resigning from the SANDF. Renier 'PP' Hugo, a seasoned operator and a new EO appointee had arrived to assist with operations. Charlie Tait would head the Air Wing with Carl and Arthur on the Mi-24 gunship. Juba was completing a quick conversion course on the Mi-24 in order to increase the flexibility amongst the pilots. A good medical team under Naas would be in place to wipe up the 'blood, sweat and tears'. It is inevitable in the thick bush and jungle of Africa that someone will be afflicted by some fever or mysterious condition, not to mention the possibility of casualties inflicted by the enemy, and it is always good to know that there is a good medical team available.

The plan was presented at EO headquarters level as we waited for the second flight of operators to arrive from Angola. On 24 May 1995 they arrived, were welcomed and stayed at Cockerill headquarters overnight before moving out the next day to BTC. Our strength now lay at approximately 140 men, including the logistic elements—a sizeable force indeed.

Jos and his team moved back to Waterloo after completing an orientation and area operation in the Mile 91 area and we started the final preparations for the offensive. By this time Brigadier Bio was becoming anxious and irritated about the build-up of the RUF and was pushing us to provide the date for the operation's D-Day.

We had, however, learnt very quickly to work strictly according to the 'need to know' principle as it was already a known fact that there was no security amongst the lower ranks of the RSLMF. Nothing was disclosed and we kept the details very close to our chests. The detailed plan was finally presented to the combat team on 5 June 1995.

Little did we know that day that EO would, over the next months, become the subject of conversations around political tables throughout the world, with their feats being discussed on talk shows in almost every developed country in the world.

TAKING KONO

Operation Waterloo

Our first operation in Sierra Leone started on the morning of 6 June 1995. We formed up in a column on the shooting range at BTC and I shared the latest intelligence picture on the RUF before we moved out towards Waterloo at daybreak. The movement had to be controlled by hand signals as it was useless to talk over the BMP-2's radios. Unlike the BMP-2s we had used in Angola, these vehicles had the bare minimum and this did not include serviceable radios.

The force moved out on the main road in the direction of Newton and then turned directly south in the direction of the coast and along the road to the Fo-gbo district which we had planned to cover and clear of RUF elements. The previous day Lieutenant-Colonel Tom Nyuma had told me that on a previous occasion the rebels had shot the shit out of him just south of Newton. He was not quite sure where they were concentrated but he assured us that they would be in the bush surrounding Yawri Bay where the Kandiga River flows into the Atlantic Ocean. The ambush site he was referring to was a mere eight kilometres from Waterloo, which in itself is a suburb of Freetown. The sound of the battle had been heard at Waterloo and BTC, the army training area at Benguema.

At Newton we passed the last of the cheering, waving local inhabitants. It had become common knowledge that EO had replaced the Gurkhas. What was also new to the local inhabitants was the fact that the BMP-2s were being used in combat for the first time. The RUF were certainly in for a surprise. As we turned southward at the intersection I looked backwards to make sure that the order of march was correct. My BMP-2 with the 14.5mm mounted machine gun was in the lead, followed by a Land Rover with a mounted 7.62mm PKM light machine gun, then a Tatra troop-carrier truck, followed by a second Land Rover and Jos as the vehicle commander of the second BMP-2 made up the rear.

There were no signs of any local inhabitants on or alongside the road—a clear indication of a rebel presence. To locate the enemy in this area would be difficult as the bush and undergrowth were very thick and the only access was provided by a number of narrow, well-used footpaths leading away from the roadside into the dense vegetation. The road surface was gravel and the bush alongside the road was thick, with impenetrable thickets followed by scattered villages, all of which were deserted. The column continued in a southerly direction, moving alongside the gravel track, until we reached the coastline at Fo-gbo after travelling approximately ten kilometres. We were not able to move in a wider formation as we often ran into a mass of marshy areas that hampered movement and kept us on the hard surface of the twin tracked gravel road. We drove straight to the last village without coming across any sign, tracks or presence of the RUF in the area.

As we turned around one of the BMP-2s got stuck in the mud. It took us a full two hours to get it out of this very vulnerable location, with no open arcs of fire for the main weapon or the other machine guns. My only reason for not deploying on the ground at this point was that we had not come across any signs at all of a RUF presence in the immediate area. The Mi-24 gunship kept us company by flying overhead and engaging targets of opportunity south of our position and across the river and the RDF in Freetown was on permanent standby, awaiting our call.

We succeeded in freeing the vehicle and were approaching an area covered in especially thick bush when a few of the men gave the hand signal indicating the presence of the enemy in the bush to the right of the direction of movement. We turned off the gravel road onto a single track that led into the thick vegetation and I knew instinctively that we were not going to be able to travel much further by vehicle. The BMP-2s tried to force their way over the thick undergrowth and around the large number of palm trees, but this resulted in the vehicles often becoming suspended in the air on a cushion of vegetation. I decided that to continue would be to give the enemy a chance to pin us down and I gave the command to return to where we had left the gravel road.

Up to this point in the operation we had reacted to intelligence and had only located a single rebel who had lost his way and believed that our vehicles had been commandeered by his colleagues. He really was in a sorry state and so ill that he was not able to run away. What a surprise he got when the weapons on our forward vehicles forced him to stop in his tracks. As we stopped to interrogate him, one of the RSLMF soldiers accompanying us fired a shot at him and killed him on the spot. The first opportunity we had to obtain any valuable information on the RUF had been taken away from us through poor battle discipline.

Instructions were carefully and clearly conveyed to the RSLMF members once again that they were only to fire when instructed to do so by us. We still had no information on the location of the enemy and I decided to move the force to a valley north of our present location. During the journey we halted at a number of villages and found that they had been deserted for some time. We also knew that if we left the villages intact the RUF would occupy them and use them as bases to dominate the whole area. We burnt the villages and chopped down the banana palms to deny the RUF any shelter and food.

I led the return movement with the aim of locating a safer area from where we could approach the operation with a different set of tactics. As we drove off from one of the villages that we had burnt down, my vehicle moved slightly ahead and a gap formed between my vehicle and the rest of the force. Jos's vehicle was stuck again and the vehicles had been held up. As I entered the next village my BMP-2 came under RPG-7 fire from a position located behind a hut. My driver got a fright and swung the vehicle off the road to the right. I gave the dead stop instruction as I realized that we were still in the line of enemy fire, despite the fact that it was not effective at all. My main concern was to stop the rest of the force and mount an attack on the enemy on foot through the village. My hand-held radio had been swept off the vehicle's turret in the excitement and I could hear the other vehicles approaching the ambush position.

By now our vehicle had come under effective enemy fire and Gaddafi, Tuma and I had been wounded. I had no other option at this stage than to carry out an immediate counterattack on the RUF ambush position. My team and I pushed forward on foot towards the small village using the tried and tested method of fire and movement. I could then hear Jos's BMP-2, which had reached the ambush site, returning fire to support me, but by now the rebels had withdrawn into the thick bush. Their tactics indicated a preference for laying ambushes and then disappearing after a few shots rather than engaging in a firefight. The closed terrain left very little space to manoeuvre and it also made the targets very small. The contact was actually a brief skirmish and none of us had had the opportunity to show our mettle. Our casevac report brought a speedy reaction and the wounded Gaddafi and Tuma were airlifted from the contact area. I had a few pieces of shrapnel in my right leg but decided to remain behind and was casevaced later as the wounds were minor.

Jos took charge of the follow-up together with his men as this had been his forte during his bush war days as a Koevoet operator in South West Africa. We realized that a follow-up with vehicles was just not possible. The area became so dense that the BMP-2s were just not able to carry out the bundu-bashing as we had done in Angola and Namibia. This was a totally different ball game. There was no alternative but to move on foot and even then it became risky as the rebels were in the vicinity, waiting for us.

I pulled the follow-up force back after a whilst, knowing that the enemy would remain in the area. We would return with a well-devised plan to overcome both the enemy and the constraints of the terrain and the vegetation. The force moved back to a safe distance just southeast of Newton, supported by the top cover of the Mi-24 gunship which was trying to locate the rebel base. Carl Alberts and Arthur Walker were a formidable team and they crisscrossed the bush in a vain effort to locate it. They reported that the vegetation was so thick that they couldn't even see the ground and suggested that we would have to sweep the area on foot. They did manage to locate an element of the enemy crossing the Kandiga River in a dug-out canoe and fired at them with the Gatling gun, putting them out of their misery.

Duncan and Lieutenant-Colonel Tom Nyuma had by this time moved the tactical HQ to BTC from where we decided to regroup and tackle the rebels from a different angle. By now Duncan had the RDF, under the command of Cobus Claassens, in the Mi-17 helicopters and had dropped them in the Fo-gbo area. Effectively this meant that the enemy had been blocked off to their east and they would have to break through our deployment to escape in that direction. The rebels were, however, very familiar with the area and were able to mix with the local population and disappear amongst the populace as and when required. Their base in this area was probably the last one before they would mount attacks on Freetown itself, and if we could threaten the area their plan to attack Freetown would be in jeopardy. They had the advantage of the terrain and this gave them the opportunity and time to rethink their attack as well.

Cobus deployed his thirty-odd men but an immediate follow-up was not possible as there was too little daylight left and they moved into a temporary base after dark. During the night Cobus lost his first man due to a misunderstanding between two guards. The situation in the temporary base had been rather tense and as the guards were changing their shift, one of the troops was shot by a fellow guard. This incident placed the RDF in a difficult position as they were forced to evacuate the area at night in order to carry out a safe medical evacuation.

The next morning we all pulled back to a poultry farm south of Newton to regroup and replan the offensive against the rebels in the area. I handed the operation and the ground force over to Jos and on 8 June 1995 Gaddafi, Tuma and I flew to South Africa together with Efraim, the deceased RDF trooper.

Over the next few days the air wing spent time conducting air reconnaissance in an attempt to locate the enemy base. By now it must have been pretty obvious to the RUF that the increase in offensive activities and a new approach by the government meant that they would have to step up their aggression to further their plan to attack Freetown. We were aware that the RUF were always keen to revisit the site of a contact to search for whatever they could lay their hands on. This allowed them to replenish their ammunition and lay their hands on whatever else they could use. Duncan came up with the plan to attack the area where the enemy had last been seen and thereafter to clear the area through area operations.

Hendri's Waterloo

Hendri, better known as Old Baldy or Pan, had received his nicknames during his tenure as a Koevoet operator. His large bald pate and even larger heart belied the physical strength and strength of character of the man. A leader amongst the men, he didn't pontificate much but when he did his wit and sayings were remembered by one and all. Loath to talk about his experiences as an operator, I encouraged him to recount his narrow escape just outside BTC whilst I was on leave. Here are his recollections:

> Colonel Roelf had left on the Mi-17 helicopter to Freetown and we had returned to BTC. Jos, Cobus Claassens and I sat together and discussed recent events. This was our first contact with the RUF and it was still too early to form a real opinion of their capabilities and compare them to the other enemies against whom we had fought in the past. UNITA had used a combination of conventional and unconventional warfare whilst SWAPO had mostly used terrorism. The RUF tactics appeared to be altogether different. They did, however, use the terrain very well and succeeded in mingling with the local population. They were proficient in the use of the RPG-7 although their fire was not very accurate, but the blast effect and the shrapnel were effective enough. Look at Roelf with RPG shrapnel in his leg and Gaddafi's stomach, full of shrapnel.
>
> Duncan and Lieutenant-Colonel Tom Nyuma were busy planning our next movement. We at least knew that the RUF was here, on the outskirts of Freetown and that they were located approximately five kilometres from BTC as the crow flies. It was also very clear that they were preparing for an attack on Freetown via Waterloo. This approach was ideal as it provided protection for an attacking force,

with the peninsula mountains on one flank and the marshy waterline of the Rokel Creek that flows into the Atlantic Ocean on the other. And, by the way, this was also the very same route used by Captain Valentine Strasser and his fellow RSLMF officers to enter Freetown when President Momoh was toppled during the coup d'état.

On 14 June 1995 we received a warning order for a mission to fix the enemy in the area southeast of Newton and destroy them in order to relieve Freetown from the threat of an attack by the RUF. The mission was simple and all we had to do was fill our 'saddle bags' with *biltong*, arrange for bullets and move out. Our earliest movement time was at 0700 on 15 June 1995.

We moved through the gate at BTC that morning under command of Jos and with the loud support of the local inhabitants. Through Waterloo we drove, turning right at Newton onto the bush road and then straight to the school where we had been active the previous few days. We passed it and moved on to where we had previously made contact with the RUF when Colonel Roelf was wounded.

I led the movement in one of the BMP-2s, with Jos within sight and behind me in the second BMP-2, followed by the Tatra truck with the Land Rover, known as 'Five-O', covering the rear. We had learnt from the previous ambush that it was important for the occupants of the vehicles to stay within sight of each other at all times. The vegetation was just too dense and the RUF appeared to know how to move in this thick jungle. The rainy season had just started and dust was not a factor as it had been in Angola.

The next sound I heard was all too familiar. I left my thoughts of Angola and returned to the present where I was in the middle of a firefight with the RUF, the bunch of cheeky buggers. My vehicle was drawing fire from positions within a number of houses on my left flank and I instructed my driver to swing the vehicle slightly to the left on its tracks. My gunner, Frans 'Flakjacket', traversed the 30mm cannon to where I had indicated and opened fire. This felt really good and I felt exhilarated as he commenced firing. Things were happening at the receiving end of Frans's shots. The 30mm cannon is, in my opinion, a really fantastic weapon.

I ordered my men to debus and form up on the vehicle's right flank. Out of the corner of my left eye I saw that Jos had moved into a position about 30 metres from me and he was also covering the left hand side of the road with his main weapon, the 14.5mm machine gun, as well as his section. The bush was thick and I knew that his men could not see what I could see.

My vehicle was located on the edge of a small village with four houses and a dense banana plantation behind them. I estimated the enemy force to be in the vicinity of 20 to 30 persons. Once we had started to return the fire the enemy immediately withdrew to positions behind the houses and disappeared into the bush. Jos's gunner, Attie, looked at me and raised his hands, palms facing upwards into the air. He was frustrated as he wasn't able to see any enemy to engage effectively. His facial expression indicated that he wasn't particularly pleased as he was being prevented from being part of the game.

We didn't really have the opportunity to get down to the hard tacks of a real firefight and a battle against the enemy as everything ended within a short five minutes after which I established contact with Jos and Cobus via the A-54 radio. Cobus and his team on the Tatra were totally out of the picture as they had scarcely had time to debus and take cover before I had given the order to cease fire.

Jos quickly reorganized the force and my men on the ground confirmed that the enemy consisted of about 30 persons, who had by now moved off in a southeasterly direction into the thick bush. It appeared that the position to which they had moved had already been prepared by them for such a contingency. They had obviously learnt from our previous skirmish that EO was not the type of force that would run away in a contact, and that we were inclined to start an immediate follow-up operation. They had not experienced the full benefit of an EO follow-up as yet and it must have been a hair-raising thought to anticipate such an event.

The bush here was our greatest enemy and our biggest problem. We were ex-Koevoet men and with EO in Angola the bush was much kinder to us as we could at least see a little distance ahead. All we could see here were banana leaves and other cursed plants that combined to form a thick blanket to our front. We would have to adapt to and master this set of circumstance very quickly indeed. The bush was so thick that during the follow-up after the contact in which Colonel Roelf was injured, a BMP-2 managed to 'climb' onto the vegetation and became suspended above the ground as a result.

The follow-up operation was initiated and Jos confirmed that it should be a silent activity. The follow-up force moved on foot, followed by the two BMP-2s, the Land Rover and the Tatra, all located a tactical bound to the rear. All my men and Jos's men had been attached to Cobus's force for the follow-up. The BMP-2 vehicle crews, including Jos and I, were the only persons left in the vehicles. Our role was to support the ground force once contact had been made with the enemy. The terrain dictated everything, as had been the case during the previous contact and it appeared once again that the RUF wanted to draw us into thick bush and fix us.

Cobus informed us that he believed the tracks of the RUF indicated that they were returning to the village where our initial contact had taken place. Jos confirmed that Cobus should continue with the follow-up and ordered the vehicles to turn around and move back to the contact area at the village. Jos led this movement aimed at occupying a defensive position and waiting for the enemy or fixing them whilst Cobus's force approached and engaged them from the rear. This plan sounded good to me. Approximately 45 minutes had passed since the first shots of the day had been fired and I was amazed that the enemy would return to the first contact area so soon. This time we would make sure that they understood us very well.

We entered the contact area in the village and Jos took up a defensive position in the road on a slight rise, with my vehicle about 20 metres behind him. All of a sudden Jos aimed the BMP-2's main weapon—the 14.5mm machine gun—and fired a burst; and, since he wasn't the type of person who would fool around unnecessarily, I just couldn't fathom what he was up to.

What I didn't know was that the RUF had already moved into attacking positions behind the houses in the village. My driver tried to reverse to get a better arc of fire but stalled the BMP-2 and I shouted to him to stop just where he was. Jos, seeing that I was in his line of fire, tried to move into a better position, but in the process his driver turned the vehicle too sharply and it threw a track. So, there we both were, not at all in the best of positions in the road, and in each other's arcs of fire. What a mess.

Jos and his vehicle crew debussed and took up positions behind their BMP-2 on both sides of the road and he and Attie, his gunner, provided support fire. The main weapon on my BMP-2 experienced a stoppage and we continued to fire using the vehicle's co-axial light machine gun.

Cobus, who was still following the enemy tracks on foot, radioed us and wanted to know what was happening. I briefed him, emphasizing that the RUF had already moved into positions within the village and that we had been exposed and fixed in the open. I emphasized that his approach to contact should be speeded up as we did not have the strength or the serviceable firepower to take on the RUF alone. All we had was Jos and Attie plus their driver and two troops at his vehicle, plus Frans 'Flakjacket', Nico and Raymond, with a medic and two more troops alongside my vehicle. I remembered that a local journalist was also in my BMP-2 but I only saw him much later, hiding inside the vehicle. Everyone debussed and hit the ground except Jos and I and our gunners. The volume of fire that we were delivering from the turrets didn't appear to have any effect on the RUF at that moment though.

Cobus warned us that he was not able to move much faster due to the thick vegetation and the strong possibility that the RUF was waiting for him in ambush. I, on the other hand, wanted him to accelerate as we, as a small group of people, were running out of ammunition. The enemy remained unseen but they were shooting from the thick bush over a wide front and I was starting to become apprehensive about being surrounded by them.

I was forced to lift my head out of the turret and observe so as to assist Frans in acquiring targets. The next time I raised my head I heard the double explosion of an RPG-7 firing from a short distance away from my location. The rocket was streaming from my right and I felt the shrapnel shoot up into my face from the point where it had detonated against the BMP-2's turret. I fell back into the turret for a moment to gather my bearings and realized that I couldn't see very well at all. I ran my hands over my face to clear away whatever was obstructing my sight but was unsuccessful. I hoped for the best and believed that this was merely a temporary thing. I called the medic closer as I was only able to observe half of what I was used to seeing. This was annoying and I didn't quite know which way to look. As he approached from his position alongside Ngombe, one of my black operators, I saw a look of shock and amazement on both their faces. I deduced that this was obviously not good for me. They were very anxious and anxiety is infectious. I indicated to him that he should throw a field dressing up to me. It was very difficult to catch the bandage as my arms appeared to be too long. I became convinced there and then that there was something wrong with my right eye. The firefight was continuing around me and I slipped back down inside the BMP-2. My left eye caught Frans's hand signal that we were low on ammunition and he asked me if I was all right. I was fine and decided that I would sort this sight thing out later. My self-confidence had received a telling blow during the RPG explosion but it returned as Frans resumed fire with the co-axial machine gun.

I contacted Cobus and anxiously enquired about their progress as we were in the shit at our location. Jos remained fixed behind his 14.5mm machine gun and he provided welcome covering fire when I asked for it. Cobus contacted us to say that we were firing in their direction now and that we should move our fire. No sooner had we moved our fire than the RUF rebels started picking up their heads. They were slowly moving closer and closer to our position as they darted back and forth across the road. With the enemy closing it was becoming all the more difficult to defend without the volume of fire and penetration of the two serviceable machine guns. Cobus should understand this. He informed us that they were located immediately behind the enemy and that the enemy had not realized this yet.

I really was concerned now as I could only see half of what I should be seeing. How must I fight with only half my sight? You shoot at what you see and you see what you aim at. I couldn't see. I peeped out of the turret to look at the rest of our men and their communication to me via their hand signals was similar, their ammunition was depleted and they needed assistance from Cobus's follow-up force.

I must say I hadn't experienced this deep-in-the-shit type of feeling for a long time and I made sure that the nine AK-47 magazines I had were easily accessible beside me in the turret. I still had a 50-round magazine on the weapon with an additional spare 30-round magazine. We were really in deep shit if everybody was concerned about their lack of ammunition. I felt the field dressing over my eye and realized that it was still sitting snugly and doing its job and the bleeding had stopped but I felt a great deal of pain deep inside my head. I started to panic as I realized that these rebels may assault the vehicles, and we, with our depleted supply of ammunition and no support from Cobus and the majority of the men, stood a chance of being overrun by them. I looked out of the turret once again and watched as Ngombe, who was on his haunches in the open in a position alongside the vehicle, fired carefully aimed shots at the enemy. The enemy was full of bravado by now and they were visible and fired more inaccurate RPG-7 rockets at the vehicles.

I grabbed Frans by the shirt and shouted that we were the only persons on or around the vehicle and that we should abandon it and pull back to the vicinity of Jos's BMP-2. The rebels were sure to hit the vehicle with an RPG rocket sooner or later and that would be the end of us. That was it. No questions asked. We slipped out of the rear of the BMP-2 and joined Jos behind his vehicle. I felt much safer there and watched our BMP-2 as the rebels pelted it with all they had. We had been in the centre of their killing ground.

Cobus's voice came over the air and he shouted that we should lie low as they had made contact with the enemy and that they were initiating an immediate attack. He also mentioned that the enemy appeared confused and their actions indicated that they were trying to get out of the fire that was coming from two directions now. This information was very encouraging and the enemy fire immediately started to abate. Cobus was talking about a rout.

We didn't cease fire totally. Despite the fact that the thick bush didn't allow us to control our fire properly, reports of enemy movement on the flanks every now and then resulted in a number of skirmishes taking place in our vicinity. Cobus eventually gave the instruction to cease fire and we all eventually gathered in the vicinity of the BMP-2s.

Jos contacted Duncan over the radio and sent a contact report, the most important part of which related to the casevac flight request to get all those with shrapnel wounds—Ndakolo, a former 32 Battalion man and I—to a doctor to receive medical attention.

The closed terrain didn't allow a helicopter to land in the immediate vicinity so we decided to forego the normal methodical search and consolidation through the contact area in favour of the preparation of a LZ for the helicopter in the vicinity of the local school. Jos and his team first had to repair the BMP-2 track that he had thrown before we could leave.

For the BMP-2 crews it was an anxious time as one is so vulnerable in these vehicles when they are immobile and without ammunition or fire power. On the other hand, the adrenalin rush was still high amongst Cobus's men who were in all-round defence of the BMP-2s. They fidgeted and talked and joked amongst each other as they relived parts of the contact. They couldn't stop talking about that fact that the contact had actually been a rout. It was very evident that the RUF had suffered a telling defeat, with a large number of casualties. Those who had seen the rebels remarked that it was very difficult to find a single piece of military uniform amongst them. They were mostly dressed in civilian clothes with red bands around their heads. We also understood why they had returned to the contact area. They had come to scavenge in order to replenish whatever they needed. The RUF strong point was its ability to ambush its opponents and this was something that we would have to deal with over the next couple of months.

Jos's BMP-2 was serviceable again and we were ready to move. Juba, one of our Mi-17 pilots, had been placed on standby for the casevac flight in the interim. At the school the LZ was made safe and Jos's white smoke grenade guided Juba to the area as he came in from the south and landed without the usual over flight prior to landing. I quickly said goodbye to the men as I was aware that I would probably not see them again for some time. The doctor would ultimately decide whether I should be moved immediately or not. I suddenly realized what a massive impact this injury was about to have on my life. I got into the helicopter together with the other wounded men and Juba lifted off for the journey to Cockerill Barracks.

I went to lie down on one of the benches in the aircraft and looked up at the innards of the helicopter just above me. Was this my last operation with the men or would it be recorded as just another contact on my totem pole? We landed and I watched as a group of people approached the aircraft. We had landed about 50 metres from the EO headquarters at Cockerill in Freetown and I was comforted, knowing that I was in good hands here. As I lay on the examination table I tried to get a number of short-cut answers from the doctor but he underlined the fact that he could only effectively conduct a superficial examination. He emphasized that he would try to limit the damage as far as was possible but I tried to force him to be totally direct with me and asked; 'Do you think that I have lost my eye?'

I suddenly realized that this was the first time that I had actually had the courage to be totally truthful with myself and tackle the subject of the loss of sight in my one eye. Blind in one eye. I couldn't believe this.

The doctor was vague about the diagnosis and they decided very quickly that I should be evacuated to Abidjan in the Ivory Coast for observation. I was airlifted by helicopter to Lungi Airport where I was transferred into an Andover aircraft for the flight to Abidjan. I was the first casevac that the aircraft had transported. It was a true privilege, especially since the aircraft had at one time in its life belonged to Queen Elizabeth II. It was equipped in a very practical way and I prepared for one more flight, with the doctor, into the unknown.

I landed on the examination table of a French-speaking doctor in Abidjan and his appearance made me doubt the links between French men and beautiful French women. I knew that this was somewhat unfair but I felt that if he could stare at me and examine me in such detail I could do the same. I didn't understand his language but the way in which he pointed his index finger in all directions concerned me greatly. I had judged him unfairly as being not good looking. My emotional condition and feeling of insecurity had got the better of me, and I just wanted the examination to end in order that I could go home to the people I knew.

My feeling of utter loneliness and abandon became even more acute when the doctors left the room to discuss my case in more detail. This feeling of desolation led me to question why this had happened to me. I had faced different enemies on the battlefield in three different countries over a number of years and had always had the upper hand. Why this all of a sudden? Shouldn't I rather have moved away from the BMP-2 sooner and sought cover to the rear once it had come to a standstill? Maybe I shouldn't have stuck my head out of the turret so often to help Frans with the fire control orders. After all Frans was a good gunner and he didn't really need my assistance.

The doctor returned and informed me that I should expect the worst, as my right eye had been severely damaged and I had lost all sight in it. It appears that a piece of shrapnel from the rocket had hit the eye socket below the eye and penetrated the eye thereafter, cutting through it and severing the nerves at the rear of the eye.

"Your eye has been destroyed within the socket," the doctor said.

I took a deep breath and said; "Let's go".

That same day we returned to Freetown to find that my movement back to South Africa had already been planned and I flew to Johannesburg via Brussels on 17 June 1975. Baba Tonkara, one of the EO coordinators in Sierra Leone, accompanied me to Brussels and I was on my own thereafter for the flight to Johannesburg.

Pollie, a former operator during the EO operations in Angola who was conducting signals duty for EO in Pretoria, met me at the airport and he took me directly to Olivedale Clinic for the operation to remove my eye.

So ended my exciting and adventurous career as a member of EO. I had met the enemy on many a battlefield throughout Africa but in Sierra Leone I had met my personal Waterloo.

The advance proper

With the sad news about Hendri's eye fresh in my mind, I returned to Freetown from Namibia, where the short leave had worked wonders. I always said to my men that I became 'green sick' in Sierra Leone and that the only cure was to take my family and camp out in the wide open spaces of the brown Namib Desert for a few days. This 'healed' me and brought back my perspective by opening up the 'channels' and enabling me to see vast distances over the plains again. I was once again able to differentiate the vast array of different, non-green colours and this enabled me to develop different approaches and innovative plans. The last couple of months had forced me into a rut; I had lost my sharpness and this in turn affected my planning, making it too narrow and unimaginative with too few options.

On my arrival in Sierra Leone I was briefed that my men had continued the sporadic contacts with the RUF in the outlying areas of Freetown under the command of PP, Jos and Cobus. There had been casualties, but fortunately, nobody had been killed. We all still hoped fervently that Hendri's eye could be saved. In time I spoke to him about it and he said that he subconsciously knew that his sight had gone forever the moment the shrapnel had hit him.

At this point Duncan was still in command in Freetown and after thorough discussions in the ops room with Brigadier Maada Bio, Brigadier Kelly Conteh, Colonel Komba Mondeh, and other operations officers, we concluded that the plan would have to be amended somewhat. The operational plan initially provided for the clearing of the enemy along the two main routes into the interior. By this time, however, the RSLMF units in the Kono District were desperate for assistance. The area was known as the bread basket of Sierra Leone in terms of its ability to provide food and, of course, it was home to the rich diamond deposits and fields. The RUF had concentrated on attacking the area regularly at exactly the right time, thereby allowing them to turn the output of the diamond washing plants to their own benefit.

Colonel Mondeh also informed me about how he had struggled to get to his troops at Koidu after they had been trapped and isolated there. At one point he had been forced to make use of a long, tortuous road detour which took him two weeks to return to Freetown via the sovereign territory of Guinea. What made the Kono district, and specifically the town of Koidu, so difficult to approach was the number of small roads that serviced the whole area. No matter where we found ourselves, we were road-bound and easily immobilized.

Just before my return the commander of the small contingent of RSLMF troops at Koidu had reported that most of his troops had deserted and if the RUF got to know that he only had a meagre 30 troops available, they could assault the town in short order. This platoon of RSLMF troops had also evacuated the town and taken shelter in an area alongside the road to the west of the town. In this position they were protected by a large marsh to their north so their defensive area of responsibility only required three flanks to be covered.

During the period that Andy Brown and I had waited for the first men to arrive in Sierra Leone we had got to know Lieutenant-Colonel Tom Nyuma quite well. He loved to order his uniforms from *Soldier of Fortune*, wear pendants and chains around his neck and emulate Hollywood action heroes. His bodyguards also saw this as the 'in thing' to do and would have hung RPG launchers around their necks if they had been able to achieve this feat whilst seated inside his official vehicle. Although they were loud mouthed and brash, they at least had a little more guts than the other officers and men I had met so far. Time would tell if this remained the case.

Tom indicated that he wished to participate in the operation to free Koidu. As pleasant a person as what he was, he did not have the benefit of having received much formal tactical military training and he tended to impulsively rush off on a tangent, expecting everyone to follow regardless. A number of times we had to stop him and first develop a number of options then decide on the best course of action to follow. Tom said that his 'gut feeling' told him what was required and he relied on it to solve tactical problems.

As South Africans, we also threw a spanner in the works by deciding that it would be best to watch the Rugby World Cup final between the Springboks and the All Blacks before starting the offensive. What a great feeling of joy it was when the Springboks won the World Cup and our sense of gratification was also shared by members of the British High Commission who watched the game with us. Not bad for British cooperation and consensus with EO.

By now two lowbed trucks had been arranged to transport the two BMP-2s by road. In addition the vehicle convoy consisted of two Tatra 10 ton cargo trucks, the two Land Rovers as well as Tom and his seven or eight bodyguards in the Nissan Safari he had commandeered from its unfortunate Lebanese owner. In support we had a single 120mm mortar, one 82mm mortar and two 60mm mortars that had been converted into patrol mortars. The advance was also supported by the two Mi-17 helicopters and the Mi-24 gunship. A few RSLMF troops had been attached to our unit, mainly to man the BMP-2s and it wasn't long before we decided to get rid of them. Their standard of training was just not on a par with ours and they were better off being utlized as riflemen. I asked Jos to give them a simple practical test by letting them fire a few rounds with the main armament of the BMP-2 aimed into the hills. They failed this test, and our men, who had vast experience with this type of vehicle in Angola, took over the BMP-2s. The RSLMF soldiers finally left us when we reached the outskirts of Masiaka.

Finally the order of march was fixed and the logistics were in place, somewhat haphazardly mind you, as nothing worked in the Sierra Leone armed forces. The best map available to us from which to navigate was a commercially available Shell Roadmap of Sierra Leone. There were a few 1:50,000 scale maps available at the geological department, but it was an excessively frustrating process to get them and we reverted to the Shell Road map—Go well, Go Shell.

It was Saturday, 24 June 1995, the Springbok rugby team had lifted the Rugby World Cup and the men were eager to get the advance underway. We hadn't left the confines of Freetown since May and we were willing, eager and hyped up to get at the RUF.

Final orders were issued on the morning of 25 June on the BTC terrain, the order of march was set up and I gave the order to start the advance. At that point it was also important for Lieutenant-Colonel Tom Nyuma to lead the advance. I actually didn't have a choice other than to travel with him in his vehicle—chiefs talk to chiefs—although I knew this was tactically wrong. Tom's Nissan Safari led the advance up to Makeni where we liaised with the local RSLMF battalion commander. Thereafter the order of march to Magburaka was adapted with PP and the two Land Rovers, each with PKM light machine guns, at the front, followed by the two BMP-2s, then Tom and I in the Nissan Safari, followed by the mortar fire support group and the two cargo vehicles with the rest of our troops. I had managed to convince Tom that commanders do not move in the vanguard of the advance, for very good reasons. There were enough men there who could lead the advance very efficiently and effectively and we were approaching a semblance of balance in the force deployment at last. Some of the men were very nervous, as they had not been under fire before. At Matotaka we stopped, enjoyed a few coconuts, had a smoke break and generally had a real, relaxing bullshit session.

It was at this point that I got to know 'Fearless' Fred Marafono. Fred was easily the oldest man amongst us. With a mane of long hair and a bushy beard as befits an ex-SAS operator, he had a wide knowledge of the world and valuable experience in a number of small team contacts. But I also came to realize that someone had sent him along with a plan. Fred had been attached to us as he had already been in Sierra Leone for some time and he knew the environment and the conditions better than we did. I had only met Fred briefly at our headquarters during the planning of the operation where he had provided input.

PP (an abbreviation for *Pantser Poes*, translated as Panzer Pussy—a reference to the fact that this former Recce operator originally hailed from the SA Armoured Corps) took the lead from Matotaka—east of Magburaka—onward, with Fred breathing impatiently down his neck. Initially PP did a good job of putting up with this state of affairs. Fred continually insinuated that PP was advancing too slowly and PP reported that Fred just wanted to rush ahead. It cost me all my diplomatic skills to resolve this difference of opinion and convince Fred that he would just have to put up with the way we advanced. I really appreciated his way of doing things but there was only one commander—Lieutenant-Colonel Tom Nyuma—and his decision to advance in a more measured, conventional fashion was how we had planned the movement in the first place. And this was how we were going to carry it out. End of discussion.

We also realized that we had the undivided attention and rapture of the local population. Tom was the orator and his bodyguards were the clowns. The people loved what they saw and heard as most had probably never seen such a convoy before, despite the fact that we only had eight vehicles. We had 'joiners' to contend with a large number of people who took a chance and tried to hitch a ride to Kono as there had not been vehicle traffic on this route for some time. To them this was an ideal opportunity to catch a joy ride, or *junter*, to Kono with the force. It also gave them the opportunity to arrive on the scene at an early stage and loot the areas that we took back. By the time we had reached Matotaka, however, they were very weary. Matotaka had not been damaged, destroyed or burnt by the RUF, as was the case in towns further east. I had also heard that Foday Sankoh's family stayed there.

The lowbed vehicles that had transported the BMP-2s returned to Freetown and we entered more mountainous terrain. I instructed PP to move at best speed, a movement technique in which we were all well versed, which provided for mutual support and an advance speed dictated by the surrounding terrain. This did not impress Tom Nyuma or Fred Marafono and I had to repeatedly remind them that we wished to achieve our objective of reaching Kono in one piece. I may not be the greatest strategist on earth but I bloody well remembered what my own commanders had taught me during my formative years in the SADF. Always keep one foot on the ground. Tom and Fred wanted to rush and PP had his hands full trying to keep Fred in tow.

With PP in the vanguard we succeeded in reading the terrain beautifully. As we approached a possible choke point PP would give me the grid reference, then Neels, our artillery officer, and I would bring the 82mm mortars into action and fire one or two mortars into the target area in question before we moved on. I had only lost one man in Angola during our advance on Cacolo—a man taken out by UNITA using a Dragunov sniper rifle from a tree. The EO men all understood the danger and I had always played this game safely, whilst always achieving my goal within the required timings. The planned duration of this operation was four days, the terrain was difficult ahead and we were making very good progress at this point. I had even started wondering whether the RUF were about to treat us in the same fashion as UNITA, by enticing us into an area and then isolating us. Only time would tell.

PP and Fred had eventually risen above their differences and were working well together now, despite Fred wanting to do something reckless every now and then. We then had to remind him that the speed of advance was not his to determine. The aim was not to locate the enemy and summarily destroy them. The aim was to advance on Kono, to bind the enemy there and destroy him, then stabilize the area and continue with area operations. Everyone eventually began to understand the work.

PP called a halt about 20 kilometres from Massingbi and indicated that the lead vehicles had observed the enemy in the distance. The terrain offered clear defiles to the enemy into which they could entice us, bind us and deliver a telling blow. I didn't want to pick up any leaks so early in the advance and lose troops. We had the Mi-24 on standby at Makeni and within minutes it was overhead. We knew that the RUF would wait for us along the route and we were aware that there were massive security leaks within the RSLMF HQ in Freetown. The terrain was ideally suited to ambushes here and we understood that the RUF were masters of this technique. A warning bell rang in the back of my head, reminding me of the Gurkha force that had been destroyed by the RUF in an ambush a few months back. We would not fall prey to this.

The Mi-24 approached along the axis of attack stipulated by PP and strafed the indicated position with its 12.7mm Gatling gun. What a feeling. The helicopter followed this up with the delivery of a number of AGS-17 30mm grenades onto the target area, and all hell broke loose as the grenades exploded on impact. PP and the advance guard troops debussed and, with the support of the main armament of the BMP-2s, cleared the objective on foot. Indications were that the enemy had deployed between 80 and 120 men in an ambush position astride the road and they had been compromised thanks to the sharp eyes of our men. The rebels had fled and PP reported approximately 15 dead rebels. I stopped the usual follow-up that we undertook after a contact of this nature as we were not here to waste time; there were troops in Kono who urgently required our help and I wanted to be there as soon as possible. I redeployed the 82mm mortar and engaged the fleeing enemy. It was also clear that the enemy had hastily set up this ambush.

We had overcome the poor operational security that was a trademark of the RSLMF headquarters and it was no longer necessary to explain our *modus operandi* to Tom. He was surprised that this contact had gone so smoothly. Of course he was. If it had been him he would have rushed blindly into the defile and lost a large number of troops at the same time. He admitted to me that if he had led the advance then his force would have been divided into two parts by now—one component on the other side of the enemy ambush position and the other well on the way home. This, he said is why he had to go out on operations—to ensure a measure of cohesion as the RSLMF troops were notorious for their inability to stand and fight.

With no time available to clear the objective and a commitment to reach Massingbi by last light, we moved on and reached our objective late that afternoon. Our arrival was too late as it didn't allow sufficient time to carry out a thorough reconnaissance of our overnight position and lay out clear arcs of fire. This was important as we were a relatively small force and the fire we would deliver had to be effective.

It was raining hard when we reached the town and Tom and I quickly liaised with the remaining occupants, and then departed to our various overnight positions. Tom and his men occupied the existing observation post that had been manned by the government troops, whilst the EO component moved into an old house with a roof that leaked so much that we may as well have stood outside in the rain. The walls did offer some protection against small arms fire though. It had been a long day and our ration packs were devoured hungrily.

Early the next morning we set up the order of march again and prepared to leave on the next leg of the advance which would take us from Massingbi to the Sewa River at Njaima–Sewafe, then a further 40-odd kilometres on to Bumpe where we would join the isolated RSLMF troops.

The movement progressed well and the greatest problem was to maintain our current level of alertness. I still valued my commitment not to lose anybody. On our approach to the Sewa River we were forced to stop once again as we expected resistance from the RUF and, as a consequence, deployed men on the high ground on the near side of the river to provide covering fire. The terrain on the other side of the river was very thick with many high trees and I decided not to engage this area with a preparatory bombardment from the mortars. We would engage the enemy as and when we drew fire.

The BMP-2s crossed the bridge and were followed by the troops on the cargo vehicles. As the troops reached the middle of the bridge a single shot rang out. The BMP-2s reacted immediately and used their main armament to fire into the bush on both sides of the road to suppress any enemy fire. I soon realized that the deployment of the troops on the far side of the river was useless as the shot that had initiated the firefight had originated from a position on the near side of the river. All at once a man jumped out of the bush on the near side of the river, with a balaclava over his head, indicating wildly to us with both hands that he was unarmed. I ceased fire immediately. The troops grabbed him and manhandled him into the road, demanding an explanation for his behaviour. It eventually transpired that he was a RSLMF troop and that there were additional troops hiding in the bush. The soldier was very upset, claiming that he had fired a single shot only to get our attention and indicate that he was a member of the RSLMF force. His excuse was immediately rejected and the RSLMF troops accompanying us got stuck into him for giving us such a scare with his ill-conceived action. He succeeded in calling the rest of his troops out of their hiding place in the bush.

On further investigation we realized that the soldier who had fired the shot was the platoon sergeant of a group that had broken away from the RSLMF base at Bumpe, west of Koidu. When he heard this Tom couldn't contain himself any longer. He descended on the sergeant and meted out a mighty swipe for deserting the force. By now the sergeant's balaclava was sitting on his head at a totally different angle and he explained once again, skew balaclava and all that he would not have survived if they had stayed at Bumpe as there had been an argument with his subordinates. Those who wished to get out alive had followed him and they hit the road. Eventually, after this long explanation he and his troops were told to mount the cargo vehicles and accompany us on the advance.

We advanced slowly now towards Bumpe, passing totally deserted towns and villages along the way. All that remained in some locations was a stray dog or chicken that, for some or other reason, hadn't scattered with the others when the town had emptied. There were no signs of human life around and it was clear that the RUF had put the fear of death into all the locals they had not murdered. We intended to arrive at our destination as early as possible in order to relieve the pressure on the small force that had been surrounded there. Our movement speed had indeed slowed and the troops had debussed due to the threat of possible enemy ambushes from the dense vegetation in the mountainous terrain. Eventually the terrain opened up and we were equally relieved to feel the sunshine again, knowing that we were close to our objective.

As the last rays of sunlight faded on 26 June 1995 we reached the road intersection at Bumpe where the RSLMF troops were deployed. The troops there had obviously heard the vehicles from afar and their abundant joy greeted us on arrival. At first they were very concerned at the appearance of a number of white faces amongst the relief column. They stood back at first, wanting to approach my black troops, but were not able to communicate with them due to language difficulties. Eventually they recognized the break-away group members amongst us and then realized that they had in fact been rescued.

Tom approached them and, without hesitation debriefed them in order to understand the situation on the ground. The picture that emerged was not favourable at all and he called me to one side. I decided there and then to hold a debriefing session with my own men once I had received more information from Tom. Our first priority now was to deploy the force for the night and this was made all the more difficult by the large areas which were under water on both sides of the road, combined with very limited manoeuvring space. A few houses were dotted around the area and it was clear that we had no alternative but to remain on the road.

Tom informed me that he had intelligence that indicated that an attack by the RUF would in all probability take place overnight or during the next morning. I called PP and the rest of my command group together and we held a quick order group as the optimum layout of our forces for the night had now taken on even greater importance. We would first have to repulse the attack then we would be able to obtain a better idea of who we were up against. The darkness had caught up with us this time.

I called Neels, my mortar commander and indicated to him that the most probable direction of an enemy attack would be from the east and that he was to deploy the 120mm mortar to enable it to fire a bomb as close as 300 metres from my position, from where I would control the fire. I also deployed one platoon on the eastern flank and located my own position behind them. Tom and PP were deployed closer to the road intersection to the west. The enemy would have to pass my position or PP's position in order to penetrate the defended location. We didn't really expect the RUF to have the capability to penetrate the defended locality but we were fully prepared for any event. Silence descended as the sun set but we were by no means at ease and no one really got much rest that night. I moved into an abandoned house on the edge of the deployment, made sure that the guard system was operational and then lay down to rest on an iron bedstead without any mattress. It was cold comfort after the day's journey.

The next morning before first light I woke and my first reaction was to dig around in my rucksack to locate the remaining few jelly beans and pieces of liquorish that were in there somewhere. The search for these treats was rudely disturbed by the sound of a shot. I picked up the crack and thump of the projectile and realized that the shot had been fired from outside our defended locality. Was this the start of the expected attack?

It was still dark as I rushed out onto the veranda and bumped into Johan, my signaller. I remembered that it was his birthday and congratulated him whilst pushing him into a firing position at the corner of the house, accompanied by words to the effect that despite this being his birthday he would have to carry out this important defensive task against the enemy as they attacked. He explained to me that his mustering was that of a signaller and that infantry defence was not his strong suit. Tough shit.

The shots were coming closer and closer to the house and becoming all the more effective. I also heard fire starting on the flank occupied by PP and deduced that we were being attacked from all sides.

I could hear that my troops were delivering carefully aimed defensive fire. I could also hear the enemy fire, and then it would stop, and start up again in a less effective manner than before. Neels requested permission to commence with a fire mission and I ordered him to fire in an easterly direction, onto the road at a distance of approximately 200 metres from my position. When the first 120mm mortar bomb exploded on the road there was absolute silence for a short period of time. I estimated that, since the majority of the incoming fire had come from that position on the road, the mortar had probably hit its target. I ordered Neels to fire five more bombs for effect at the same target, then to move the fire outwards along the road. The enemy fire was erratic by now and I knew that the firefight in my vicinity had been won.

I could also hear that PP and Tom were still heavily engaged in a firefight at their position. As I crossed the road to see if there was any fire close to my own position I drew fire from the bushes close to the house. I ranged the mortar fire back to a distance approximately 100 metres from the house and gave a target indication of an area adjacent to the road. Silence fell after the bomb exploded.

I then decided to launch an immediate counterattack and mustered all my troops. I left the two BMP-2s behind, prepared the two Land Rovers and started the follow-up in an easterly direction. I also saw Tom and PP approaching with their troops and they explained that they had concluded the firefight on their front in their favour and that they wished to accompany us on the follow-up. The speed with which we undertook the follow-up was such that the RUF had no other choice but to scatter in an unorganized fashion and the battle turned into a rout with the RUF running for their lives. We located our 120mm mortar target area as well as a number of RUF bodies lying next to the road. There must have been approximately 150 rebels and everywhere we could see how the effective mortar fire had forced them to scatter head-over-heels into the thick bush, abandoning their weapons and equipment as they ran. This was something out of the ordinary as the rebels would usually return to a contact area to scavenge weapons, ammunition and equipment that had been left behind. In this case they had fled the area completely.

I decided to occupy the small airfield a few kilometres away at Yengema as we completed the follow-up and deployed there without a shot being fired. PP and I caught up on the progress he had made on his front during the contact and it was evident that the rebels had tried to penetrate the defended locality on his front but they had ended up receiving a hiding as well. We both decided then to return to the contact area and, on arriving, located the bodies of nine rebels who had actually penetrated the defended locality.

One rebel was still alive and we interrogated him. It soon became clear, however, that he was in no condition to answer any questions—his one leg had been shot to pieces and he had to deal with the pain of a burning stick rammed up his anus by the RSLMF troops. I voiced my strong opposition to this type of treatment of prisoners to Tom, stating that this was not how we in EO worked. Apart from losing the opportunity to obtain valuable information from him, we just didn't believe that this was the right thing to do. Tom's troops had cut the penis and testicles off the bodies of the other dead rebels and stuffed them into their mouths. Tom conceded that this was a common practice on both sides.

As we progressed with the clearing of the area I realized that the result of the morning's activities would enable us to continue the advance immediately and reach Koidu town itself. I issued instructions to PP to form up, continue the advance to Koidu and occupy the town.

As we approached Koidu we discovered a number of dead bodies strewn all over the place along the road at a village. Some were the bodies of rebels who had died from their wounds during the contact that morning whilst others had been in their final resting places for some time. The streets were riddled with pools of dried blood where the RUF butchery had taken place a few weeks earlier. Looted military equipment lay scattered all over the place. The rebels must have had a whale of a time. Tom also informed me that Corporal Foday Sankoh, the rebel leader had named this attack Operation Pay Yourself.

Within two hours we reached Koidu and slowly entered its precincts to find that it was a ghost town. Whereas Koidu could easily have housed between 20,000–30,000 people, it was devoid of any human activity. Decomposing bodies, half-eaten by dogs, pigs or vultures were scattered everywhere. As we entered the town proper we came across the first traffic circle and it was decorated with human skulls. The town was clearly a pro-NPRC establishment as could be seen from the advertisement boards supporting the leaders of the coup d'état with large portraits of Captain Valentine Strasser and Brigadier Maada Bio. No wonder the destruction of human life was so violently visited on these people by the rebels.

We slowly ventured deeper into the town but still could not locate a single soul. The total population of the town had fled, some northward and others eastward across the border into Guinea. Throughout the town the doors of businesses had been broken open and the property that the looters had not taken had been torched. I stopped at a mosque and together with Cobus Claassens located two handicapped children who had been abandoned there. It was evident that their parents had seen no other alternative for themselves or the children other than leaving them and hoping that the rebels would not enter the mosque. They had fled, leaving their most valuable possessions behind.

I had seen enough. My head was swimming as I tried to grasp the enormity of the devastation and the scale of the task that lay ahead for me and EO. It is very difficult to grasp and accept the cruelty that had been visited on these people by their own families and compatriots. With the standard of the RSLMF troops not much better than that of the rebels I had a lot to ponder regarding how my men and I were going to sort out this chaotic situation.

That evening I decided that we should occupy an area of high ground in the middle of the town. The terrain we selected housed the premises of the old casino and it enabled us to establish a robust defence against any possible counterattack mounted by the rebels. Tom kept on telling me that the rebels had never been thrashed the way that they had been that morning. What a wonderful advance this had been—no own forces wounded and no losses. I emphasized to Tom that this was the correct way to approach this type of operation—patience and movement at best speed.

A Mi-17 helicopter visited us from Freetown and resupplied us with ammunition and drinking water. At sunset the guards approached Tom and I with a visitor who hailed from Freetown. This was unusual as we had believed that all the Freetown visitors had left in the Mi-17 but here she was, all on her own amongst a whole host of soldiers. She approached me and introduced herself as Agnes, a freelance American journalist. Tom wanted to know how she had managed to hitch a ride on the helicopter from Freetown. She responded to this question in a cool and calm fashion, saying that surely Tom was aware of how easy it was for a woman to persuade a man to do something he didn't really want to do.

We realized immediately that she had guts, and that her African-American origin would also have played in her favour. It was not difficult to see how she would have found it relatively easy to persuade someone, especially the RSLMF troops. So, here she was, and it was becoming very evident from her behaviour that she had a lot of time for Tom and I. Tom was not persuaded at all and she then moved the focus of her attention to me. Once I had told her that EO does not provide information to journalists she shifted her focus back to Tom. Her tactics became all the more clear as dusk approached and she still did not know more about how it was possible that our force managed to sweep the RUF out of the way and occupy Koidu so rapidly and efficiently. She didn't relish the thought of sleeping on the rock hard floor that night and as a final resort she zoomed in on Tom. I believe that she didn't achieve much that night.

We all rose early the next day, secure in the knowledge that the absence of a RUF counterattack the previous evening had strengthened our deduction that they had received a thrashing from us the previous day. Later we learnt from information sources in Guinea that the rebels has sustained between 180 and 190 losses during the two days. Those rebels who had not been killed on the spot had been evacuated, as and how they could, to Guinea where many died from the wounds they had sustained during the fighting.

On the day after our arrival a group of militiamen arrived out of the bush to find out what the situation was on the ground and to confirm that it would be acceptable to allow the local inhabitants to leave the bush and return to the town. The militia, known as the Kamajors, had been raised during the time that Britain had held great sway in Sierra Leone. In short, one could describe them as a tribal police force but as the war between the government troops and the rebels progressed they became part of the conflict as well. They had been armed with shotguns and were required to protect the tribes—the Konos in this case—from human and animal threats. It was only to be expected that they would use the weapons to hunt and as a result the wildlife in the area had been decimated.

The Kamajors were clearly delighted with what we had achieved and they immediately returned to the bush to spread the good news. This was obviously a change from the normal depressing news that had been conveyed to the locals up to this point. This time it was due to the efforts of men from the south of the continent that the rebels had been driven out. On top of this, there were white men present as part of the force.

Early on the morning of the third day we received another visit. Men of stature in the area had ventured forth from the bush to establish who this group was, and they were accompanied by the same Kamajors who we had met the previous day. The visiting group arrived at our defensive position on the hill totally unaware that we had been prepared to defend the area with maximum force. We realized that this type of visit to our defensive position could not happen again as the enemy could very easily infiltrate the group and make life very difficult for us.

Notwithstanding this minor concern we bade the visitors a warm welcome. The first person to introduce himself was Chief Abu Kongoba II, the paramount chief of the Lhei chiefdom on the Guinea border. He was a large, bearded man with an imposing presence, who spoke with grace and measure. He was also the chairman of the Council of Chiefs and in this capacity he had the mandate to speak on behalf of all the chiefs in the area. He was accompanied by a former Minister of Defence, a former head of local government and other senior persons who had been in control of the country during the 1980s, when President Siaka Stevens had been president of Sierra Leone. The delegation expressed their abundant joy and happiness and immediately promised their full cooperation. They praised us for the amazing success we had achieved and in the same breath pleaded for protection against their own brothers in the RUF.

One man went so far as to state that he was very pleased that the colonialists had occupied the area once more, as things had not gone well with them up to this point in time and they were ready for a change. Tom and PP promised that we would quickly reestablish order in the town and expressed the hope that all the town's inhabitants would return as soon as it was safe to do so.

Over the next few days the town began to live again as the local people returned from the bush. Many of the returnees went directly to their homes to see what was left of their property, whilst others began searching for their loved ones who had not returned with them from their sojourn in the bush. As we patrolled the town and its surrounding area over the next few days we watched as returnees desperately searched amongst the burnt out houses and decaying bodies for loved ones and personal possessions. This was the greatest tragedy that Koidu had experienced to date. During previous invasions the rebels had come into the town, made themselves at home between the local populace and then used the men to wash diamond grit for them, raped the women and stole their possessions. Never before had the rebels massacred the populace on as large a scale as this.

By the end of the first week after our arrival at Koidu the people were still streaming back to the town in their hundreds. I noticed a large number of troops accompanying the returnees out of the bush, a clear indication that the cohesion amongst the RSLMF troops had disintegrated and, without any leadership, they had sought their safety and future amongst the locals. It was really disappointing to see how the leadership element had deserted their own troops, leaving them to their own devices, whilst they escaped to the relative safety of Freetown.

Tom, together with his officers and men, returned to their battalion base at Gayia, approximately five kilometres to the west of the town. He did set up an office in the town itself though. In anticipation of the arrival of additional fresh troops at Gayia, he eagerly awaited the arrival of the commander of the Eastern Province and we reconnoitred the terrain in and around the town thoroughly.

SECURING AND DEFENDING
THE KONO DISTRICT

Meeting the people of Koidu

Time had moved on since we had occupied Koidu 10 days previously and large crowds of people were arriving from far and wide to greet us, see who we were and find out what the fuss was all about. I wanted to deploy inside the town whilst at the same time being in a position to protect the surrounding area and to this end we had reconnoitred and come across a very suitable base area within the confines of the town. The local inhabitants would also be able to provide some measure of early warning. The EO force in Koidu only numbered 49 men and I needed to extend our line of defensive as far outwards as possible. I had learnt from UNITA that it is wise to utilize the local population to the maximum and to look after them at the same time. Our base was located on top of the hill where the district commissioner's house had been built. The house was adjacent to the jail and there was sufficient space for three helicopters to land with ease. The area was easy to defend, with a good view over a wide front and it was strategically located. I was satisfied with the location and set up our head office. It would also be convenient to meet and obtain the cooperation of the local inhabitants and leaders to defend and administer the district.

It became obvious that there was an urgent requirement to communicate with the local police, the RSLMF and the local inhabitants as soon as possible. The best way to do this would be to speak to them all during a public gathering and we set about arranging it in short order.

The day of the public gathering dawned and thousands upon thousands of people from all corners of the district arrived to witness the occasion. It was also very evident that they were full of joy at the new status quo. I was introduced to the more eminent inhabitants, the paramount chiefs, the subordinates, even the Lebanese businessmen came to meet us and introduce themselves. We had selected a position on the second floor of the best-placed building in the town to address the people and to this end we installed loudspeakers. There were journalists from Freetown, and representatives from other international radio stations, including the Voice of America. People from far and wide had come to see the soldiers who had chased the rebels from the Kono district.

The public gathering was a long, drawn out affair. EO, the authorities who had sent EO and the South African government were officially welcomed by each and every speaker. As the people made the connection between the EO soldiers and Bafana Bafana, the South African football team, everyone who hailed from the southern part of the continent was given a loud applause and made to feel welcome as a result. Everyone on the 'stage' had a turn to speak and naturally everyone awaited my address with great anticipation.

Almost all of us had grown beards due to the lack of the opportunity to shave and the crowd appeared to be anxious to hear from the bearded men. My address was short and to the point. I repeated what I had said on Voice of America the previous day. EO would drive the enemy out of Sierra Leone before Christmas 1995 and the Kono district would be free of the RUF—from Koidu to Gandorhun and Kenema. This was greeted with load applause, especially amongst the younger generation and joy was evident on everyone's faces.

Once the meeting had adjourned Tom and I had another discussion before he left for Freetown. Now it was time to start working, as the expectations of the local inhabitants had been raised and they would have to be met. We were not going to disappoint anyone, no one's contribution was going to be turned away, and all efforts would be combined into one total, directed effort. Tom agreed that all operations would be conducted on EO level. No operations would be conducted by the RSLMF battalion in isolation; the control of all operations would be taken over by EO and we would determine the how and where forthwith. Both Tom and the local RSLMF battalion commander accepted this. I knew, however, that this would not be an easy task and somewhere in the future I foresaw that the RSLMF would deviate from the agreement and try things on as only they could.

To help maintain the momentum, my men undertook a patrol westward on the main road to Freetown on 19 July 1995 and made contact with the RUF just west of Bumpe. They killed six rebels without sustaining any casualties or injuries on their side. The incident caused my troops to be seen as better than the local RSLMF troops despite the fact that no local observers were on the spot to witness the contact. The sound of firing was, however, proof enough to them.

From the outset I cleared the town of any RSLMF troops who had taken up residence there instead of at the battalion base. It had become clear early on that the RSLMF troops preferred to live in the town itself and when manpower was needed for military tasks they simply didn't show up. This move soured our relationship somewhat but I persevered and cleaned up the town to the absolute delight of the local inhabitants. I realized then that I would have the total cooperation and support of the local inhabitants if I succeeded in bringing about a number of basic changes. It was clear that the RSLMF held sway here and elsewhere in the country, and the police were either totally absent or subordinate to the RSLMF. There was no order and no proper administration. In short, the government had collapsed here.

Very few instructions or guidelines were received from the government at this point. EO was in command here and this was exactly how we wanted it. Contrary to Angola, where we were constantly plagued by the interference from local and second-level government officials, we had the opportunity here to get the complete situation under control as we deemed necessary. Some guidelines regarding mining in the district did emerge though and the ministry of mines decreed that there was to be no mining until further notice. Femmi Kamara, the district mine engineer, was located in Kono at that stage and he informed us that the minister would not allow mining activities of any nature to take place and that we were to strictly enforce this policy. The intent was to enact new mining legislation before any new mining activities would take place. This was not necessarily a good decision as the primary source of revenue in the area had effectively been cut off.

My first orders to my men were to get the total area in and around Koidu under control and to discourage any mining activities. Whilst this was happening I would focus my attention on the stabilization of the district. The EO patrols throughout the mining areas would also dominate the area, allowing a tactical requirement to be satisfied as well. I received enthusiastic feedback from far and wide as the locals now realized that the RUF would no longer be able to sneak into the area unopposed. I also received an understandably mixed reaction from the Lebanese businessmen as they wanted to mine and trade in diamonds. The old dilemmas surrounding the Lebanese presence in Sierra Leone—were they a stabilizing factor or did they actually contribute to the instability of the country—resurfaced but I didn't pay much attention to them at the time due to more pressing priorities.

Birth of the Kono Consultative Committee (KCC)

Carl Dietz, our intelligence officer who had taken over from Andy Brown, paid us a quick visit from Freetown to exchange intelligence and to brief us on the situation in the capital. The rebels had not recovered from the shock and their losses as yet. Foday Sankoh had spoken with his lieutenants and had calmed them down; stating that the RUF would re-occupy Kono and the people of the district would pay the price. It was clear that Sankoh was very annoyed at being humiliated here, partly because he didn't expect such an ambitious move from Freetown to Kono, and partly because he didn't expect the execution to be so violent. Around Freetown he could fully understand that, with the means at their disposal, the government would be able to defend vigorously, but not here in the remote areas on his own doorstep. After all, he had prevented Tom and a group of people from entering Koidu in the recent past. Foday Sankoh wanted to know who was behind this sinister move against him. Carl had brought good news indeed.

I briefed Carl on the first Joint Operations Committee (JOC) meeting that I had held with the local RSLMF commanders. A clearer picture of the overall situation in the district was slowly emerging and I intended to use the total local population to help drive out the RUF and help themselves reestablish the district. We would be the catalyst and set the tone but the energy would also have to emanate from them. We would fight the RUF and assist on an administrative level but the local inhabitants would have to step up and exhibit the will to rise out of this mess. Carl and I discussed a suitable name for this action and decided there and then to establish the Kono Consultative Committee (KCC). The KCC was destined to play a pivotal role in the times ahead for EO as well as the total Kono district and its people. There were, of course, people here who did not like what was happening and I was able to identify who these opponents were. They were by and large the very government officials whose corrupt hand would no longer be filled or tolerated under the auspices of EO.

I approached Lieutenant-Colonel Sena, the RSLMF commander in Kono; Inspector Sesay, the police commander and Chief Abu Kongoba II, and arranged for the first meeting of the KCC. During this short meeting I briefed them on what had happened on my level and I gave them an overview of the enemy situation. I mentioned that my forces had made contact with the enemy twice over the last few days and that during the contact on 13 July 1995 two rebels had been killed and nine RSLMF soldiers had been wounded. On 19 July 1995 our forces had killed six RUF rebels without any own forces casualties. For a moment or two this news appeared to flabbergast them, as it was clear that they had never been informed in such precise factual detail via a formal channel like this before. I had their full attention thereafter but they were also very unsure as to how we should all fit in and work together.

I informed them that I wished to establish the KCC with the purpose of bringing about order amongst the local inhabitants to enable them to continue with their daily lives and to obtain information regarding their knowledge of the area. We were very aware that the rebels had family members in Kono and in this fashion we would obtain the correct information. Heads nodded in enthusiastic agreement and they all agreed that we should go ahead with this initiative. I also agreed to act as chairman for the first few meetings, after which either the RSLMF commander or the police commander should take over from me.

The next meeting of the KCC was scheduled for the coming week and the turnout was so overwhelming that we were forced to lock people out. Everyone, from all walks of life within the district, wished to make a contribution. They all wanted to hear what the people who had not been stopped by the rebels had to say as they were short of good news and solid solutions. I spent the duration of this meeting explaining the goals of the committee for the next three months and confirmed that at the end of the three months we would review the situation and our progress and then decide if it was necessary to continue with the KCC or not. The attendees were very receptive and supportive of the KCC and it did me personally, as well as EO, the world of good to commence with these actions. I received strong support from my headquarters in Freetown, and from Eeben Barlow and Tony Buckingham.

I also activated the Kamajors, the armed tribal police force, through the KCC and ensured that they were represented on the KCC as well. Their first representative was Randolph Fillie Fahboi, a veteran former APC politician who had been forced to go to ground as a result of the coup d'état. Randolph Fillie Fahboi and I were destined to become very good friends as time passed.

As KCC chairman I set clear objectives and I could see the expectation of the end results on the faces of the attendees. They looked forward the most to the briefings and the feedback given by EO as they were, for the first time, regarded as important people and they were being handled in a fair, even-handed and humane manner. They were like people who had just had their fortunes read by a fortune teller; previously they had survived in a cocoon and had been subjected to punishment and violence. Who were these white people and their trusted supporters who arrived out of the blue and brought only good news? They were literally eating out of my hand. I had the full support of Chief Abu Kongoba II and his council, as well as the local inhabitants. They were in absolute awe of us and it was a pleasure to work with them. At the same time my men patrolled the area around Koidu and I received even better cooperation as a result.

The news had spread far and wide that Kono was safe and that those who had fled could return. Naturally we were also concerned that the rebels would use this as a means of returning as well and there wasn't really much we could do about this except wait for the local inhabitants to identify them for us. As the people's confidence returned and they visited, and even returned to their fields and villages further afield, we began to receive reports that the rebels were visiting these areas and killing people.

The first time we were called out to a location on the main road to Njaima–Sewafe southwest of Koidu. When we arrived, the force followed up on the available information and the Kamajors who accompanied us took us along such a wide detour that the men began believing that they had been taken for a ride. However, with the du Preez brothers and Simon Witherspoon in the EO group nobody would be likely to attempt this and get away with it unharmed. Eventually the group was led silently into a village where one of the Kamajors pointed out a group of rebels on the far side of a number of houses. The EO group immediately opened fire, knowing that the rebels would rather avoid a direct confrontation. Four rebels were killed and one was captured before the group returned to Koidu. The badly malnourished, captured rebel was tied to a pole for the night but the information we exacted from him thereafter was of little real value. He stated that the rebels had intended to infiltrate the area again and target their own families; and that they were aware of the fact that they were up against a serious force who they wished to avoid in favour of attacks on soft targets.

The rebel was of no further use to us so I called Lieutenant-Colonel Sena and recommended that he should take the rebel under his care. With a shrug of his shoulders he stated that there wasn't much more that they could do with the prisoner, as inevitably they are shot. We had seen evidence of this when we had come across desecrated rebel bodies in Bumpe and scenes of decapitated rebel bodies on the battlefield. He decided that the rebel should be killed and he took the man a short distance away from my office to a position adjacent to the old unused prison. I realized, however, that he was not very keen to commit this act himself, and he looked at me in an expectant manner. I explained to him that we would run into unnecessary problems in the future if the word got around that we had simply lined up a prisoner and shot him. This could be construed as murder if one did not give the man the chance to defend himself and we would have to come up with another plan. I sent the driver up to my office to fetch one of Lieutenant-Colonel Sena's troops. This troop had no reservations about pulling the trigger but we didn't realize what a poor marksman he was. The first shot hit the rebel and forced him to his knees. Lieutenant-Colonel Sena shouted to his soldier to put the man out of his misery and four shots followed before the rebel's life ended. I now understood better why things had gone so badly for the RSLMF during the conflict. The soldier couldn't fire a single telling shot at a distance of two metres. The rebel had also dug his own grave before being shot and he was summarily piled into it, without any ceremony, or even a cross.

The rumours about EO actions in the district ran far and wide. We had been successful in our latest contact with the rebels and the security forces had killed a rebel. The Kamajors drew strength and motivation from this and eagerly participated in actions to secure the area thereafter. They had a pressing need for shotgun cartridges though. I reported this to Brigadier Bert Sachse in Freetown and we subsequently received a large consignment together with a budget to be used in the deployment and employment of the Kamajors. I decided that the ammunition would only be issued when the Kamajors were on operations and when they were attached to the armed forces. This plan worked excellently and it received a rowdy approval from the Kamajors. I also promised them that if they killed rebels then I would issue the captured AK-47 to them and provide 7.62mm ammunition for continued operations. This was seen as a massive incentive on their part and I put it into action despite the disapproval of the RSLMF.

We began to receive more and more information from the local inhabitants during the KCC meetings and I realized that this forum had been a singularly successful initiative that had produced exceptional results.

The EO operations were not without the odd mishap though. On 23 July 1995 I learnt from our headquarters in Freetown that the helicopter that Charlie Tait, one of our pilots, was flying had taken a bird strike whilst he was en route to Kono. Fortunately he managed to land the aircraft safely amongst the palm trees near Magburaka in the central areas of Sierra Leone. He was on a rat-run mission to Kono when the incident took place and the aircraft was also loaded with a number of sacks of maize meal for the Kamajors. The crew of the downed helicopter were stranded but since EO always operated with two helicopters at a time, the second helicopter picked up the crew and flew directly to Makeni, where they informed the RSLMF there of the position of the stricken aircraft and requested a guard, before returning to Freetown. This had not been a good day as we had never experienced something like this in Angola. Helicopters shot down? Yes. But no bird strikes. Fortunately the helicopter was not an EO Mi-17. It belonged to the RSLMF and Major King, who was in control of the RSLMF Air Wing, was not impressed. On the other hand, no one had any control over this situation. The loss of the aircraft was serious as it had been a converted Mi-17 with the added advantage of having rocket pods, something that our helicopters did not carry. The next day a replacement Mi-17 was tasked to deliver the rations.

For the first time since we had started the advance from Freetown there was the opportunity to take a little time off to relax over the weekends and the men were always on the lookout for an opportunity to have a few beers. Logistically we were very well looked after. When a rat-run arrived at our base in Koidu a set of priorities kicked in. First it was the postbag, then the cargo was offloaded and we all keenly waited to see what meat had been packed for the first braai. We always had a braai on the first night after a rat-run and there was usually a braai pack of meat specially packed for each man. That evening the war was set aside for a whilst, a fire was lit and beers were consumed whilst the meat sizzled. The men switched off and relaxed, whilst we relied on the Kamajors and the local population for protection. Whilst the smell of meat permeated the air and the cold beers flowed, war stories of things that had happened down south were told and retold by storytellers in fine form. Jos and a few experts had, on request, built a bar above the area where we lived and we enjoyed many relaxed evenings there.

Gaddafi earns his flak jacket

On some occasions our weekend routine changed for operational reasons. One Friday evening at last light I received a message that rebels had been observed in a small village south of Koidu. The sun was already setting and I tasked Neels with his 82mm mortar team and a protection element to move out and fire approximately 20 bombs all along the road to the village as the rebels would in all probability use the road especially if it was after dark. I estimated that they would want to carry out a last light attack in order to regain some prestige. The successful EO mortar fire mission that evening was in all probability the reason why we heard nothing from or about the rebels for another two weeks at least. We knew that they would return though, as Foday Sankoh didn't have much sympathy for his men and he was desperate for a breakthrough. The rebels then captured two local men and questioned them about the armed force that was in the town and we realized that they were very keen to find out about us and determine what our capability was. One of the captured men told the rebels that the force consisted of a white leadership element with approximately 40 black troops. He was branded as a liar by the rebels and summarily executed. The other man was tasked by the rebels to inform EO about this event.

About ten days later, at approximately 1400 on a Friday afternoon, I received a message from Randolph Fillie Fahboi, the head of the Kamajors, that a number of the local inhabitants had reported that the rebels were once again planning to enter the town from the south. He had received this information from Kamajors who had run into the rebels whilst en route from Baiama.

The right man for this job was Jos Grobler and after I had issued a set of quick orders the force under his command left on the mission. A vehicle transported them to a location outside a village close to the town and dropped them once they had been met by a guide. Jos decided that they should follow a route that would bring them around and to the rear of the rebels but, according to Jos, the du Preez brothers did not agree with this approach as they had followed this tactic on a previous occasion without any success and they were not looking forward to being fucked around again. Jos persevered as he believed that this was the right decision and he was not in favour of being the victim of any rebel ambush, hence the detour to move into a position behind them. By the time Jos and his men had found the rebel tracks it was starting to get dark. Jos deduced from the tracks that the rebels were up ahead of them. Two alternatives presented themselves. They either had to set up an ambush and wait for the rebels to return the next day or they could continue to move and make contact with the rebels ahead of them. The latter course of action was selected.

The bush alongside the track was so thick that it didn't provide any opportunity to manoeuvre in a battle formation. Nevertheless, they made the best of the situation and moved as tactically as possible. It wasn't long before the forward troops shouted that the enemy was up ahead. Jos's instincts took over, as had always been the case from his first days as a Koevoet operator, and he attacked. The battle raged and threatened to get out of hand but the EO fire was more sustained and accurate than the return fire. Jos didn't have many RPG-7 rockets to fire, and in any event there were too many own forces in the area, so he relied largely on small arms and PKM machine-gun fire. Jos's troops won the firefight and ahead of him his men felt the urge to get at the enemy as this day had been a long time coming. The previous time that the two forces had clashed over such a short distance had been outside Freetown where Hendri had lost his eye and the feeling had been that the rebels had made the EO troops work hard for their money that day. Today seemed to be a similar occasion but it was now time to resolve this outstanding issue with Foday Sankoh's troops before dark.

The bush was very thick and the tried and tested drills could not be effected as desired, so Jos decided to phase the attack. The rebels had made use of a few houses as cover in a nearby village but they were not expecting an attack from the rear. Notwithstanding this the rebels had their fair share of dare devils whose bravado was undoubtedly fuelled by a mixture of marijuana and the locally brewed *pega pak* gin. A little later Jos received a message that Gaddafi, one of our true characters, had been seriously wounded and he gave the order to bring down heavy fire from the area where Gaddafi lay. This forced the rebels to move back into the bush, their fire became inaccurate as a result and the contact petered out and ended.

Jos and his men estimated that up to 30 rebels had been killed as compared to one seriously injured EO soldier. The bullet that had wounded Gaddafi had entered his body through the upper part of his one shoulder alongside the shoulder blade and, without so much as touching the backbone, exited along the other shoulder blade and shoulder. He was carried in the darkness all the way back to Baiama and evacuated to Freetown later that night. There was no argument about the risk of bringing a helicopter into Koidu at night as Gaddafi had to receive the best treatment. He was a brave, courageous man, was highly regarded by one and all and bore the scars of wounds sustained during a previous ambush at BTC outside Freetown.

Jos had decided not to search the contact area as the evacuation of Gaddafi was the priority. It was already dark and additional losses during the search would not have been acceptable. Since it was known that the RUF would return later the chances of an additional contact were high.

Since the noise of the battle could be heard as far away as Koidu, EO was lauded by all after Jos's force returned that evening, and this carried on for a number of days. Information we received over the next few days indicated that we had been conservative about the number of enemy killed in the contact. The local inhabitants related that up to 45 rebels had been killed and the scene of the battle had been strewn with blood, discarded ammunition, uniforms and lost equipment. During the next KCC meeting feedback was received that the Kamajors who had visited the site of the contact had counted more than 50 decaying rebel bodies and that they had come away with a number of AK-47 rifles with which to enhance their arsenal.

During the contact Gaddafi had earned the right to the title of 'Flakjacket No. 3' amongst his colleagues. The title of 'Flakjacket' was normally conferred on a person due to the large number of shrapnel wounds they had sustained in combat. Lafras had earned the first title as he could not pass the security scanners at an airport without being called aside and strip searched until, after promising that he had not swallowed anything, he was allowed to pass through.

The 'Flakjacket No. 2' title belonged to Frans, my signaller during the operations in Angola.

He had received the title, not because of the shrapnel that he had p... almost superhuman efforts to avoid picking up any shrapnel. In the EO... we would often be on the receiving end of incoming fire from the UNITA D-30... first sign or sound of incoming fire, Frans would dive for his flak jacket, put it on and t... get to the trenches and, because there wasn't always time to grab it, he would wear this heavy burden for the rest of the day, irrespective of whether there was any incoming fire or not. We jokingly tried later to convince him to sleep in it, just in case.

EO insisted that RUF radio traffic should be intercepted. This was done in a clandestine fashion as there were many opportunities for this type of intelligence to be leaked from our military headquarters in Freetown. We were provided with very good interception equipment and our signallers were assisted, as far as language was concerned, by a Staff Sergeant Conteh of the RSLMF. From the intercepts we learnt that Foday Sankoh used three radio frequencies; one for operations, one for logistics and one for general use. He was very active on the networks and used, or misused, the ether to harangue and motivate his people on all levels. At first we learnt that he was still very disappointed at the RUF's performance at Kono. After these disastrous actions, where he had lost his best troops, he was very annoyed with Lieutenant Mosquito, a popular young rebel, who became the target of Sankoh's shouted insults.

We had been very successful with the intercepts and began to provide information to the headquarters in Freetown. We didn't trust Staff Sergeant Conteh though and were not in favour of the transfer of information to him personally, so we allowed him all the more leisure time in order to minimise the possibility of security breaches. If Sankoh had learnt that we were intercepting his radio communications it would have become all the more difficult to establish his comings and goings.

After Gaddafi had been evacuated we really put our heads together. It was evident that the rebel force was regrouping and that they had withdrawn troops from other provinces in order to retake Kono. The dusk attacks, ambushes and the harassing of the local population were all signs that they had some capability and that they were serious in this endeavour. The RUF then deployed a forward headquarters at Gandorhun, approximately 30 kilometres southeast of Koidu. Their intent was to use this as a base from where they could launch actions to retake Koidu. During the KCC meetings, the Kamajors provided valuable information to us on RUF activities and very often we would put our heads together to resolve this. Randolph Fillie Fahboi was exceptional and fought the negative perceptions about EO tooth and nail. He developed a very close and open relationship with EO and we remained friends and comrades long thereafter. From time to time I would assist him with a bag of rice or so for his contribution. The KCC meetings progressively became a cornerstone without which we would not have been able to operate as successfully.

After the latest KCC meeting, I attended an important meeting in Freetown where Brigadier Bert Sachse, Brigadier Maada Bio and I agreed on a broad strategic plan and associated support to neutralize the RUF around Kono. Phase three of the Sierra Leone operational plan—the clearing of the main roads to the Liberian border—would have to wait a whilst.

Whilst I was in Freetown I met up with Fred Marafono and he invited me to his home to

Sam Hinga Norman, with a large number
...cy to brief them unofficially on the reasons for
the background to the organization. They were
. expertise with which we had carried out our plans
vholeheartedly. I also realized that Sam Hinga Norman
...evated status amongst his peers.

...ext day with renewed energy, a new strategy and a number of
...od news that EO had also obtained a push-pull Cessna 337 aircraft
to .   ...onnaissance missions forthwith.

The defence of Baiama

Once again the KCC provided a snippet of reliable information on the whereabouts and intent of the rebels and on the strength of it I decided to involve the Kamajors in the defence of the front. Randolph Fillie Fahboi and I gathered about 80 Kamajors together, briefed them on the plan I had in mind and equipped them for the defence of Baiama, a village approximately 15 kilometres south of Koidu. I planned the operation in such a way that the EO force would take the target and thereafter hand the location and the surrounding area to the Kamajors. I also realized that the terrain had not been occupied before and we would have to ensure that it was safe before bringing in the Kamajors. This would also be the first operation in a long time in which we would be using the BMP-2 infantry combat vehicles. The closed terrain limited the effective use of the BMP-2 and its vulnerability here was severely exposed, particularly in the mountainous and marshy terrain, but we decided to use the vehicles mostly for their firepower.

I appointed Major Cobus Claassens as the operation commander. I would accompany the force but would not interfere with the conduct of the operation itself. Cobus, a former paratrooper, had already displayed the necessary courage during previous operations and I wanted to give the younger men an opportunity to develop without having autocratic leaders breathing down their necks.

The movement to the target area proceeded successfully despite the very thick bush. The EO troops debussed from the BMP-2s and we moved on foot at a snail's pace with the vehicles in support. Once we had reached a fork in the road where we were due to turn to the southwest to Baiama, Cobus decided that the area held a threat and he gave orders for a stand-off fire mission by the 82mm mortars, with a bridge as the target. The fire mission was soon completed, the bridge was secured and the movement continued. Then something happened that made me singularly unhappy. Just as we were closing with Baiama the advance came to a halt and I asked what was happening up ahead. Cobus came walking back to my position and informed me that he had stopped the movement and that he wished to cancel the attack if that was acceptable to me. I made it very clear that the advance to contact should proceed and that we couldn't stop here. Cobus disagreed and said that we should turn back and supported his point of view by stating that the BMP-2s would not be able to turn around if we moved ahead any further. This was a huge disappointment to me. Up to this point in my military career I had never turned back during an operation for whatever reason. I felt that Cobus could possibly have been intimidated by his subordinates as he had painted himself into a corner with his very close relationship with some of his mates over whom he had been appointed as commander.

There had always been a measure of animosity between Cobus's group, as the helicopter-borne group and Jos's group who manned the combat vehicles on the ground and I had been required to resolve a number of disputes between them in the past in a diplomatic fashion. Within EO the forces were composed of a large number of specialists on tactical level and each wanted to follow their own head, leading to differences of opinion that had to be managed. The command structures in EO were also continually reminded of the fact that EO was not an army and that the rules and regulations that governed an army were not applicable here. This was a true dilemma and it required a commander to exhibit a mature, more democratic, yet firm leadership style. I granted Cobus's request and ascribed it to the fact that on this occasion EO had not had the will or inclination to do battle with the rebels. Was it a case of battle fever? I was not convinced. We had lost this battle to the rebels without even firing a shot and this opinion was shared by a number of the men.

The day had started badly; one of the BMP-2s had not started without a tow and during the ensuing actions to get it started Nico, one of the du Preez brothers, had been injured in the ribs by a towing cable. I had watched the incident and had believed that he had surely broken at least one rib. Nico believed otherwise and decided to continue with the operation. This had probably led to the decision by Louis, his twin, not to participate, due to Nico's injury. The twins were very close and were considered to be a popular combination amongst the rank and file. They also exerted some influence on this level. Two good men, but they needed a strong leader to keep them motivated and aligned in the correct direction, something that Cobus had failed to achieve that particular morning. I closed this chapter and ended the day hoping that something of this nature would not happen again. We shelved the operation, knowing that at some stage in the future we would have to carry it out.

I also decided that it was unwise to deploy both the helicopter-borne and vehicle-borne groups together as an integrated force as their different approaches were difficult to reconcile and this would have an adverse effect on operational effectiveness. We returned to Koidu having experienced one of the lowest points in my life.

On 8 August 1995 Lafras sent me a message to the effect that a well-know war journalist was on his way to visit us. He had agreed that the journalist could interview us, subject to the fact that any material to be published would be cleared by EO headquarters prior to it going to press. This removed some pressure off my shoulders as it was always difficult to maintain operational security during these types of visits. The journalist turned out to be Al J. Venter and on his arrival I briefed him on the train of events that had taken place up to that point. He came across as an affable man and insisted that he wanted to accompany us on our operations. I then decided that this was the time to undertake the Baiama operation, only this time we would have two Mi-17 helicopters at our disposal.

Venter decided that he would move with the ground force, which I had placed under the command of Cobus once again.

This time I decided to use the Kamajors to support the operation and they deployed a tactical bound behind the forward troops. The intent was for the EO force to attack in a southerly direction and that, once the objective had been taken and secured, Cobus would deploy the Kamajors tactically on the terrain and, after a day's training, he would leave them there to occupy and defend the terrain forthwith. The EO force would then leave and return to Koidu.

The attacking force left the next day to dislodge the RUF from Baiama and Venter made himself comfortable amongst the troops. I was located in the helicopter flown by Charlie Tait and as the ground force approached the objective the two Mi-17 helicopters flew a holding pattern in readiness to support them. The Mi-17 was armed with a 7.62mm PKM light machine gun, a handy weapon when rebel resistance is experienced. Cobus and his men came up against light resistance from a number of rebels who had underestimated the EO force. Four rebels were killed and the remainder, approximately 60 in total, decided to give way and leave the terrain. The Mi-17 helicopters were the target of relatively accurate RPG-7 fire from the rebels but this was neutralized through indirect fire.

The target had been overrun with relative ease and we were cleared to land at a designated LZ that Cobus had secured on the objective. We then cleared the Kamajors to enter the target area and Cobus deployed them on the terrain. I walked around the target area and deduced that the rebels had built a very large base here, to the extent that it could probably house a force of approximately 200 RUF members. This concerned me somewhat as it could indicate the strength of the enemy against which we would be pitting the Kamajors once the rebels had regrouped. I instructed Cobus to do a thorough job of familiarizing the Kamajors with the terrain and how to defend it. This would not be achieved in a day, of course, but we had to put our best effort in to make the most of the available time. I also realized that there were in all probability a large number of rebels in the surrounding countryside and that the battle was not nearly over yet. The rebel base had been well prepared with good overhead cover against indirect weapons and good observation over all the access routes and approaches, as well as good all-round defence. I also realized that any thoughts of attempting to attack a RUF base of this nature without adequate support fire would have to be shelved forthwith. I did not have enough men to write off in this type of rash action and, in any event, this was not the type of tactic employed by EO. I also concluded that I would have to rely all the more on good information in the future and concentrate on stand-off bombardments with indirect weapons to intimidate the enemy and to harass them until they had left the area. The vegetation was simply too dense, jungle warfare techniques would take too long and I didn't have that luxury. I had declared that EO would have the RUF under control by Christmas and that was what we were going to achieve. I gave Venter a lift back to Koidu in the helicopter and from there he flew back to Freetown.

Cobus returned to Koidu a day earlier than planned with the assurance that the Kamajors were in position and that they were battle ready. I would have preferred him to have stayed that extra day to ensure that they were totally familiar with the front and the situation. I didn't have much time to reflect, however, before my fears were confirmed when an exhausted Kamajor arrived with the news from Randolph Fillie Fahboi that the rebels had attacked the positions at Baiama again that morning. The Kamajor firepower had been insufficient to control the rebels and the defenders had scattered. I had feared this would happen. I had, after all, warned Randolph Fillie Fahboi that it would require a supreme effort on the part of his men to deny the positions to the enemy. As an infantryman of many years standing I knew very well how long it takes to train an infantryman, let alone make him comfortable with the infantryman's role in battle, and teach him how to apply the fundamentals correctly. One principle is that the front should be covered by the fire of all available weapons, not by troops. Indirectly I blamed Cobus and I was of the opinion that he did not like the idea of being saddled with the Kamajors. I lowered my head in shame and made a promise to myself that we would have to make good for this. This was not what EO stood for. We stood for quality, for daring, and for continuous achievement, not failure.

I confirmed that the Kamajors would not be deployed or utilized on their own again as this gave the rebels a hold over us and it contributed to a fall in the morale of the troops. My words of reassurance had hardly been uttered before we received the next piece of discouraging information. Whilst the Kamajors were scattering during the chaos of the RUF attack, a group had tried to cross a nearby swollen river whilst under RUF fire. Five Kamajors had drowned and, to make matters worse, 12 weapons had been lost during the attack. We had by now realized that in Sierra Leone one could afford to lose a man, as he would inevitably have a brother, but once a weapon has been lost it is gone forever.

The next day I visited Captain Johnny Moore, the acting commander of the RSLMF unit at Gayia, near Bumpe, and discussed the matter with him. I knew that the RSLMF soldiers and the Kamajors were not on the friendliest of terms, and he repeated this opinion to me. I asked him to provide me with a platoon of RSLMF troops to deploy at Baiama until we could open up the front to the south and secure it further in a southerly direction. Understandably Captain Johnny Moore was not very happy with this request but he actually had no choice and he provided the troops.

In the interim I readied a section of EO troops to accompany me on a reconnaissance mission to the north of Koidu. Our tiffy (mechanic) had managed to get an old Isuzu truck going and I wanted to test its performance during the task as the two Land Rovers did not have the capability to transport more than ten men. I had heard that the road was not passable and decided in any event to check if this was actually the case. The patrol left early the next morning and proceeded in a northwesterly direction of the Bafi River which we crossed without any trouble, to enter the Sandoh chiefdom, the second largest chiefdom in Sierra Leone. Our initial information about the state of these roads, however, was indeed correct—they were impassable. The road allowed us to travel to Kayima, the main town, but on turning south after reaching the town we came across swollen rivers and were forced to stop and retrace our steps. The reconnaissance mission did bear some fruit; however, as we had made good contact with the people along the way and I had formed a good idea of what was happening to our north. The area was not popular with the RUF due to their fear of the Kamajors with their ever sharp cutlasses or machetes. It was also cut off from the southern part of the Kono district by the Bafi River, locally known as the 'killer river' as many locals had drowned here. A heavy dugout canoe is necessary in order to cross it due to the strong currents. This was in fact a blessing to the people of the Sandoh chiefdom.

ADMINISTERING THE KONO DISTRICT

A new concept of operations

I was due to take my annual leave down south during September 1995 but, unfortunately, that was not to be. The much anticipated leave had to be postponed until much later during the year as there was work to be done.

The operations that we undertook after the stabilization of the area around Kono were of an opportunistic nature, with RUF targets of opportunity being sought and engaged. The operations undertaken by the rebels were so flexible that it was perhaps more accurate to classify them as impulsive. To retain the initiative thus, we had to be able to react immediately to such rebel operations. This was contrary to the principles of offensive action that I had been taught during my days at the Infantry School in Oudtshoorn, South Africa. It is difficult not to become nostalgic for those days here, but I cannot help it. These principles had been drilled into us and we learnt to apply them naturally and practically without even batting an eyelid, on all levels, from my first days at the SA Army Gymnasium in Heidelberg, South Africa where we as young national servicemen learnt to 'fix bayonets', to the formation-level operations we planned during my staff course.

We gradually developed a practical strategy against the RUF that produced the desired outcome. We knew that to try and fix and confront the rebels on foot would be an impossible task due to their ability to disappear into the jungle and we focussed instead on where they would undertake their next logistic replenishment. Whether the target was the local population or government forces, this was where they would score, as this had become their method of survival. A number of sporadic attacks by the rebels at first appeared to give them a sense of enormous power and this kept us very busy, but once I had started a series of stand-off bombardments of the known RUF locations on an irregular basis, in addition to the engagement of RUF opportunity targets, we realized that we had unsettled them completely. Previously they had not had to contend with such threats and this new development forced them to inhabit only a few bases and to move on as soon as there was any indication of a threat to the base. On the contrary, we should actually rather talk of the hunger and the need for ammunition which got the better of them and forced them into offensive action.

With the arrival of Paddy and his push-pull Cessna 337, we undertook many reconnaissance flights over the entire Sierra Leone to the extent that I think PP eventually became fed up with all the flying. The origins of a number of new approaches were conceived as a result of the aerial reconnaissance undertaken, the use of night vision equipment and a GPS. Numerous night flights were undertaken and once the enemy had been located, the information was relayed to the applicable unit in real time, the operation was then planned and it took place as quickly as possible thereafter.

This new concept of operations heralded the death knell of the rebels as an organized force as we now had the perfect procedure to pin the enemy down in order to engage them. The Kamajors picked up enemy movement in the general areas when they visited their normal hunting grounds and reported this movement to us. In addition, we also had the radio intercepts to confirm their presence and we then followed this up with the deployment of the Cessna 337 and PP. All that remained once the information had been confirmed was the planning and execution of the offensive operation thereafter. The reaction time until the execution of the operation was usually between two and three days.

Whilst this worked excellently and was perfect for Sierra Leone, I believe that in Angola it could only have worked a few times before it would have to have been changed as in that theatre of operations such a tactic had a limited shelf life before UNITA would cotton on to it and take counter-measures to neutralize it. Know your enemy, sir. This was the mantra we had learnt as young soldiers—know your enemy and his capabilities.

On two occasions I participated in such flights and I must say, after the experience, I saluted PP who had the unenviable task of conducting them repeatedly. In fact, he did it so many times that Paddy and some of the other pilots even handed the controls over to him.

The new concept of operations also highlighted the importance of helicopter operations, as the mortar teams were placed on alert to operate in conjunction with these aircraft when necessary. The successes were phenomenal and it became very apparent that the RUF didn't have a solution for this type of action, except to maintain better discipline when making fires at night and spend less time in their temporary bases.

The operations were short-lived and the successes were unbelievable. Here full credit and appreciation must go to PP, the mortar teams, the link-up forces and the pilots who would land the Mi-17 helicopters in the most impossible places. Credit was also due to all the men who assisted with the planning of these successful operations, from the Kamajors, the local inhabitants and chiefs of the various chiefdoms, who passed on the necessary information timeously during the KCC meetings, to the streams of local inhabitants who evacuated areas to move closer to towns and assisted us when they met us.

We couldn't sustain these types of operations over the long term, however, and we were convinced that the RUF would want to plan some type of countermeasure.

The Gandorhun attack

The elements of an offensive operation were developing in the Gandorhun area, south of Koidu, by the end of September 1995. Radio intercepts had confirmed that Foday Sankoh continued to pressurize his rebel troops to reach Koidu. In addition, the local population of the Baiama area were also pressurizing us to secure the Gandorhun area and thirdly, PP had located a rebel force marching from the south towards Koidu.

Fred Marafono joined us to participate in the operation and despite the fact that I had informed him that the ground force would only consist of RSLMF troops he insisted on taking part. In addition, we were joined by Jim Hooper, a journalist who had spent a lot of time with the Koevoet members during the conflict in South West Africa.

The order of battle for the operation consisted of the tactical headquarters, a tactical group, and a ground force. The tactical headquarters, under my command, was where the planning and execution was undertaken by Carl Dietz, Lieutenant-Colonel Tom Nyuma (RSLMF), two Russian pilots (former lieutenant-colonels) and a Russian interpreter. The tactical group, under PP Hugo, consisted of the medical doctor, the 120mm mortar team, a protection element and Jim Hooper. The ground force was led by 'Fearless' Fred Marafono and it consisted of an infantry company from 16 Battalion, RSLMF. Jos Grobler commanded the EO cut-off groups to be deployed to the south of Gandorhun.

The planning for the operation took place on 23 and 24 September at the EO base at Koidu. I carried out the initial planning and decided on the day before the operation to include additional professionals—Carl Dietz, Tom Nyuma as well as the two Russian pilots—to refine and round off the plan. I presented the plan to the military commanders on the morning of 25 September 1995 and briefed the council of chiefs thereafter. They duly performed a complete ritual, speaking to their forefathers, and we received the blessing of the local traditional leaders.

Fred Marafono engaged in a brief discussion with the RSLMF troops, speaking to them very sternly about the fact that in the past they had fled very quickly when contact was made with the enemy and he promised all hell would break loose if they deserted him this time. The first phase of Fred's operation was to reach Woama that night and to continue from there the next morning.

On the morning of 26 September 1995 I deployed the tactical group but the weather was against us. After 20 minutes in the air I saw the Mi-17 helicopters returning and landing and Charlie Tait informed me that the weather was too bad to deploy the tactical group on the summit of a granite hill, known as Gandorhun, about three kilometres northwest of the main target. Time was still on our side and we could afford to wait another 30 minutes before a decision to abort the operation was required. The second attempt at deploying the troops was also unsuccessful and Tait was forced to return to Koidu. By this time, Fred had informed us that he was approximately three kilometres from the target and we were forced to halt him there. The deployment of the tactical group had to take place first in order to allow them to engage and soften the target before the ground force could attack it.

The third attempt at deploying the tactical group was successful. The Mi-17 landed all the troops and equipment and it didn't take long before PP and the mortars were on target. By the time the first mortar bombs had fallen, Fred was already on the move and his force took over the fire on the main target whilst the mortars moved to the next target south of Gandorhun. Fred's force didn't encounter much resistance and it became obvious that once the rebels had heard the first bombs they had evacuated the target area to a temporary base west of PP's force on top of the granite hill.

That night PP could clearly see the RUF troops entering and occupying the base through his night vision equipment and it wasn't long before he was on target with the 120mm mortars once again. This must have been the last straw for the rebels. They had clearly not expected to be attacked by the RSLMF in the first place, only to be harassed by accurate mortar fire, even after they had escaped the target area.

We decided not to follow the enemy any further as this was only something we did if it was absolutely necessary. The scorecard didn't look too bad though with only four RSLMF men being wounded.

In time it became clear from our radio intercepts that the RUF had vacated the front south of Koidu and returned to their headquarters at Joru. We had achieved our objective of clearing the RUF from Koidu before December 1995.

Strange visitors

EO had become well known to the international media by this time. The nature of our task was such that any contact with the media was governed by strong guidelines from the EO headquarters in South Africa. In essence, we didn't talk to the media in Sierra Leone. Having said this, EO had indeed become a target for the more brazen media types, particularly those of the fairer sex and we had received very explicit warnings from the Freetown headquarters about a pair of ladies who were hunting for information on the comings and goings of EO.

One morning as I was descending the hill from the EO base on my way to a meeting with Femmi Kamare, the mines department engineer stationed at Koidu, I met Kassim Basma's minibus on its way up to the base. Kassim was one of the major diamond buyers in the district; in fact he was probably the biggest diamond buyer in Sierra Leone at that point. We had met under the auspices of the KCC and he appeared to be a pleasant enough person, who was friendly towards EO in a guarded fashion as he had probably realized that EO was actually in full control of the Kono district. Nothing happened in the district without EO and I deduced that he had sent his minibus driver to ask a favour of us. It was evident that the generous Black Label whiskies that we had shared previously had given him the courage to approach us with a request.

Kassim's driver stopped the vehicle, exited his minibus and approached my vehicle gingerly, stating that the person who he was transporting in the vehicle would like to talk to me. Before I had the opportunity to react to the request, a woman jumped out of Kassim's minibus, approached me and introduced herself.

"Hi, I'm Khareen Pech, and you are the Colonel van Heerden everybody's talking about," she said in Afrikaans.

"I am," I replied. "Who are you and what brings you here?"

"Yes, I want to make an appointment with you and can you make it today please as I must return to Freetown tomorrow," she replied.

I was clearly somewhat taken aback by the way this 'cat' was addressing me. She obviously knew what she was up to and she knew exactly what she wanted. I made it clear to her that there had been restrictions placed on external communications, but that she could interview me although I would only be in a position to provide limited information to her. We agreed to meet at Kassim's house and she confirmed that she was planning to overnight at this location.

That evening I visited Kassim's home to attend to the appointment. We received and enjoyed the best fare from Kassim's kitchen, washed down by the best of whiskeys. Khareen and I talked between the various courses and the whiskeys and she tried to find out as much as possible about our activities. She also mentioned that she had met a number of the traditional leaders that morning and that they had all confirmed their high esteem of EO. She confessed that she had been surprised that the local population had been so enthusiastic about us and supportive of us. She maintained that it was generally accepted that armies and, in our case, mercenaries do more harm to the local inhabitants and area than good and they tend to be a source of great unhappiness. She had concluded that the opposite was true in our case.

During the meal I had the opportunity to evaluate the female journalist who had appeared out of the blue. She was easy to get on with and could probably be even more so if one played one's cards correctly. She did have a somewhat waspish side and one had to tread warily. After the meal I thanked the host, said my good nights and returned to the EO base before the curfew.

This was by no means our last contact. Within days she was back, asking if she could visit me at the EO base. I received her there in a friendly manner and she introduced me to another person she had brought along with her by the name of Elizabeth Rubin, a New York based journalist who worked for Harper's Magazine. She explained that although they were together, each was on their own mission.

Khareen started off by asking me if I could shed any light on a massacre that had taken place at a village by the name of Njaima Nimikoro, where a large number of women and children had died. I replied that I had troops in the vicinity of the village who were patrolling the area and that it would be best to visit the village itself and talk to the local villagers to find out for herself. That afternoon I took her on the hour-long journey to the village in my own vehicle. She interviewed the local people about the so-called massacre and learnt that once the EO and RSLMF forces had moved on from their area of operations south of the town, the RUF forces had come to the conclusion that the local inhabitants were to blame for their misfortunes and they had exacted some measure of retribution from them.

What ensued indeed amounted to a massacre. The RUF had attacked the village then rounded up all the women and children they could find, locked them all into a house and set fire to it. Only one of the approximately 120 villagers who had been locked in the house made it out alive—a baby who had been extracted from beneath the smouldering rafters and dead bodies the next day. The boy had been christened Colonel Roelf. I didn't, however, believe this to be that appropriate, especially as I had felt profoundly moved by the fact that the remainder of the group of villagers had been killed and we had not been in a position to save or help them.

On the way back to Koidu she asked if I would drop her off at Ahmed Shamel's home—another diamond buyer—where she and Elizabeth, were staying. Ahmed and a South African by the name of Rich Verster were in business together and the latter had invited them to stay there. When we arrived at the house she asked if I would wait a moment to allow her to check whether Elizabeth was there or not. Within a very short whilst she returned to the vehicle and I could clearly see that she was very upset. I decided there and then that she could be a devil if one rubbed her up the wrong way. I also made a mental note to the effect that journalists do not necessarily regard one another as colleagues, particularly if the subject at issue related to 'mercenaries' in 'darkest Africa'.

"Tell me," she shouted in a heated voice, "how do you say 'cunt struck' in Afrikaans?"

At first I didn't believe what I was hearing. I would have expected a deranged person to express such sentiments.

"*Poes bedroef,*" I replied.

"Yes, well that's exactly what's wrong with Elizabeth," she said.

She went on, saying that she was very angry as it appeared that Elizabeth had tried to gain access to her laptop computer whilst she had been on the visit to Njaiama Nimikoro. This lady was really upset. Was it anger or merely a question of professional jealousy between the two journalists over a 'mercenary scoop'? I left her to her own devices and returned to the EO base.

The next day I was due to leave on a patrol eastward to cover a smuggling route that I was investigating at the request of the local police. Before I had a chance to leave I was surprised to find the two women and Rich Verster at the base, ready to join me on the patrol. I did the unthinkable and invited them to join the patrol with a view to allowing them to visit the region where voodoo was reportedly widely practiced. We arrived at the smuggling route where large quantities of cigarettes and surely diamonds are smuggled into Sierra Leone from neighbouring Guinea and succeeded in confiscating large numbers of cigarette cartons worth thousands of Leones. There were so many cigarettes that I didn't have sufficient men to carry the load. The smugglers had fled and we decided to leave the cigarettes there and send a RSLMF force with the police to pursue the case further.

That evening after we had returned to Koidu I was just about to breathe a sigh of relief that our 'visitors' were probably too weary to enjoy the evening meal with us, when they arrived at our bar to have a few drinks. The effect this had on the men was entirely predictable. Their eyes followed every move the women made. Both were very attractive and Rich had a hard time trying to convince the men that Elizabeth did not want to strip for them, whilst Tommy, our tame chimpanzee, wanted to know more about what went on under Khareen's skirt. The evening did not end on a pleasant note, though, as a number of the men had by this time indicated to both Khareen and Elizabeth how they felt about them. What they found out, however, was that Rich had pre-empted this and felt somewhat possessive over the two ladies. In short Rich left the bar under a barrage of threats about the status of his future safety at the base. Despite this, though, he did manage to get the women safely into the car and away. The two women were forced to work in such close proximity to each other forthwith that they had left for Freetown by the end of the week.

We next saw Khareen when she visited Koidu whilst we were evacuating child soldiers and war orphans to Freetown. What I do remember of this visit was that she actually became physically involved and guided some of the children onto the helicopter. What I didn't know at that point was that Khareen wanted to return to Freetown that evening with the same helicopter that was transporting the children. On hearing about her request I actually gave the approval for her to join the helicopter flight although this was against EO policy. I was also due to leave for Freetown for my liaison visit to the headquarters and I made the trip with the children to the airport at Lungi in the capital as well. I sat at the front of the helicopter between the pilots and during the flight Carl, the pilot, asked me if I was aware that Khareen was also on the flight. I answered in the affirmative, stating that the press and other coverage we would receive from this undertaking made the risk of transporting her on the helicopter worth the whilst. I deduced at the time that Carl was not very enamoured with her at all.

It was dark by the time we landed at Lungi and we wasted no time in handing over the children to the church representatives at the airport. As we prepared to take off again we realized that Khareen was missing and I asked Carl to wait for a moment. I deduced from his facial expression that he, as the pilot, had other ideas. Without hesitating, he wound the helicopter up and we took off. Khareen obviously had heard the helicopter preparing to take off and had run out of the airport building towards the aircraft, only to be confronted by the downwash of a disappearing helicopter.

During the flight I learnt that Carl and Khareen had met each other one evening at Paddy's, one of the more popular watering holes in the capital, and they had had a serious misunderstanding, from which Khareen had emerged the victor. Tonight had been payback time. If one is ever stranded on Lungi airport at night, the only thing one can do is hunker down somewhere on the floor for the night and hope that there is a lift available the following day. Was this a fitting punishment for a girl? I leave you to be the judge. I did, however, hear that after the helicopter incident Carl had to bear the brunt of Khareen's humour one night at Paddy's in front of a crowd of eager witnesses. Such is life.

I met Khareen once more on another of her visits and learnt that she did not have enough material for her 'story'. The story lacked additional 'facts' and at her insistence some of the EO staff accompanied her to a Koidu disco one night together with SK, one of her Lebanese 'connections'.

Time spent in the bush in Sierra Leone does make things difficult for some of the men, and being away from home for such extended periods of time on a regular basis can make one's mind move one in strange and unnecessary directions. Some of the men who had followed such a path found that this approach wreaked total havoc on their marriages. The type of work we did required the men to be strong physically and mentally, and know where to draw the line as far as personal behaviour was concerned.

One of the oldest tricks in the book is the honey trap and it is far easier to succeed if the target has been isolated from female company for long periods of time. Far be it for me to moralize about what was successful or unsuccessful but, judging by the content of some of the magazine articles on EO that I have read, some of the men did indeed succumb to this trick.

War children

An obvious feature of this war was the large number of children—mostly young boys— who had been armed with weapons from both sides. At first I thought that it was merely a case of young children who wanted to be associated with the soldiers and had become camp followers, but as time passed I realized that this was actually a permanent feature of the conflict. Was this a result of the socialization process or was there something else behind it? Only time would tell.

The matter surfaced again one evening in Koidu when the guards called me and informed me that a woman wished to see me. I approached and found the very same young African-American freelance journalist who had jumped out of the helicopter and made a bee-line for Lieutenant-Colonel Tom Nyuma and I on the day we took Koidu. We exchanged greetings and she informed me that she was staying with Father Mondeh, the Catholic priest in Koidu, and that she wished to raise a matter that the church felt should be resolved.

Child soldiers were no longer a strange phenomenon or an aberration in Sierra Leone. This caused one to almost believe that the community had accepted the situation and that they had never really seen it as socially unacceptable. I wasn't too concerned about this, despite the fact that I had two sons of similar age as many of the child soldiers. It did make me ponder the matter somewhat though. Having child soldiers fight in a conflict such as the one being settled in Sierra Leone could only be the source of serious social problems for the individuals in the future. In addition, the boys should be at school, not in uniform, and the longer this continued the greater the social problem would become, creating social havoc for a generation of future adults.

I agreed to discuss the matter with her and said that, since the days ahead would be busy, it would be advisable to discuss the matter immediately. This request didn't surprise me as I had realized that EO was slowly but surely becoming more than just a force that operated at the sharp end and took no shit from anyone. All that would happen was that this would become another task on which to focus our attention and I would manage it through the auspices of the KCC.

Since it was dusk the men were already in their stand-to positions as was our routine. My guest and I moved to my office and as we sat down in the light I confirmed that she was indeed the same attractive lady who had arrived at Koidu just after we had taken the town. She re-introduced herself as Agnes and informed me that she wished to become involved in the search for a solution to the problems associated with the child soldiers. We discussed the issue and she informed me that the church had already done a lot of work in gathering the affected children together and that they were experiencing serious logistical problems. I duly informed her that this matter was not really part of the EO remit and that in the event that we did become involved, this could lead to other repercussions and consequences. I was actually thinking of the consequences for the NPRC government and even the Red Cross. EO could become the focus of criticism, either for not staying focussed on our primary mission, or for interfering in matters that belonged to organizations such as the Red Cross.

Agnes explained that this situation has been a throwback from the RUF, who had many child soldiers in their ranks. It was relatively easy to commandeer children due to their needs; children are so much easier to influence and it is even easier to introduce them to drugs. This is where the lasting damage was done. Marijuana was freely available in Sierra Leone and there was no way that it could be effectively policed due to the many other law and order priorities. Marijuana was not the only drug available; *pega pak* was also provided to the child soldiers before an operation and there were unconfirmed stories of other drugs, including opium.

We discussed various solutions and it eventually came down to the fact that success would depend on the degree to which we communicated the matter to the local inhabitants and the degree to which they were able to identify the phenomenon as an evil. I undertook to meet the church leaders and to discuss the matter with my higher commander. I knew that I would have to justify such a request very well so that Eeben and Lafras would grasp its importance. I was also aware that we would have to indicate up front that we would still be able to carry out our tasks and responsibilities as per the contract whilst engaged in this humanitarian activity.

Over the next two days I met the church leaders in Koidu and expressed our sympathy regarding the unnecessary and tragic exploitation of the local children by the RUF. I visited the hospital and met some of the children who had been admitted for treatment after they had borne the brunt of unsuccessful recruiting drives by the RUF. They had paid a high price and had lost their hands in the process. This affected me deeply, despite the fact that I was a hardened soldier who had seen and experienced death on many a battlefield. I also realized that this must have generated fear and anguish in the villages where these activities had been practiced.

It would also be relatively easy for the RUF to reverse the fear in the children and indoctrinate them into believing that they were the ones who should cause fear amongst their targets. This thus 'enabled' the young children to become fearless, and ruthless rebels. I must also admit that this philosophy of fear was to a greater or lesser extent practiced in the ranks of the RSLMF. I approached the matter with great seriousness and had a feeling that it would be approved by my commanders. What was required, however, was to develop the means to actually do something about it.

Agnes and I got on well and we shared a few precious whiskies from the stock of gifts I had received. Whilst savouring her drink she made me understand in no uncertain manner that she would never forget the first few days after she had met Lieutenant-Colonel Tom Nyuma and I in Koidu. On the contrary she intimated that she had a very soft spot for mercenaries, despite the fact that I had tried very hard to convince her that we were not the type of mercenaries that she had in mind at all. As attractive as she was, and as available as what she ostensibly was, I brought the conversation to a close and said that I would ensure that she was returned safely to her lodgings at the home of the church leader before the curfew.

I arranged with Pikkie to take an old Unimog vehicle that we had recently acquired and, together with a few escort troops, return Agnes safely to her lodgings. We shook hands and she held onto my hand as she moved towards the Unimog. I realized then that she was serious about spending the night with me but I resisted the temptation and made as if I didn't understand. She needed very badly to rest and Pikkie was harmless, at least that was what I surmised when I heard the Unimog return to our base shortly thereafter.

I discussed the war children with Brigadier Bert Sachse and we received the authority to provide assistance to the church. I also made arrangements that a helicopter mission that was scheduled to bring us rations and stores would pick up the child soldiers and fly them to Freetown on the return leg of its journey. That day I saw for the first time that more than half the group of war children consisted of orphans whose parents had either been murdered during the war, or who had been separated from their parents. The rebels would usually attack a village at the most inopportune moment and everyone would flee into the night, with the slower children dropping out along the way. I agreed with the church elders that the youngest children should be evacuated first as this would alleviate the greatest logistic pressure on the Catholic Church. I also agreed that for those who couldn't be accommodated on the flight there would undoubtedly be an opportunity at a later stage. The flight took off and the children were safely transferred to Freetown where they began a new, more hopeful life away from the fear and trauma of the conflict.

Soldier, sobel, rebel, Bicycle

It didn't take long after our arrival in Sierra Leone to realize why there was very little stability in West Africa. In the beginning, when Andy Brown and I had maintained a low profile in Freetown, the frustration used to get to me and I alleviated it by jogging or going for a drive. Before I left I would always describe the route I intended to follow to Andy so that he could start searching for me in the correct area if I didn't return on time as expected. Mostly I would run along the main road past the RSLMF headquarters and barracks, then down to the beach, along the beach and then back to the house. On those occasions that I ran past the military headquarters I would invariably be subjected to comments made by the guards or emanating from the troops who used to shout at me and pass comments from the back of passing military vehicles. We often used to run into RSLMF road blocks as well and if it hadn't been for the fact that we had been in uniform we would in all probability have had a difficult time at the hands of these soldiers. We actually had no idea initially how difficult it must have been for the local inhabitants in the vicinity of these road blocks.

As time passed, though, I began to understand what I had been told by senior sources, namely that there was an underlying fear about the composition of the armed forces in Sierra Leone. Before Brigadier Momoh's time, the armed forces had been a smaller, more effective organization. The escalation of the conflict against the RUF had brought about impulsive and unplanned recruitment and in some cases people were even press ganged off the streets. Poor discipline was endemic as the number of soldiers in the armed forces rapidly increased to 13,000. This figure also included many young criminals recruited out of the jails and deployed on the front to counter the RUF.

Foday Sankoh, the RUF leader, was a former corporal in the RSLMF whose message of making the country ungovernable may even have resonated well with many of the RSLMF soldiers and there were doubtless a number of them who believed that they could achieve the same notoriety or fame as long as they had a weapon in their hands. The long history of military coups in Sierra Leone didn't do much to dampen their enthusiasm either. The armed forces were, therefore, part of the problem as well and, for unknown reasons, the Sierra Leone Police (SLP) as a force were unarmed and were unable to be of any assistance.

They were more like sitting ducks than anything else. From the outset EO experienced no difficulty with the RSLMF forces, mostly because our way of doing things was new to them and they couldn't believe how we applied iron discipline in our own ranks. Our ranks were filled with hardened, professional men in their late twenties and early thirties. The RSLMF men watched in awe.

After the first couple of months in Koidu it became very evident that the RSLMF soldiers in the Kono district were becoming a real problem. As the combined forces would occupy an objective and hand it over to the RSLMF forces, so the matter would begin to boomerang right back into our faces. For example, during the reorganization phase in Kono, RSLMF forces were deployed and given the responsibility of ensuring safety on the outskirts of Koidu. One afternoon a group of Kamajors came to see me at the EO base in Koidu and asked for assistance as there had been an attack on a village in the direction of Kainkordu, a village approximately 30 kilometres east of Koidu. I hastily gathered a section of the standby men together and they left to investigate the matter only to come across the bodies of a number of villagers who had been felled as they were trying to hold on to the meagre possessions they had grabbed before fleeing. The only person that the attackers hadn't touched was a mentally handicapped child who was not able to move at all. The village was deserted and eerily quiet with not even a chicken in sight, the food baskets had all been emptied and there were no witnesses either. We investigated and followed the tracks of the departing raiders until sunset and I realized there and then that we would have to try a different tack. I recalled the men to the EO base without having completed the task.

What was of interest was the fact that the matter had been reported by the people in the vicinity of the village and some of the younger children had hinted that they had identified the aggressors as RSLMF soldiers. I approached Chief Abu Kongoba II and through his good offices managed to get hold of the children who had reported the invasion of the village. I also requested Lieutenant-Colonel Sena, the commander of 16 Battalion, RSLMF, to attend after having discussed the matter with him and gaining his total cooperation. With his assistance we gathered the troops from the checkpoint closest to the village and moved them to the EO headquarters. Once they had arrived I asked the young children, who were hidden and protected by EO troops, to identify any of the soldiers who could have been involved in the attack on the village. They identified a large number of the soldiers as the perpetrators of the attack on the village and provided graphic details of where they had been seen and what they had done. This enabled us to confront the guilty soldiers with hard facts and they were summarily transferred to Freetown in an EO helicopter. This may have been a small victory but it certainly appeared that this type of aberrant behaviour was part of a general trend.

A difficult time followed for EO as we became involved in many more incidents where our troops were required to point out RSLMF troops as criminals. This of course led to a sense of disunity, and tension began to build between EO, the RSLMF, the Kamajors, the traditional leaders and other state authorities. I was forced to hear, for example, that certain RSLMF officers in Freetown had teams of soldiers in the Koidu district mining diamonds for them. These soldiers would then go out and 'recruit' young men to do the spade work for them. There was no effective control over the troops here by the RSLMF—they could have been anywhere—in their barracks, mining or elsewhere. Nobody seemed to know or care.

Another example of this malaise took place on the main route between Koidu and Njaiama–Sewafe. The reaction group from 16 Battalion at Gayia was tasked to patrol the route and they restricted their patrols to the vicinity of the main road as their reaction vehicle happened to be a Toyota Dyna truck fitted with a 12.7mm heavy machine gun. The vehicle commander was a soldier known locally as 'Yellow Man' as he had dyed his hair a yellow colour.

Yellow Man's shelflife expired when he and his accomplices tried to pull a stunt on the locals. On the route between Koidu and Njaiama-Sewafe they approached a village alongside the road, approximately 35 kilometres from Koidu. At a distance of approximately 500 metres from the village, Yellow Man offloaded his first troops, who were clothed in the same garb as the RUF, including red armbands. They approached the village on foot along the road. Yellow Man kept the vehicle behind the troops so that he could approach the village behind them. It was late afternoon—the same time that the RUF would have attacked the village. Once the troops reached the first houses they started firing indiscriminately in all directions. Their purpose was not to kill but to instil fear in the villagers and force them to flee into the bush. They didn't waste time and went about pillaging the few shops in the village before disappearing into the bush again.

What Yellow Man didn't know on this particular day was that one of the shop owners had decided that he was not prepared to be separated from his wares. He hid amongst his meagre provisions inside the shop and was saved on the day as the soldiers raided the more profitable, better stocked shops. As the pillaging was taking place Yellow Man brought the reaction vehicle into the village and carried out his own raid as he most probably believed that his troops were not bringing him enough of the spoils as agreed before the raid. The hidden shop owner's establishment was spared once again and more importantly the shop owner was able to identify the vehicle and the fact that the raiding troops were RSLMF.

EO got word of the incident via the KCC and it was openly discussed during the meeting. Yellow Man was identified and it was made public knowledge that the RSLMF was guilty of conducting rebel activities against defenceless citizens for a few hundred Leones and food from the shops. Major Kamara, the next commander of 16 Battalion at Gayia, didn't play open cards with us and tried to dismiss the event as an unsubstantiated rumour which EO had contrived in order to create friction between the RSLMF and the local population.

In the end EO benefitted from the matter as he was discredited, and both the RSLMF and the NPRC lost the support of the local inhabitants. I pursued the matter with the EO headquarters in Freetown as well as the Sierra Leone Police and other local leaders. Yellow Man was summonsed but denied any illegal activities. Major Kamara was pressurized and increasing demands were received from Freetown for Yellow Man to report to the military authorities there.

The whole mess—the defenceless local inhabitants, the increasing involvement of EO— led to an atmosphere where the only loser was the local inhabitants. Increasing pressure was being brought to bear on EO as more and more incidents of this nature were reported and revealed during KCC meetings, and the RSLMF were increasingly forced to try and defend their untenable position.

In the interim, Lieutenant-Colonel Robert Koroma, the PLO for Mines, Minerals and Energy, had issued the instruction to EO that they were to assist the mines' engineer, Femi Kamara, in controlling the diamond mines in the Kono district. All mining activities were to be stopped until the government had made adjustments to the mining legislation. As a consequence, EO became actively involved in the enforcement of the prohibition of mining activities throughout the Kono district. This was in itself a massive task and EO sent daily patrols out to enforce the ban. We really had insufficient troops and vehicles with which to carry out the task effectively.

The inevitable happened; the protection tasks as well as the area domination actions were prioritized. The consequence of these priorities and the fact that EO had increasingly become entangled with the undisciplined RSLMF meant that the RUF began to realize that EO had indeed become occupied by domestic-type activities. The RUF had received an opportunity to get their foot in the door once again and they used this time to continue their illicit diamond mining activities.

It was also during this time that sobels—soldier rebels—began arriving in the district from far and wide to share in the spoils of illicit diamond mining. Cargo vehicles loaded with people from as far afield as Freetown descended on Kono to obtain any benefit they could from the unstable environment. Chaos was evident everywhere. Illegal military roadblocks continued to function and the streams of people seeking their fortune in Kono were robbed and abused by RSLMF soldiers even before they had arrived. The philosophy of the new arrivals was that they truly believed that whatever they had lost on the way would be regained during the time they worked on the diamond fields in the Kono district.

Grafton Mining, an Italian mining group, managed by a man known to me as Tony, was the first to approach EO and report that RSMLF soldiers were engaged in illegal mining on its concession. The company's concession was located in the area immediately surrounding Koidu and it was the most vulnerable as a result. Koidu itself was bursting at the seams as a result of the streams of new arrivals from the length and breadth of the country as well as from Guinea, Liberia, the Ivory Coast and Ghana, all seeking their personal Eldorado. The place had become a true Sodom and Gomorrah. The district, which had once been the bread basket of the country, had once again become an attraction due its relative safety—the curse of success. I received the mine engineer's authority to act against the illegal mining and that same afternoon I gave Jos orders to send a patrol out to the area that night. Lieutenant-Colonel Robert Koroma was in Koidu at the time as well.

Jos took a section of ten men as we had calculated that there was a possibility that the patrol would have to be strong enough to arrest people. It was envisaged that the task would be relatively simple and straight forward. By midnight Jos and his men were on foot in the vicinity of Monkey Hill on the southern outskirts of Koidu and as they approached the area they realized that the Grafton Mining concession was a hive of activity. During the hours of darkness 'manholes' as deep as three metres were being dug to reach the gravel level below the layer of surface soil. The diamonds were located in this gravel and, since the gravel was not far from the kimberlitic pipe, the chances of locating a diamond were relatively good. A profitable undertaking under the noses of the authorities.

Jos and his section observed as the illegal miners worked under torchlight, and candlelight, in the holes. Superficially one could perhaps mark these activities as minor infringements of the law, innocent yet illegal, and Jos assumed that he would merely be required to approach the miners, arrest a few people, and then transfer them to the police holding facilities before the word got around the next day that the law was being strictly applied.

As Jos informed the men in the first 'manhole' that they were under arrest and that they should get out of the hole, his section drew automatic fire from a position on the other side of the diamond workings. The sound of the shots raised the alarm and chaos ensued as mining activities ceased and miners scurried out of their holes and ran in all directions to escape. The automatic fire was a signal to the illegal miners that the place was being raided and they should disappear. What complicated matters was the fact that the automatic fire, from a 7.62mm PKM light machine gun was so effective and accurate that Jos's force was required to return the fire. During the exchange of fire, Bicycle, one of the EO men on the patrol, was wounded in the arm and hip. The situation on the ground had deteriorated into absolute chaos and the section was being subjected to accurate fire from the front. In view of the injuries to Bicycle, Jos ordered his men to return fire and the sound of shots reverberated throughout the district.

Jos then ordered his men to cease fire and the area became eerily silent as the illegal miners scattered back to the town with their torches still ablaze. Here and there one could hear the sound of a few bursts of AK-47 fire as the RSLMF soldiers tried to protect the withdrawal of the miners. The only people who had any idea of what was happening were EO and the faction who had been involved in this mini-war. The rest of the town were readying themselves for a hasty retreat into the bush as it had sounded to them as if the RUF had returned and were attacking Koidu.

The morning arrived and we put the word out that this had been the work of the sobels and that RSLMF forces were in danger of being killed if they continued to engage in illegal activities for personal gain.

Bicycle was evacuated to the EO headquarters in Koidu, stabilized and flown to Freetown as his wounds were more serious than we had initially thought. Fortunately the doctor was able to stabilize him until such time as the EO Boeing 727 reached Freetown and evacuated him to South Africa where he received the required specialist treatment.

I visited Femmi Kamara at daybreak, as I knew that it would be more effective to report the matter directly via the PLO of Mines, Minerals and Energy than through the commander of 16 Battalion. Lieutenant-Colonel Robert Koroma was already at the mine engineer's office and he found my report very disturbing. He didn't want to believe that the whole endeavour was being backed, supported and even orchestrated by the RSLMF. He stated that an investigation *in loco* would have to be undertaken as EO had been forced to respond to effective fire, and the result of their response to the fire had not been investigated in the darkness once the firefight had ended. I mentioned to him that the matter would probably become very complicated because own forces had become involved in the fire and not RUF as we would have preferred. The inspection *in loco* by Jos thereafter revealed that three illegal miners had been killed during the short exchange of fire.

I mentioned to Lieutenant-Colonel Koroma that I had already reported the matter to my headquarters but the seriousness of the matter evidently escaped the RSLMF and they could not identify any soldiers who had fired their weapons the previous evening. Here was clear evidence of the unskilled and irresponsible corps of officers in the RSLMF. The incident was summarily made to look as if it was insignificant and we didn't hear much about it until much later in 1996 when I was forced to recall the incident in an effort to rescue one of my men.

The point had been made loud and clear that illegal mining would elicit a very serious response from the authorities and EO applied the government's order to implement the mining policy hereafter with little patience. Many EO operations followed and a number of these mini-wars were fought, always with the approval of the government. The effort did not however lead to the complete cessation of, or control over, illegal mining activities but it did lead to the transfer of Major Kamara to Freetown and his temporary replacement by Captain Johnny Moore, a much improved call.

Our actions against the sobels only served to bolster the image and perception of EO amongst the local inhabitants to the extent that they demanded the presence of EO throughout the area as this had become the only way to achieve any semblance of safety and stability. What these actions failed to eradicate was the sobel attitude amongst the RSLMF and incidents and reprisals still took place.

Our actions also led to a meeting with Randolph Filly Faboi—veteran politician and former APC party member—who was the current Kamajor administrator in Koidu. He wished to convince me to issue those AK-47 rifles that we had recovered during contacts with the RUF to the Kamajors. His justification lay in the argument that the rifles would lend that little extra firepower to the antiquated arsenal of Kamajor shotguns of which the ammunition had become old and unserviceable. I also calculated that I was justified in assisting the Kamajors to defend themselves, especially if the sobels became aware that the Kamajors did in fact have AK-47 rifles. Randolph and I would just have to control the process efficiently.

Efforts continued to eradicate the sobel evil within the conflict but they were met with mixed success and the evil practice did continue over a wide front, with the isolated and vulnerable local inhabitants as the tragic losers. The locals continued to report sobel activity and the over-extended SLP would regularly call on the assistance of EO. As the commander of the EO force I regarded the matter as being of a very sensitive nature and tried as far as was possible to pass it on to the SLP as the correct government agency to enforce the law.

In any event, what was EO to do with the sobels that were handed over to them by the local inhabitants? EO had no policing authority or responsibility and to hand the transgressors over to the RSLMF—their brothers in crime according to the SLP—served no purpose at all as they were never prosecuted.

I liaised regularly with the commander of 16 Battalion to formally hand over sobels and express our utter disgust at their actions. They didn't deserve a place in society and were an evil visited on the people of Sierra Leone, particularly when one is confronted by the sight of a young boy or girl with a severed hand or leg, with very little to look forward to in the future. In some cases where EO personally handed over sobels, the battalion commander would take the matter further and the case would inevitably end with the guilty party being ordered to dig his own grave, followed by one shot which would send him on his way to eternity. No feathers were ruffled, no mercy was shown or given—life was cheap.

Fort Pega—The House of Pain

Towards the end of 1995 the EO contract in Angola came to an end and a large number of men were scheduled to transfer from Angola to Sierra Leone. The additional manpower was welcome as we had been thinly spread in certain areas and this had led to the over-utilization of some of our sub-units. Our strength was just over 140 men now and the men all deserved a pat on the back for the work they got through and the results they had achieved.

The approximately 300 men who were due to arrive were required mainly to bolster the operations conducted in the southeast of Sierra Leone and this gave EO the capability to operate autonomously—a great relief as we found it very difficult to conduct operations together with other forces. This difficulty had developed over a period of time. In Angola, for example, we first had to convince the FAA forces that we were fighting on their side. In addition to the issue of trust, which was understandable, there was a massive difference in battle discipline and doctrine between EO and the FAA forces. I must admit that the FAA forces did not hesitate to make a contribution to the overall effort but they fell far short of the level of the EO operators. In addition there was a language gap, which was somewhat overcome by the presence of ex-Angolans in the EO ranks. Furthermore approximately 75 percent of the EO force was composed of black soldiers, for no other reason than they had the skill and experience—excellent fighters, who I placed in a class well above the FAA and RSLMF troops. The EO troops were there for the cause and the camaraderie and above all because they had chosen to be there. The additional EO troops in Sierra Leone would enable us to achieve more, take more objectives simultaneously and undertake area operations.

The new men were deployed at the various existing call signs—Golf 1 at Koidu, Golf 2 at Sumbuya, Golf 3 at Sierra Rutile and Golf 4 at Bumbuna Dam, approximately 50 kilometres north of Magburaka. A further deployment area, later referred to as Romeo 4, was envisaged in the Bo vicinity. The men already deployed in Sierra Leone were also reshuffled. A number who had been with us over the long run were promoted and transferred to various call sign locations, whilst others who had come in fresh were given the opportunity to operate from some of the well respected and notorious call sign locations.

Sumbuya soon became the EO transit base; a place to overnight on the way to or from leave as Freetown had become just too small for some of the men. Sumbuya also became known as Fort Pega and the House of Pain. These two nicknames were coined from the practice which saw PP welcome EO travellers with his own special brand of good cheer in such a way that it could not be refused. The welcoming beverages of locally brewed *pega pak*, mixed with whatever else he saw fit, ensured that visitors remained out of action for some time, at least for the time that they spent in the transit area in anticipation of the arrival of the Boeing. And heaven help the visitor if he stayed over for longer than a day. Only those men with a constitution as strong as a horse could survive.

Sumbuya also claimed other casualties that year. The first EO victim of Sumbuya was one of PP's men, who had been accidently killed by his own hand grenade. The tragedy happened whilst the men were on a water patrol. The victim, who formed part of the patrol's protection detail, jumped off the Land Rover to take up his defensive position and as he did so, his web equipment caught the side of the vehicle, the safety pin of a grenade inside one of the web pouches caught as well and was extracted by the force of the jump. Once this became evident pandemonium broke loose, with everyone shouting advice to him. The unfortunate soldier, whose webbing was still attached to his body, tried to extract the grenade from the pouch in order to throw it as far away as possible but the effort was in vain and he died in the subsequent self-imposed explosion. What a tragic way to meet one's maker after having faced enemy soldiers in the heat of battle in both Angola and Sierra Leone.

The second victim was Manuel, another of PP's men, who became a party in a tragic love triangle. One afternoon whilst he was about to visit his local girlfriend in a village adjacent to the base, he was flabbergasted when he came across a rival suitor in the form of a RSLMF soldier. A difference of opinion occurred between Manuel and the soldier and it escalated out of control. Manuel was summarily threatened with a rifle and he naturally regarded this as totally unacceptable. He left the scene, hastened back to the EO barracks and, telling himself that no one would come between himself and his girlfriend, grabbed his own AK-47. On his return to the village the RSLMF soldier persisted with his threats and it was evident to Manuel that the lovelorn local soldier was not prepared to be scared off by a foreigner. One thing led to another and Manuel became the target of a burst of fire from the RSLMF soldier's weapon. He was lucky to escape unhurt and returned the fire with a number of deadly shots, whereupon he turned on his heel, left the area and returned casually to the barracks, without making too much of a fuss about the whole affair. The local RSLMF troops were so trigger happy when they were drunk that the shots didn't really raise any alarm at all, especially amongst the EO rank and file.

At dawn the next morning PP was indeed surprised when he was confronted by a particularly violent threat from a bunch of RSLMF troops who had decided to actually attack the EO barracks on behalf of their dead comrade. The first indication that something was terribly wrong came when a number of shots were fired at the EO base from across the road. Without any knowledge of the preceding events and without any choice in the matter, call sign Golf 2 was attacked by the RSLMF and it took all PP's skills to bring the situation under control. He grabbed a white T-shirt and with great courage and daring waved it above his head whilst sprinting into a position between the warring factions to bring the attack to a quick halt.

I arrived at Sumbuya on my way to Koidu just as the shooting had been brought to an end.

I had been scheduled to overnight at Sumbuya the previous evening but had been requested by Chief Hinga Norman to visit him at his home in Freetown instead. As I pulled up I could see that some of the EO men were still pretty uptight and a pall of acrid smoke still hung over the area. I had been fortunate to have missed this incident.

Once the matter had been explained and clarified between EO and the RSLMF, Manuel was arrested and detained in the RSLMF detention facility at their headquarters at Cockerill Barracks in Freetown. One day, much later and towards the end of our contract, his name was mentioned in the context of the fact that we were unable to obtain his release. A visit to the military police revealed that the man had been locked up in solitary confinement and that he didn't dare mix with the other prisoners due to the nature of his alleged crime and the difficulty in understanding their language. We decided to pursue the matter with the government authorities and PP discovered that Manuel had been charged with murder and that he would have to appear in court.

On our visit to the attorney general we conveyed the facts of the case to him, to which he responded with a very forceful conclusion that Manuel would probably be able to get away with a lifelong jail sentence and that he would end up at Pademba Road, Freetown's notorious jail. We had been told that the circumstances at this institution were far from ideal and that if the dark, stinking passages there are one's future then one had better get used to accepting that sunlight was a privilege and not a right.

I asked the Attorney General if there was any parity at all when it came to the practice of law in Sierra Leone. I was referring to the incident where Bicycle had been wounded by RSLMF troops during a patrol to evict illegal diamond miners and, had it not been for the work of our medical orderly and our casualty evacuation capability, he would have died. Why then would Manuel be guilty and the RSLMF troops who had done the shooting in Bicycle's case had not even been arrested? The man was shocked to hear about the Bicycle incident and assured us that it was the first he had heard of it. I mentioned to him that the authorities knew of the incident and that it had been reported to the police as well. Both PP and I instinctively knew that we were on to something here in that we could bring some pressure and leverage to bear. The Attorney General requested us to visit him again in order to discuss the matter further.

When we visited him a week later he referred us directly to the office of the Director General in the Ministry of Defence, who knew the facts of the matter but stated that his greatest concern was that we had woken sleeping dogs by taking the matter up via official channels and that we would have to follow the correct channels forthwith. He asked us to leave the matter in his hands and assured us that he would see how it could be managed with the least amount of damage on all sides. We informed him of the Bicycle case as well and he stated that this would not make Manuel's case any easier but he invited us to visit him again after a week.

PP was of the opinion that we were not going to achieve much here and this was compounded by the fact that, with the return of some semblance of law and order to Sierra Leone, government officials were once again following the correct channels. We discussed the matter at length and ideas were thrown back and forth. No official wanted to touch the case. In short Bicycle and Manuel had been involved at different ends of the same type of crime during two different eras in Sierra Leone—the former as victim was involved during the era of chaos where everyone could literally get away with murder, except EO, that is. The latter era had come about as a result of our success. We had brought order to the chaos. The matter was sensitive but we formulated an approach where we would press for both matters to be either settled in court or abandoned. PP and I shared the approach with our commanders and received the green light.

We made the proposal—allow Manuel to go AWOL and EO would resolve the matter so that the authorities in Sierra Leone would never hear of him again. The AWOL incident was arranged and one evening Manuel mysteriously disappeared from the detention barracks and found his way back to South Africa under a blanket of secrecy, never to set foot in Sierra Leone again.

The hunt for the 530-carat diamond

Our progressive successes against the RUF had enabled the government to regain some measure of control over the provinces and the mining sector understandably received the most attention. Under the direction of Dr Harding, who later became the Minister of Mines, Minerals and Energy, momentum was gaining rapidly but these efforts did place some strain on the use of the EO helicopters, as government officials made use of them whilst the roads were still unsafe. I had met Dr Harding on a number of occasions and we had reached a broad agreement on a number of aspects, including the use of EO to help the government exercise better control over certain areas of the mining industry.

One evening he invited me over to his home in Freetown and revealed to me that he had received information that a large diamond had been discovered in the Kono district. He asked me if I knew anything about it and I replied that diamonds were not our business. EO was feared somewhat by the mining community, particularly as a result of the implementation of the no mining rule after we had taken Koidu. It was, therefore, highly unlikely that people would share their diamond mining secrets with us. The diamond mining industry in Sierra Leone was indeed a secretive business and information about finds, quality and quantity was kept highly secret. Everybody knew that the Lebanese businessmen were behind most of the mining activities, controlling them remotely yet with a firm hand.

Dr Harding told me that his information indicated that the diamond in question was in the range of approximately 500 carats. His request was that EO, as a tool of the government, should assist him in locating the diamond before it slipped through the hands of the authorities. He was of the opinion that the diamond was probably owned by a legal miner but he agreed that the opposite could also be true. We were requested to assist in chasing down the diamond and bringing it, plus its owner, to appear before the minister. I knew that, apart from being very difficult to locate, this diamond story could be a load of bullshit as well.

With the minister's backing and authority, I discussed the matter with the EO pilots and since Brigadier Bert Sachse was not in the country at the time, I proceeded with the matter. The dilemma was where to start. If we were not able to locate it in a day, that very same diamond would disappear as mist before the sun. The word would spread like wildfire and it would not surface again until it was in Liberia or the eastern parts of Guinea, or even as far away as the Ivory Coast and Nigeria. I had to act swiftly and bulldoze my way to the core of the issue.

I decided to go to Koidu, as that was where anybody with a find of this magnitude would start the business of moving the diamond. I knew by now that boys from the countryside never go to Freetown with their diamond finds unless they had some power or person behind them who could back them up with knowledge and authority, as the Freetown buyers were ruthless when it came to inexperienced sellers. I landed in Koidu and decided to visit the big daddies of the buying cartels. There were only two big buying cartels in Koidu and both belonged to Lebanese buyers. I made a calculation and deduced that if I were to sell a stone, I would go to Cassim Bassma. He had taken over from Ahmed Shamel as the bigger of the two buyers. Ahmed was also not very favourably disposed towards EO as he regarded the company as a threat to his business.

When one opens the door of Cassim's office one normally finds a number of dealers sitting in the waiting room. These dealers are normally supported by a Lebanese businessman, who commissions them to do the mining itself and then bring the product to his office. This support is universally regarded by the Lebanese dealers as a type of goodwill and generally speaking, if the miners don't locate any diamonds, the dealers would feel free to visit the office and maybe even receive a free bag of rice for their work to date. If the miner was not successful in begging for a bag of rice, he could still request 'transport' as it is known in the business. This means that he had tried his best and that he would still be able to buy a plate of jollof rice for 1,000 Leones on his way home.

I was normally invited right through into Cassim's office and made to feel at home. I'm sure he used my visits to obtain some sort of security from the fact that the commander of EO was one of his acquaintances. This meant a lot in Koidu. I did spend time showing respect to all the businessmen in the town, including the diamond buyers, the taxi association and the greengrocers association. The result was that I had free access throughout the town.

Cassim was not in town and I was invited by his eldest son to sit and enjoy some delicious Lebanese coffee. I told him about my mission and he registered great surprise, stating that he had no knowledge of such a diamond. He also promised me that he would keep me informed if he did happen to hear anything. I made it very clear that I didn't want to have to return to this office to pick the diamond up later as I was in a great hurry. This was not the best approach to take as his father and I were good friends, but this time the situation was somewhat different and of a serious nature. What was always very clear to all the Lebanese business people and their families was that EO was straight and to the point in everything that we did. This was another example we set for the people of Sierra Leone—EO is focused on our goal, we stay neutral and refrain from corrupt issues.

I stood outside Cassim's buying office for a whilst, not quite sure where the next port of call should be. I then decided to check with Ahmed Shamel's buying office as well. I was travelling by taxi and on the way decided to drop in on Femi Kamara, the mine engineer. On my arrival at his office, I was overwhelmed by the number of people there who came to greet me and I decided to play devil's advocate. I informed one and all that they would be arrested that very same day if I wasn't able find the 'big' diamond in Kono. To my utter surprise, and within a minute, a member of the staff informed me that I should visit my close friend, the paramount chief of the Sandor chiefdom, as he was the owner of the diamond. I was also confidentially informed that the paramount chief was the miner of the diamond as well, as it had been located on his land. I should not expect to find the diamond on him though. This is all the man could tell me and thereafter he disappeared mysteriously into the crowd. Well, at least I had some sort of an idea where to start the search. What concerned me, however, was that since it was noon already I'd have to start soon otherwise I would not locate the diamond before the end of the day. I may have been a little too optimistic in believing I would find the diamond that very same day. Nevertheless, I wasted no time, skipped Ahmed Shamel's office and headed for the pilots waiting for me at the helicopter pad.

I informed the pilots of my findings and said that we should fly to northeast to Kayima, the main town in the Sandor chiefdom, as we would have to see the paramount chief himself about this matter. The pilots told me that this flight would have to be the last leg as the fuel in the helicopter would be just enough to get us to Freetown thereafter. This meant that, if I was unsuccessful, I would have to return the next day or on another occasion and the chances of locating the diamond seemed more remote as the day wore on.

We wasted no time and flew in the direction of Kayima, hoping to meet the chief. From my experience I know that they cover vast distances in their chiefdoms and it would be down to good fortune if we were able to find him in his village. I flew directly to his house and landed adjacent to it in a small maize field. Luckily the chief was at house, conducting meetings with his people and he was indeed surprised to see me. I informed him that I was on a diamond locating mission, and that I was acting on the authority of the Minister of Mines, Minerals and Energy.

The paramount chief was an old soldier himself and we had engaged in many conversations on soldiering in the past. We had lots in common and he was always happy to be associated with EO. We never disagreed on anything; he was always supportive at the KCC meetings and provided as many Kamajors as he could when requested to do so during a crisis.

Today, however, I came up with a different request and to my surprise he immediately confirmed that the diamond did in fact belong to him. He gave me the details of the stone as far as he could. My surprise turned to astonishment when he informed me that he was not in possession of the stone as he had left it with one of the buyers—none other than my friend, Cassim Bassma in Koidu. I told the chief that the minister's orders had been that I was to bring the owner of the diamond to him as it was not to be confiscated, but merely identified. The truth was a little more complicated—the government required the stone's owner to pay due taxes on the gem. The chief stated that he had no problem with this and confirmed that he would give his full cooperation and accompany us.

Everything had worked out perfectly. We landed back in Koidu town, hailed a taxi and headed directly to Cassim's office to locate and pick up the diamond. The moment we walked into the office Cassim's son knew that he had made a grave error earlier in the day. He was so overwhelmed that all he could do was raise both arms in the air and beg me not to take this up with the authorities as he was merely following his father's instructions on how to handle the matter. I told him that we were there to pick up the diamond and nothing else.

I knew how Cassim operated and he was fond of showing me his big diamonds when I visited him. He always told me that behind each Lebanese, corrupt or not, there sat an even more corrupt Sierra Leonean. He revealed to me how things had started out in Sierra Leone when diamonds had first been discovered. Cassim, who was in his seventies, told me he was born in Sierra Leone in the town of Masingbi, a location which I knew very well. He also warned me that Sierra Leone had a long history of corruption and, in order to be able to survive, the Lebanese had to play the game themselves, and the Lebanese in Sierra Leone were indeed true masters at this game.

In any event, I still had to locate the diamond. Once Cassim's son had laid eyes on my entourage, he realized full well that he had to come up with the goods and he asked me if he could be excused for a moment. On his return, he locked the door behind him and, in the presence of the chief, revealed the diamond to us.

It was the first time I had seen a diamond that size—a round, brownish stone somewhat larger than a golf ball, weighing a whopping 530 carats. Cassim's son pointed out that it was unfortunately not a high quality diamond.

I informed Cassim's son that we had to produce the stone for inspection to the minister. I could see that this news caused him to worry as to what the reaction would be when the way in which the diamond had been handled to date became known to the minister. But, on the other hand, I also knew the most probable course of action that his family would follow. Somewhere, somehow some palm greasing would take place and that would be the end of the difficult situation in which Cassim and his son had found themselves.

The paramount chief and I flew on to Freetown with the diamond and we visited the minister at his home that evening to hand it over. He was truly surprised that we had been so successful within one day. I told him that if it had not been for the clear cut, straight-down-the-line way in which EO had worked in that district, we would never have been successful. Our hands were clean and our approach and actions were exemplary in all respects and that is why we could go in, ask straight questions and obtain straight answers.

I never heard what the eventual outcome of the 530 carat diamond saga was or whether the paramount chief received his rightful share of it or not and, of course, I never heard what happened to Cassim regarding the manner in which the diamond had been reported or handled.

Order group at the EO headquarters at Koidu. Lieutenant Tom Nyuma is sitting in the centre, with Carl Dietz on the right. Ukrainian helicopter pilots are sitting with their backs to the camera.

The thick vegetation on the way to Baiama didn't allow much room to manoeuvre.

PP discussing an upcoming operation with EO troops at Koidu.

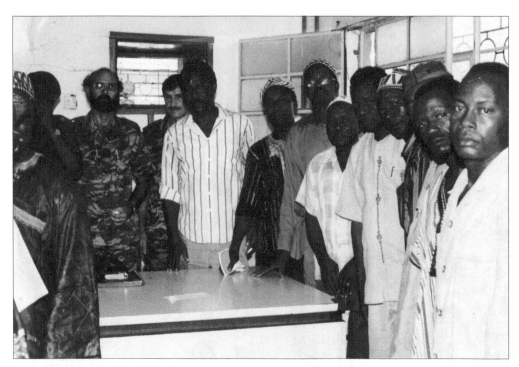

A meeting of the Kono Consultative Committee (KCC), an organization established by EO to administer the Kono district. To my left is Nick du Toit and Chief Abu Kongoba II, the Paramount Chief of the Lhei Chiefdom, and Chairman of the Council of Chiefs.

EO men preparing the two Land Rovers before a patrol from Koidu. Jos Grobler is standing at the driver's door of one of the vehicles.

One of the Mi-17 helicopters, on a rat-run mission, landing at the EO base in Koidu. One of the two BMP-2 infantry combat vehicles is in the foreground.

A Soviet-designed, single-engine light, multi-task utility aircraft, the Antonov-2 seen here on the airfield at Yengema, close to Koidu, was often chartered to provide us with rations and other logistic support.

On my best behavior at Koidu, complete with the RSLMF rank insignia of a full colonel.

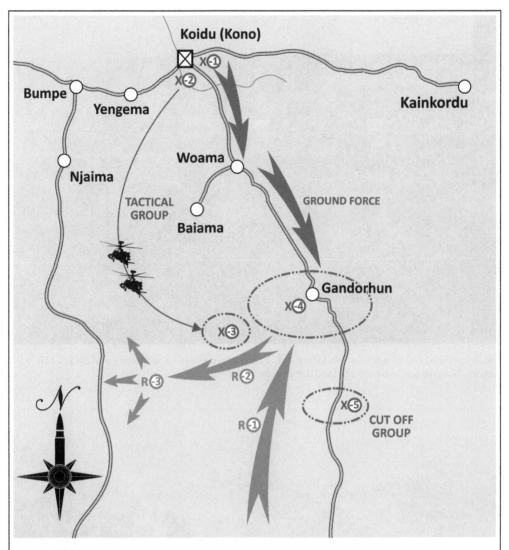

NOTES:

x① EO HQ: EO and RSLMF prepare here for attack
x② Force: Tactical HQ (Roelf van Heerden);
      Tactical Group (PP Hugo, mortars & protection element);
      Ground Force ("Fearless" Fred Marafano + Infantry company, 16 Battalion, RSLMF);
      Cut Off Group (Jos Grobler)
x③ Tactical Group deployed on high ground. Bombards RUF positions with mortars
x④ Ground Force advances, forms up and takes Gandorhun
x⑤ Cut Off Group deploys; cuts off RUF escape southwards

R① RUF deploy to Gandorhun to launch operations against EO/Kono with +- 150 rebels
R② During EO/RSLMF attach the RUF withdraw westwards
R③ RUF scatter after Tactical Group mortar bombardment of their position

Graphic representation of the operation to remove the RUF from Gandorhun

Celebrating the successful attack on Gandorhun with 'Fearless' Fred Marafono and members of the RSLMF company. Note the sign in the top left-hand corner of the photograph.

Discussing a problem with the local RSLMF commander and the chief of the Sierra Leone police at Koidu.

NOTES:

X-1 : OP JORU
: Aim - Disrupt RUF HQ in Joru area
: Forces - EO, ECOMOG, Nigerian Air Force, Kamajors
: Commander - PP Hugo (EO) at Kenema

X-2 : OP GH134
: Aim - Locate and attack RUF forces west of Kono
: Forces - EO, including 82mm mortars, Land Rovers & MI-17 support
: Commander - Roelf van Heerden (mobile)

X-3 : OP LEVUMA
: Aim - Locate and attack RUF forces at Levuma
: Forces - Combined EO/RSLMF attack, supported by 82mm mortars & MI-17 helicopters
: Commander - Nic du Toit (EO)

R-1 Joru: RUF HQ forces did not defend as most were at Levuma

R-2 Makali: Possible RUF distraction force

R-3 Masingi: Possible RUF distraction force

R-4 Levuma: This RUF force intended to conduct a surprise attack towards Freetown to pressurize the SL Government to negotiate

Graphic representation of the operational plan for Operation Zenith.

Visit by EO members from Freetown. From left: myself, a Ukrainian helicopter technician, Andy Brown, Duncan Rykaart, Jos Grobler and PP Hugo.

I take leave of Major Kamara (shaking hands), the RSLMF commander at Koidu, and welcome the new commander. Inspector Sesay, the Koidu police commander behind me, looks on. Major Kamara later joined the Armed Forces Revolutionary Council (AFRC) which, after taking over the country in a coup d'état, allied itself with the RUF. When the elected government was restored, Major Kamara was apprehended, charged and, together with other officers, shot on the beach at Freetown by ECOMOG officers.

So true

The end of 1995 arrived suddenly. I could still remember the radio interview I had given six months earlier during which I had stated that we would overpower the RUF by December. Looking back I realized that we had actually pulled it off with a combination of high quality EO men, innovative tactics, the assistance of the local inhabitants and the RSLMF. Here was proof once again that EO was not just a concoction of bloody-minded, renegade mercenaries who operated purely for money. We had penetrated Africa with a new concept and had delivered the results. In Sierra Leone we had moved into the heart of the diamond fields and, against all odds, defeated the RUF, to the astonishment of the local inhabitants, the government and the RUF themselves. Once again the right calibre of men, correct professional approach and high level of training and expertise, coupled to clear objectives, enabled us to achieve this.

In the Kono District the local inhabitants south of Koidu informed us that the rebels had approached them and asked what the people looked like who had visited such defeats upon them. The local people usually answered that EO consisted of a few men who looked exactly like everyone else—no different—carried the same weapons and ate the same food. The RUF was not happy with this answer at all. The Kamajors located just south of Koidu, in the vicinity of Baiama, reported that the RUF had shown their distaste for the answers they had received by lopping off the hands of some of the local inhabitants and chasing them into the town to return with better answers. This behaviour was unacceptable and we would have to act. Fortunately, time was on our side.

We also knew that the time would come when the RUF would have learnt enough from their confrontations with us to be in a position to respond with counterattacks. We would have to be prepared for this at all times from now on. I knew that this would not disturb us that much but I had my doubts about the readiness of our allies in this regard.

Reflecting on the original plan of the campaign, I would agree that we had been required to amend certain components over the last six months, but the overall plan itself remained intact. The plan for the stabilization of the Kono district had of necessity changed as it couldn't wait until later and we were working under time constraints. We probably had embarked a little prematurely on this venture, but nevertheless the results we achieved had made up for it. The initiative had been wrested from the RUF sooner than we had anticipated and the pressure on the main routes had been relieved.

As far as the wider conduct of the war in Sierra Leone was concerned, EO was indeed satisfied with progress and rebel activity had been significantly reduced. Our intelligence indicated that the RUF had lost direction and this was exactly what we had wanted. The key was to maintain the momentum and keep the rebels on their knees. If the radio intercepts were to be believed, then we had them by the short and curlies. In addition, they were very aware that even the hours of darkness could no longer protect them and they had been scattered all over the bush. We also knew that they would in all probability regroup and come with a renewed assault against vulnerable or soft targets on the two main routes, in the form of ambushes, in order to replenish their supplies.

Pamela and the Tusk

We all spent long periods of time away from our loved ones without any contact except by post. This eventually changed and we were all eternally grateful to our signaller, call sign Romeo 1, who made it possible for us to talk to our loved ones in South Africa on a regular basis.

Using his initiative during a leave period in Cape Town, South Africa, he registered a seafaring yacht, call sign *Pamela*, with the authorities there. In this fashion the 'sailors on the yacht' were able to contact the authorities at Silvermine, the maritime communications facility in Cape Town, who were only too pleased to put us in telephonic contact with our loved ones via a South African landline. Admittedly, we first had to win the northern hemisphere high-frequency band war before we got a single message home. I still don't know who we fought with over the airwaves to get our voices in edgeways but, judging from the many foreign languages and the direct manner in which those voices addressed us, no love was lost between the various call signs at all. I don't know if they understood us at all but the key was to stay calm and talk back 'directly', indicating that we understood what they were saying. The key was not to give our position away in the northern hemisphere and the conversations were therefore always rather ambiguous and 'thin', but our families at least knew that we were alive and kicking.

It was my turn to return home, as provision had been made for each man to spend time at home over Christmas or over New Year. In practice this was carried out in most cases. For those men who had been home two or three times that year, the chances of spending the holiday season at home were, of course, less likely. I hadn't been home for six months and I was really looking forward to seeing our two sons and eighteen month old daughter, Amoret, who I had seen twice since her birth. My wife and children found the long absences difficult, as did the other families, but we didn't complain. We had signed up for this and if anyone was to blame it was ourselves.

The process of going on leave from Sierra Leone was an escapade and experience fraught with great joy, exuberance and good cheer. The EO Boeing 727 would fly from South Africa via Luanda to Sierra Leone and arrive during the late afternoon in Freetown. The aircraft then overnighted at Lungi airport and took off on the return flight to South Africa at 0500 the next morning.

In preparation for the arrival of the Boeing, the men who were due to take leave were transported by various means from all over Sierra Leone and, after overnighting at Fort Pega, if required, were gathered together in Freetown before emplaning. It is hardly necessary to mention that they were elated at the prospect of a well-earned break and their spirits soared as they gathered in the capital to await the arrival of the aircraft. Men who had not seen each other for some time met up, new men arrived and there were many, many reasons, real and imagined to raise a glass of good cheer. Consequently, it was a real mission to get the men into the Boeing in one piece, and on their way to South Africa.

If we were still located in the interior of Sierra Leone on the night before the Boeing started the trip back to South Africa, we would have to get up very early the next morning and prepare for the flight to Lungi airport in the Mi-17 helicopter. It was actually better to stay awake all night and know that you would make it to the helicopter in time rather than risking the possibility that someone would forget about you in the rush, excitement and high spirits. It was a greater sin to miss the flight in the Boeing than it was to forget to take leave of the EO commander and hold your breath so as not to asphyxiate him with your rum and garlic breath.

To get to the airport we made use of the EO ferry, to transport us from Freetown itself across the waters of the Sierra Leone River mouth to Lungi Airport, with Vissie as our guard and vessel commander. We would board the vessel at the yacht club and then a period of level headedness had to prevail as a number of things had to happen simultaneously; stay dry for the flight to Johannesburg; keep your kit high above your head in one hand, shoes in the other hand and remain upright as the rubber duck ferried us to the Lungi side. All that remained thereafter was to get yourself onto the Boeing in one piece.

On this occasion I was not destined to have things easy at all. I had made it all the more difficult for myself by bringing a souvenir or two with me, making a total of five items of luggage over which I was very possessive. The items consisted of a role of Konti Krot, a clothing material that the Kamajors made from the bark of a specific tree and rolled up like a bandage; a very old meteorological instrument that I had saved from a ruin, two python skins and an elephant tusk. The tusk had been carved and Chief Mani of the Lhei chiefdom had brought it and hastily handed it over to me in Koidu as the helicopter was about to take off for Freetown. The tusk was my greatest concern. I hadn't had the opportunity to prepare it for the journey, and I wrapped it roughly in a T-shirt and stuffed it into my carry bag. It was, nevertheless, very difficult to conceal due to its length and it stuck about a half metre out of the bag. I did, however, make it to the Boeing in one piece and decided to face the inevitable questions about the tusk and other souvenirs during the journey.

We stopped in Luanda to refuel and the key for the smokers amongst us was to try and get out of the aircraft and have a smoke on the tarmac without being spotted by the Angolan Police, who found great pleasure in inviting one to accompany them to their office, where cash would make everything go away and work wonders for the offenders.

I had the opportunity to chat with Simon Mann on the tarmac whilst we were refuelling. We had last seen each other during the Soyo offensive. He approached me and asked a few questions about the Sierra Leone operation and especially about the veracity of the humanitarian operation we had conducted. I confirmed that we had indeed conducted such operations, emphasizing that it had been difficult to win over the local inhabitants and even more difficult to maintain such good relations. Not everyone wanted to conduct such operations, I told him, but we hadn't actually had a choice. We had been drawn into this mode of operation due to the prevailing circumstances and we had benefitted tremendously from it. I also mentioned to Simon that we had managed to gain the support of the Lebanese community as well, due to the fact that we had been successful in gaining the support of the local inhabitants first. The Lebanese community was dependent of the goodwill of the locals, and they could only prosper if the locals were on their side. The emphasis had changed somewhat—the locals were stretching a hand of supplication to EO in the hope that this force would help to make their lives a little more bearable. As was the case with Eeben, Simon was concerned about the media image of EO. I assured him that the local media in Sierra Leone were supportive of EO, but that the international media were a different kettle of fish. It was for this very reason that I had engaged the international media rather than avoiding them which, to my mind would have been counterproductive.

We eventually landed in Johannesburg and my fears about the contents of my baggage returned. Things went surprisingly well as it was very late and the customs officials were probably too weary to investigate the odd shaped item that protruded from my kitbag. I had made it and rewarded myself with a few beers as I waited for my flight to Windhoek in Namibia the next morning. I didn't actually have much choice but to bed down on a bench and experience the silence of a massive building that is usually a hive of activity. Some of my colleagues had decided to visit a well know watering hole in Johannesburg known as 'The Ranch' and in so doing missed the next morning's flight to Windhoek.

As I lay on the bench in the dead of the night the devil began to get to me and convince me that I was in the shit as far as the tusk was concerned and that the customs officials at Hosea Kotako Airport in Windhoek were already waiting for me. The night was long and the bench holding the elephant tusk kitbag cushion was very hard. What concerned me the most was that I wouldn't have enough US dollars to make the customs official in Windhoek happy enough to ignore the strange shaped kitbag. Time to make a decision. I walked to the nearest toilet in the international transit lounge, entered one of the stalls, went through the drill and happened to forget the tusk there when I left.

The next morning I commenced the last leg of my journey homeward without my beloved tusk. Nevertheless, it was Christmas and I was safely at home with the rest of my memorabilia. The two weeks' leave passed too quickly but it was a pleasure to be home and spend what is known as quality time with my family. The good times were captured on a video for posterity, something that brought deep sorrow and heartache years later when I eventually viewed them. The damage that is done to family relations by this type of life is severe and long lasting. This is the price that one pays for embarking on such a career.

Refreshed and rested I returned to Sierra Leone after saying goodbye to my family once again.

The palace coup, 16 January 1996

During the late afternoon on 16 January 1996, I was occupied with tasks in the EO office in Freetown when Lieutenant-Colonel Tom Nyuma arrived on foot. Tom and I got on well and we didn't hide any secrets from each other. We had a mutual respect for each other— Tom respected me for the professional approach EO demonstrated and their focus on the achievement of the contract and I must say I respected him for the fact that he had the guts to do what he and his colleagues had done regarding the coup d'état. But that's enough of that for now. Tom asked me to step outside the office with him for a minute and I obliged, although this behaviour was somewhat strange. If he wanted to talk to me in private he usually closed the office door and we discussed whatever there was to be discussed. In addition, the office was not occupied by anyone else at that stage as it was after 1700 and the troops had all knocked off for the night.

We exited the office and he asked me to listen carefully to what he was about to say. He mentioned to me that the head of state, Captain Valentine Strasser, would retire to the officer's club, known as The Oval at the RSLMF headquarters at Cockerill later that afternoon to relax and have a few drinks. Members of the NPRC and senior staff officers at the RSLMF headquarters, plus the various bodyguards would probably be present.

Tom then asked me not to interfere in anything that might happen that evening, no matter what. I found this odd at the time. After all, I had been in Sierra Leone for some time now and had worked closely with the senior members of the RSLMF as a trusted colleague. It may have been that this was the very reason why he had hastened over to the EO office and conveyed this puzzling message to me. The more I thought about it the stranger it seemed and, since I believed that if it was something that was of such high security value that it would affect the whole offensive then I should know about it. I left it at that and he started to leave in somewhat of a hurry.

"Oh," he said just before leaving. "Before I forget, could you get the Mi-24 on standby please?"

I reminded him that the Mi-24 helicopter would surely not operate in isolation.

"Do exactly as I say," was his answer.

This was really odd. I returned to the office, got hold of the VHF radio and called the standby pilots. Juba, who was on call, wasn't too happy that a possible mission had materialized at the end of the day without any earlier indications thereof. I said that I would explain this odd behaviour to them after they had arrived.

Whilst I was making arrangements for the MI–24 and the pilots, I happened to hear the sound of a single shot from the vicinity of The Oval, followed by shouting and then silence. I wondered what was happening but decided that this could be the result of someone's alcohol intake. At the same time I was still wondering why Tom had asked me not to interfere. I kept my inquisitiveness under control and remained in the office. Juba and the other crew members arrived and the Mi-24 was readied for the mission. The helicopter had been refuelled when the standby period started, as was the drill, and Juba and his men sat and looked me in the eye, waiting for their orders. I was, however, just as mystified as they were.

Suddenly Tom Nyuma and Major King, the head of the RSLMF Air Wing, appeared and inquired as to whether the helicopter was ready to fly. The mission they described was simple— take passengers to neighbouring Guinea. All diplomatic, bureaucratic and political matters would be handled by the passengers. Whilst we were being briefed I saw a group of men exit the building housing The Oval and swiftly move towards the helicopter LZ adjacent to the Cockerill headquarters. I couldn't believe my eyes. I saw someone being led out of the building by armed men. The mystery deepened and I didn't realize it at the time but I was witnessing the January 1996 palace coup in Sierra Leone. Here, in front of my very eyes was Captain Valentine Strasser, still in uniform but with no rank insignia, being led away under armed guard to the

Mi-24 helicopter. I tried to see who the other people were but this was made difficult by the surrounding bodyguards who wished to get the helicopter into the air as fast as possible.

Lieutenant-Colonel Tom then walked over to me and said, "Just get the men in the air and get them out of here. And please, we don't need any stunts from you. This is an internal, in-house matter. Thank you for understanding."

The helicopter powered up, took off and commenced the flight to Guinea without any further incidents. That was the end of it. The helicopter offloaded the passengers in Guinea, returned safely and we learnt that Brigadier Maada Bio, Valentine Strasser's second-in-command, was now the new head of state of the Republic of Sierra Leone. I didn't have too many problems with this news as I had dealt with him from the start.

I had only met Captain Strasser on two previous occasions and I will never forget the day when Lafras, Andy Brown and I were invited to his birthday party. This was something special as we had not yet become acquainted with the country or its way of doing things, but there must have been a reason to invite us so we attended the celebrations at Brigadier Maada Bio's mansion, which had at a time belonged to one of the first Lebanese millionaires in Sierra Leone. I must say that the 'after party' was better than the formal affair. Valentine Strasser's wife was in the USA at the time and he was well known amongst the young, attractive ladies in the city as 'the bachelor' and they were there in their droves to meet him.

By the Monday following the coup things had returned to some semblance of normality and there was no real feeling that much had changed. Brigadier Maada Bio did a good job—a skilled man as Chief of Defence Staff and now the Head of State as well. EO regarded the chapter as closed.

Over the next few days, however, I began to piece the story together from snippets of information I received from the bodyguards after I had solemnly promised that I would not divulge the details. The shot that had been fired was intended to warn Captain Valentine Strasser's bodyguard to back off, as the latter had tried to interfere with the takeover process. It appears that only a select inner circle of men, led by Brigadier Maada Bio and Lieutenant-Colonel Tom Nyuma, were involved in the coup. An unknown number of unnamed, 'on-side' senior staff officers were also included in the group and were not identified as they had feared reprisals from members of the pro-Strasser faction.

The story that unfolded told of the Head of State arriving at The Oval and proceeding directly to the officers' bar as was his custom. As he entered the bar his bodyguard, who accompanied him at all times, was refused entry and halted at the door. The bodyguard put up a strong resistance and the only sure way to quieten him down was to fire a warning shot. This had been a last resort as it was well known that Strasser and his bodyguard were inseparable. By this time it had become evident to Strasser what was happening and he was summarily told that Sierra Leone had to move on now without him at the helm.

I must say at this point that EO was actually receiving information which indicated that Strasser had become less involved in the affairs of state and more involved in irregularities and self-enrichment.

Unconfirmed reports had it that at about the time that Sierra Leone had picked itself up from the ashes and was relieved from the total grip on the country imposed by the RUF, one of the EO administrators had visited Strasser to receive the agreed payments for EO services rendered to date. No payments had been made to EO by this juncture and the government's financial indebtedness to EO was mounting by the day. During the discussions between Strasser and the administrator, the former told the administrator that any reminder of the state's financial indebtedness to EO was not the correct way to deal with a head of state. The administrator was also reminded in no uncertain terms that Strasser was, after all, the head of state.

The administrator allegedly replied thus. "You are only the head of state of Sierra Leone because EO is keeping you there."

On another occasion I visited Strasser to present a plan to him with Duncan and PP. During the presentation it was very clear to me that he was more concerned about when the next smoke break would take place and the plan was not approved. So, all in all, I did not hold too many pleasant work-related memories of him. His birthday party was enjoyable though.

The opposite was true in the case of Brigadier Maada Bio. He would always lend an ear and, from his contribution, one realized that he was focussed on how things physically happened on the ground, the exact spot where we wanted things to happen as well.

A NEW HORIZON FOR
SIERRA LEONE, 1996

Stepping up before the election

Although I didn't really want to think about work whilst I was on leave during the festive season, I involuntarily found my thoughts turning in that direction fairly regularly and more often than not the injustices and issues associated with Sierra Leone came to mind. The lack of local development grieved me the most about Sierra Leone and over the last couple of months this had taken most of our attention. It required large amounts of energy and concentration on the part of the men as well. I could have made things easy for us by merely throwing the ball back in the direction of the RSLMF with the excuse that this was not part of our contract. I could have stated to the RSLMF that they were required to show us where the enemy was and we would defeat them, nothing more, nothing less. But I was well aware that this would have been a recipe for disaster, despite the fact that a number of the EO men in Freetown had begun to form an opinion that Roelf van Heerden was currying favour with the locals. I knew that if we didn't keep the local inhabitants positively disposed towards us we wouldn't be successful at all and this would not enable us to achieve our objectives. I wasn't the only EO commander who had realized the value of this approach. Brigadier Bert Sachse and Jos Grobler were two equally strong proponents of making things work through the local structures. The disadvantage of this approach was that it took so much effort and this was what was bothering me as I stared into the far corners of the open Namibian desert whilst on vacation. This approach was exhausting us.

Back at Koidu I was full of new ideas and energy as the break had done me the world of good and the changed environment had inspired new ideas. It was time for the KCC and the Kono Defence Committee (Kondecom) to meet. The Kondecom was a newly formed committee similar to the management committee of a civilian organization in that it consisted of the heads of the uniform services, was smaller than the KCC, more confidential, and discussions could be kept short and to the point. Once we had differentiated between security members and non-security members, the Kondecom meetings were even shorter. When we just had the KCC, a meeting would last up to four hours as there was so much interest and everyone wanted to contribute to the proceedings. It had just become too much. Now, with the Kondecom I could keep the meeting short. The discipline at the meeting amounted to paying attention, listening and speaking only when one had something to say.

I started changing the structure of the KCC as well. Initially EO had chaired the meetings and this was the correct thing to do as it worked for us and all the participants wanted it that way as well. The chairmanship could of course have rotated or have been passed on to the military or to the police but this was summarily returned to EO during the time I had tried to offer it to other uniform branches. EO had to accept the permanent chairmanship of the KCC.

Times had indeed changed, the military situation was under control and the time had now arrived to systematically prepare all the state structures and hand them over to a new, democratically elected government. The winds of change had been blowing stronger and stronger about the necessity of the upcoming election and the two main political parties—the APC (All People Congress) and the SLPP (Sierra Leone People's Party)—were squaring up to each other. Smaller parties sought coalitions and everyone wished to talk to EO as we started to become a vehicle for the political parties during the election campaign. It was to be expected as we were currently the big brother with whom all the younger brothers wished to be associated. Interesting times were ahead and the APC, who had been the previous government during the corrupt period before the conflict, had some stiff opposition. The electorate was tired of war and they tended to believe that the root cause of the conflict was the corruption within the APC. The people wanted change, and a total change at that.

The senior district officer (SDO) in Koidu was the first person to approach me in this regard. He was a long serving member of the APC, well known for his corrupt ways, and a person who certainly knew how to utlize the state machinery to his personal advantage. This type of approach had contributed in no small way to the initial coup d'état and the conflict thereafter. I should also mention that he was the first person to flee seven months ago, when the rebels had threatened the Kono district, deserting his administration and hastening its collapse as a result. Now that matters were under control he was anxious to return to his former role. I received him in my office and he duly informed me that he was unable to continue with his task as SDO as long as EO and I were in his district. He also stated that I was actually occupying the dining room of his official residence and that he required me to vacate his home as soon as possible. In response to this I happened to mention that EO had actually fought to regain his district from the rebels and once we had achieved this there had been no functioning administration to which we could have handed the administration. EO had, in the absence of an administration, taken over the role and I would be fulfilling that role until such time as the government of Sierra Leone asked me to go. I had, by this time, become rather annoyed with his approach and decided to invite him to attend the next KCC meeting where I would table the matter for discussion. He asked for an opportunity to address the members and I undertook to place the matter on the agenda.

During the next KCC meeting I gave him his opportunity to address the members. He obviously had not expected to receive the reaction that he did on that particular day. The majority of the attendees actually advised him to stay away from his office until such time as the new government reaffirmed his appointment as SDO. He was not welcome in his own district, to put it mildly. The chairman of the council of chiefs, Chief Abu Kongoba II, had given me his opinion of the man, stating that the traditional leaders would prefer to keep him out of office for as long as possible and continue the existing arrangement where EO kept the district under strict security measures until the electorate had made their decision.

I had also felt that the time had arrived for the SLP to take over the security of the town itself. The Chief Police Officer (CPO) stated categorically that he was not in a position to do this as the majority of his men had not returned after fleeing from the RUF and, in any event, on their return the RSLMF would only overwhelm them as before. He asked me, unofficially, to continue as the chairman of the KCC and the Kondecom. I didn't have a choice. It was also vital to keep the group of figureheads together in a cohesive unit for as long as possible and it was equally important to give the people of Kono some hope now that they were returning in their thousands.

I decided to engage the community better and, to this end, visited the hospital with the Council of Chiefs, Shahid Khalil, the Lebanese community representative, and Dr Siddiqi, the man who was achieving medical wonders on a regular basis under very trying circumstances. The Lebanese community had even promised to provide funds to the hospital in order to allow them to obtain the most necessary medicines until such time as the government could take over. Here all praise is due to Cassim Basma and Ahmed Shamel, the two diamond buyers, and Shahid Khalil the chairman to the Lebanese committee, who summarily bought up all the most necessary medicines, such as bandages and antiseptic lotions, off the streets and handed them over to the hospital. EO also promised to help medically where possible, despite the fact that we were also under pressure to deliver in the security area. This gesture was really appreciated on the part of Dr Siddiqi, the head of the Koidu hospital. The local women's organizations also came forward and offered what little help they could. It was a revelation to see a community, who had barely recovered from the trauma of the conflict, declare their willingness to help. They had just needed the extra helping hand and encouragement to take the first step.

EO was not responsible for delivering humanitarian aid to the local people but on several occasions we intervened despite the fact that it placed additional pressure on our logistic system as well as the EO helicopter pilots, and search and rescue teams who I pleaded with to take unauthorized humanitarian passengers or cargo on board. This was initially prohibited by my commander but later I received the full support from all, including Eeben and Lafras, as this began to contribute substantially to our intelligence gathering effort. Eeben later called me personally over the radio and requested my involvement and, having discussed the contents of the activity, he gave his full support. This was a tremendous relief as it had been frowned upon previously due to the pressure exerted on the pilots as they were going out of their way to assist my call sign.

The February 1996 national elections in Sierra Leone were a huge success and the SLPP won the majority of the available seats in parliament. This was a clear sign that the people of Sierra Leone were fed up with the civil war which pitted families against each other and spawned atrocities for which Sierra Leone would become notorious throughout the world. As predicted, Ahmad Tejan Kabba, the SLPP presidential candidate, was inaugurated as president of the newly formed government and, as a former United Nations administrator, received the necessary support and recognition from this body as well. What remained now was to achieve an acceptable political solution to the RUF problem.

Kay's curse

On my return to Koidu I was also confronted by a somewhat unique human problem. Kay, one of the men under Jos's command had become ill and the conventional, prescribed medicine was not working. Kay, a well-built, pleasant young Himba man, who I had known since my young days in the Kaokoveld region of Namibia, was summoned and in the presence of the medical orderly he stated that he wished to consult his traditional doctor in Namibia. EO's medical policy did not provide for traditional healers and the medical orderly also reported that the EO doctor in Freetown had already informed Kay that there was nothing medically wrong with him at all. Before me stood Kay, a man who had obviously lost a lot of weight and looked ill, despite the fact that the EO doctor had diagnosed his malaise as a psychological matter. I knew that there were various types of traditional healers and doctors in Sierra Leone and it could be a preferred outcome if Kay first visited a local traditional healer and then confessed to this visitation once he saw his own traditional healer in Opuwa, Namibia during his next leave period. I agreed to this course of action and the search for a traditional healer commenced.

A suitable traditional healer was found and since he lived in the voodoo headquarters of Sierra Leone, some distance from Koidu, I tasked a patrol under the leadership of Rocco to accompany Kay during the consultation. The consultation was to take place at a certain large granite hill that we were familiar with as it lay astride the so-called smuggling route. I made it clear that the patrol's task was to follow up previous incidents and reports of smuggling and infiltration activity and if they happened to bump into the healer then they should ensure that the consultation took place.

Rocco and his section left Koidu in an easterly direction at the crack of dawn and completed the patrol and the consultation successfully. For some or other reason Rocco also managed to become exposed to the traditional healer's medicine and he had coughing attacks for some time thereafter. In any event, Kay was not required to pay for the consultation on the spot but was requested to leave 100 US dollars and a white chicken at a certain address in Koidu within two weeks.

Kay was of the opinion that the medicine had helped and that he had recovered. We also saw that he had started eating again. We did find out much later that his loss of weight was actually due to the fact that he had stopped eating because of a feeling of guilt. He had become rather friendly with a Himba friend's wife in Namibia. It appeared that in his absence the friend had ordered a local traditional medicine man to put a spell on him and Kay must have come to hear of this. Kay never really fully recovered, even after he had approached the same healer who had put the original spell on him, and commissioned him to allow him to escape from the spell. Kay was, however, not destined to recover and he died from the spell some time later. Adultery had brought about the guilt that had made him mentally unbalanced and he just couldn't recover from it.

I had learnt about this phenomenon during my days as a young captain in the South African Army in Namibia as I watched the Himba troops become embarrassed and coy when, on returning from leave, they were required to explain their red, ochre-smeared bodies. What emerged is that the Himba hostess for the evening usually required that the guest's body be smeared with red clay to indicate that he was the evening guest and that he had penetrated to the objective, with the permission of the hostess's legal husband. There were, however, times when this practice was misused and the traditional healer or sorcerer was consulted to make things right. Once the spell had been cast the news spread like wildfire and the message reached the far corners of the continent, even Sierra Leone, affecting the cursed person's appetite, visiting him at night, and driving him into the hands of foreign sorcerers until the repetitive cycle of demons and spirits overwhelmed him. There is only one solution. Return to the sorcerer who cast the original spell and pay him to end it. The Himbas were superstitious and their forefathers played a substantial role in their everyday lives. They were not alone, mind you.

TT recalls road movement losses

On the war front the silence in the weeks after New Year was a source of concern to us as it was generally accepted that the RUF would stick their head out somewhere. We didn't sit and wait for them to do so though. Our intelligence picture was updated once again and it indicated clearly that the RUF was intent on avoiding EO at all costs, but that they would once again attack targets where they knew EO had no presence. It also became known that the RUF would concentrate on key points, such as the Bumbuna Dam, the two main routes from Freetown towards the east and of course on retribution operations against all the local inhabitants who had sold them out.

The training of RSLMF forces that Pine Pienaar, the oldest EO yuppie, had carried out together with Basie Riekert had produced results. The new leader groups were of a better quality and a certain Second Lieutenant Ngauga and his platoon were detached to Koidu where we utilized him with good results. The additional force levels did allow us to deploy an EO platoon, under command of Wessie van der Westhuisen, to the large Bumbuna Dam, approximately 50 kilometres north of Magburaka.

The redeployment activity placed a large burden on the use of the helicopters as a means of transport and logistical supply and this forced EO to also make increasing use of the road to move to and from bases. In the south of the country we were also fortunate to be able to resupply the call sign at Sierra Rutile by sea, and Vissie, a former commander in the SA Navy, enjoyed these nautical trips immensely.

EO had been fortunate in Sierra Leone so far in that we had only lost one man in battle. This was destined to change on 9 February 1996. The Mi-17 helicopters were dedicated to other tasks and the air wing was under increasing pressure to be more available for government use—this at a time when the RUF was due to concentrate anew on the main routes. The EO force at Kono had two Land Rovers, each fitted with a 12.7mm DShK machine gun and a 7.62mm PKM machine gun. The vehicles had no protection and we had to rely on the application of operational procedures and the men's aggressive battle skills to keep us out of trouble during any rebel actions whilst we moved by road.

The enemy picture at that stage had started to crystallize and information provided by the locals indicated that the main routes were indeed RUF targets; especially in the Lunsar area. I took part in the first road movement on the Koidu—Makeni route and between Makali and Magburaka we surprised the rebels where they were restfully engaged in preparing their midday meal consisting of smoked monkey meat, also known as bush meat. We had been travelling very slowly in the two Land Rovers in the hilly area when the 12.7mm machine gunner suddenly opened fire. The gun's flash hider was located just above my head and the shots and powder smoke in my face brought about a sudden heightened situational awareness of the area around me. A short exchange of shots ensued but the rebels had been caught unaware and they disappeared into the bush. The tracks that Phillip Katanka, our tracker for the follow-up operation, found indicated that the rebels had fled into the thick bush to avoid contact with us. I decided that the number of daylight hours left favoured us and we pushed on to reach our destination before last light.

It was a well-known fact that, in the area west of Makeni, the route passes through a number of road cuttings in the rolling terrain—ideal places to ambush vehicles. Cobus Claassens was the next to travel on the route and Tshisukila Tukahula de Abreu, fondly known as TT, one of EO's most respected operators and a participant in the operation, takes up the story:

> This next operation undertaken by Cobus was to become the worst incident that took place in the time that EO was in Sierra Leone. It can be blamed on poor information or the fact that the RUF had already liberated an area and were in full control of it, or the stubbornness of the commander or the possibility that immediate action drills were not carried out by the EO troops.
>
> Whilst Cobus and his men were travelling by road towards Makeni they stopped at a village and his men obtained information about the presence of RUF rebels in the area. Cobus was required to make a decision at that point—was he to carry out proper closed area drills on foot or would he continue driving through the area and ignore the obstacles and cuttings alongside the road. The cuttings are dead giveaways of a potential ambush area and if taken seriously will take time to pass if the correct drill is applied. The terrain and the potential obstacles were not that important to Cobus and he wanted to push on to the next target as time was of the essence.
>
> One of the men who accompanied the force was Koekies Koekemoer, a radio operator and the driver of one of the Land Rovers. Little did he know that on this day he would not make it to Freetown. As the force drove through one of the cuttings all hell broke loose as accurate RUF fire was brought to bear on the vehicles from the cutting above them. A poor tactical decision had been made and the EO force was under strength as well. The RUF ambush covered the length of the cutting and their protection against sight allowed them to take up positions very close to the road itself. Cobus immediately called a halt and the enemy fire was returned. It was, however, very difficult to bring effective fire to bear on the

RUF forces. Return fire from the vehicles was only effective if a rebel showed his head over the edge of the cutting and little could be done unless Cobus and his force drove out under the fire, regrouped and counterattacked. The EO men had been pinned down and were sitting ducks. All that they could do now was fight their way out of this situation.

Tragedy struck as a RPG-7 was fired at a vehicle by the rebels at relatively close range and the projectile hit the Land Rover on the front grill, exploded and penetrated the vehicle. The driver, Koekies Koekemoer, who had opened his door to get out of the vehicle, was hit and the shrapnel from the explosion tore into him, severely wounding him. This was indeed the mother of all firefights. Return fire was only effective if one fired from the middle of the road, a position that exposed one to enemy fire. Toshimbeni, the 12.7mm gunner on the one Land Rover remained behind his weapon and fired in whichever direction he was asked to fire. Without any protection, he was exposed to enemy fire as he manned the weapon. This ultimately cost him his life, as he was also severely wounded by RUF small arms fire and fell back onto the floor of the vehicle. The loss of the 12.7mm gunner made things that much more difficult and no one had the courage to run to the vehicle and man the machine gun in the exposed position.

The loss of the machine gun fire allowed the RUF rebels to move forward to the edge of the cutting and this proved to be a fatal error on their part. Cobus and his men could now see them clearly and they brought effective fire to bear on the rebels. When a cobra is cornered it is at its most dangerous. Cobus and his men fought back furiously and drove the RUF rebels off, killing seven and wounding many others. Only now were the teams able to return to the Land Rovers and make a clean break from the contact area. A contact report was sent and an urgent casevac was requested.

As Koekies and Toshimbeni, (nicknamed Michael Jackson), were carried to the casevac helicopter they left streams of blood trailing behind them. Both men were already in a coma and their chances of survival were not good at all. A few of the other men in the group had also been wounded and were attended to immediately on the ground. An unhappy feeling spread amongst the men standing around. Koekies Koekemoer and Michael Jackson were flown to the Cockerill headquarters at Freetown where Dr Naas's EO medical team attended to them, but to no avail, and we lost two brave men.

As the Mi-17 helicopter took off from the contact area I was standing on the helicopter LZ at Golf 4 (Bumbuna Dam) waiting for the aircraft to complete the casualty evacuation so that I could catch a ride to the contact area to provide additional support to the force on the ground.

By the time I eventually landed at the contact area there was not much left of the RUF rebel presence. A follow-up to the closest village usually brings some clarity. The RUF usually returned to a contact area to see if anything was left that is worth scavenging. They would remain in the area until they believed it was safe to search the contact area. I accompanied the follow-up force and as we reached a village, movement was picked up by the scouts and with minimal planning we attacked the village. The next day the bodies of nine rebels were identified in and around the village.

At the EO headquarters in Freetown a sombre mood had set in as arrangements were made to fly the two dead men to South Africa. These were the second and third casualties suffered since the battle with the RUF rebels had started in Sierra Leone. The loss weighed heavily on the men as the group was a close knit unit. The chances were good that most of the survivors had seen the expired men return from leave shortly before the incident or had shared a beer with them the night before the operation had started. Cobus's critics at EO noted that all the casualties during the campaign so far had taken place whilst he had been in command of a force. Was this just his bad luck or had he refused to listen to his men warning him of the enemy presence in the cutting?

Many questions were asked, although we knew that they would not necessarily be answered satisfactorily. The bitterness, however, remained amongst those few who had fought shoulder to shoulder with their colleagues who had paid the ultimate price. Those who had not been part of the contact looked on in admiration at the fighting spirit and heroism displayed by the survivors. This particular firefight was continually talked through and analyzed over and over by the men around camp fires and relived at other locations where silent reflection took place.

We will never forget Koekies and Michael Jackson.

What stood out was that Cobus's way of doing things had failed on two occasions and it had brought about EO casualties. In addition, the fatalities had taken place long after the more intense operations against much larger groups of rebels had ceased. These operations had all been successful with no EO fatalities. I believe that the root lies in the fact that Cobus no longer applied the drills that we had all learnt and applied during our time in the SADF and thereafter. Nevertheless, his actions did come to the attention of Dolphin—Nic van den Bergh—and Cobus was awarded the EO Dagger for meritorious performance.

Mi-24 action in Kangari hills

During the second quarter of 1996 the RUF avoided contact with EO and concentrated on areas where we were not deployed, using ambushes against the RSLMF forces as a means of resupplying their logistic requirements. In addition they decided to occupy the Kangari hills area, alongside the main route to the Kono district and patrol the sparsely populated area east of Makali. From a military perspective the Kangari hills were the first major obstacles one encounters on entering the Kono district from the direction of Freetown.

The NPRC did not wish to allow the RUF any territorial gains and EO was tasked to undertake immediate offensive actions to keep the RUF out of the area in dispute. Due to the time scales and the focus on other areas of importance, EO decided to complete this operation in short order.

PP was deployed in the Cessna 337 and he located the RUF in an area amongst a cluster of hillocks in the Kangari hills. We used to fly over this area quite regularly and the fear was that they might even deploy anti–aircraft means against us. Brigadier Bert Sachse drew up a quick plan and it was carried out using the Mi-24 gunship to strafe the dense bush on the hilltops.

Not much time was spent in the target areas themselves and the pilots returned without even being shot at. The action spelled the end of the rebels in the Kangari hills though. We learnt later that they had vacated the area with what was left of their men and belongings for at least the next three months. Although the Kangari hills area is located relatively close to the town of Magburaka, apparently the birth place of Foday Sankoh, it never really came under any RUF threat for the duration of the conflict. Interesting.

Sobels at Njaiama

Njaiama, in the Nimikoro chiefdom southwest of Koidu, was a little town that had been the base of a diamond mining company known as the Sierra Leone Selection Trust (SLST). The town was also situated adjacent to the Nimini hills and was very fortunate to have a paramount chief, Chief Maturi, who demonstrated a great deal of courage and character. Blinded at an early age, he stayed on as the paramount chief despite his handicap and he appointed a strong Kamajor-speaker for the chiefdom by the name of Sahr Bufa. They formed a strong team and the chiefdom was a prosperous haven until the war broke out and Chief Maturi was forced to move to Freetown.

During June 1996 the commander of 16 Battalion approached me and told me that the Nimikoro chiefdom was still unpopulated, making it difficult for the security forces to obtain information on the RUF in the area. We decided to visit Chief Maturi in Freetown, and whilst there, ask him why his people were not returning to the town. Interestingly enough he stated clearly that his people would not return until he had returned. I discovered that in fact he really was anxious to return but that he lacked the support, partly due to his blindness. It was clear that we needed to assist him to make this possible, and we did.

On 18 June 1996, Major Jan Joubert and I, with the help of Lieutenant-Colonel Mansaray of the RSLMF, the chief police officer, the senior district officer, Sahr Bufa and representatives of the Kondecom made it possible for Chief Maturi and his people to return to their village. Chief Maturi, and those who wanted to return, were invited by the security forces to the small town's church, which was still in good repair, to attend a service. It was a very emotional day for the chief as this was the first time in a long period that he had returned to be with his people. It was also the first time some of his family members and many of the villagers had seen him.

Within a month the town began to show signs of life again as people slowly started to resettle and rebuild their homes. Security was stepped up and 16 Battalion deployed an element there to ensure that the local people could restart their lives in relative safety. Chief Maturi decided not to stay in the village on a full time basis though and commuted back and forth from Freetown due to his state of health. He remained a good friend to EO and we visited his chiefdom on a regular basis.

After Chief Maturi's return the RUF tried to harass the people in the area on a number of occasions and the RSLMF had to stand their ground to prevent any further chaos. On one specific day I received a visit from one of the Kamajors in the chiefdom, who stated that there had been an attack on the town and that the RSLMF soldiers had run away. This information, together with other reports that we received were not at all clear and I decided that it was necessary to undertake a quick investigation. I gathered a few men from the duty staff and drove to the town as quickly as possible. On my way there I came across a number of RSLMF soldiers who reported that the rebels were attacking the town. Scores of people were fleeing with the few possessions they had managed to grab as they fled. This was truly a sad sight to see, only a month or so after we had brought the people back and resettled them.

When I saw the chaos, I returned to the EO base in Koidu and ordered a section to carry out a proper patrol and report back to me. Later that day the men reported back and the message I received made me very angry. It appeared that the RSLMF had issued a false alarm to scare the local inhabitants and, once the people had started fleeing, the soldiers had used the opportunity to start looting. What an absolute disgrace. On arriving in the town my men had found an element of the locally deployed platoon of 16 Battalion preparing food for the day. Their response to the questions from my men was that the guilty men must have been pissed. In addition, the platoon commander didn't appear at all concerned about this, saying that he had heard a few shots fired in the distance but that no enemy had been reported.

There is no easy or simple way to turn such a fiasco around and at my next 'mothers meeting' with the Officer Commanding 16 Battalion I voiced my anger and disappointment vehemently, underlining that the people of Njaiama would never trust the security forces again.

This was yet another example of the root cause of Sierra Leone's malaise—the people feared their own security forces. It took weeks for the people of Njaiama to return once again and EO was forced to deploy a number of the Kamajors in the town itself as a stabilizing force. We couldn't trust the RSLMF.

Preparing for the cessation of hostilities

By now the RUF had started to talk to the newly elected government about a ceasefire agreement and measures were put in place to make sure there would be no breach of the agreement once it had been concluded. We knew that this phase would give the RUF valuable time to rethink their position and, as a bush organization, there would be much to do in order to organize themselves as a political party. These were interesting times for Corporal Foday Sankoh and his top structure. At least they had time to catch up on some good meals and visit their families as they would have to come out of the bush and start appearing in public so as to be perceived as being there for the people. EO knew from our experience in other conflicts that this was the time that the enemy would go flat out to reorganize and reposition themselves, so that when the time was ripe they could take up arms again in a decisive onslaught on the government of the day. We tried to warn the RSLMF and pointed out to them that they should do likewise and prepare for the resumption of hostilities.

We also told the RSLMF that we as EO must be given the opportunity to regroup as a single force and be ready to conduct counterattacks where and when needed.

We all understood that this was a sensitive time on both sides but it was not the right time to be naïve about the peace process. We were unable to convince the RSLMF that the peace agreement would be a painful process, one in which things would deteriorate before they improved. Would Sierra Leone be able to withstand the test during this time?

One issue that made us sit up and take notice was the government's insistence that EO should be more 'legal'. Initially EO had been given carte blanche to enter and exit the country freely, but this was followed later by a measure of passport control. We now learnt that the Minister of Home Affairs had issued instructions to have all EO movement into and out of the country monitored. We were required to have our passports stamped as was the case with any person leaving or entering the country. This wasn't really an issue but it took some valuable time from us when we wanted so badly to get on the plane to start our well-deserved leave. We tried to speed up the process by getting our passports stamped in bulk the previous day by the immigration authorities but, as always with a new government in Africa, corruption had already raised its ugly head. There was always that very irritating set of last few words as one is leaving an official's office, "Bring me something?"

How do you tell someone to piss off, if by stamping your passport he actually thinks he has done you a massive favour? The two major culprits here were the principle immigration officer, Solomon D. Musa and his assistant, Morie Lengor. They gave me the creeps at that time and, true to form, a number of years later they both played a major role in a corruption scam in an attempt to get me locked up and expelled from the country.

During this period of time we limited unnecessary movement and avoided any action which would give Corporal Foday Sankoh an excuse to get us evicted from the country. We used the time to catch up on smaller issues such as outstanding leave, the redeployment of forces and, most importantly to stack the most important logistic requirements. Contingency plans were revisited and updated before we declared ourselves ready for any eventuality.

EO was also tasked to provide escorts for government ministers during their visits to various parts of the country. This played a very important role as the populace were generally not in the picture at all as to what was going on in the country. For most of the people nothing had changed for many years; they knew of the NPRC government, but they never saw any head of state, nor were they visited by any ministers. To the normal man in the street the country and the government were being run by a few soldiers. So, the new ministers needed to explain the election results and the new dispensation to the population.

Chief Sam Hinga Norman visits the Eastern Province

On 5 July 1996 I was instructed by EO to assist Chief Sam Hinga Norman, the deputy minister of defence, on a trip to the eastern province of Sierra Leone to visit Bo, Matru, Kenema, Kono and a few other areas over a number of days. On the previous occasions that we had met he had forecast that this position would be offered to him and he had been right. The Mi-17 helicopters were made available to us and we attended a large number of meetings on local government level.

During the visit Chief Sam Hinga Norman informed me that he had been approached by the NPRC to be part of the coup that had put Captain Valentine Strasser in power, but he had refused. He told me that he really wanted to participate in freeing his people from the dictatorship of the previous two presidents, Siaka Stevens and Brigadier Momoh, but the time he spent in jail and later in the bush in Liberia had made him slow down a bit. He had known that his time would come though.

Chief Sam Hinga Norman was equal to the occasion when he was approached by Ahmed Tejan Kabba, the newly elected President. In addition, he had the support of the Kamajors. The Kamajors were his firm base and with them behind him he was a powerful man. This power returned to haunt him later though as he became too powerful for a number of cliques in parliament.

The main message that the Deputy Minister conveyed during the trip was to inform the local population about the security situation and the coming peace process.

What amazed me as a representative of EO was the manner in which he respected and revered the people. This absolute respect was reciprocated by the people wherever he went. At the same time, and due to the fact that EO was associated with him, the people's respect for EO grew as they had someone whom they could trust. EO in Sierra Leone had done good work and their presence and operations were greatly appreciated by the local inhabitants.

It was an eye opener to travel with the Chief and see the masses of Kamajors gathering from all over to come and pay their respects to him. These bush hunters really served Chief Sam Hinga Norman and they showed it by their prayers for him as well as their dancing in the streets and the bush. The visit was a great moment for them and Chief Sam Hinga Norman was a proud man. It was also a breakthrough for EO and the respect that the people showed us was absolutely phenomenal. They stared openly at us and you could see the amazement in their faces. They had heard about the foreigners and here we were. I wish I could have saved the occasion somehow and taken it back to share with the rest of the EO operators. They would really have appreciated it.

The message was clear to all members of the community as well as the security forces and the police—everyone had to be more aware of the critical period ahead and the importance of preventing the RUF from ruining the peace.

During this period EO had been tasked to deploy Romeo 4, the last EO call sign, in the Bo area. PP was appointed to bring EO operations up to speed there and make sure that the liaison with the ECOMOG forces in the vicinity proceeded smoothly. Chief Sam Hinga

Norman had also travelled to Bo to ensure that there were no obstacles between the different groups of soldiers who were deployed in the area. PP was an easy and capable officer and the headquarters was soon established in Bo from where operations could be coordinated. The deputy minister also attached the local Kamajors under the command of EO and this was something that they were very proud of. Cobus and his men, now operating from Sierra Rutile, were also placed under the operational command of the Bo headquarters.

The last leg of Chief Sam Hinga Norman's journey took him to the Kono district and during the majority of these meetings he used the platform to thank EO for what they had achieved. After the visit, Major Jan Grobler took over command of the Kono district from me as I had been assigned to undertake other activities in Freetown.

Keeping presidents safe

During August 1996, Brigadier Bert Sachse called PP and I and a number of other EO officers into his office and informed us that President Kabba was due to leave the country for a peace conference in Abuja, Nigeria and that he would be away for an unknown period of time. The president had requested EO to pay a visit to him, during which time he had entered into a quiet conversation with Brigadier Bert Sachse. In short he had sworn Bert Sachse to secrecy and had requested him to conduct a specific task under the utmost secrecy. President Kabba stated that as the newly elected president he was not at all sure whether or not the security forces would attempt to topple him whilst he was outside the country. As a consequence of his uncertainty he would like EO to hold a number of strategic points and maintain the status quo until he returned.

The most important strategic areas to cover were the international airport at Lungi and the RSLMF headquarters at Cockerill Barracks in Freetown. The mission was short and powerful; deploy to the Lungi airport in such a way that the ECOMOG forces and any other group or persons do not realize that EO had achieved this, and be in a position to take over the airport before last light that same evening.

The planning for this operation was handled strictly on a need to know basis and PP and I were ordered to occupy the Lungi airport in a clandestine fashion by late that afternoon. We had no insight into what the other group was planning regarding the military headquarters. There was little time to plan in detail as we would normally have done and it was a question of getting the 25 men ready, together with an 82mm mortar for indirect support and moving to the airport as soon as possible.

We loaded two Land Rovers onto the ferry at Government Wharf in Freetown that same afternoon. This proved to be a mission in itself as we were totally on our own with no assistance from the local police or traffic department. Dino, the driver of the leading Land Rover, was instructed in no uncertain terms to get us to the ferry on time. This was no mean feat through the ill-disciplined traffic and we decided to take the shorter, narrower route to the ferry via Hill Cut Road. If the traffic en route was at a standstill one had no choice but to sit and be patient. We didn't have this luxury as the ferry would not wait for us and we pinned our hopes on it being late as usual. I told Dino not to be a gentleman in the traffic—he was to drive as badly as the taxi drivers and show the bull bars on the front of the Land Rover to any competitors. I can clearly remember him looking at me as he took the indicator light off a vehicle in front of us whilst squeezing past it. As the pieces of plastic scattered and fell to the roadway, those inside the vehicle looked back and were about to start yelling at us when their faces froze at the sight of this hostile bunch of soldiers giving them a beady eye. Dino, a quiet person and ever the gentleman, lifted his dirty right hand in acknowledgement of the mishap and we pushed on.

We eventually reached the ferry but it was already in the process of being loaded and appeared too full for our vehicles. PP went over to the person in charge of the loading and exchanged a few firm, choice, but urgent words with the man. The words triggered much talking, hand gestures followed by more pointing and gestures and before we knew it PP was showing us onto the ferry. PP was indeed a man who knew how to express himself. He could convey the letter and spirit of a message in such a way that it was crystal clear. We parked on the ferry and took our seats on the top deck. A fresh breeze from the sea cooled us as we took our seats for the 45-minute journey to Lungi.

During the crossing PP and I discussed how we would conduct the short operation. We knew that it could last for a few days but it could also be extended for a period of up to ten days or more. We decided that we would adapt the plan as time passed.

Once we had reached the Lungi side we drove the vehicles in a very relaxed manner along the main road, passed Lungi Airport and stopped at a fishing village about five kilometres to the west of the apron. If stopped by the local security forces our cover story would be that we intended to conduct a patrol to the border between Sierra Leone and Guinea. We calculated that the local population would not be unduly concerned as they were used to seeing troops all over Freetown and Lungi.

We had to disguise our intent and play it cool at the same time. We achieved this by keeping a few men and the mortar team on a standby basis on a rotation schedule whilst the rest of the men relaxed and swam in the sea. Our beach camp was idyllic and isolated, with sufficient palm trees to keep us cool and hide the weaponry at the same time. Nobody complained about the location of this mission.

There was still a lot for PP and I to plan. How would we physically occupy the airport once the order had been received? What made it difficult was that we couldn't conduct a thorough military appreciation the way we wanted. The closest we could get was to carry out a reconnaissance around the outskirts of the airport and look for approaches to the administration areas and the control tower. We know how the set up looked inside the main building but it was the outside areas that we needed to learn about in order to make the plan.

I jumped into a Land Rover and took a trip inland to reconnoitre the area around the airport in order to pinpoint the deployment of the ECOMOG troops there and find a place from where we could access the airport without having to enter through the main gate. We calculated that this gate would certainly be blocked by any element who wished to keep the airport under their control. We also knew that to take over an airport as part of a military coup would require the application of surprise. The EO force would be too small to stage a huge firefight and we in turn would have to rely on surprise as well by gaining access to the airport along an unexpected approach route and prevent the occupation of the control tower as this would be the first target of any attacking force before they attempted to obstruct the runway. From there, matters could proceed in any number of directions and we would need to be flexible.

We calculated that the ECOMOG forces would not play any part in such a chaotic event, but the fact that they might know of our presence might make it more difficult for us to execute our plan. They might start spreading rumours about our deployment and this was not what we wanted. Our plan was basic—allow the president's aircraft to land safely in Sierra Leone. I scouted the area using a roundabout route so as not to bump into any ECOMOG guard posts and at the same time I had my cover story well rehearsed. I located ECOMOG troops deployed mostly on the corners of the airport property, close to where the locals were staying, in order to be closer to women and booze. This suited us perfectly and I located promising access points at various locations as a result—exactly what we wanted. My plan was simple. During chaos, create more chaos and confusion, and maintain the element of surprise.

Back at the deployment area we continued to surf and relax on the beach and I naïvely believed that we didn't have any booze. Did I really believe that these men wouldn't be able to organize as simple a thing as booze? I don't really think so.

By the end of the third day into this low profile exercise it started to become so boring that I had to think of ways of making life a bit more interesting. PP and I decided that whilst this was the day on which the president was scheduled to return, we would surely come to no harm if we approached the police at the airport and asked them if they could confirm the president's arrival details. At the same time, we were aware that this was actually classified information and there was a good chance that we would be none the wiser after the visit. We arrived at the police station on the airport and entered the premises without any problems as we were regarded by them as special guests. We entered the station commander's office and learnt that they were totally unaware of our beach party or our presence on the beach. They did tell us that the president's flight was expected at any moment and asked us to excuse them as they had certain official tasks to fulfil as part of his return process.

The president's aircraft landed without any mishap and he returned safely to the country. PP and I hitched a ride on one of our helicopters, leaving the younger officers to return to Freetown with the vehicles and the rest of the men. On balance, however, the few days on the beach were a welcome break from the dusty roads of Kono, the cloying heat of the interior and the daily grind of resolving the problems that beset the area.

On another occasion, EO received another unusual call, this time from across the border in Guinea, though not much has ever really been said about the matter to date. We had become known far and wide and it must have crossed the mind of many an African head of state that, if it came to the push, that there was a source of reliable assistance available with which to counter revolutionary problems and help improve the capabilities of the armed forces.

President Lansana Conteh of Guinea, a former military man, was no exception. As a friend of Sierra Leone and the permanent host to two exiled former Sierra Leonean leaders, the thought must have crossed his mind that he too could fall in a putsch.

One day I received a call from the EO headquarters and, in confidence, was told to be prepared to be flown out from Koidu to Conakry, the capital of Guinea, with 20 to 30 men to evacuate the president of Guinea to a position to be indicated later.

I prepared quick orders for an activity of this nature and identified the members of the Rapid Deployment Force, who were under my command at the time, as the force to carry out the mission. No orders were given, no names were taken, and I waited for the operation to start. I did do a mental scan through the available men and conducted a brief period of mental war gaming to think through the possible contingencies I would have to manage. I felt very comfortable with the men who had been identified for the task. They were not an easy bunch to deal with and one had to lead from the front with them. I had worked with some of them from the very first operations in Angola and I knew that this type of operation was ideally suited to them.

I didn't bother much further about the operation but kept the men ready, reduced their deployments on other operations to the extent that they were cleared to carry out day-long tasks close to the headquarters at Koidu. In the end, though, we never received the call from the president and in retrospect I somehow regret that it never came.

OPERATION ZENITH,
OCTOBER 1996

The concept of operations

During the few weeks that I had been away from Koidu much had happened. I was extremely happy to hear that the government had approved that operations against the RUF in the southeast of the country should continue. As we had predicted, the RUF had violated the ceasefire agreement on a number of occasions in order to infiltrate their units into positions that would enable them to commence offensive operations immediately, should the negotiations fail. Rebel sightings were being reported from all over the country. They were also concentrating their forces in areas that they had previously avoided and had deployed as far west as the forested area west of Taiama, the main road around Masingbi, at Bama and Konta to the south of Njaiama–Sewafe. This development confirmed our greatest concern—it would take a concerted effort to get them under control again.

We achieved consensus, however, that EO, in conjunction with ECOMOG and RSLMF would participate in a high-intensity operation to be conducted over a widespread set of targets for a short period of time. This would bring about confusion in the ranks of the RUF, disrupt their effort and stop their planned movements to deployment areas prior to the final political negotiations.

The overall plan, referred to as Operation Zenith, provided for offensive operations against three targets as follows; disruption of the RUF headquarters in the Joru area (Operation Joru); disruption of the RUF forces between Magburaka and Njaiama–Sewafe (Operation Golf Romeo 134) and an assault on the RUF in the Levuma area east of Moyamba (Operation Levuma). Operation Joru was scheduled to be carried out first and the remaining operations would follow thereafter. For command and control purposes Brigadier Bert Sachse kept me in the Kono district, PP remained at the EO HQ in Freetown with him, and Nick du Toit was deployed at the tactical headquarters at Kenema for the Joru target, with the ECOMOG element in the Sierra Rutile mine area. This command and control arrangement was set to change once the attacks on the first two targets had been completed.

Operation Joru

D-Day for Operation Joru was set for 11 October 1996 and the attack was due to commence with an artillery bombardment on the Rotifunk area by 76mm M1942 medium guns manned by Nigerian soldiers from ECOMOG. A rebel presence in the area had been reported by the Kamajors who described the deployment as being spread over a wide area so as to block all access to the east of the country. The artillery fire was meant to harass and confuse the RUF

234

forces at Rotifunk to enable the attack on Joru to be executed without their support.

During the air reconnaissance in the Joru area it was confirmed that the operation would be difficult as access was only possible on foot. The plan was to send in a clandestine element to locate and mark the Joru headquarters area but in the end this was not possible due to the early warning posts that the RUF had set up, allowing the their forces at Joru to vacate the position and disperse in good time after receiving early warning of the security force presence. We had appreciated that the forces at the RUF headquarters would not defend the area but would withdraw deeper into the forests on the Liberian border.

In the end the operation was conducted through the use of artillery harassing fire on a number of widespread secondary targets surrounding Joru, followed by an air attack by Alpha Jets of the Nigerian Air Force (ECOMOG) and an Mi-24 helicopter gunship flown by EO pilots.

This operation effectively closed down the RUF headquarters and it took a few days before Corporal Foday Sankoh's voice was heard over the air again.

Operation Golf Romeo 134

On 24 October 1996 my operation, staged from the Bumbuna Dam area in the Makeni district, started and we moved by helicopter and by road in the two Land Rovers fitted with 12.7mm DShK and 7.62mm PKM machine guns. My tactical HQ was airlifted to the helicopter pad at the old construction camp on the dam site. My force, consisting of 25 men, occupied the small office block and rooms that had been prepared by my men who had kept a presence at the dam over the past few months. The facility was well kept by an Italian government para-statal organization and the dam was in the final stages of completion, but the war had prolonged the final touches and it had become a strategic target for the RUF. The lodgings were the best accommodation I had lived in away from Freetown. What a pleasure.

The operation had a tight schedule to be run over just three days before the final operation in the Levuma area was due to commence. I named the operation Golf Romeo 134 as we had only one sub-unit which, over a period of three days was required to take four possible targets.

What made the operation difficult was that we had no intelligence on the RUF presence in the entire area designated for clearance. The Kamajors had reported that local inhabitants had been killed in the area south of Masingbi and in the Bumbuna Dam area itself. This is why we had decided to start from Bumbuna and work our way south, then east along the main road as we were confident that the rebels would want to lay ambushes to replenish their provisions, ammunition and weapons. The difficulty with so little information was that we had no real idea where we should start the operation.

I decided to bait the rebels in the hope that they would play their cards. We knew that they would operate from a base in the area and we assessed that it would be located in the Kangari hills forest and south of the main road, but we had not pinpointed it as yet.

We decided to move south to the main road and then carry out a patrol in the direction of the Kono district and see if the rebels had the balls to attack us. The patrol was commanded by Nico du Preez and they left early the next morning whilst the rest of the team, consisting of the RDF force, waited on standby at the tactical headquarters at Bumbuna Dam. The Mi-17 helicopters were also on standby in Freetown from where they could reach us within 45 minutes.

Around midday I received a radio message from Nico that they had received information from a number of Kamajors in the area that the force should continue along the road as the rebels had set a number of ambushes in anticipation of any road movement. The road was not being used without military escorts and it appeared that this rebel element had been waiting for a number of days in well-prepared positions.

We agreed that the force should continue along the route until they made contact with the enemy, and then test them before we followed up to eliminate them. Nico ran into an ambush on the main road east of Masingbi shortly thereafter and, from the volume of incoming fire he determined that there were a large number of rebels deployed in the killing area. Nico's force tried unsuccessfully to break up the main rebel group in the killing area of the ambush as the area selected by the rebels for the ambush was perfect; they had deployed on the high ground and were firing down at the road—a good position with good observation over the area and clear arcs of fire. Nico withdrew his force, sent a contact report and requested assistance. Within about 50 minutes the Mi-17 helicopters landed at my position at Bumbuna Dam. We emplaned the remainder of the RDF, together with the 82mm mortars and headed out towards the ambush site.

On our arrival we linked up with Nico and he gave me a quick situation report whilst the 82mm mortars deployed alongside the road and the helicopters powered down. We were going to use the helicopter pilots as airborne forward observation officers for the mortars whilst we attacked the ambush area. At that stage it was very clear to us that the rebels were still in the area and that the hilltop behind them was also being used as a base from which they could react quickly and enter into the ambush position once early warning had been received. The area was very dense and attacking the position from the road would not be an easy task. The road was also separated from the hill by a marshy area that would act as another perfect killing area for the rebels.

With the mortars in place, the MI-17s took off and we moved on foot along the road to make contact with the enemy. Once the rebels realized that the mortar fire was being directed from the helicopters they opened up with all they had on the aircraft. We could hear the pilots indicate targets and correct the fire and it soon became clear that the rebels were in trouble. The pilots complained that the RPG-7 fire made it impossible for them to get any closer than 1,000 metres from the target. We could see the RPG-7 rockets detonating in the sky around the helicopters as the self-detonating fuses exploded at 975 metres from the launcher. The RUF were firing with all they had to prevent the helicopters from coming any closer and this allowed them to withdraw to the rear slopes of the hilltop and escape to the north.

When we tried to enter the area on foot from the east, to consolidate the ambush area, we found that the rebels had already vacated the area. The ambush had been in a perfect location but they had sprung it too early, giving our men the gap they needed. We spent the rest of the afternoon undertaking a follow-up of the rebels but they had scattered into the bush. We sustained no casualties on the day and withdrew to Bumbuna Dam to overnight.

That evening we held a debriefing prior to planning the next day's actions. We concluded that we would have to be flexible and agile in our approach and adapt to the situation, as the enemy picture was changing rapidly.

We planned a mortar attack on a probable rebel target to the south where the Kamajors had indicated that the RUF might have a base. Time was not on my side and the Mi-17 helicopters would be needed for other operations so I would have to do whatever I needed to do as quickly as possible within the next two days and then call an end to Operation Golf Romeo 134. It was clear that maximum benefit could be gained from disrupting the enemy over a wide front and keeping them on the run, preventing them from organizing their activities and penetrating other areas.

For the attack on the possible rebel base we flew the RDF, with the 82mm mortar teams, to the town of Makali on the main road and started gathering intelligence from the local inhabitants who were still in the vicinity. We found that they were scared about giving any information, saying that the rebels might come back and leave them battered and limbless for choosing sides in the conflict. It took a lot of patience on our part as these villagers had not worked with EO forces before. Eventually we managed to piece together a picture which indicated that the rebels had occupied a hilltop base not far from the town. The location was secret and nobody was supposed to know about it but the rebels' need for 'women and wine' had compromised its location. The base was, as always, perfectly located at the top of a hill with lots of overhead cover against sight.

We would need more men to attack the base effectively and cut off escaping rebels. Once again I decided to show them that we had located them, then smoke them out with the mortars and scatter them so that they would have to look for a new base area. With one more day left we needed an end result without any own-force casualties and the watchword was simplicity—a simple operation with calculated risks.

Quin was in command of the RDF and he complained about the risks involved in the operation. EO had been operating for three years and I had partcipated in the majority of their operations. As a consequence I knew that there would be risks involved but we would just have to be able to handle them. After all, this was why EO was what we were. As long as we had the advantage of surprise on our side we would be in a position to achieve the desired result against superior opposition numbers. I heard him complaining about putting the troops and the helicopters in danger and this made me somewhat confused about the man. It was clear that he, as a new kid on the block, was not used to these kinds of operations, not even in the SADF. I was convinced that we could conduct them successfully. It was a little late now for him to complain as we were already into the deployment and I refused to stop the operation. We pushed on.

We organized the attacking force into two groups—the mortar group and the all-round defence group—boarded the helicopters and lifted off on our way to the designated area. The operation would involve a standoff mortar attack on the most probable location of the

RUF base. It would last approximately 20 minutes and then we would return to the tactical headquarters at Bumbuna Dam. My only concern was that we would not find a suitable LZ for the helicopters. If this was the case we would just have to squeeze in amongst the foliage as we had done before, then drop the teams one by one and return to pick them up after the job had been completed. This was the application of the element of surprise. If this was not possible then the operation would have to be aborted. I was not convinced that an air reconnaissance was possible if we wanted to surprise the enemy.

Whilst flying into the target area, we located an open area about 2,000 metres from the hilltop and about 300 metres in diameter. Carl, the pilot, dropped the all-round defence group and then took off in order to make room for the mortar group to be deployed by the second helicopter. I exited the first helicopter and remained on the LZ to meet and join the mortar group. As we started to prepare the mortar base plate positions, we found that the earth consisted of solid rock and instinctively knew that the operation would take longer than planned. The helicopters were supposed to wait in the holding area or make dummy drops in a safe area. The longer we spent on the ground the more fuel was being consumed and if the rock delayed our mortar deployment we would have to abort the mission due to the risk of low fuel levels in the helicopters.

I had to think quickly and discussed the matter with the waiting pilots, then asked them to conduct a quick reconnaissance around the area where we were to see if there were any easy approaches for the rebels. They reported that apart from being very dense, the area was also surrounded by a lot of water. The mortar bombardment went ahead and I ordered the two helicopters to land on the outskirts of the landing area. At this stage Quin confronted me once again with his views about the operational risks. I replied that we could discuss this matter at the base later that evening but that since we were nearly through the mortar ammunition we would complete the mission on the ground.

As we fired the last few bombs and the white phosphorous smoke hung thick over the hilltop area, I ordered the evacuation of the whole force. That night Quin told me that I had endangered their lives during the operation. He did not have the support of all the men though and, feeling that he was pushing an empty wagon, he stood down. With this we left the Bumbuna Dam area the next morning, and the deployment area was handed back to Wessie and his team.

Operation Levuma

On 5 November 1996 I handed over to Major Jan again as I had to go to Freetown during the few days prior to the final operation in the Levuma area. I would assist with the coordination of the operation, and the operation commander, Nick du Toit, was also assisted by PP.

This operation was due to be conducted jointly by EO and the RSLMF. We knew from the start that it would be problematic as the quality and approach of the two forces were totally different. We believed that we could manage the differences if we deployed each force on its own separate axis of attack, but we had miscalculated a few things.

The target was a RUF area around Levuma, approximately 80 kilometres to the east of Freetown. The terrain selection by the RUF had been thorough and it left them with a number of escape routes. Escape routes were always carefully planned to enable them to scatter and vanish in the opposite direction to the incoming fire whilst at the same time giving them a choice as to whether to return the next day to search for whatever had been left behind.

The intelligence picture on the enemy was vague regarding rebel force levels and their actual location. It was assumed that the rebels would be in the area and that they would defend a specific position. Their main objective would be to occupy a position east of Freetown in order to be able to launch an attack on the capital.

The first phase of the operation was conducted from an area north of the suspected rebel base by a force consisting of a RSLMF protection element and an EO mortar group. The moment that the mortar group was in position, the second phase—a joint attack by an EO force under command of Cobus, supported by a RSLM company along the southern axis—would get underway.

As soon as the mortar fire was on target, the southern force moved into position to make contact with the rebel group. This ground force was supported by the two Mi-17 helicopters and the Mi-24 gunship, which was on call from Lungi Airport.

As Cobus and his men pushed forward slowly towards the target area they came across some resistance and small pockets of rebels popped up all over the area carrying out minor harassing attacks on the EO element, which was leading the attack. Cobus and his force had to walk in single file due to the thick vegetation. The rebels honed in on the EO force stretched out over a considerable distance, making mutual support very difficult. Rebels started appearing from a number of positions to ambush the whole attacking force and firefights broke out all over the area. The EO guys tried to keep control but it soon become impossible as the RSLMF members of the attacking force were on another mission. They decided that this was not for them and they pulled out, leaving the EO troops to their own devices. There are different ways of dealing with this situation—one is to make a stand and see it through and die like flies, or to pull back, reorganize and mount a counterattack as the rebel location and their plan had become known.

It also became very clear to Cobus that there had been heavy casualties amongst the RSLMF troops and that they were scattering. This didn't leave him with much of a choice and he decided to pull his men back to a safe area.

As they reached the safe area, Cobus could see that this situation needed some serious rethinking and he reported the matter to Nick du Toit who was airborne in the Cessna 337 above the area. The report from Cobus referred to the disarray, confusion and bewilderment amongst the RSLMF troops. Cobus also stated that it would require time before the force could be patched up, regrouped and the operation replanned.

What happened next was, I believe, not the solution. However, I was not in command of the operation and I had no influence over it so I kept my cool. I respected the ground commander's observation but this was to have serious consequences for EO in what was to happen in the next few hours.

Cobus demanded to be pulled out of the area as it had became very dangerous and he was concerned that the RSLMF troops might start to accidently shoot at the EO troops. The RSLMF troops were totally out of their depth and had become petrified for their lives. Cobus regrouped his men and withdrew to the rear, called on Nick to get the MI-17s in to airlift them out of the area, and leave RSLMF troops behind.

The first Mi-17, with Charlie Tait behind the controls, came in for the landing in an open patch adjacent to a number of houses in a village and the first EO stick ran to embark just as the unforeseen happened. In this utter confusion and chaos the RSLMF forces saw the EO troops withdrawing and began to believe that the Mi-17 helicopters were meant to evacuate the casualties on hand. Chaos broke out and all the RSLMF troops—wounded, unwounded, and scared—ran in one mass towards the helicopter. Control disintegrated and the situation began to spiral out of control.

Charlie Tait got the message and lifted off just to get his aircraft into the air. He was running the engines of the Mi-17 at full power, and, although he had been given the thumbs up to lift off, his effort was in vain and he realized that the aircraft was overloaded. He decided to try and lift off in any event. The effort brought the helicopter into a forward motion but he couldn't gain sufficient height nor could he hover and the rotors clipped the roof of a house in the helicopter's flight path and sustained damage. Charlie immediately decided that the aircraft was not safe and he landed and shut down the engines whilst chaos broke out around him. Some of the RSLMF troops were even sitting on the helicopter's external fuel tanks. During the debriefing session thereafter, an estimate was made that in the region of 90 men were in and on the helicopter, including those hanging on outside.

This all happened in a few seconds and quick thinking was required to get an alternative plan in place. The second Mi-17 was circling the area and Juba, the pilot, had observed what was going on. It was decided jointly that Juba would land the Mi-17 some distance away and that only the EO personnel would be accommodated in it and extracted from this chaos. They would, however, first have to escape from the mess on the ground and then run towards the other helicopter that was waiting for them in the distance.

All hell broke loose in the Cockerill headquarters in Freetown as this incident took place and the garbled messages received led to confusion. By sundown it had become clear that the RUF had actually instigated the chaos.

The next day Juba, as brave as ever, decided that he would return to the area and fly out the crippled Mi-17 helicopter. A search and rescue team was put together to protect the rescue operation and they left for the LZ, prepared for the worst and knowing full well that they could be surprised by the RUF once they had landed. As the Mi-17 approached the area, the pilots searched for any signs that would give them an idea of what the situation on the ground would be before a quick plan could be made. They located the crippled helicopter in the distance but saw that it was on fire. The RSLMF troops had left the area the previous day and the rebels had claimed this position and set the helicopter on fire. It was a sad day for EO and it reminded me once again of the Camaxilo disaster in Angola.

Back at Cockerill we held a debriefing session to determine exactly what had really happened on the ground and what could have been done differently to prevent the chaos. It soon became clear that the feedback to the RSLMF commanders was different from what we were hearing from our own men. The RSLMF were blaming EO for the unplanned withdrawal and they maintained that this had put their troops in danger. On the other hand Cobus explained that once the RSLMF troops had started to evacuate their positions during the attack, it had weakened the whole operation.

One of the main weaknesses of the overall plan was that EO had not actually conducted any joint attack operations with the RSLMF before and the huge differences in training and experience levels had probably caused the cohesion to fall apart. The RSLMF sustained heavy casualties and they then broke contact, leaving the small EO force to fend for itself. The RSLMF troops had been pushed into battle with little or no training or rehearsals with the other participating forces and it had left the EO forces no other choice but to withdraw.

The other EO men who had made up the mortar group deployed to the north of the target related a familiar set of circumstances. The RSLMF troops had believed that they were in command of the operation and it was clear that the orders that had been given on the top level for the operation had never reached the troops on the ground. In addition, the RSLMF troops had no idea of what to expect from EO, nor did they know what the attack plan, to be conducted by Cobus and the remainder of the RSLMF force to the south, entailed. Weak leadership on all levels lead to the loss of control and cohesion. The loss of a very valuable EO aircraft came as a serious blow and EO was forced to operate with only one helicopter thereafter.

Needless to say, the debriefing session in Freetown did not go well. Not only were we required to defend the actions we had taken; we were also forced to defend the reputation of a number of EO men in leadership positions during the attack. One thing became very clear. EO should not conduct joint operations with RSLMF forces. We had not done so to date, and we would not do so in the future. Brigadier Maada Bio and the newly appointed Chief of Army Staff, Brigadier Hassan Conteh, were not happy with the outcome of the debriefing at all. They really wanted to place the blame on EO for pulling out of the battle and they had no understanding of the fact that their troops had run away during the contact with the RUF. The outcome was painful for both EO and the RSLMF.

The end in Sierra Leone

Operation Zenith was the last operation conducted against the RUF by EO. As a unit we never did get the opportunity to complete the final two phases of the original plan—the attack on the RUF headquarters at Joru, followed by area operations. Instead we were handed a number of ad hoc tasks which, to my mind, never really achieved much due to the lack of a clear overall purpose.

The RUF did, however, decide to temporarily suspend military operations and an all-out effort by all parties to gain the lion's share in the subsequent power sharing deal ensued. This was not an easy task for the RUF as they had been dispersed throughout the country. Their biggest issue now was to try and get EO out of the country. This put real pressure on the government as there was widespread support for the presence of EO and in some provinces there were demands that EO should stay. On a number of occasions the local leaders pleaded with us not to leave the area as they felt that there was no hope without EO. In the Kono district, for example, the Lebanese businessmen even raised money to keep us in place, even if it was on a reduced level, and they were prepared to keep an element there that they could afford. It was tragic to see people begging for safety.

With the end of the contract in Sierra Leone many seasoned, really good soldiers whose whole life was soldiering, who knew nothing else, had to face the stark reality of unemployment with families to support. The cessation of hostilities was agreed on 30 November 1996, I left the services of EO in December 1996 and EO had left Sierra Leone by March 1997.

This was not the end of the saga or the violence in Sierra Leone though, and many sad days followed for the people of the country. The negotiations were still in the early stages and there were clear signs that both sides were not happy with the situation. Eventually the negotiations failed despite the fact that Corporal Foday Sankoh had claimed the position of vice president and control over the lucrative mining sector. Even this did not work out in the end and the RUF decided to take up arms again. With Corporal Foday Sankoh back in the bush, and with a large number of soldiers and rebels on the rampage, a group of soldiers under the command of Major Johnny Paul Koroma (JPK) who referred to themselves as the Armed Forces Revolutionary Council (AFRC) joined hands with the RUF and formed a front against the government and ECOMOG. Since EO was not in the country any longer it was a piece of cake to turn the tide in their favour.

Worse was still to come, if that was at all possible, and the country's pain and suffering continued. In the following months the responsibility to combat the enemy fell on ECOMOG and with the help of the British Government they managed to wrest power from the mob and restore the elected government by July 1999. Many people lost their lives in the process and towns were totally destroyed.

The Kono district, where EO had worked so hard and achieved so much, was hit the worst and the AFRC/RUF coalition exacted special retaliation on the population for what had befallen the rebels during the EO period. The town of Koidu was razed to the ground. Not a single roof stood and not a single well was without its fair share of bloated, floating corpses. For the RUF it was payback time. What a shattering end to such a promising beginning.

Reflections

By the end of the twentieth century, in an age of supplicant political correctness, the unflattering profile and notoriety associated with mercenaries in general and with EO in particular had become somewhat universal. But, were members of EO mere 'dogs of war' who fought for pleasure and money or was there more to us than offered by the general perception? The mercenary vocation is one the oldest professions and, whether one likes it or not, the mercenary will undoubtedly survive for the foreseeable future. A more balanced view of the profession thus would be to accept the inevitable fact that in times of conflict the mercenary was, is and will be in demand and that the past indicates that there is little likelihood that the world will be rid of conflict in the future.

The essence of the meaning tied up in the word mercenary was the source of general argument and debate within EO itself. And, as hard as we tried to avoid it, disguise it, defend it, change it, or accept it, the world only had an appetite for the negative connotations associated with the profession and the sensation-hungry public's cravings were fed by a media which roundly condemned EO without a balanced view or analysis at all. In the long run, and despite our efforts to change perceptions, the die had been cast against us from the outset and on the ground in Angola and Sierra Leone we accepted this.

So, what did it take to be a member of EO? When I reflect on this my thoughts inadvertently return to the Soyo and Cafunfu operations and the fervour with which a host of ex-soldiers, free booters, opportunists and others clamoured to be part of the adventure. I also remember those who quickly decided that this profession was not for them and beat a hasty retreat to South Africa once the crack and thump of incoming fire became a reality.

It took an inner strength to be a member of EO. This characteristic was most often displayed by former members of South African Special Forces units, 32 Battalion, Koevoet and those paratroopers who had previous battle experience, as well as a few others who had faced and overcome their limitations whilst under enemy fire or under adverse circumstances.

In my own case I believe that the fact that I had successfully completed the SA Army Command and Staff Course, as had a few other EO members, and had battlefield experience in both conventional and counter-insurgency operations stood me in good stead as a commander. This enabled me to approach the vastly different operational requirements in Angola and Sierra Leone with a balanced, flexible and practical ability to apply the principles of warfare. The application of conventional warfare solutions to achieve the success of the mechanized advance on Cafunfu in Angola contrasted by the more people-orientated military administration of the Kono district in Sierra Leone are but two examples that come to mind.

Another hallmark of success was the adaptability of the EO men to their circumstances and physical environment. In Angola the pace of the advance was frenetic and the application and adherence to what is generally referred to as battle discipline, as opposed to parade ground discipline, was required. In Sierra Leone, however, once the pace of operations dissipated the application of strict discipline and parades was required in order to ensure the cohesion and direction of the force.

Prior battle experience in Africa was to my mind a necessary ingredient of our success in the two countries, as was the fact that we were all sons of Africa. This signified two things— an instinctive understanding of the continent as applied to their own circumstances and a knowledge of how warfare is waged here. Together these elements enabled us to get on with things without having to agonize over and overcome first world prejudices and approaches to warfare that were unsuited to the job at hand.

On a more mundane note, EO men had to be comfortable with long periods away from home, danger, poor accommodation, climatic extremes, a short career planning horizon and numerous changes of plan at a moment's notice.

Above all, though, the EO member had to love what he was doing and be able to relieve the stresses associated with the lifestyle through a real sense of humour.

Finally, the sense of achievement, the lift and the exhilaration a soldier experiences during and after an engagement with the enemy, particularly at close quarters, is and will always be unmatched in any other profession. This, in my view is why soldiers, whose future in a garrison-type military organization, to which the South Africa armed forces aspired in the 1990s, left to take up the EO challenge to close and engage with an enemy on the open savannahs and under the jungle mantles of Africa.

I believe that national armed forces outside Africa have no particular wish or desire to engage with any enemy in Africa, especially at close quarters, and immerse themselves in military operations that would erode their thin veneer of respectability and principled reputation in the perceptions of their electorate. Politicians after all are not keen to sully their carefully constructed facades and convenient rhetoric.

In Africa there is still a desire to seek political solutions within the framework of the local culture, sense of time and unique way of doing things. Africa has its own particular style, somewhat outside the ambit of the developed world, which abandoned it at the time of decolonization. In essence, the leaders of African states exhibit a predilection to grasp onto and keep that which they could lay their hands on and fight for political survival until such time as they are toppled, often through violence. To prolong their survival in the political storms that beset Africa, political leaders often engage foreign military forces, mercenaries and military leaders of the ilk of Colonel Mike Hoare, Colonel Rolf Steiner and Colonel Callan. I must say that on the surface, EO may even have fitted into this mould to a greater or lesser degree. After all, could our operations not be regarded as an infusion of military skills to prolong the survival of an existing African government? Notwithstanding this, EO was indeed the correct solution to the existing dilemma in Africa—there at the right time, with the required professional approach, providing an African option with unprecedented success.

So, were we really mercenaries? I leave it to you, the reader, to form your own conclusions. I should caution you, though, that the chances are equally possible that you may not arrive at a clear answer after turning the last page of this book. Life is usually a case of more gray than black or white, and after all, what's in a name?

Further reading

During its heyday Executive Outcomes was portrayed by some news media as a villain whilst others regarded it as a prince, and the wider public perception of the organization was influenced accordingly. Very little energy has since been devoted to a systematic and serious analysis of the actual military operations undertaken by the organization in Angola and Sierra Leone. It is, therefore, the purpose of this section to assist the serious reader by providing a select, yet informal, reading list of book titles which could be consulted to establish a more measured account of these operations.

To date the author has located one publication which recounts the military operations of Executive Outcomes in both Angola and Sierra Leone (and elsewhere, including Indonesia and Papua New Guinea) in detail. *Executive Outcomes: Against All Odds* by Eeben Barlow, the founder of Executive Outcomes, was first published by Galago Publishing (Pty) Ltd, Alberton, South Africa in 2007 and it covers the lifecycle of the organization. A second edition was published as recently as 2010.

Regarding the military operations undertaken by Executive Outcomes in Angola itself, Jim Hooper's book, *Bloodsong! An Account of Executive Outcomes in Angola*, was first published by HarperCollins Publishers, London in 2002. The author combines a set of interviews with six members of Executive Outcomes into an account of the actions of Executive Outcomes during the Soyo raid, the operation to take Cafunfu and the Cacolo offensive. Jim Hooper visited Roelf at Koidu in Sierra Leone.

To date no book has been published which is exclusively devoted to a description of the military operations undertaken by Executive Outcomes in Sierra Leone. This void was partially filled by Hamish Ross and Fred Marafono who authored *From SAS to Blood Diamond Wars*. Published by Pen & Sword Military, Barnsley, the authors recount the exploits of Fred Marafono—to which Roelf has also referred—during and after the Executive Outcomes era in Sierra Leone.

Two somewhat different views of the events surrounding the Executive Outcomes/Sandline assignment in Papua New Guinea in 1997 are described in some detail in Tim Spicer's autobiography, *An Unorthodox Soldier: Peace and War and the Sandline Affair* published by Mainstream Publishing, Edinburgh in 2000 and Sean Dorney's book *The Sandline Affair- Politics and Mercenaries and the Bouganville Crisis*, published by ABC Books in 1998. Roelf did not participate in this assignment. This reference is provided for the sake of comprehensiveness.

Finally, two other publications are included here by virtue of the fact that they can be regarded as a sample of the more general, yet distinct, approaches followed by commentators to add to the body of knowledge on Executive Outcomes. The first publication was authored by Al J. Venter, who visited Roelf at Koidu, and is entitled *War Dog: Fighting Other People's Wars*. The book was first published in the United States in 2003 by Casemate, Havertown, PA and sections of the contents are devoted to the activities of Executive Outcomes. The second publication is a compilation of chapters on the privatization of security by ten different authors under the auspices of the Institute for Security Studies, entitled *Peace, Profit or Plunder:*

The Privatisation of Security in War-torn African Societies. Edited by Jakkie Cilliers and Peggy Mason and published by the Institute for Security Studies, Halfway House, South Africa in 1999, one of the authors—Khareen Pech—visited Roelf at Koidu and her twenty-eight-page contribution on Executive Outcomes is included as one of the chapters in the volume.

Wisdom grows from knowledge and understanding.

Andrew Hudson

Index

Lightning Source UK Ltd.
Milton Keynes UK
UKOW06f1531160516

274334UK00004B/22/P